Social Innovation and Impact in Nonprofit Leadership

Tine Hansen-Turton, MGA, JD, FCPP, FAAN, and **Nicholas D. Torres, MEd,** are both serial social entrepreneurs. They met in 2008 as Eisenhower Fellows in a conference on education and health care best practices and innovation in Brazil. Since then, they have founded several organizations and social enterprise movements.

Education-Plus, Inc. (www.educationplushealth.com) improves and scales education and health outcomes and disseminates innovations and best practices, including school health clinics, high school to college access and completion pipelines, K–12 blended learning with a focus and emphasis on special education students, and dissemination of innovative social practices toward social impact.

The *Philadelphia Social Innovations Journal* (www.philasocialinnovations.org) is the first online publication to bring a public focus to social innovators. The *Journal* leads the Philadelphia region's dialogue regarding social and public innovations and inspires the innovation and execution of new models within the government, not-for-profit, and social enterprise sectors by sharing expertise, strategies, and ideas about topics such as leadership, human capital, and disruptive innovation.

The Social Innovations Lab (SIL; www.socialinnovationslab.org) is a social enterprise that nurtures social enterprise models from ideas to implementation by providing a low-risk opportunity to test, vet, and realize strong ideas across the social sector, social enterprise, and government.

The Philadelphia-based SIL provides instruction, mentoring, support, and expert guidance to Lab participants in developing viable blended value models—social impact and financial sustainability. The Lab takes social enterprise models from ideas to implementation across a 3-month series of workshop modules.

Education Plus Academy Cyber Charter School (www.edpluscharter.org) is an independent, free, public K–12 college preparatory school. It is designed to provide extraordinary educational opportunities to students with specific learning disabilities such as dyslexia and dyscalculia and/or who are struggling academically in traditional school settings. Education Plus Academy uses research-based intervention strategies demonstrated to be effective with students with learning differences and capitalizes on advances in technology to advance learning and produce students prepared to be successful for college.

Finally, Tine Hansen-Turton and Nicholas D. Torres both teach Leading Nonprofits and Social Innovations and co-direct and facilitate the SIL at the University of Pennsylvania's Fels Institute of Government (www.fels.upenn.edu).

Social Innovation and Impact in Nonprofit Leadership

Tine Hansen-Turton, MGA, JD, FCPP, FAAN
Nicholas D. Torres, MEd

Editors

SPRINGER PUBLISHING COMPANY
NEW YORK

Springer Publishing Company, LLC
11 West 42nd Street
New York, NY 10036
www.springerpub.com

Acquisitions Editor: Stephanie Drew
Production Editor: Michael O'Connor
Composition: Newgen Imaging

ISBN: 978-0-8261-2178-3
e-book ISBN: 978-0-8261-2179-0

14 15 16 17 18 / 5 4 3 2 1

The author and the publisher of this Work have made every effort to use sources believed to be reliable to provide information that is accurate and compatible with the standards generally accepted at the time of publication. The author and publisher shall not be liable for any special, consequential, or exemplary damages resulting, in whole or in part, from the readers' use of, or reliance on, the information contained in this book. The publisher has no responsibility for the persistence or accuracy of URLs for external or third-party Internet websites referred to in this publication and does not guarantee that any content on such websites is, or will remain, accurate or appropriate.

Library of Congress Cataloging-in-Publication Data

CIP data is available from the Library of Congress.

Printed in the United States of America by McNaughton & Gunn.

We dedicate this book to our families and the millions of passionate individuals who work or have worked in the U.S. and international nonprofit sectors.

CONTENTS

CONTRIBUTORS

ORGANIZATION CONTRIBUTORS

The Alliance for Children and Families

The Alliance for Children and Families is a national membership association of nonprofit child and family services agencies across America. These agencies collectively provide services in thousands of communities and serve millions of people. The Alliance, headquartered in Milwaukee, Wisconsin, supports nonprofit agencies through direct services to members and through policy leadership out of its Washington, DC, office.

The Bridgespan Group

Founded in 2000, The Bridgespan Group is a nonprofit advisor and resource for mission-driven organizations and philanthropists. The group collaborates with social sector leaders to help scale impact, build leadership, advance philanthropic effectiveness, and accelerate learning. The group works on issues related to society's most important challenges breaking cycles of intergenerational poverty. Our services include strategy consulting, leadership development, philanthropy advising, and developing and sharing practical insights.

The Children's Village

The Children's Village is a charity devoted to keeping vulnerable children and youth safe, and families together. Founded in 1851 to shelter youth in New York City who had committed petty crimes, The Children's Village has evolved to become an innovative leader in strengthening the most at-risk youth in the child welfare and juvenile justice systems.

Community Wealth Partners

Community Wealth Partners (CWP) is a leading management consulting firm that emboldens and equips leadership teams to innovate, grow, and sustain impact. It offers strategy and implementation services to social sector organizations looking to achieve dramatic improvement in community outcomes. At Community Wealth Partners we dream of a world in which all people thrive. To realize this dream, we help change agents solve social problems at the magnitude they exist. For more than 15 years we've helped diverse, inspiring change agents make lasting progress in their organizations and communities. Working side by side we reimagine what's possible and promote new ways of thinking. Through this spirit of intense partnership, we help change agents accelerate the pace of change and carry their dream forward. As a Share Our Strength organization, we bring the successful practices of one of the nation's leading antihunger, antipoverty organizations to hundreds of change agents nationwide.

Conservation Economics Services

Conservation Economics Services was founded by Clifford David to identify and pursue opportunities that blend economic development with environmental sustainability. The company works with private individuals, corporations, family offices, and nongovernment organizations to identify and then implement strategies that produce a financial return while at the same time enhancing a property's environmental conditions.

Education-Plus, Inc.

Education-Plus, Inc. improves education and disseminates innovations and best practices by supporting schools through consultation regarding general and special education, tutoring, testing, and other services for children and adults; engaging in the promotion of general health and knowledge through educational health activities; and disseminating best practices through articles and publications of educational journals.

Eisenhower Fellowships

Chaired by General Colin Powell, Eisenhower Fellowships (EF) brings two groups of approximately 20 outstanding mid-career Fellows (aged 32–45 years) drawn from 47 different countries to the United States annually for an intensive, individually designed program in each Fellow's professional field. In addition, approximately eight to 10 high-achieving mid-career U.S. citizens or legal permanent residents are sent abroad for a similar program in the country of their choice. Since the founding of EF in 1953, approximately 1,900 emerging world leaders have become Eisenhower Fellows who better the world around them through their individual actions as well as their collaborations within their countries and across national borders.

Fels Institute of Government, University of Pennsylvania

Penn's Fels Institute of Government has educated students committed to making a difference in the world for almost 75 years. Its approach is distinctive; its small class sizes and unique setting make the Fels program personal; and its practice-based curriculum, taught by practitioners and some of Penn's most distinguished faculty, keeps it closely focused on the tough but critical questions of how to get things done and how to achieve real-world results in challenging political environments.

Hillside Family of Agencies

Hillside Family of Agencies is a family and children services organization that provides child welfare, mental health, youth and family development, juvenile justice, special education, and developmental disability services across central and western New York and Prince George's County, Maryland. Hillside Family of Agencies comprises affiliates Crestwood Children's Center, Crestwood Children's Foundation, Hillside Children's Center, Hillside Children's Foundation, Hillside Work-Scholarship Connection, and Snell Farm Children's Center.

The Independence Foundation

The Independence Foundation is a private, nonprofit, philanthropic organization serving Philadelphia and its surrounding Pennsylvania counties. The foundation's mission is to support organizations that provide services to people who do not ordinarily have access to them. The foundation also has two special initiatives—public interest law fellowships and fellowships for visual and performing artists.

Independent Sector

Independent Sector is a leadership network for charities, foundations, and corporate giving programs committed to advancing the common good in America and around the world. Independent Sector serves as the premier meeting ground for the leaders of America's charitable and philanthropic sector. Since its founding in 1980, Independent Sector has sponsored ground-breaking research, fought for public policies that support a dynamic independent sector, and created unparalleled resources so that staffs, boards, and volunteers can improve their organizations and better serve their communities.

Nancy Moses Planning+Development

Nancy Moses Planning+Development provides strategic, feasibility, marketing, and fund-raising plans to help organizations start up, revitalize, and turn around. The firm has helped clients establish new museums, philanthropies, and tourism entities; launch civic and heritage tourism initiatives; and create academic centers and digital learning labs. Clients range from national cultural treasures and foundations and agencies of all levels of government to community arts and development organizations.

OMG Center

The OMG Center provides innovative, high-impact solutions that accelerate and deepen social impact by blending successful business and practice insights with on-the-ground realities. The OMG Center builds more effective philanthropies, nonprofits, and government organizations by leveraging insights gained from evaluation and research to determine which programs are working best and why, and then developing strategies to drive these best practices to scale.

The Philadelphia Foundation

Since 1918, the Philadelphia Foundation has linked those with financial resources to those who serve societal needs. The Philadelphia Foundation supports the intentions of individual, family, business, and organizational donors who have established 800 permanent charitable funds. The foundation invests and administers those funds and awards the distributions—about $20 million a year—to nearly 1,000 area organizations in the form of grants and scholarships. It is overseen by a volunteer board of leading citizens and is run by professionals with expertise in the region's needs.

Philadelphia Social Innovations Journal

Philadelphia Social Innovations Journal (PSIJ) focuses on the region's current and emerging leaders of social entrepreneurship, nonprofit organizations, foundations, and social sector businesses, and the principles they have developed to create, manage, and promote social change. *PSIJ* highlights the accomplishments of local leaders and social entrepreneurs who set the standard for regional nonprofit organizations and policy makers, providing an opportunity for these leaders and their agencies to publish their innovations and share best practices and lessons learned.

Public Health Management Corporation

Public Health Management Corporation (PHMC) is a nonprofit public health institute that builds healthier communities through partnerships with governments, foundations, businesses, and community-based organizations. It fulfills its mission to improve the health of the community by providing outreach, health promotion, education, research, planning, technical assistance, and direct services. With nearly 2,000 employees, 250 programs, 11 subsidiaries—one with programs throughout Pennsylvania, and another nationwide—70 sites, and 250,000 clients served annually, PHMC has become one of the largest and most comprehensive public health organizations in the nation.

Skipta, Ltd.

Skipta, Ltd. specializes in the development of niche professional, social, and private networking platforms. Utilizing proprietary Skipta technology, the company incorporates social media with customized interactive applications into a digital powerhouse designed to optimize communication for and between like-minded audiences.

Social Impact Exchange

The Social Impact Exchange is a community of funders, practitioners, wealth advisors, intermediaries, and researchers interested in developing practices for funding and implementing large-scale expansions of top-performing nonprofit programs and organizations. The exchange serves as a focal point and gathering place for those interested in further building the field of scaling social impact and as a platform that facilitates the efficient flow of capital to scalable social solutions. The exchange was established by Growth Philanthropy Network in partnership with Duke University and with primary funding from the Robert Wood Johnson Foundation and a group of charter members.

TCC Group

Since 1980, TCC Group has developed strategies and programs that enhance the efficiency and effectiveness of foundations, nonprofits, corporate community involvement programs, and government agencies. From offices in New York City, Philadelphia, and San Francisco, the group offers hands-on support in designing and implementing solutions that combine objectivity with enthusiasm, direction with responsiveness, and discipline with flexibility.

The Urban Institute

The Urban Institute gathers data, conducts research, evaluates programs, offers technical assistance overseas, and educates Americans on social and economic issues in order to foster sound public policy and effective government. The institute builds knowledge about the nation's social and fiscal challenges, practicing open-minded, evidence-based research to diagnose problems and figure out which policies and programs work best, for whom, and how.

The Wharton School Leadership Program, University of Pennsylvania

Wharton's leadership program, which includes the Undergraduate Leadership Program, the Graduate Leadership Program, and the Center for Leadership and Change Management, seeks to develop global leaders who exemplify leadership at its best— their visions are strategic; their voices, persuasive; their results, tangible; and their impact, global. The program strives to develop world citizens—global leaders with an understanding of how they and their organizations can make a positive difference for investors, customers, employees, and communities regardless of national setting but with a deep appreciation for the distinct cultures at play. The shared focus is to advance Wharton's distinctive blend of coursework, coaching, experiential learning, and conferencing to develop the personal leadership capacities of constituents at all stages of their careers.

Your Part-Time Controller, LLC

Founded in 1993, Your Part-Time Controller, LLC, provides expert bookkeeping, accounting, financial consulting, controllership, and CFO services to nonprofit organizations. With offices in Philadelphia, Washington, DC, and New York City, Your Part-Time Controller helps make nonprofit organizations more successful by building stronger financial management and financial reporting systems.

INDIVIDUAL CONTRIBUTORS

Jennifer Alleva, CPA

Jennifer Alleva is a Certified Public Accountant and a Partner at Your Part-Time Controller, LLC. Frequently asked to speak about nonprofit financial issues, she has developed and taught classes for the Pew Charitable Trusts, the Center for Nonprofit Advancement in Washington, DC, the National College Access Network, the Delaware Division of the Arts, and the Jewish Federation of Philadelphia. Alleva is a graduate of the Boston College School of Management, where she received a BS in accounting.

Dina Wolfman Baker, BA

Dina Wolfman Baker serves as Director of Marketing and Communication for PCG Public Partnerships. Her expertise includes public/media relations, advertising, branding, public affairs, internal communication, change management, funding and development, e-marketing and e-business, strategic planning, and client services. Baker serves on the boards of various organizations and as a mentor to young professionals; she is director of professional/leadership development for the Boston chapter of the International Association of Business Communicators.

Ken Berger, MBA

Ken Berger joined Charity Navigator in 2008 after nearly 30 years in the nonprofit sector. He has held leadership positions at a variety of human service and health care agencies, both large and small, and has operated programs serving the homeless, the developmentally disabled, the mentally ill, substance abusers, the medically underserved, and persons with HIV/AIDS, among others. He earned his bachelor's degree at the University of Buffalo, a master's degree in psychology from Antioch University, and a master's degree in business administration from Rutgers University.

Sara Brenner, MBA

Sara Brenner is president of Community Wealth Partners, where she helped develop and is implementing the firm's new strategy to solve social problems at the magnitude they exist, while leading a sales team that grew revenue by more than 45%. She is a frequent presenter at conferences on nonprofit sustainability, social impact, and philanthropy and the author of "The Art of Sustaining Social Innovation," published in the Massachusetts Institute of Technology-based *Innovations* journal. She received her MBA from Georgetown University's McDonough School of Business and a BA in history and history of culture from the University of Wisconsin-Madison.

Mark Carnesi, PhD, MEd

Mark Carnesi is the senior director of international programs for Eisenhower Fellowships. Prior to joining Eisenhower Fellowships, he served in a variety of positions related to international exchange both in the United States and abroad.

David Castro, JD

David Castro is a graduate of Haverford College (1983) and the University of Pennsylvania Law School (1986). In 1993, following a successful career both in private practice and as a Philadelphia prosecutor, he was awarded a Fellowship in the Kellogg Foundation National Leadership Program. He devoted his Fellowship to the study of community leadership and its relation to improving quality of life. Based upon this work, in 1995 he founded I-LEAD, Inc., a school for community leadership development that has served several thousand emerging leaders across Pennsylvania through its affiliation with Pennsylvania Weed and Seed. In 2002, in recognition of his work on behalf of Pennsylvania communities, he was awarded an Eisenhower Fellowship, which he used to study leadership and its impact on economic and community development in Turkey. In 2009, in recognition of his development of an accredited associate's degree program in leadership delivered in underserved neighborhoods through innovative community-education partnerships, he was inducted as an Ashoka Fellow by the Ashoka Global Funds for Social Change. Ashoka is an international community of the world's leading social entrepreneurs. A teacher at heart, he is frequently consulted as a speaker, serving on panel discussions and contributing regularly via blogs and articles posted through the Kellogg Fellows Leadership Alliance and the Ashoka network.

Fernando Chang-Muy, MA, JD

Fernando Chang-Muy is the Thomas O'Boyle Lecturer at the University of Pennsylvania School of Law, where he teaches international refugee law. He also teaches courses on nonprofit management and immigration at Penn's Graduate School of Social Policy and Practice. In addition to teaching, as principal and founder of Solutions International, he combines his experience in academia and operations to provide independent management consulting, facilitation, and training to philanthropic institutions, nonprofit organizations, and government entities.

Michael Clark, MPA

Michael Clark is the executive director of Germantown Systemic, a social impact venture in Philadelphia. Michael has advised faith-based communities in the areas of impact investing and has developed social-innovation finance legislation for the state of New Jersey. Prior to this, Michael worked in a variety of roles in K-12 urban education in Philadelphia including strategy, resource development, and teaching. He also served as a Peace Corps volunteer for two years in Bulgaria. He holds a bachelor's degree from the University of Scranton and a master's of public administration from the University of Pennsylvania's Fels Institute of Government.

Richard Cohen, PhD, FACHE

Richard Cohen is the CEO of Public Health Management Corporation (PHMC), where he leads 1,400 employees, over 250 public health programs, and numerous subsidiary organizations that have become affiliated with PHMC during more than 20 years of mergers and acquisitions. He is also a nationally recognized authority in nonprofit public health management.

Paul Connolly, MPPM

Paul Connolly is a senior partner and chief client services officer at TCC Group. He is an expert in organizational capacity building, strategic planning, grant-making, evaluation, and social enterprise. He is author of *Navigating the Organizational Lifecycle: A Capacity-Building Guide for Nonprofit Leaders* and coauthor of *Strengthening Nonprofit Performance: A Funder's Guide to Capacity Building*. He received his master's degree in public and private management from Yale School of Management, where he was awarded the Jess Morrow Johns Memorial Scholarship, and a BA with honors from Harvard University.

Maria Cristalli, MPH

Maria Cristalli is the chief strategy and quality officer of Hillside Family of Agencies. She has 20 years of experience in planning and quality assurance in nonprofit social service organizations. She holds a master's degree in public health from the University of Rochester School of Medicine and Dentistry and a BS in biology from Utica College.

Clifford C. David, Jr., MS, BS, BA

Clifford David has built his career as an innovator, combining a nonprofit mission with for-profit financial incentives to transform land management through conservation. His distinguished and groundbreaking work as a senior leader of a regional land trust and other nonprofit and for-profit organizations has advanced the cause of natural resource conservation and historic building preservation. He holds a BA in psychology, BS in botany, and an MS in organization and management.

Liz Dow, MBA, MA, BA

Liz Dow has been president and CEO of LEADERSHIP Philadelphia since 1993. She writes a column for the *Philadelphia Social Innovations Journal* and is the author of *Six Degrees of Connection*. She earned an MBA from the Wharton School and an MA from Cornell University.

William Foster, MBA

William Foster is a partner at The Bridgespan Group, where he heads the consulting practice. He is coauthor of "Should Nonprofits Seek Profits?" (*Harvard Business Review*, 2005), "How Nonprofits Get Really Big" (*Stanford Social Innovation Review*, 2007), "In Search of Sustainable Funding" (*Nonprofit Quarterly*, 2007), "Money to Grow On" (*Stanford Social Innovation Review*, 2008), and "Ten Nonprofit Funding Models" (*Stanford Social Innovation Review*, 2009). He earned his undergraduate degree in social studies from Harvard College and his MBA from Stanford University's Graduate School of Business, where he was an Arjay Miller Scholar.

Tine Hansen-Turton, MGA, JD, FCPP, FAAN

Tine Hansen-Turton is chief strategy officer for PHMC. She also serves as executive director of the National Nursing Centers Consortium, a nonprofit organization of over 250 nurse-managed health centers members nationally and is cofounder and executive director of the Convenient Care Association, a national trade association of more than 1,300 private-sector retail-based convenient care clinics. She cofounded the *Philadelphia Social Innovations Journal*, is a recipient of an Eisenhower Fellowship and the *Philadelphia Business Journal*'s 40 under 40 Leadership Award, and has been named a Philadelphia Connector and American Express NextGen Fellow.

Erin N. Hillman, MEd

Erin N. Hillman is the director of USA programs for Eisenhower Fellowships.

Undraye Howard, MA

Undraye Howard is the vice president of the center on leadership for the Alliance for Children and Families, with primary responsibility for creating, supporting, developing, and delivering knowledge, products, and services that move the human services sector forward. He also serves as a faculty member at the University of Wisconsin-Milwaukee School of Continuing Education and Ottawa University. He holds a BA in business and marketing and a master's degree in communication with a special interest in training and development.

David E. K. Hunter, PhD

David E. K. Hunter consults internationally to funders, ministries, and direct service agencies in the nonprofit and public sectors. His practice builds on more than three decades of experience using performance management systems to improve the quality and effectiveness of social services. He has written and edited numerous books in the social sciences. He has recently developed Web-based tools for nonprofit and public sector agencies to assess their capacity to manage performance and take stock of their readiness for evaluation.

Jason Hwang, MD, MBA

Dr. Jason Hwang is an internal medicine physician and chief medical officer of PolkaDoc, an online clinic that provides low-cost primary care services to patients via their smart phones. He is also the cofounder and was previously the executive director of health care at the Clayton Christensen Institute for Disruptive Innovation. Together with Professor Clayton M. Christensen of Harvard Business School and the late Jerome H. Grossman of Harvard's Kennedy School of Government, he coauthored *The Innovator's Prescription: A Disruptive Solution for Health Care*, the American College of Healthcare Executives 2010 Book of the Year and recipient of the 2011 Health Service Journal Circle Prize for Inspiring Innovation.

Peter Kim, MPP

Peter Kim is a manager in The Bridgespan Group's New York office. He is the coauthor of "Ten Nonprofit Funding Models," which was recognized as the *Stanford Social Innovation Review*'s most widely read article of 2009. He earned his undergraduate degree at the Woodrow Wilson School of Public and International Affairs at Princeton University and a master's degree in public policy from Harvard University.

Jeff Klein, MBA

Jeff Klein is the executive director of the Wharton Leadership Program and a lecturer at the Wharton School and the School of Social Policy and Practice at the University of Pennsylvania. He holds an MBA from the Wharton School and a BA and BS from The Pennsylvania State University.

Lisa R. Kleiner, JD, MSS

Lisa R. Kleiner is a senior research associate with PHMC's research and evaluation group. She has more than 20 years' experience conducting all phases of formative and summative evaluations of health and social service programs, including after-school and child care programs. She holds a JD from Temple University's Beasley School of Law and an MSS from the Bryn Mawr Graduate School of Social Work and Social Research.

Jeremy Christopher Kohomban, PhD

Jeremy Christopher Kohomban is president and CEO of The Children's Village and The Center for Child Welfare Research at The Children's Village Institute. The Children's Village provides a continuum of programs, including evidence-based support for families, shelters for homeless youth and immigrant children, alternatives to incarceration, nonsecure detention, alternative schools, affordable housing, and specialized services for more than 9,000 children and families in community settings and more than 1,000 children in residential settings annually. He was honored by the Alliance for Children and Families with the 2011 Samuel Gerson Nordlinger Child Welfare Leadership Award and currently serves on the boards of the Alliance for Children and Families, the Child Welfare Watch, the Child Welfare Organizing Project, the Annie E. Casey Foundation's Center for Effective Family Services and Systems, the Council of Family and Child Caring Agencies, the Youth Work Center, and Charity Navigator's Advisory Panel.

Jeff Mason, MBA

Jeff Mason is vice president of Social Solutions, where he has been instrumental in the company's evolution from a software provider for nonprofits to a facilitator of performance management across the human service sector. He holds a BS in marketing from The Pennsylvania State University and an MBA from Loyola College.

Jill M. Michal, BS

Jill M. Michal is president and CEO of United Way of Greater Philadelphia and Southern New Jersey, an organization committed to driving measurable, lasting impact that no one person or organization can achieve alone. She serves as a board member of the Greater Philadelphia Chamber of Commerce, Fox Chase Cancer Center Foundation, and the Philadelphia Council for College and Career Success. She also serves on the Audit Committee of the Philadelphia Jewish Federation and the advisory board of Graduate, Philadelphia. She earned a bachelor's degree in accounting from The Pennsylvania State University.

Nancy Moses, MA

Nancy Moses developed the Wharton School's Social Impact Fellows for MBA candidates and founded a women's giving circle. She is the author of the award-winning book *Lost in the Museum: Hidden Treasures and the Stories They Tell*. She holds a master's degree in American civilization from George Washington University.

Tess Mullen, MPA

Tess Mullen recently completed her master's of public administration at the University of Pennsylvania's Fels Institute of Government. Prior to attending Fels, she worked in Congress for nearly six years, serving as a communication director for U.S. Congressman James Altmire (PA-04) and a deputy press secretary for U.S. Senator Tom Harkin (D-IA). She graduated from Harvard College with a BA in English.

Suzy Nelson, LSW

Suzy Nelson is a licensed social worker and graduate of the University of Pennsylvania. Her professional background includes mentoring youth, counseling elementary school students, and case management with homeless individuals. She is also an avid writer and frequent blogger.

Farrah Parkes, MPA

Farrah Parkes is a senior program officer in PHMC's management services division. She has extensive experience in a variety of areas of nonprofit management, including organizational development, fund raising, strategic planning, program planning, and development, as well as project management. She holds a master's degree in public affairs from the Woodrow Wilson School of Public and International Affairs at Princeton University and she completed her undergraduate studies at the University of Pennsylvania.

Robert M. Penna, PhD

Robert M. Penna is an independent outcomes consultant, the author of the forthcoming *Outcomes Toolbox*, and a member of the Charity Navigator Advisory Panel.

Gail Perreault, MBA

Gail Perreault is the director of learning and performance management at the Jacobson Family Foundation. She is a coauthor of "How Nonprofits Get Really Big" (*Stanford Social Innovation Review*, 2007). She received a BA in mathematics and physics from Bowdoin College and an MBA from the Tuck School of Business at Dartmouth College.

Marissa Prianti, MPA

Marissa Prianti recently completed a master's degree in public administration at the University of Pennsylvania's Fels Institute of Government and now works for the U.S. Senate. Prior to attending Fels, she worked for a nonprofit that provides legal and social services to low-income immigrants in New York City and surrounding areas. She graduated from Bryn Mawr College with a BA in political science.

Meg Rayford, MS, PhDc

Meg Rayford is a technology and business journalist, as well as a communications consultant, in the Washington, DC, area. She is the editor of Tech Cocktail, a media company covering technology news, start-ups, and entrepreneurship, and she works with financial and technology companies to refine and implement their communication strategies.

Caroline Ridgway, JD

Caroline Ridgway is currently regulatory and legal analyst and compliance officer for HealthSpot, a telehealth company based in Dublin, Ohio. Prior to joining HealthSpot, she spent more than 5 years as the policy and communications director for the Convenient Care Association, the national trade organization representing the retail-based convenient care clinic industry, based in Philadelphia, Pennsylvania. She also served as a managing editor for the *Philadelphia Social Innovations Journal*, an academic journal focused on promoting social innovation and entrepreneurship in and around the Philadelphia region. She completed her JD at Temple University's Beasley School of Law and her BA at Haverford College.

Theodore Search, PharmD, RPh

Dr. Theodore Search is the president and CEO of Skipta, Ltd. He is known as an expert on the topic of "professional networking," is invited to speak at various conferences around the country, and received a "40 under 40" award for his achievements in social media. He received his doctor of pharmacy degree from the University of Pittsburgh.

Willa Seldon, MBA, JD

Willa Seldon is a partner at The Bridgespan Group and leads Bridgespan's work on collaborations. She recently coauthored "Five Ways to Navigate the Fiscal Crisis" with Daniel Stid (*SSIR*, Winter 2012). She holds an MBA from Harvard's Graduate School of Business Administration, a JD from Yale Law School, and a BA from Bryn Mawr College.

Susan Sherman, MA, RN, FAAN

Susan Sherman is president and CEO of the Independence Foundation, a private foundation dedicated to supporting programs in Philadelphia-area counties that provide services to people who ordinarily do not have access to them. She has received a number of commendations—the Keystone Foundation Award, the 40 Leaders Award, MANNA's Outstanding Community Leadership Award, the Women's Way of Philadelphia Moving Women Forward Award, the Pennsylvania Legal Services Excellence Award, the New York University School of Nursing Alumni Award, the University of Rhode Island Nursing Alumni Award, the American Academy of Nursing Civitas Award, and the Ross Laboratories Institutional Long Term Care Award.

Daniel Stid, PhD

Daniel Stid is a senior fellow at the William and Flora Hewlett Foundation, where he is leading the development of a new foundation initiative to support the democratic process in the United States. Prior to joining the Hewlett Foundation, he was a partner at the Bridgespan Group, where he helped coordinate that organization's engagement with government agencies. He has an MPhil in politics from Oxford University and a PhD in government from Harvard University.

R. Andrew Swinney, MHA

R. Andrew Swinney has been president of the Philadelphia Foundation since 1998. He currently serves on the Professional Development Committee of the Council on Foundations and the Appeals Committee for the Council's Community Foundation's National Standards Board. He is the recipient of the 2010 Distinguished Service Award from Philadelphia Youth Playwrights, the 2007 Carl Moore Leadership Award from PHMC, the 2006 "Men Making a Difference" Humanitarian Award, the Greater Philadelphia Cares 2005 Leadership STAR Award, and the 2004 Good Citizen's Award from the Potter's House Mission.

David Thornburgh, MPP

David Thornburgh is the executive director of the Fels Institute of Government at the University of Pennsylvania. He has received a number of awards for his professional and civic leadership and is a frequent commentator on public policy and regional development issues. He holds a BA in political science from Haverford College and a master's degree in public policy from Harvard University's Kennedy School of Government.

Nicholas D. Torres, MEd

Nicholas D. Torres is a cofounder of the *Philadelphia Social Innovations Journal*. He also serves as a senior fellow for Public/Private Ventures and is the president of Education-Plus, Inc., where he scales 9 to 14 college-access and completion models for low-income students, and school-based health centers, and quality education interventions for specialized populations via learning blended models.

Peter York, MSSA

Peter York is the founder and chief executive officer of Algorhythm and has been a recognized leader of social impact evaluations and creator of evaluative learning tools and systems for almost 20 years. For the past 15 years, York has served as director of evaluation, chief research officer, and senior partner at TCC Group, a national and international philanthropic consulting firm based in New York. He began his evaluation career as the project manager of the first ever application of the theory of change approach to evaluation for community change initiatives while working at the Center on Urban Poverty at Case Western Reserve University. He also worked as a research officer at the Center for Assessment and Policy Development, a nonprofit evaluation and policy think tank based in Philadelphia.

York specializes in leveraging research design techniques, psychometrics, and predictive data modeling to design evaluations, evaluative learning tools, and systems for philanthropies, nonprofit organizations, social enterprises, and corporations. He has served in this capacity for a variety of philanthropies, nonprofits, and corporations, including The California Endowment, Atlantic Philanthropies, The James Irvine Foundation, The David and Lucile Packard Foundation, Camp Fire, Big Brothers Big Sisters, Girl Scouts, Points of Light, The Philadelphia Zoo, Target, Gap, Inc., Wachovia/Wells Fargo, the Corporation for National Community Service, and so on.

York is the creator of the nationally recognized nonprofit organizational assessment tool, the Core Capacity Assessment Tool (www.tccccat.com). York leveraged cutting-edge predictive modeling to create the tool, and the data and findings have been used by numerous leading organizations and groups to study the nonprofit sector—for example, Grantmakers for Effective Organizations (www.geofunders.org), Reimagining Service (www.reimaginingservice.org), the Weingart Foundation, and so on.

York has authored, coauthored, and/or been cited in numerous journal articles, media articles, papers, blogs, and reports and is the author of the book *A Funder's Guide to Evaluation: Leveraging Evaluation to Improve Nonprofit Effectiveness* (Fieldstone, 2005). He is a popular speaker with numerous engagements at conferences such as the Council on Foundations, Grantmakers for Effective Organizations, and the Council of Southwest Foundations. He serves on the board of the Alliance for Nonprofit Management; as a member and past research committee cochair of the national Reimagining Service Council; as an advisory board member of the Easter Evaluation Research Society; and as a member of the national Alliance for Effective Social Investing. He is also an editor for *The Journal of Nonprofit Management*.

FOREWORD

It is not the strongest of the species that survives, nor the most intelligent, but the one most responsive to change.
—Charles Darwin

Our world is becoming increasingly complex, uncertain, and dynamic. To flourish in this environment, leaders in the nonprofit sector will, as Darwin points out, need to fashion organizations highly responsive to change. They will need to nurture in them a culture of innovation that embraces strategies that achieve measurable results, jettisons practices that fail to do so, and capitalizes on emerging opportunities. Equally critical will be partnerships with both like-minded and dissimilar organizations as well as the ability to respond quickly to rapid changes. These demands will require leaders with the courage and vision to build organizations that are (1) adaptable, (2) learning focused, and (3) meaningfully networked. Future leaders will thrive *because of*—not in spite of—the myriad ways that our world is reinventing itself.

Change

A number of global trends have reshaped our world over the past decade. Addressing these trends could easily fill all the pages of this book. For our purposes, two trends—economic globalization and geopolitical shifts—warrant mention, along with the stunning advances in technology that are driving them.

Like the Industrial Revolution of the 20th century, technology has transformed (and will continue to transform) the way we live our lives, interact with others, perceive the physical world, and accomplish our everyday work. Today, more information races through the Internet in 24 hours than passed through it in an entire year in the mid-1990s (Houle, 2010). Personal computing has restructured whole industries by reducing the need for administrative support and increasing the need for IT departments. E-mail (to many people's dismay) has become the de facto means of communicating in the workplace. In short, technological tools have transformed the modern world in ways that only a few years ago we could not have imagined.

Technology is also responsible in part for accelerating a number of global trends, including economic globalization (loosely defined as the distribution of goods and services worldwide) that connects international markets in unprecedented ways. Individual entrepreneurs who were once limited to local markets now sell their products worldwide through online services. Logistical chains and distribution hubs keep consumers and suppliers informed in real time; a network disruption caused by, say, an earthquake in Japan results in delayed deliveries of auto parts around the world. Globalization has also spurred emerging markets in places like Brazil, China, and India where a new middle class is bursting with possibility while contributing to grave inequities between rich and poor.

Over the last decade or so, technology has caused tectonic shifts in geopolitics, the relationship between a government and its territory. The terrorist attacks of September 11, 2001, as well as the United States' subsequent involvement in Afghanistan and Iraq underscore the fact that conflicts transcend geographical borders. Al-Qaeda is essentially a stateless network with followers bound more closely by ideology than by a particular nation. The two oceans on the United States' coasts no longer serve as the buffer zone that they did in previous conflicts.

Technology has helped people mobilize in the face of oppression and injustice. While only the history books will fully capture the extent to which social media ignited the democratic revolutions in Egypt, Tunisia, and elsewhere, many people, myself included, watched the Arab Spring unfold day by day, if not minute by minute. We saw the choppy cell phone videos filmed in Tahrir Square, read tweets about upcoming protests, and followed blogs describing the fighting.

Modern technology provides a window to the world very unlike that offered by traditional media outlets. Courageous citizens in Syria, for instance, have been documenting their government's ferocious crackdown. Although war correspondents have for centuries put themselves in harm's way, there is an added degree of authenticity when a shopkeeper on a cell phone describes the shelling of Homs in western Syria. Each time a bomb hits, we hear the man yell over the wail of distant sirens or the cries of mourners as he offers us a real-time update. Unlike reading a newspaper or hearing the level voice of a professional journalist, we are transported to the scene of ghastly destruction. We sense, in an almost palpable way, the immense danger and feel outrage at a dictator's brutalization of his own people.

Beyond war zones, technology is reshaping the geopolitical landscape by enabling families and loved ones to stay in contact even when they are worlds apart. In my organization, we have staff members who were either born or have relatives in Cameroon, Egypt, Ethiopia, Ghana, Hungary, India, Mexico, Nigeria, the Philippines, Sierra Leone, Scotland, and South Africa. Through video teleconferencing, Facebook, e-mail, and other means, they may stay deeply involved in each other's lives. In addition, remittances have grown substantially in recent years, due in part to the ease of moving money securely. A May 2011 Gallup poll of 135 countries found that 3% of adults worldwide receive remittances, with sub-Saharan Africa topping the charts (Pugliese & Ray, 2011).

America and its nonprofit sector are, of course, subject to the ebb and flow of global transformations and the information revolution that fuels them. Technological tools have changed how organizations in the charitable community marshal funds from online donations, measure their impact in communities, and mobilize grassroots support for their causes. Gone are the days of megaphone communications in which organizations loudly broadcasted one-way messages to a vast, unidentified audience, hoping someone would hear them. Today, social media allows organizations to converse with hundreds of thousands of participants in real time and to tailor each message to particular audiences or even different individuals. Visual mapping and crowd sourcing—tools not even imagined 5 years ago—are changing the ways organizations convene through networked coalitions or virtual meta-groupings capable of surging together to surmount a crisis and then disbanding as needed.

With the retirement of the baby boom generation (people born between 1946 and 1964), the nonprofit sector may need as many as 80,000 new leaders by 2016.[1] Demographic trends illustrate the need to cultivate the capabilities of younger generations more fully as well as the potential to tap into the vast work experience of baby boomers who may be seeking encore (second) careers in the sector.

Hybrid organizations seeking to "do well and do good" are further changing the nature of the nonprofit and philanthropic communities. Because these entities draw on characteristics of both for-profit and nonprofit organizations, they are challenging traditional notions of how charities operate. Specifically, they are raising questions about whether the charitable community is the only place (or the best place) to try to improve people's lives and make communities healthy. Some point to enduring social problems— tens of thousands in deep poverty, an education system failing millions of children, and the treatment of marginalized groups—and argue that the nonprofit sector has been unable to remedy these troubling issues. Others point out that the sector itself draws on the work of for-profit partners to achieve its missions. Some nonprofits have even created for-profit subsidiaries to help them achieve their goals. In addition, a number of foundations pay for-profits to advance their missions. These new forms and structures are particularly relevant to younger workers, who tend not to define themselves by the sector in which they work but rather by their passion for a cause. Because these workers may not distinguish among government, business, and the social sector, lines between sectors are becoming more ambiguous and uncertain.

Some are skeptical of the laws that define what types of organizations warrant a tax exemption. They ask whether a well-intentioned organization that is clearly unable to show concrete, measurable results should be eligible to receive favorable tax treatment. If organizations are lowering high school dropout rates or curbing methamphetamine use in cities A, B, and C, should they receive greater tax exemptions than less successful entities in cities X, Y, and Z? Which government officials (and at which levels) should decide such issues? What about the tax treatment of prosperous universities or hospitals, both nonprofit entities that seem to receive more than ample funding at a time when lifeline service organizations cannot help the unemployed factory worker or homeless veteran?

There is no one right answer to these questions. We do, however, know that more people are experimenting with new organizational models as a way to serve the common good. Two of them, the certified benefit corporation (B corps) and the low-profit limited liability company (L3C), have grown steadily over the past few years. InterSector Partners (an L3C that defines itself as a socially responsible, low-profit business) recently listed 587 L3Cs in nine states, an increase of more than 200% since 2008. B Lab, a nonprofit committed to "business as a force for good," reported that there are over 520 certified B corporations in seven states, a significant increase of over 315% in the past 4 years.[2] It appears as though the trend of forming hybrid organizations will continue to grow. Legislation to permit L3Cs and B corps is pending in 15 and 7 states, respectively.

Given the unpredictable nature of our changing world, combined with the massive inflow of information and lightning-quick changes in technology, what essential competencies do leaders need to help their organizations survive—and even thrive—in the future? The extent to which we are likely to fashion new solutions depends on how well we grasp the dynamic nature of our complex world, how disciplined we are about our goals and strategies, and how committed we are to becoming inventive leaders who work together to find new ways of serving people and communities.

This is no easy feat. How can a leader try to move an organization forward when he or she is seemingly bombarded with decisions from all sides? However talented, smart, or capable, no one can make the right decision every single time—doing so will be nearly impossible as information flows speed up and complexities mount. Instead, successful leaders will build organizations permeated by a culture of innovation at every level and an intrinsic recognition that teams of people working together are more likely to succeed than even the most inventive individual working in isolation. This will enable organizations to excel by making smart decisions or, in contrast, to learn and recover adeptly from poor ones.

Innovation

Henry Ford studied the sewing machine, the meat-packing industry, and Campbell's Soup, and then he and his team invented the assembly line. Albert Einstein developed a theoretical framework based on previously unconnected ideas about matter and energy. He said, "Combinatory play seems to be the essential feature in productive thought." Johannes Gutenberg combined the wine press and coin punch to create the printing press. In each case, the inventor "stood on the shoulders of giants" by tapping existing materials or theories to fashion something new.

Thomas Edison's lab in New Jersey included mechanics, engineers, scientists, and tradesmen working side by side on wooden workbenches, often tinkering with each other's inventions. Their lab ultimately produced over 1,000 U.S. patents. Although Edison himself did much to propagate his reputation as a lone inventor, most of his inventions were the product of many minds.

The leaders who will blossom in the coming years will reward innovation in an effort to maximize organizational strengths, deepen staff knowledge, and sharpen strategies to compete in a complex world. They will fashion organizations that are adaptable, learning focused, and meaningfully networked—the three legs of a stool that can offer some degree of stability in a dynamic world.

Adaptability

Organizations described by their hierarchies and operating through bureaucracies are, by nature, slow. Thorough and predictable as they may be, they lumber along while the world zips past. As a result, they may miss out on the potential for greater efficiency and impact afforded by new methodologies. Successful leaders will trim unnecessary structures, cumbersome processes, and old patterns of working that inhibit their organizations' abilities to be agile and forward leaning. They and their staffs will strive to harness evolving technologies in service of their missions and remain flexible in light of changing external conditions.

Such leaders are essential if the nonprofit sector is to be successful in tackling enduring—and looming—problems like world hunger, environmental degradation, and the widening gap between the "haves" and "have-nots." They will need to enact multiple solutions to remedy mega-problems.

Learning Focus

Vibrant organizations will be able to function in a world in which the pace of new knowledge is constantly accelerating. In this environment, there will be value in deliberations that foster a learning environment defined by iterative processes that identify what works and what does not. As a result, leaders and staff members will be able to make the best possible decisions at any given time.

Courageous leaders will shun a workplace culture that is overly risk averse, knowing that, for example, Edison's team discovered 1,800 ways not to create a light bulb before they were successful, and many of their failures led to new inventions. Successful leaders see the world as a place not spiraling out of control but spinning off endless new combinations of old and new that require experimentation for fresh learning to occur.

Meaningful Networks

Broad forces such as information diffusion, international commerce, and consumerism are driving our world toward previously unknown levels of interdependence. Sharp leaders will position their organizations as nodes within a larger constellation of organizations when and where it makes sense—to advocate for a public policy change, to garner additional resources, and to rally grassroots support behind a cause. Doing so may mean seeking partners with complementary (not duplicate) capabilities who agree on a shared objective and the strategy to make it happen. Meaningful networks may include like-minded organizations, unlikely allies, or both.

Leaders who will succeed in the coming years will recognize that some problems are too big to solve alone. They will participate in meaningful collaborations that maximize the assets of multiple organizations, deepen the group's collective knowledge, and move together in ways that also fulfill individual missions.

CONCLUSION

As you turn the pages of this book, imagine a sector driven by leaders who govern organizations capable of pivoting adroitly in the face of complexity. Imagine leaders who see in failure a chance to learn and prosper. Imagine leaders who share a vision across fields of practice, forge networks to tackle ballooning social problems, and cultivate an entrepreneurial environment throughout the social sector. Imagine the high caliber of a workforce that reflects the rainbow of diversity across America and, in doing so, becomes more innovative than ever.

Darwin said, "It is not the strongest of the species that survives, nor the most intelligent, but the one most responsive to change." This text is filled with examples of leaders who have been responsive to change. They have built adaptable, learning-focused, and meaningfully networked organizations that are flourishing. I encourage you to determine which aspects of their experiences are most suitable to your circumstances and cultivate the essential competencies of leadership that will propel your organization forward in a 21st-century environment of dynamic transition and endless possibility.

Diana Aviv, MSW
President and CEO, Independent Sector

NOTES

1. Mikaela Seligman, IS Leadership presentation, September 27, 2011.
2. www.bcorporation.net/what-are-b-corps/the-non-profit-behind-b-corps

REFERENCES

Houle, D. (2010, July 2). *China's calling you: Dealing with digital overload* [Web log post]. Retrieved from www.oprah.com/world/David-Houle-Deals-with-Digital-Immediacy-and-Overload/2
Pugliese, A., & Ray, J. (2011, May 6). *Three percent worldwide get international remittances* [Web log post]. Retrieved from www.gallup.com/poll/147446/Three-Percent-Worldwide-%20International-Remittances.aspx

PREFACE

Everyone associated with this book would agree that working in the social sector is one of the most fulfilling careers one can have. We have had the opportunity to work in the government and private sectors, and we can say with confidence that the nonprofit sector is much more complex and demanding. The U.S. nonprofit sector is unique because it serves as a broker between the government and private sectors, a role filled by the government in most Western countries. This is also what makes it fun and challenging, however, and what inspired us to assemble some of the brightest minds from the U.S. sector to help write this book. In our many years of nonprofit-sector practice, we have come across some amazing leaders who have mentored us and taught invaluable lessons. Some of these lessons (all practical) we share in this book.

The world is undergoing one of the worst recessions in decades, and this has had a profound impact on both the U.S. and international nonprofit sectors. The good news, however, is that the nonprofit sector is very resilient. Moreover, tough economic times provide any sector with an opportunity for self-reflection and the implementation of changes that are often long overdue. Although not everyone can weather the storm, the best agencies and leaders are able to push through the tough times, surviving with fewer resources. The leaders of the organizations discussed here seem to be good at figuring out how to push through tough times while still meeting their missions, providing quality services, and realizing the outcomes that make their services relevant to funders, self-sustaining, and even profitable.

Central to the book are the concepts of social innovation and impact, contexts in which nonprofits are thinking differently to create high-impact and financially sustainable models. Around the globe, leaders and managers are in search of high-impact solutions and financing mechanisms to address the most challenging problems. In an emerging trend, the government, for-profit, and nonprofit sectors are looking to identify the most effective services and provide the capital to replicate them. This text describes and explores the process of creating, sustaining, and replicating innovative programs to achieve high social impact.

The book defines and discusses the competencies needed by leaders to lead and create change in the evolving nonprofit sector. Unlike the for-profit sector, there are only a few leading textbooks on nonprofit leadership, and most of these focus on management competencies. We have attempted to provide a comprehensive framework for leadership within the nonprofit sector that takes theories and demonstrates how to put them into practice. Our goal is to give anyone interested in working in the sector, or already in it, tangible tools to ensure that it continues to thrive.

Tine Hansen-Turton and Nicholas D. Torres

ACKNOWLEDGMENTS

In every sector, there are the visible leaders but also the lesser-known ones who just as importantly, and sometimes more effectively, create change and innovation over time. As with most of the projects we engage in, we could not have done this without the many inspiring people and leaders whom we have been fortunate to get to know over the years. We especially want to acknowledge and thank all of the chapter contributors and authors. Each of them has provided an authoritative voice from their own experience, style, organization and university affiliation, and prominence. They are all unique, some are known and some less so, and most are extremely busy leading change within the social sector.

We want to acknowledge the Fels Institute of Government's faculty and students who have provided us the playground in which to research and study the social sector and nonprofits, both as professors and through the work we do at the *Philadelphia Social Innovations Journal*. Much of what we have learned and what served as a foundation for this book has been the result of the enormous amount of research and study that went into each article that was published in the journal and the combined knowledge we have gained from the foundation leaders who are driving social change. We want to acknowledge the *Philadelphia Social Innovations Journal*'s funders and investors, specifically, Andrew Swinney of the Philadelphia Foundation; Susan Sherman of the Independence Foundation; Jill Michal and Ann Schmieg of the United Way of Southeastern Pennsylvania; Susan Hansen of the Greentree Community Health Foundation; Joe Pyle of Thomas Scattergood Foundation; Jan Shaeffer of the St. Christopher's Foundation for Children; Kim Allen of Wells Fargo; Tina Wahl of the Barra Foundation; Donna Frisby-Greenwood of the John S. and James L. Knight Foundation; Steve Fera, Sheila Hess, and Lorina Marshall-Blake of the IBC Foundation; Richard Cohen of Public Health Management Corporation and Public Health Fund; Gavin Kerr of the Inglis Foundation; Laura McKenna of the Patricia Kind Foundation; David Thornburgh of the Fels Institute of Government; John Kimberly of the Wharton School of Business; and Kenwyn Smith of the University of Pennsylvania's School of Social Policy and Practice. We also want to acknowledge and thank the dozen writers and volunteers who support the journal.

We want to thank the staff of our partner agencies, many of whom wrote for the book, including contributors from the *Stanford Social Innovation Review*, The Bridgespan Group, Public/Private Ventures, Community Wealth Partners, Independent Sector, Eisenhower Fellowships, Urban Institute, TCC Group, OMG, and National Alliance for Social Impact.

We also want to specifically acknowledge Dr. David Hunter, who has been a leader and has provided a vision to ensure that we achieve the social impact we all desire.

We want to thank Ann Deinhardt for serving as our supporting editor—particularly for keeping us consistent and on track—and Marissa Prianti and Nandi Brown for their editing assistance as well.

Finally, we would be remiss if we did not acknowledge and thank our families, on Nick's side, Maria-Paula, Ema, Evaluna, and Amelia and on Tine's side, Brian, Nikolaj, and Kristoffer, who are always supportive of all of our new ideas, projects (big and small), and nonprofit business ventures.

Social Innovation and Impact in Nonprofit Leadership

INTRODUCTION AND OVERVIEW

Marissa Prianti, Caroline Ridgway, Nicholas D. Torres,
and Tine Hansen-Turton

> You are not here merely to make a living. You are here to enable the world
> to live more amply, with greater vision, and with a finer spirit of hope and
> achievement. You are here to enrich the world, and you impoverish yourself if
> you forget this errand.
> —Woodrow Wilson

PURPOSE AND AUDIENCE OF THE BOOK

This book seeks to define the competencies needed by leaders to create change in the 21st-century nonprofit sector. The target audience includes students who desire to become nonprofit leaders, current nonprofit leaders, faculty who teach about the nonprofit social sector, and policy makers seeking to create social change through legislation.

The book helps readers identify, lead, and manage social change through ethical business practices, the application of business principles within the nonprofit sector, and the creation of social change via policy. Through case studies written by practitioners who have employed innovative principles to organize, create, and manage social change ventures locally, regionally, and beyond, readers will examine these tactics in depth.

Why Focus on Leadership Through Social Innovation and Impact?

Social innovation and impact have become popular terms to describe collaboration between businesses and nonprofits to create social enterprise, defined as a blending of financial investments and social impact. The creation of the White House Office of Social Innovation and Civic Participation, the National Alliance for Effective Social Investing, and the *Stanford Social Innovation Review* represent nationwide efforts to provide structure (best practices, standards, etc.) for rapidly evolving social enterprise.

In the United States and abroad, leaders are in search of high-impact solutions and financing mechanisms to address the most challenging domestic and global problems. Managers in the government, nonprofit, for-profit, and philanthropic sectors are looking to identify the most effective services and provide the capital to replicate them. Little is known, however, about the process and framework for creating and replicating innovative programs with social impact.

Issues Explored by the Book

In a watershed moment after World War II, America turned away from the European model of a welfare state. While the government grew steadily on a diet of universal taxation, public policies encouraged nonprofits to provide services (paid for with public funds) to targeted populations deemed in need of and worthy of such services.

Due to its inherent flexibility, the nonprofit sector lacks well-defined functions. The nonprofit sector, which has historically filled a number of educational, charitable, and membership roles, is being fundamentally reshaped. The primary factors contributing to this reshaping include increased scrutiny from Congress, state legislatures, and the Internal Revenue Service (IRS), advances in technology, expectations that nonprofits will fulfill social needs formerly met by the family, and demands by some donors to articulate and measure social impact. This book explores these issues and the efficacy of various responses.

HISTORY AND EVOLUTION OF THE U.S. NONPROFIT SECTOR

Charitable giving and provision of services for the needy were part of the country's social fabric prior to independence from Great Britain (Hayman, 2011). Colonists relied on one another for survival and, as a result, volunteerism became ingrained in their way of life. Despite regular if informal philanthropy and volunteering, however, "nonprofits" as we know them today were not even on the horizon (Renz, 2005). The legal structures of corporations and trusts were in place, but there was no impetus to expand beyond their for-profit functions. At this stage, there was minimal distinction between public and private, and a great deal of "volunteering" was actually compelled by law or done via barter, such as militia service or the construction of buildings and roadways.

Beginning in the 18th century, the picture began to change (Renz, 2005). The population was growing and the economy was becoming more complex, with more trade and commerce and less self-reliance and barter. Society became more compartmentalized and less unified. Increased contact between England and the colonies led to the diffusion of philosophies about freedom of speech, assembly, and worship. As colonists gained more knowledge about the operation of law and economic rights, they began to question the role of government. The number of volunteer associations grew, and a variety of religious denominations rose to prominence.

These trends, in combination with persistent social mores about volunteerism and the influence of wealthy private organizations, ultimately became the backdrop for the Revolutionary War (Renz, 2005). Many states, particularly in the South, actively opposed private charity, limiting the formation of trusts and amounts that wealthy individuals could leave in bequest. In contrast, some New England states cleared the legal way for private associations. Reforms enabled the creation of universities, libraries, hospitals, and museums. As a consequence, New England grew into an early leader in academic and medical endeavors. It was not until after the Revolution, however, that charitable activity underwent a substantial shift toward formalization. As Robert Glavin put it, "The lack of a nobility or an autocratic state made self-governing group action a principal means of building our society" (Hayman, 2011, p. 11).

Despite legal obstacles and public opposition in many areas, volunteer associations witnessed strong growth during the first half of the 19th century (Renz, 2005). Political parties became influential, and membership in churches and fraternal organizations flourished. As immigration increased, the Roman Catholic Church assumed a larger role, founding numerous schools and orphanages among other social initiatives.

The Civil War and its aftermath spurred an expansion in national volunteerism as well as private organizations to meet the overwhelming need for assistance. During the war, the need for support, especially medical assistance, was especially critical. The U.S. Sanitary Commission and U.S. Christian Commission were founded to provide medical care, funds, and other aid to troops as well as to support infectious disease control (Hayman, 2011; Renz, 2005). After the war, Reconstruction led to the formation of numerous organizations to educate freed slaves and develop a new industrial base for the South, among other endeavors. It was at this time, which coincided with the founding of the Ku Klux Klan, that the negative aspect of associations first became publicly evident (Renz, 2005).

By the late 1800s, universities had expanded in number and scope, founding robust research programs and graduate schools. New associations and philanthropic ventures were established in affiliation with universities. The economic depression of 1873 witnessed a growing representation among labor unions and radical political groups.

With volunteerism and associated activity on an upward trajectory, albeit constrained by lingering legal obstacles to the expansion of private philanthropy, charitable giving underwent a radical shift at the behest of wealthy industrialists like Andrew Carnegie. Believing the existing charitable model to be ineffective and wasteful, Carnegie argued for a new philanthropic approach based on the use of wealth to fundamentally change social circumstances (Hayman, 2011, p. 12). As a businessman, Carnegie maintained that "it shall be the rule for the workman to be Partner with Capital, the man of affairs giving his business experience, the working man in the mill his mechanical skill, to the company, both owners of the shares and so far equally interested in the success of their joint efforts."[1]

Carnegie adhered to this philosophy in his role as a philanthropist. He said, "The problem of our age is the proper administration of wealth, that the ties of brotherhood may still bind together the rich and poor in harmonious relationship." In his essay *The Gospel of Wealth*, Carnegie set forth his theory about the wealthy as "trustees," stipulating that those with money were obligated to disburse their wealth during their lifetimes to enhance society at large and opposing large bequests to heirs or posthumous distribution (Carnegie, 1889/2008).

Following Carnegie's lead, many Americans made wealthy by the Industrial Revolution became involved in formal philanthropy (Renz, 2005, Chapter 1). To enable the growth of foundations and large-scale charity to reach its full potential, however, legal changes still needed to occur. Concerns also remained among private citizens and some government officials about the influence wielded by wealthy philanthropists through private foundations. This influence caused foundations to become secretive about their donations and sources of support.

Despite these residual obstacles, the national outlook on charity, volunteerism, and associational influence had reached critical momentum. The first foundations formed in the early 1900s. The Cleveland-based Community Chest, precursor to United Way, established a model of collective fund raising with committee-based fund allocation, a model that became widespread. Business leaders subscribed to the notion of "welfare capitalism" and gave generously to charity in addition to founding employee pensions and otherwise supporting workers through educational, athletic, and social activities. Membership in fraternal organizations reached an all-time high, and social reform movements continued to expand.

The nation was entirely unprepared, however, for what was to come. The stock market crash of 1929 and the ensuing Great Depression triggered unprecedented social challenges. Public works programs became critical to recovery, and a new progressive tax system encouraged charitable giving among the rich. Progressive taxation, in combination with Roosevelt's New Deal, laid the groundwork for substantial government involvement in the provision of social services, stimulating rapid growth in foundations and nonprofit organizations.

The influence of government on the post–World War II nonprofit sector is evident simply from the increase in the number of nonprofits (Renz, 2005, pp. 18–19). From 1940 to 1980, the number of tax-exempt nonprofits increased from 12,500 to 320,000. The number of foundations has likewise grown from 203 in 1929 to more than 100,000 today.

Public attitudes about the roles of foundations and nonprofits were mixed. Many believed that policies enabling the rich to evade taxes were irresponsible and inappropriate and canceled out the benefit of services made possible by donations. This perception gave rise to a series of congressional investigations during the 1950s and 1960s. These issues aside, however, foundations and nonprofits contributed significantly to the public sector.

In addition to broad-based criticism, the increase in the influence and number of foundations and nonprofits was accompanied by a rise in the number of special interest groups dedicated to public advocacy. The postwar era also witnessed the birth of grassroots advocacy.

As the Civil Rights movement gained momentum, social activism became a potent tool.

Compared with social reform groups of the 19th century, however, these organizations were vastly more sophisticated, centralized, and businesslike in scope. In contrast, with the exception of religious groups, which continued to grow in variety and number, fraternal organizations declined as civic engagement shifted away from the traditional volunteer-based model. The modern nonprofit had taken shape and began to mature in its role in society.

The next substantial shift came during the 1980s and 1990s, when political pressures from conservative Republicans made it more difficult for nonprofits to receive federal funding (Hayman, 2011; Renz, 2005). From the time Reagan assumed office through the mid-1990s "Contract with America," conservative politicians limited federal funding for nonprofits. The widely held belief was that government support of nonprofits hampered private-sector solutions and that for-profit initiatives would compete for resources, thereby encouraging efficiency.

Ultimately, these policies did not cause a significant contraction of the nonprofit sector. These policies did, however, lead to additional centralization, formalization, and professionalization among nonprofits, which suddenly needed to compete for greatly reduced funding.

Today, many nonprofits team with other nonprofits, government agencies, and for-profit, private-sector entities. There is also a strong focus on performance metrics. Nonprofit programs must be evidence-based and outcomes quantifiable. Social entrepreneurship, the application of entrepreneurial principles to the solution of social problems, has become common. The nonprofit of today is nearly unrecognizable from its colonial predecessors, while the nonprofit sector has gained substantial influence in modern society.

THE 21ST-CENTURY NONPROFIT SECTOR

In its short modern history, the nonprofit sector has undergone substantial changes. In response to economic and social shifts brought about by globalization, the conception of what a charitable organization is and does is once again changing. Increasingly, multinational nongovernmental organizations (NGOs) respond to natural disasters, acts of war, economic crises, and the like. These global assistance networks simultaneously broaden the reach of nonprofits while stretching their ability to effect meaningful relief and lasting change. As nonprofits learn to survive on fewer and often more contingent resources, the concept of social entrepreneurship has taken root. Doing social good and breaking even or making a profit are no longer mutually exclusive.

Modern attitudes toward nonprofits are mixed. Many Americans rely heavily on the services they provide and laud their contributions to the nation's well-being. Others, however, accuse the government of enabling a welfare state, contending that those offered charity will never become self-sufficient. Although it is inaccurate, this perception persists among certain constituencies.

Despite the current challenges facing nonprofits, including the Great Recession and its aftermath, social pressures, and increased competition for government funding, the nonprofit sector is likely to survive. The very circumstances that have limited nonprofits' capacity to effect social change, however, have also increased the need for their services at the local, state, and national levels.

Size, Characteristics, and Economic Impact of the 21st-Century Nonprofit Sector

According to the National Center for Charitable Statistics, there are currently 1,574,674 tax-exempt organizations in the United States, including 959,698 charitable organizations, 100,337 private foundations, and 514,639 "other" organizations like chambers of commerce and professional associations.[2] The majority of nonprofits in the United States are 501(c)(3) organizations. They can encompass public charities and private foundations.[3] Private charities include large organizations such as hospitals, academic institutions, and museums as well as small organizations such as community theaters and neighborhood groups.

In addition to the 501(c)(3) category, common classifications include social welfare organizations—501(c)(4); agricultural, horticultural, and labor organizations—501(c)(5); business leagues—501(c)(6); social and recreation clubs—501(c)(7); and fraternal associations—501(c)(8). Of these, social welfare organizations and business leagues are the most numerous. AARP, formerly the American Association of Retired Persons, for example, qualifies as a social welfare organization. Many health care organizations also fall under this designation. Business leagues include chambers of commerce, trade and professional associations, real estate boards, and other entities "formed to improve conditions."[4]

The impact of the nonprofit sector on the U.S. economy is substantial (Renz, 2005, Chapter 1). In 2009, nonprofits accounted for 5.4% of gross domestic product (GDP) and 9% of total wages and salaries. Also in 2009, expenses and revenues for public charities totaled $1.40 trillion and $1.41 trillion, respectively. The majority of public charities' revenue (76%) came from "program service revenues," including government fees and contracts. The balance was attributable to contributions, gifts, and government grants (22%), and to "other" sources including dues, rental income, special event proceeds, and the transfer of goods (11%). Public charity assets amounted to $2.56 trillion in 2009. These numbers were driven by a 25% increase in nonprofits between 2001 and 2011.[5]

There is an indirect economic and social benefit from the nonprofit sector in terms of private charitable giving and volunteer hours contributed. In 2010, donations from individuals, corporations, and foundations amounted to $290.89 billion (Renz, 2005, Chapter 1); of that, $211.77 billion came from individuals. More than one-quarter of Americans older than 16 years—approximately 26.3%—volunteered through a nonprofit from 2009 to 2010. According to an Urban Institute report, in 2006, nonprofits benefited from 12.9 billion volunteer hours, which equates to 7.6 million full-time employees earning $215.6 billion in wages (Blackwood, Wing, & Pollack, 2008).

A FINAL NOTE TO THE READER

As the reader will discover, this book presents a new and vigorous model, one that urges NGOs to see themselves as successful business enterprises and to utilize the same methods of efficiency, impact, financial rigor, entrepreneurship, and critical evaluation as the business world. As with all methods, however, these methods can and do fail. Indeed, in the context of the 2008 financial crisis, they have failed us miserably. The NGO world, on the other hand, has successfully borne the burden of ensuring a safety net for the most vulnerable despite being under the terrible constraints of reduced government funding and donations.

The reader will also discover that the case studies illustrate successes and demonstrate how they were achieved. Mistakes, of course, occur all the time: There are inadequate employees, chief executive officers who do not utilize their employees well, donors who micromanage, and strategies that fail. This book, however, is about best practices and helping practitioners to emulate them.

Finally, the contributors to this book come from varied backgrounds. As a result, they sometimes have different definitions for the same terms and contrasting views on concepts. None of these definitions or views is considered "correct" but is rather shaped by varying perspectives.

NOTES

1. carnegie.org/about-us/foundation-history/about-andrew-carnegie
2. nccs.urban.org/statistics/quickfacts.cfm
3. nccsdataweb.urban.org/nonprofit-overview.html
4. nccsdataweb.urban.org/PubApps/showOrgsByCategory.php?group=subsection&code=06
5. www.urban.org/nonprofits/more.cfm

REFERENCES

Blackwood, A., Wing, K. T., & Pollack, T. H. (2008). *Facts and figures from the nonprofit almanac 2008: Public charities, giving, and volunteering*. Washington, DC: The Urban Institute. Retrieved from www.urban.org/UploadedPDF/411664_facts_and_figures.pdf

Carnegie, A. (2008). *The Gospel of Wealth*. Gloucester, UK: Dodo Press. (Originally published as "Wealth" in *North American Review*, June 1889.)

Hayman, D. R. (2011). *Nonprofit management 101: A complete and practical guide for leaders and professionals*. San Francisco, CA: Jossey-Bass.

Renz, D. O. (Ed.). (2005). *The Jossey-Bass handbook of nonprofit leadership and management*. San Francisco, CA: Jossey-Bass.

NONPROFIT ACCOUNTABILITY, TRANSPARENCY, GOVERNANCE, FIDUCIARY RESPONSIBILITIES, AND ETHICS

Jennifer Alleva, Jill M. Michal, and Nicholas D. Torres

The noblest question in the world is what good may I do in it?
—Benjamin Franklin, *Poor Richard's Almanac*

Benjamin Franklin had the right question in 1737, but he never asked another important question: "How do we know if we are doing good?" The nonprofit sector's thought leaders have long pondered this question. According to Berger, Penna, and Goldberg (2010), the two most important questions facing the sector are how to define the value of work being done and how to measure that value. The third most important question is how to ensure that revenues, public and/or private, maximize returns on investment and are spent according to the highest standards of accountability and transparency.

Had the realities of the nonprofit sector and national economy not changed, it is probable that the debate over how to measure value and impact while ensuring maximum investment returns would have continued unnoticed. The field, however, is changing, and nonprofit funding is increasingly taking the form of investment in organizational impact. Good stories are no longer enough; organizations need to become outcome driven and accountable to investors.

ISSUES FACING THE NONPROFIT SECTOR

Berger et al. (2010) offer three observations about the nonprofit sector. The first is that much of the effort aimed at addressing social problems over the past few decades has not been thoughtfully designed to produce results. Rather, these efforts have been activity driven, applying promising ideas to social problems without the necessary follow-up and confirmation. As Len Bickman, professor of psychology, psychiatry, and public policy at

Vanderbilt University, wrote, "All too commonly, programs seem to grow from notions and ideas [rather than from a testable theory]…Many programs lack an explicit theory; or the theory they espouse [is] implausible" (Bickman, 1987, p. 6). In other words, many nonprofits are engaged in the social equivalent of alchemy: substituting wishful thinking for demonstrated impact. The good news is that there are now practicable, affordable, and useful methods for evaluating program efficacy, and many funders are beginning to recognize the value in supporting such evaluative efforts as a way of scaling what works.

Second, for much of its history, the nonprofit sector has not invested in change but rather relied on the concept of making services available as a mechanism to stop harmful behaviors and alter negative conditions. Dr. David Hunter, a consultant to funders, ministries, and direct service agencies in the nonprofit and public service sectors, observed that "nonprofits do what their funders tell them to do" (Hunter, 2009, p. 1). This is inarguably true, and if one wishes to trace the course of the sector's mistakes, one source stands out: government. Government underwrites social investment, and the elected officials who approve the budgets from which so much grant and program funding is primarily drawn are primarily interested in three things:

- Appearing to do something about the social problems that bedevil our society
- Equitable distribution of resources among issues and the organizations that exist to address them
- Keeping within the letter of the law

As a result, most social service organizations and their elected funders are activity driven and activity oriented, focusing on the "how many?" questions: How many meals were cooked and served in the soup kitchen to how many people? How many middle schoolers attended the after-school program? The advent of categorical funding inexorably led to a focus on head counts. These funding streams were created by law to provide X services to Y population. Thus, documentation was produced to show that money was spent as required. Emphasis shifted from concerns about effectiveness to concerns about compliance. Many nongovernmental funders have followed this pattern, focusing on "how much?" and on their own versions of compliance. This is a dead-end pattern from which the sector must escape.

There are those who worry that performance measurement may become just another meaningless form of compliance, a condition for grant payment. Instead, this approach must be recognized as vital if nonprofit leaders wish to know which programs and delivery models work best so they may be supported, replicated, and made widely available. While there is no perfect cure-all for the issues addressed by the nonprofit sector, some solutions are more effective than others. The challenge is to increase support for the former while minimizing resources wasted on the latter. The only way to achieve this dynamic is the implementation of meaningful evaluation systems throughout the sector.

Berger et al.'s (2010) third point stems from this belief. Many donors want to know which is the preferable investment, the one likely to provide the most impact. There are two ways to answer this question. The first is for organizations to be held accountable for the claims they make regarding the changes they are bringing about. With this answer, performance measurement is a necessity, and every nonprofit must be able to answer three basic questions:

- Is it using targeted results in the design, management, and measurement of its efforts?
- Are its targets "reasonable?" Are they meaningful, sustainable, and verifiable?
- Is the organization achieving desired results, and how does it document those results?

The second critical element is for information regarding performance to be made not only available but readily accessible to the public.

A NEW BREED OF INVESTORS

While donors give for a variety of (often emotional) reasons, they are increasingly seeking guidance regarding the effectiveness of the organizations to which they give. So-called impact investors differ from the philanthropists of the past and have expectations about appropriate financial and social returns. There are also more social entrepreneurs, defined as those who use business to solve social issues.[1] These new funders represent a shift regarding how to create measurable social impact. They often use intermediaries, such as the University of Pennsylvania Center for High Impact Philanthropy, that have emerged to advise investors on getting the most good for their philanthropic "buck." Intermediaries apply the concept of cost per impact as the fundamental measure of any philanthropic investment. Social impact is measured by specific, objective criteria for success.

Intermediaries have started to influence investors and social entrepreneurs through rating criteria. For example, Charity Navigator (CN), an intermediary with more individual donors using its site than any other in the world, has been at the forefront of judgments regarding the performance of nonprofits (Cohen, 2010). CN and others believe it is essential for the nonprofit sector to identify high-performing nonprofits and direct donor contributions to them. CN is not alone in its quest. Some of their fellow travelers have charged that, for its $1.5 trillion a year in revenue, the nonprofit sector has provided little credible evidence that many of its organizations produce any social value at all. CN is firm in its belief that

- Charitable donations should not be mere monetary gifts but rather social investments.
- An informed donor is the best social investor.
- Effective organizations represent the wisest and most meaningful investments.
- An organization's constituents deserve the best information to guide social investment decisions.

Distinguishing among similar organizations presents a challenge for social entrepreneurs. High-impact organizations are able to define the value of their work and how to measure that value, but this does not necessarily help an investor to determine which delivers better results.

Issue No. 1: Inconsistent definitions of outcomes across funding streams make it difficult for decision makers and nonprofit practitioners to develop a clear picture of overall program results.

Issue No. 2: Most organizations/services do not track long-term participant impact (e.g., employment beyond 3, 6, or 9 months; college completion; college transition into the workforce) due to funding limitations.

Issue No. 3: The customized technology systems of different investors require duplicate, time-consuming data entry by nonprofits, often without providing "apples-to-apples" reports or useful data to improve services.

Issue No. 4: Performance standards and comparisons that do not account for program differences make it difficult to know what constitutes "good" performance.

Issue No. 5: Nonprofit practitioners need centralized expertise to develop and maintain an internal culture of continuous improvement.

Despite these obstacles, investors and intermediaries are creating benchmarks within the nonprofit sector. One method of creating benchmarks is a theory of change, defined as all of the building blocks required to bring about a given long-term goal. This process is elaborated on in Chapter 3.

EFFECTIVELY MOVING AN ORGANIZATION TO EXCELLENCE IN FINANCIAL MANAGEMENT

Financial management is the cornerstone of nonprofit accountability, transparency, governance, and ethics. Donors may be attracted to a charity by the emotional content of its marketing or by the results of its services, but if the fiscal infrastructure is unsound, those programs and services will not be credible or sustainable.

Financial management systems need not be unnecessarily complex or expensive—in fact, sometimes the simplest solutions are the most effective. Failure to provide these systems, however, is an immediate red flag for auditors, donors, grant-making institutions, the general public, and the communities being served.

One of the most significant challenges of fiscal management is the absence of financial expertise among board members and nonfinancial managers. Particularly in smaller nonprofits, the chief executive may not have formal training in financial management. Boards of directors are often selected based on the "three Ws"—wealth, work, and wisdom—or for their social connections, but expertise in reading and analyzing nonprofit financial statements may be lacking. Even when board members possess financial backgrounds, they may be unaccustomed to the accounting intricacies of the nonprofit world. While this is a reality for many nonprofit organizations, it does not absolve the board or management of its fiduciary responsibilities. Can be a highly effective strategy for smaller nonprofits that lack an accounting department, it does not absolve the board or management of their fiduciary responsibilities. Therefore, it is vitally important that board members and nonprofit managers learn the basics of proper nonprofit fiscal management as well as ensure that their organization's accounting and financial management are performed by experienced professionals, whether in-house or by an outside provider.

Dangers of Poor Financial Management

In the worst-case scenario, improper financial management can cause an organization to lose its tax-exempt status. Even short of such a catastrophe, however, the absence of sound financial management risks the loss of public trust. Nonprofits are the stewards not only of other people's money but also of their hopes and dreams. All too often, boards and executives let this component of their work slide.

Leaders may not know what questions to ask, or they may not feel comfortable asking the accountant for clarification; if leaders do ask, they may get so much accounting jargon that they are embarrassed to ask for clarification. It is also possible that the accountant or bookkeeper truly does not know what he or she is doing but is too fearful to admit it. Jargon is never a substitute for clear information, nor are excuses ever a substitute for timely, accurate information. If the leadership cannot understand what is happening, more digging must be done.

The Fundamentals of Financial Management

Figure 2.1 illustrates the basic components of effective financial management.

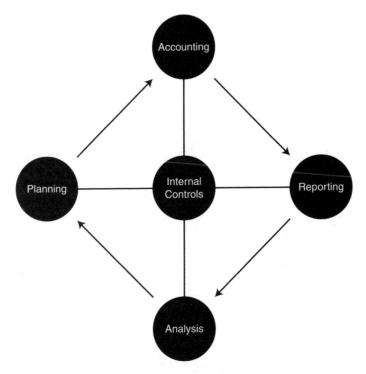

FIGURE 2.1 What is financial management?

Accounting

Accounting is the tracking of all financial activity within the organization. Financial activity includes checks to vendors, invoicing to funders, receipt of checks and cash, and employee payroll. Activity is tracked via an organization's bookkeeping, typically by hand or using an accounting software package. Many nonprofits use Intuit QuickBooks for their accounting systems, but there are many other systems, such as Sage 50 (formerly Peachtree), Sage 100 (formerly MIP), and Blackbaud Financial Edge. Regardless of the software used, it should be compatible with the size and complexity of the organization.

Reporting

Once transactions are in an organization's system, staff must make sense of them. What do they say? This is the financial reporting part of the process. Many types of reports are needed, but the most important are balance sheets, income statements, and cash flow statements.

Analysis

Once reports are complete, they will give information about an organization at a point in time or over an extended period, but they do not tell the story of how an organization is doing against its budget or against grant requirements or in comparison with peer agencies. This is where analysis—the interpretation of the numbers—comes in.

Planning

The fourth element of financial management is planning—budgeting, forecasting, and strategic thinking about how to run the organization in the near future and for the longer term. Budgeting is typically static, but in recognition of the fact that situations continually change as the fiscal year progresses, regular, often monthly, course corrections are made in the form of forecasts for the remainder of the year.

Internal Controls

All of these functions surround a system of internal controls—the checks and balances that ensure that things are done properly. For example, one control is segregation of financial duties: No one person should be responsible for inputting the information, signing checks, reconciling the general ledger, and so forth. In a small nonprofit, this can be challenging, but it is essential to spread responsibilities to avoid the centralization of power.

Best Practices

Best practices in financial management entail (a) the right people; (b) the proper systems for accounting, reporting, analysis, and planning; and (c) a strong internal control structure.

The Right People

As noted earlier, ultimate responsibility for financial management rests with the board. The board sets the tone for the entire organization, not only in terms of mission and policies but also through structure and the individuals charged with executing day-to-day functions. The board sets policy and delegates management to an executive director (ED) and a chief financial officer (CFO) or a controller, accountant, or bookkeeper, depending on the size of the organization, to ensure that its policies are carried out. Several characteristics are important to board members and managers:

- **Care**: High-ranking individuals should attend meetings regularly, exercise independent judgment, and remain informed about the workings of the organization. Board members should not typically become involved in day-to-day operations but rather set mission, strategic direction, and policy. They should then delegate daily operations to management and staff, providing follow-up as needed.
- **Loyalty**: Board members and senior staff should not have conflicts of interest that could compromise the ethical standards of the organization. They should also exercise confidentiality by not revealing sensitive organizational, financial, or human resources information.
- **Obedience**: Board members and managers should believe in the mission of the organization and protect it.
- **Stewardship**: Individuals should participate in the creation of accountability mechanisms in the organization's policies, programs, outcomes, efficiencies, and finances.

It is advisable that there be a finance committee separate from the board.

This committee's importance cannot be overstated. It should comprise more than one person, and members should have strong accounting and financial management backgrounds.

The finance committee's responsibilities typically include

- Oversight of financial accounting, reporting policies, and organizational controls
- Reviewing internal financial statements on a regular basis
- Guiding and supporting management in preparing the annual budget, then approving and monitoring the budget
- Reporting significant financial matters to the full board
- Selecting the audit firm and meeting with it at least twice, generally at the beginning and end of the audit, to review findings. (This and the next responsibility may also be performed by a separate audit committee.)
- Reviewing IRS Form 990

If there is no finance or audit committee, the board should still require that these activities take place.

Other levels of fiscal responsibility include the organization's leader. Along with the board of directors, the organization's leader is charged with setting the tone of the organization from the top. Fiscal responsibility rests with managers at the senior, department, and program levels because they typically have budget and grant responsibilities. Unfortunately, many organizations have budgets created by management and sent down to various departments without any bottom-up input. Because they are responsible for their departments' costs, department managers should be part of the budgeting process.

Whether hiring internal accounting staff or engaging an outside contractor, there are several considerations for management. What is the level of financial expertise of the individual or firm? Who is responsible for supervision? How long should bookkeeping and accounting tasks take? What is the cost?

When making the decision to hire a professional accountant, be prepared to spend a lot of time interviewing candidates to get the right person. When choosing an outsource solution, select a firm that is reputable and that has references and a nonprofit specialty.

Proper Systems

To ensure accountability, transparency, and fiduciary responsibility, open communication is essential. The "accounting department" (whether one individual or a team of people) should not operate behind closed doors but rather as an integral part of management—not only with the preparation of monthly financial reports but also in the crafting of budgets and grant applications. The accounting department should facilitate information sharing among program managers, developmental staff, and the ED. It needs to work closely with the development department throughout the budgeting process to remain apprised of fund-raising efforts. Fund raisers must know which funds will be restricted, how they may need to be tracked separately, and how this information will be communicated to stakeholders. There should never be a disconnect between the people responsible for raising money and the people responsible for accounting for that money.

It is the responsibility of the accounting department to understand the business model of the nonprofit. What is the revenue—grants, dues from members, fees for services, sales of products, fees from events, donors' contributions, or planned gifts? What type of expenses—salaries, rent, insurance, and so forth—does the organization have? The accounting department must know how to properly record all of these items and determine what format the financial statements should take.

The accounting department also needs to understand the capital structure of the organization and how to properly report it. What makes up the organization's reserve funds? What is the organization's equity or net assets; that is, what is left after liabilities are deducted from assets? Reserve funds may be unrestricted, to be spent as management sees fit; restricted for certain uses or until a specific time period has elapsed; or permanently restricted, such as endowments, in which donors expressly dictate that the principal can never be touched but that the nonprofit may use revenue generated by its investment. Responsible, ethical financial management not only balances current operational needs against future forecasting but consistently honors the intentions of donors.

Even a very small organization should have a written manual describing the processes by which financial transactions take place: how bills get paid, who approves them, who signs checks, how money is deposited, and so on. Regardless of the size of the accounting department, there are three levels of operation with increasing responsibility that may be performed by one individual or an entire team depending on the size of the organization. Figure 2.2 represents a simple model.

At the base of this pyramid is the bookkeeping function, which is used for regular transactions. At the next level is the controller, functioning as "the discipline." Controllers ensure that accounts, especially cash, are reconciled and that all agree with the balances. The controller is also responsible for preparing monthly financial, operational, and restricted fund reports for the board, management, and funders. If possible, the bookkeeping and controllership functions should not be performed by the same person; there should be a segregation of duties, but often this is not possible in smaller nonprofits. The role of the CFO is more strategic, centering on planning, analysis, budgeting, and forecasting. The CFO usually facilitates the audit and preparation of 990 forms. He or she also consults regularly with the ED and makes presentations to the board and the finance committee. Finally, the CFO is responsible for establishing internal controls as well as departmental policies and procedures. Figure 2.3 depicts the relationships among all of an organization's financial management roles.

Transparency and accountability can be achieved only if an organization maintains an adequate system of record keeping for all financial information. Proper accounting

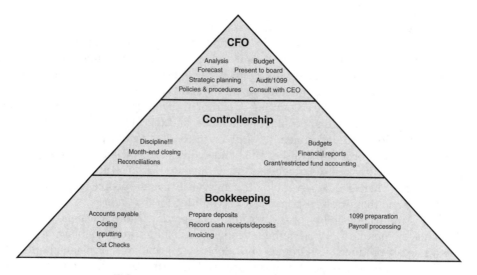

FIGURE 2.2 Accounting department functions.

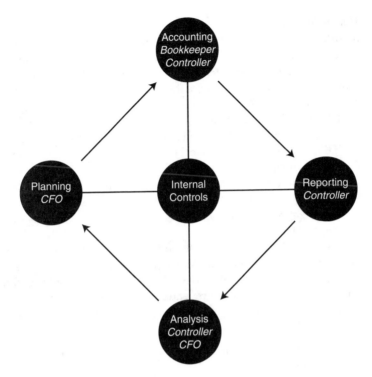

FIGURE 2.3 Financial management roles.

software is needed and, as already noted, many excellent products are available. Regardless of the software package used or the accounting department's degree of sophistication, record keeping must be disciplined: All transactions should be recorded immediately or very shortly after they occur. "Closing the books" must be a priority and be done at least monthly.

Effective processing of transactions and record keeping frequently involves the use of forms, calendar schedules, checklists, and work papers. A form may be used to clarify a standardized approval process, outlining who is authorized to incur an income or expense, who is required to approve it, the code for the account into which it will be placed or from which it will be paid, and the name of the donor or vendor.

A schedule or calendar of events is a way to set up a consistent timing for recording transactions that occur on a regular basis and to generate reports, such as grant or financial reports. Even if they do not look at reports until the last minute, boards feel more comfortable with and confident in the staff and their processes if they get information several days in advance. The schedule of financial management activities should be driven by the finance person in charge and coordinated with other departments involved.

Checklists are roadmaps, itemizations done on a regular basis, such as the month-end closing out of books. They detail the specific steps for reconciliations, who is responsible for what, and when it needs to be done.

Work papers are a means of documenting reconciliations and account analysis. Each month, all journal entries, reconciliations, trial balance details, and financial statements should be saved electronically in an organized format to provide a proper audit or paper trail.

Financial Reporting Best Practices

Financial reports should be formatted in a way that makes them transparent and easy to understand. While some external reports, such as Form 990, have standardized formats that must be used, internal reporting systems can take many forms provided the objective is met: information must be clear and give the reader an accurate snapshot of the financial position of the organization. As noted, the format should follow the organization's business model: How does the organization get its money and how is it spent? A best practice is to ask users what information they need and to tailor reports accordingly.

A financial management system works from a chart of accounts. These are the basic building blocks of financial reports. Account classifications are assets, liabilities, equity or net assets, revenue, and expenses. Many organizations have an excessive number of line items in their reports, information that is not necessarily useful but that was historically included. An organization should examine its reports and try to determine the appropriate level of detail needed.

The key is to determine how to track finances for internal and external reporting purposes that makes reporting efficient. Many organizations break out their revenues and expenses by standard functional categories such as administration, programs, and fundraising. Some organizations break out revenue and expenses by department.

There are several standard financial reports that all nonprofits should produce. These are:

- Balance sheet or statement of financial condition—a picture of the organization at a specific point in time.
- Income statement or statement of activities—a picture of the organization over a period of time. This can be used to compare actual results to the organization's budget.
- Cash flow statement—a picture of the organization's cash position.

Financial planning and management begin with the organization's budget. The annual budget process enables an organization to determine its programs and activities for the coming year and to anticipate expenses and revenue, which may be based on historical experience or new assumptions.

A budget looks at the entire organization and each program, activity, department, and function. It helps to determine operating costs and the resources available to cover them. It should be driven by strategy—namely, what the organization is trying to accomplish in the next fiscal year as driven by the board and the ED. Everyone who has budget responsibility, such as the program managers and development director, however, should be part of the budget process.

The accountant's job is to pull everything together, communicate the timeline to all concerned, and present the finished product back to the entire team. Once management is comfortable with the budget the finance committee and then the board should approve it. Once the board approves the budget, it is typically set for the fiscal year.

Advanced reporting systems may include forecasting on either a cash or accrual basis. As an organization moves through the fiscal year, it can forecast based on more current information and compare the forecast to the original budget to identify significant variances. Then the real analysis can begin: Why are there such variances and what can an organization do about them?

Financial reporting may also include a written narrative in each month's financial statement that synthesizes data and makes sense of patterns, describes significant variances between budgeted figures and actual results, and explains events that occurred. Explaining to the reader why things happened is crucial to gaining a clearer picture of the organization. Again, a best practice is to ask users what information they need and then tailor reports and analysis accordingly.

Internal Systems

There are many reasons staff, management, volunteers, and board members could take advantage of a nonprofit. Situations that can lead to fraudulent behaviors are illustrated in Figure 2.4, commonly called the "Fraud Triangle."

In some cases, theft or misappropriation occurs when unforeseen circumstances create an incentive. An individual may face a sudden need for money due to family illness, mounting debt, divorce, gambling losses, substance abuse, addiction, and so forth. In other cases, the mere absence of internal controls, or a breakdown in these systems, affords individuals the opportunity to find a weak spot in the organization's armor to pilfer or steal. Still others involve individuals such as disgruntled employees, who justify their theft because of long hours worked, inadequate pay, or lack of recognition for achievements.

Fraud takes many forms, all potentially catastrophic for a nonprofit. Examples include:

- Concealment of information
- Use of organization credit cards to pay personal expenses
- Paying off personal credit cards with organization funds
- Insurance scams
- Paying oneself with organization checks

Ethical issues that may or may not be clearly fraudulent must also be guarded against. Some nonprofits spend restricted funds and manipulate financial statements to meet funder requirements, inappropriately placing costs into different functional allocation categories with the rationale that this is permissible because "everyone does it." Others feel they have to "use it or lose it," spending funds in a particular year's budget or for a particular program, even if it is inappropriate, simply because the money is available.

Therefore it is very important for a nonprofit organization to have a strong system of internal controls. The primary features of excellent control systems are:

- The "tone at the top" is one of ethical behaviors
- Regular and continual oversight of all financial transactions
- Regular reviews of bank and investment reconciliations and statements
- Regular reviews of payroll

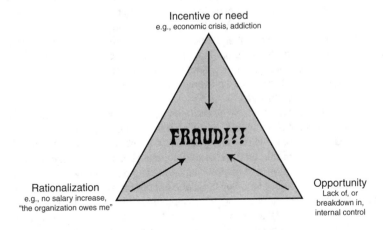

FIGURE 2.4 The fraud triangle.

- Segregation of duties so that no one person has enough power to be able to carry out fraudulent actions without being discovered
- Establishment of appropriate policies, procedures, and training that are continuously updated and conveyed to all new employees, board members, and volunteers, particularly in organizations with frequent turnover
- In some cases, outsourcing of accounting and bookkeeping functions to ensure that they are carried out by qualified individuals

CONCLUSION

Financial management lies at the heart of nonprofit accountability, transparency, governance, fiduciary responsibility, and ethics. With a solid system of bookkeeping, accounting, reporting, analysis, and controls, transparency for both internal and external stakeholders can flourish and the organization can enjoy a credible reputation, even in difficult economic times.

CASE STUDY: UNITED WAY OF SOUTHEASTERN PENNSYLVANIA (REFERRED TO HEREIN AS UNITED WAY): BECOMING A PERFORMANCE-BASED ORGANIZATION

Anyone who has ever played Monopoly knows that players hope to land on the Community Chest because good things happen when a player really needs them. Community Chest, Red Feather, United Fund, and numerous other organizations came together nearly a century ago to form United Way—an organization that works to make sure good things happen when people need them most.

Like every organization with a long history, United Way has evolved and adapted to meet the changing needs of communities and donors over the last 100 years. Once exclusively a fund-raising organization that distributed funding to a set of member agencies, United Way ultimately realized that giving via payroll deduction was no longer revolutionary and that the value of being able to collect and regrant funds to worthy nonprofits was not the future. The strength of United Way lies at its core—its ability to unite and inspire local communities to collective action. Thus, it has shifted its mission and vision toward becoming a social change agent, with fund-raising being one of several ways in which to drive change.

This transformation took research and conversations with the community to determine not only where the needs were greatest but where United Way, with its unique ability to bring together a diverse set of stakeholders willing to define themselves more by the problem they are trying to solve than by the organizations or constituencies they represent, could have the greatest impact. The setting of a new agenda had to be about ensuring that the problem took more than money to solve and that, by investing in United Way's Community Impact work, donors were "buying" something they could not get on their own through direct giving. In 2007, United Way of Southeastern Pennsylvania developed the Agenda for Community Solutions, on which all of the work the agency would do over the following years would be based.

Since 2007, there have been many changes and iterations, but no change has more fundamentally compelled revolution instead of evolution than the need to demonstrate results. The social service sector has spent many years talking about the number of lives it "touches," but donors want to know how many lives are *changed*. In the mid- to late-1990s, donors began looking at the draws from their checkbooks and then their communities and seeing a mismatch between their investments and the ongoing challenges still faced by thousands of people all across their region.

This sentiment grew exponentially after September 11, 2001, and peaked during the recession of 2008. The stark reality that the only option for the foreseeable future was to do more with less drove United Way to two key decisions: focus investments and invest in results.

Moving to Focus

The need to focus may seem obvious, but in a community and a country where the prevailing donor sentiment for the past 30 years has been more personal control and choice, the idea of narrowing some of those choices was borderline heretical less than 20 years ago. After 9/11, the idea of rallying a critical mass of organizations and individuals around a set of common causes to drive real, lasting change made more sense. The pendulum eventually began to swing back to the middle—people wanted some level of control and engagement, but the "me" generation had blended with the "we" generation to understand that there is greater value in collective action.

As a result, United Way shifted to a framework built on the fundamental building blocks for quality of life—education, income, and health—recognizing that in different communities across the country, the particular challenges might be different but they all exist within this broader framework. United Way Worldwide adopted these pillars because they clarify United Way's brand position, reinforce the sense of interdependence necessary to advance society as a whole, and demonstrate how United Way aims to achieve lasting change.

Within this framework, each United Way considered the specific challenges facing its community. In Southeastern Pennsylvania, United Way used community surveys and other tools to determine the greatest needs. The list was ultimately narrowed to issues on which United Way was credible and uniquely positioned to make an impact, issues that required more than money and on which United Way would not duplicate the work of other effective organizations.

One example of how these choices played out was in the health arena. There were many spirited debates as to whether United Way would tackle health as an issue and, if so, what specifically it might address. Many challenges threatened the health of the Southeastern Pennsylvania community—specific diseases, access to health care, and so forth. As each of these issues was discussed, staff determined that they were not optimal for United Way.

In the case of diseases, United Way is not a credible expert on any given disease and does not do research or other work to find solutions. Access to affordable health care was looked at as well. United Way recognized that Southeastern Pennsylvania is home to some of the preeminent health care institutions in the country, institutions working on health care access within the constraints of the ever-changing world of health services. While there are always improvements to be made, it was uncertain that United Way's limited pool of resources and lack of expertise in the health care field were likely to create the kind of systemic change that would have leveraged donor dollars.

In looking at health in terms of social services, it quickly became clear that seniors are the most vulnerable population. Pennsylvania is one of the oldest states in the country, and the social infrastructure is not prepared to support the growth of this population over the next 20 years, nor can it withstand the financial and socioeconomic pressures that placing economically disadvantaged seniors in institutional care would put on the state, the region, and seniors themselves. There are alternatives, such as in-home and community-based care, that are much less expensive and preferable, but they are often not well known, understood, or available through government-funded programs. These are issues United Way can tackle—where the connective tissue between programs and services is critical and where people are needed to raise money, their hands, and their voices— to give, volunteer, and advocate for change. This is just one example of the many discussions that have taken place and that continue to evolve as United Way learns more and refines strategies accordingly.

Even after much debate and discussion, actually making the shift was difficult because whenever an organization focuses, some issues are bound to be priorities and thus favored over others. Despite its challenges, focusing was simple in comparison with the task of investing in results. The problem is not that organizations are not getting results but rather that it can be remarkably difficult to demonstrate those results.

Investing in Results

In many ways, the world of philanthropy has remained true to its roots—people helping people. Over the years, however, needs have become more complex, and multifaceted solutions require a collaborative approach that takes more than just a helping hand; the phrase "it takes a village" holds true. Some organizations are "the" solution for certain issues, but more often, each organization is part of a larger solution that moves individual lives forward. As a result, measuring direct impact can be a challenge.

In 2008, United Way announced its 3-year commitments in greater Philadelphia. These grants were the result of an open, competitive process that invited all 501(c)(3) health and human services organizations in the region to apply. United Way received over 2,000 applications from more than 500 organizations for general operating support grants and hundreds more for more specific, targeted investments.

Some readers may have paused for a moment at the phrase "general operating support" grants. This appears to be the same thing United Way has always done but with a new slogan. On the contrary, it is something that has almost never been done, by United Way or any other organization that has come before. One of the biggest downsides of philanthropy has been the perceived necessity for donors to take control of how their dollars are spent. If that is the right approach, should investors call Bill McNabb, the CEO of Vanguard, and tell him how they would like a portfolio manager to select the stocks in the mutual fund they have chosen for their retirement? Or better yet, should investors call the CEO of the company issuing those stocks and tell him or her how to run that business so that they get the greatest return? The reader may laugh, but this is what donors, governments, and foundations do to nonprofits every day. In the end, it is about outcomes—if you're investing in the market, you personally get the return on investment and you don't care how the CEO got it (provided it was ethical). If you're investing in the community, you want to ensure that the people who are being served get results. Investors who see those results keep investing because, unlike with the stock market, past performance *is* a very reliable predictor of future results in the social service sector.

The shrinking pool of flexible funding that allows nonprofits to do some of their most critical work is sometimes difficult to obtain because donors would rather pay for food for a hungry family than for the maintenance of the building where the food is stored. The increasing number of strings attached to donations has resulted in some painful "mission creep" and a challenging balance between what is important and what is popular. Social service organizations rarely fail because their programs are not important or needed—they fail because they cannot pay for the leadership, strategy, development, and support that the for-profit sector takes for granted.

It is important to note that this was not venture capital money. United Way did not set out to use these resources to pilot new ideas or take significant risks. It aimed to invest in what was working, and agencies could use the money as they saw fit provided they continued to deliver results. However, many organizations use United Way money to pilot innovation, because flexible funding is the only funding with which they can take risks to gain potentially greater rewards. Because United Way grants are 3-year commitments, the ability to drive innovation is enhanced because organizations have sufficient time to get their work off the ground.

After spirited debate, United Way's board decided it would consider the unthinkable: Let agencies decide how to use the money but demand outcomes. This was much more difficult than funding a budget line item for which it would be certain that each dollar "bought" a particular output. The board recognized, however, that, because of the decline in sources of unrestricted revenue, the nonprofit sector was struggling to innovate and attract talent and leadership.

United Way's team went to work designing a funding process in which grantees would be selected based on their ability to demonstrate results against United Way community priorities *but* the grants would be awarded as unrestricted dollars. If an agency could prove it was delivering results, United Way would invest in those results rather than restricting their investment to simply "buying" just the direct services. To ensure that the funding process was beyond reproach, United Way recruited over 100 outside volunteer content-expert reviewers to analyze the grant applications.

As with any other volunteer effort, expectations and parameters were important. To ensure objectivity, a rating rubric was created and three reviewers (generally, two external and one United Way staff member) reviewed each application. Once the ratings were complete, the groups of reviewers were brought together to discuss any conflicts and minimize discrepancies resulting from varying interpretations of information.

The grant application asked each agency to describe three things: how its work was aligned with United Way's priorities; how it was demonstrating best practices in its field; and whether it was able to demonstrate that it was achieving results against those priorities. In addition to closely evaluating the programmatic work of each agency, using a team of 14 volunteer certified public accountant (CPAs), United Way also conducted a financial review of each applicant's audits and other key financial information. It also gathered information related to the leadership and governance of each agency. All three components were utilized to make final investment decisions.

As with any good funding process, however, the work did not end when the grant was issued. There have been ongoing dialogues, participation in programming, and annual reviews of outcomes against the scope of services outlined in each agency's contract. If the agency performed, it continued to receive funding for the full 3-year cycle (contingent on campaign results). Agencies could use funds to repair a roof, hire a CFO, or start a new program as long as they continued to deliver results.

It has been rare for an organization to be defunded midcycle, but there have been programs that closed down because of imprudent fiscal or strategic decisions or changes in government funding that would have prevented the organization from achieving results.

Results and Questions Raised

In many ways, United Way is a lot like Vanguard. Just as Vanguard is an investment management company, offering mutual funds that seek to maximize investment returns for its clients, United Way is a charitable mutual fund, enabling its donors to maximize social return on their investments. During the first 3-year funding period, over 85% of funded organizations achieved their contractual results. In any other 3-year period, one might consider that a mediocre return. In the toughest economy since the Great Recession (2008–2011), these results were outstanding.

As with any new process, however, United Way discovered some barriers to achieving its vision. In addition to the general operating grants, United Way made investments designed to drive systemic change through collaboration, leadership, and/or leveraging resources to form the connective tissue that integrates the work of individual organizations into a system able to effect change at the community or regional level.

One of the best examples of this integration is early childhood education. While data show that investment in children yields the greatest dividends before age 5, the most formative years of brain development, this is also the age range in which the United States invests the fewest resources in children's academic and social development. Research also shows that children need more than just babysitters: They need quality early childhood education that addresses the needs of the whole child. Only 10 years ago, Southeastern Pennsylvania relied on a group of well-intentioned but painfully underresourced child care centers to start children off right. There was no way to objectively assess the quality of services or to tap into the government or private resources to raise standards. United Way, however, understood the need for a rallying point for early childhood education—one that inspired the community, united providers and government officials, and marshaled resources to invest in building and motivating a cadre of business leaders to champion the cause. This is the "connective tissue" and what United Way refers to as Community Impact.

The biggest challenge in endeavors such as this is that giving is never a choice between right and wrong. It is a choice between right and right, which makes giving much more difficult. There were some hard choices—How to measure outcomes versus outputs? Abandon the safety net, leaving behind the handout in favor of the hand up? Choose a series of priority strategies to get to the desired outcome, or choose the outcome and invest in whatever strategies result in that outcome?

People who fall into the safety net are sometimes going to need a handout before they even have the strength to use a hand up. United Way split its funding into two pieces and established different criteria for funding safety net services versus funding services that would be considered interventions. For example, food cupboards and emergency shelters were not evaluated on the end result of individuals served but rather on the quality of the ways in which outputs were delivered. To receive the highest rating, an agency would have to demonstrate that it provided comprehensive food or meal services that included an intake process, needs assessment, and on-site case management. It would have to both identify persons in need of services and actively reach out to those individuals. Further, the format, duration, frequency, and accessibility of the agency's services needed to be field-recognized as the most effective way to meet the program or service goals as well as client needs. The agency would be required to have any appropriate licenses to operate its program and a comprehensive outreach strategy that involved fostering relationships with social service providers and others who could connect with its target population. The organization would be staffed by individuals with case management experience and have a system in place for internal quality improvement that includes training and professional development for staff. The agency would be accredited by, a member of, affiliated with, or receive funding from a national, federal, state, or local entity that regulates its fields.

Investing in results and achieving community impact is an iterative and evolving learning process that is proactive in vision but reactive to community needs and changes in those needs. It is about turning outward, talking to and listening to stakeholders and partners.

If those who follow this path look to one guidepost, the one that had the greatest influence on United Way's process was, "Good outcomes come from 50% good strategy and 50% good communication." The process was all about transparency and frequent and linear communications. The old saying "Tell them what you're going to tell them, tell them, and then tell them what you told them" exists for a reason. Changing 90 years of philanthropic history means constantly providing context for change and then leading the way.

For United Way, that meant that each Community Impact strategy committee and board meeting (and there were many) followed a path laid out at the beginning of the process, with each decision built on the one before. Following this process but disagreeing with the end result would have meant questioning the process itself, which had already been agreed upon. This doesn't mean that processes shouldn't be revised if the results don't make sense, but rather that they should not be revisited simply because the results are unpopular.

In a process that is all about accountability and results, decision making cannot sacrifice accountability or results. A critical underpinning of United Way's Community Impact grant-making process was that absent any error, the organization would not alter results and the board would neither champion its favorite causes nor succumb to political pressure. If any exceptions had been made, the outcome of this case study would have been far different or, more likely, the study would not have been written at all. The board agreed that any alteration or violation of the guiding principles would put the credibility of the entire process at risk. In the end, it was a strong shield against any criticism that came after.

The fundamental level of discourse in the sector has changed, and, nearly 4 years later, the grantee agencies are showing remarkable results and outcomes and a level of clarity around impact that has never been seen before. Some organizations changed business models to define and focus on key organizational outcomes. Others changed measurement processes to more clearly demonstrate their impact. During the first cycle, United Way was able to fund nearly every organization that was able to demonstrate results at the desired threshold. The decisions were numerically easy though politically hard. The second time, however, the decisions were much harder: The primary task was deciding between good and great, which was the best outcome of all.

NOTE

1. www.forbes.com/sites/helencoster/2011/11/30/forbes-list-of-the-top-30-social-entrepreneurs/

REFERENCES

Berger, K., Penna, R. M., & Goldberg, S. H. (2010, May). The battle for the soul of the nonprofit sector. *Philadelphia Social Innovations Journal*. Retrieved from www.philasocialinnovations.org/site/index.php?option=com_content&id=163:the-battle-for-the-soul-of-the-nonprofit-sector&Itemid=31

Bickman, L. (Ed.). (1987). *Using program theory in evaluation*. San Francisco, CA: Jossey-Bass.

Cohen, R. (2010, April 8). Who let the charity watch dogs out? [Web log post]. *The Nonprofit Quarterly*. Retrieved from www.nonprofitquarterly.org/index.php?option=com_content&view=article&id=2163:nonprofit-newswire-who-let-the-charity-watch-dogsout&catid=155:daily-digest&Itemid=137

Hunter, D. E. K. (2009, October). The end of charity: How to fix the nonprofit sector through effective social investing. *Philadelphia Social Innovations Journal*. Retrieved from www.philaso-cialinnovations.org/site/index.php?option=com_content&id=36:the-end-of-charity-how-to-fix-the-nonprofit-sector-through-effective-social-investing&Itemid=31

EVALUATING ORGANIZATIONAL IMPACT AND OUTCOME MEASUREMENT

David E. K. Hunter

> Greatness is not a function of circumstance. Greatness, it turns out, is largely a
> matter of conscious choice, and discipline.
> —Jim Collins, *Good to Great and the Social Sectors*

Nonprofit organizations are required to meet public needs, but they have not done well in determining whether or to what degree they are doing so. This chapter discusses how organizational impact can be evaluated, focusing on organizational effectiveness with regard to the ability to produce intended outcomes reliably and sustainably. Basic terms are defined, including inputs, outputs, outcomes, and impacts, as are the preconditions for driving organizations to impact: strategy and theory of change. The need for performance management and the differences between performance and evaluative data are discussed. Steps are outlined for understanding the likelihood that a service will have impact, which include determining the following: the evidentiary basis for claims about the effectiveness of the programming, how closely the program adheres to the models or practices implemented, and how well the organization is able to deliver its programming with fidelity.

EVALUATING ORGANIZATIONAL IMPACT

Introduction

In the United States, nonprofit organizations are an artifact of the Internal Revenue Service (IRS) tax code, which lists three criteria that will justify an organization's designation as a 501(c)(3) nonprofit charity: It must have an independent board of directors, it cannot distribute profits to the board or staff, and it must meet public needs (Hall, 2006). It is the latter criterion that is the focus here.

What does the concept "meet public needs" mean? In its most general sense, it must include either doing something of high quality that is of societal interest (e.g., operating a symphony orchestra or dance troupe that enjoys critical and popular success, managing a teen drop-in center offering recreational opportunities, delivering hot and healthy meals to stay-at-home persons) or undertaking a set of activities that improve conditions or prospects that are of concern to society or segments of society (e.g., improving the environment, public health patterns, neighborhood safety, high school graduation rates for underachieving populations, social and emotional competencies of elementary school children, employment rates for newly discharged prisoners; or driving down gang membership and violence, homelessness among groups such as former foster care youth or war veterans, child abuse rates, the prevalence of low birth weight in babies born to teenage mothers, pet abandonment). Another way of saying this is that to meet the requirement that they are addressing a public need, nonprofits must either do things very well (provide high-quality services that people want simply because they are so good) or do them effectively (provide services that yield either improvements to or diminish negative developments in specific domains that policy makers, funders, grassroots organizations, and/or people on the street have targeted). While it is rare that organizations can work effectively without also working at high levels of quality, the opposite need not be true: High-quality activities need not necessarily produce socially significant changes (note the examples given earlier)—or what will henceforth be called outcomes.

Since this chapter is about evaluating organizational impact, it will not be addressing issues of quality management as a stand-alone concept; rather, it will focus on organizational effectiveness with regard to the ability to produce intended outcomes reliably and sustainably and will consider issues of quality only when they are directly pertinent to the matter at hand. Finally, while the approach to measuring impact presented in this chapter applies to all realms in which nonprofit organizations work, for clarity of presentation and coherence of discussion the definitions, examples, and explanations used herein will be confined to the domain of social services.

A Case in Point

A few years ago, the following conversation took place between a national funder and a national (well regarded and well funded) youth development organization[1]:

Funder: So, tell us about your work and the scope of your impact.
Nonprofit: Last year, we touched over four million young people.
F: Four million young people? That's really amazing. How were you able to do this?
N: Well, we got over four million hits on our website.
F: Oh. Do you know for sure all the hits were from young people?
N: No…it would be impossible to determine that.
F: And when you say you "touched" young people…are you claiming that you actually made a difference in their lives?
N: We put a lot of work into creating interesting, interactive elements on our website, and we like to think that young people who go there will be intellectually stimulated and learn important things that they need to know to succeed in life.
F: But let's be clear. First of all, you don't know who the people are who visit your website, second, you don't know whether any are repeaters, and third, you don't know what they have learned as a result of their visits to the website. Or are we missing something here?
N: No, you are right in what you say. But we think that our website is doing a lot of good.

While this example may strike many readers as extreme, it illustrates a pervasive problem in the nonprofit sector: Namely, that more often than not, nonprofits have not developed (and are even less likely to have implemented) reasonable ways for assessing how effectively they are producing the outcomes they have targeted. Yet they expect to be funded to continue doing whatever they are doing and however they are doing it. And more often than not, funders comply (Hunter, 2009).

Some Basic Terms Defined and Discussed

Before going any further, we need to define and consider some fundamental terms. While alternative definitions of these terms enjoy widespread use, the definitions presented here are not in themselves controversial, would be recognized as valid by most practitioners who concern themselves with these matters, and are used in one of the most well-regarded books about nonprofit effectiveness to have been published in recent years, *Leap of Reason: Managing to Outcomes in an Era of Scarcity* (Morino, 2011). Below is a list of terms that will be used as the building blocks of the discussion about evaluating organizational impacts, along with some observations about the state of the nonprofit sector with regard to them.

Inputs
The resources—money, time, staff, expertise, methods, facilities—that an organization utilizes to produce intended outputs, outcomes, and impacts.

Nonprofits generally are quite aware of their inputs and track them in order to maintain solvency and satisfy funders who want to know how they are obtaining and spending their money. Notably, a great deal of attention is paid to the perceived need for revenue diversification and to understanding what percentage of a nonprofit's funds go toward supporting frontline service delivery and what part goes to paying administrative, infrastructure, and other overhead costs.[2] Probably because of the nonprofit sector's origins in charity work (mostly by religiously affiliated groups), there is a strong and widespread prejudice that almost all monies given to nonprofits should be spent directly on programs and services and very little on overhead. Many funders structure their grants and contracts to allow no more than 10% to 12% of the total to be used for overhead—perhaps half as much as most high-performing for-profit corporations spend (especially when counting in the costs of research and development, which nonprofits also do under the rubric of "pilot programs"). Among other things, this leads many nonprofits to "rob Peter to pay Paul"—that is, to use operational funds from one grant to pay the overhead for the programming supported by another or to hide large parts of overhead costs by listing them under program costs. As nonprofit leaders will acknowledge when speaking candidly, these shell games are ubiquitous, are enervating to the nonprofits, and lead funders into wildly unrealistic beliefs about what it *really* costs to change people's lives and prospects for the better.

Outputs
The number of people served, activities performed, and/or items produced by an organization.

One output that social service agencies tend to keep track of is the number of people they serve each year. However, it must be said that many do so poorly, with duplicated counts in which serving one person multiple times is counted as seeing multiple clients. Sometimes called a "turnstile" number, this kind of count tells us nothing about, for example, how service recipients benefited, what percentage achieved these benefits, or how many people received intense enough services or participated long enough that it could be expected that they might benefit.[3] Yet most government contracts and grant requirements settle for reports on turnstile counts as sufficient to indicate that a nonprofit organization is doing its work well—as long as it meets the quota of people it is expected to serve. *To put a fine point on the matter, turnstile numbers are a pervasively used indicator for social impact in the nonprofit sector—an indicator that, in reality, tells us nothing at all about how or to what degree there has been any societal benefit produced!* Thus, as seductive as a gross turnstile count might be, it is not a meaningful measure to calculate the social good generated by a program (Hunter & Koopmans, 2006).

The same can be said for any counting of outputs—be they in products produced (such as HIV or smoking prevention pamphlets printed) or activities undertaken (pamphlets distributed, meals served, etc.). By themselves, these have little intrinsic social value because no sustained changes arise from their production and/or distribution alone—and *hence outputs cannot be used as a measure of social impact.* This poses a problem for funders and practitioners alike because grants and contracts pay for the purchase of outputs (activities and products) and, in fact, cannot ever be used to purchase outcomes: No amount of money spent will ever buy healthier families, better educated children, safer neighborhoods, fewer teen parents, employment for the chronically unemployed, psychological stability for people with severe psychiatric disorders, or any other outcome. *Money buys outputs. Smart, intentional, and relentless management of outputs generates outcomes!* So, from the perspective of producing social impact and understanding the costs and benefits of doing so, linking revenue to outputs simply will not do the job. From this perspective, even though it will inevitably be indirect, the funding of outputs always must be linked to their use(s) in the achievement of outcomes.

Outcomes

The expected, measurable, sustained, and monitored changes undergone or achieved by people participating in social programs or receiving social services—generally comprising changes in attitudes, knowledge, skills, behavior, status (e.g., having graduated from high school with a diploma), and social or personal conditions (e.g., living in poverty [social condition] or having lung capacity loss due to cystic fibrosis [personal condition]); furthermore, these changes must be directly linkable to the organization's intentional efforts and be a key metric through which the organization holds itself and its staff accountable.

This definition of outcomes is framed from the point of view of performance management. Evaluators would not care whether they were measured and monitored by a given organization or program itself as part of its operations or whether they were used as the basis of an accountability system. Rather, the only questions evaluators would ask concern the degree to which these changes occur (the number and percentage of service recipients who manifest them) and the extent to which they are attributable to the specific program or service. It is convenient to think about outcomes in terms of time and to designate them as short term (or immediate), intermediate, and long term (or ultimate).

Measuring outcomes is a lot less difficult than most people seem to think. The hard part is settling on what the optimal outcome sequence is for members of a (well-delineated and deeply understood) target population. Once this conceptual work is done (and it is essential that any agency claiming to help people improve their lives or prospects do so), then the means to measure short-term and intermediate outcomes become quite obvious: one either counts things (e.g., days of school attended per week), scales things (e.g., improved academic self-efficacy), or makes yes/no determinations (e.g., either a young woman is pregnant or is not; either she has graduated from high school with a diploma or she has not). Measuring long-term outcomes also is not conceptually difficult, but problems are significant with regard to collecting such data.[4]

- Long-term outcomes are those changes in service recipients that constitute the ultimate expression of the social value created by an organization.[5] Usually these are assessed at some period after program participants are no longer receiving services. Hence, long-term outcomes are not under an organization's direct control but rather are expected to be achieved because the services have sufficiently prepared or equipped participants so that, all other things being equal, they have a high likelihood of achieving them (much like a vaccination equips people to resist disease). For example, Youth Villages, headquartered in Memphis, Tennessee, tracks outcomes for its program participants 6, 12, and 24 months after they are discharged. Youth Villages currently serves high-risk (risk factors include mental illness, substance abuse, criminal behavior and other legal issues, and having experienced domestic violence and/or abuse) children and teens and their families in 12 states through residential and community-based services. At 24 months after discharge, 85% of service recipients (who received at least 60 days of service) are in high school, have graduated from high school, or are in GED classes; 82% have not been in trouble with the law; and 81% are living at home with family or independently while 18% of youth younger than 18 years are in state custody. Of those in school, 88% have mostly passing grades, 88% have not been suspended or expelled, and 91% are not truant.[6]
- Intermediate outcomes are the changes in service recipients that one expects to see at specific points or intervals while they are participating in a program. These are convenient milestones for knowing that participants are benefiting as intended from services and making progress in a timely manner. These intermediate outcome(s) mark readiness for discharge from the program—and strongly predict the likelihood that the participants who are discharged will go on to achieve the organization's targeted long-term outcomes. Consider, for example, Children's Aid Society (CAS), a large and well-established multiservice agency in New York City that recently reassessed its approach to working with children from low-income households and decided to focus on academic attainment. For its adolescents and young adults, the intermediate outcomes that CAS will track are as follows:
  ○ The child gets into what CAS regards as a good high school
  ○ The child/youth is fluent in English
  ○ The high school student passes regency examinations
  ○ The high school student passes advanced placement courses
  ○ The high school student achieves good enough PSAT/SAT scores to qualify for college matriculation
  ○ The high school student graduates with a high school diploma
  ○ The high school dropout earns a GED
  ○ The young adult enters postsecondary education

These intermediate outcomes constitute a logical sequence of necessary milestones to track the progress of teens toward the ultimate outcomes that CAS has targeted: At age 26, the service recipient will either have graduated from or enrolled in and be on track to complete postsecondary education or will be employed full-time and living above poverty.

- Short-term outcomes are immediate, incremental changes that service recipients achieve in direct and easily understood relation to the services they receive or program activities in which they participate. High-performing service providers track such data weekly or even daily in order to be sure they are optimizing their influence on the progress made by intended beneficiaries, and making immediate (real-time) adjustments in what they are doing, how they are doing it, or how much they are doing if clients are not making progress at targeted rates (a key performance standard). For example, WINGS for Kids, an after-school program that originated in Charleston, South Carolina, works with elementary school children from low-income families to help them develop social and emotional skills (widely regarded as essential building stones for subsequent academic and social success). WINGS has codified a sequence of very short-term outcomes that it measures daily and tracks weekly for every participant:

   i. The kids know about social and emotional learning (SEL)
- Kids can recite one element of the WINGS creed[7]
- Kids can recite two elements of the WINGS creed
- Kids can recite three elements of the WINGS creed
- Kids can recite four elements of the WINGS creed
- Kids can recite five elements of the WINGS creed

   ii. The kids understand SEL
- Kids can give a meaningful example of one creed element from their lives
- Kids can give a meaningful example of two creed elements from their lives
- Kids can give a meaningful example of three creed elements from their lives
- Kids can give a meaningful example of four creed elements from their lives
- Kids can give a meaningful example of five creed elements from their lives

   iii. The kids pass [frequent] tests demonstrating their mastery of
- Self-awareness
- Social awareness
- Responsible decision making
- Relationship skills
- Self-management

Or consider the Center for Employment Opportunities (CEO), which works with prisoners leaving incarceration in New York State, placing them on transitional work crews in order to help them become job ready and avoid recidivism. This is how the agency discusses "tracking participant outcomes" on its website[8]: *Once participants have begun transitional employment on CEO work crews, their daily attendance* [i.e., a program performance standard], *as well as their progress in developing appropriate on-the-job behaviors and basic skills* [short-term outcomes] *is noted daily in their Passport to Success booklets. Collected Passport data are then entered into the Salesforce.com database and analyzed to determine when participants have achieved baseline preparation for full-time employment* [intermediate outcome] *in the competitive workforce. Once this milestone is achieved, participants are considered "job start ready" and begin interviewing for full-time positions developed by Job Developers in CEO's vocational services teams.* CEO's long-term outcomes include permanent employment and not having reoffended up to 2 years after completing the program—an issue we shall return to shortly.

Impacts

Outcomes that can, using experimental research methods, be attributed (with a great deal of confidence, generally 95%) to the effects on participants of a program or service.[9]

Whereas measuring outcomes only requires tracking program participants, understanding impact requires that the outcomes achieved by service recipients and the percentage of program participants who achieve them be compared with those of similar—or, if possible, identical—groups who have not received these services. This is the only way to eliminate alternative explanations for individuals or groups having achieved the changes that are being tracked—such as, for instance, that people make progress on their own. Going back to a previous example, until WINGS for Kids compares how much SEL its program participants have mastered with how much SEL is exhibited by similar children who are not in its programs, it will be impossible to know whether the SEL outcomes that the organization tracks for participating kids really are due to the programs or simply come about as a result of normal and expectable family, neighborhood, and school experiences.[10]

Or consider the fact that a majority of the job placements (impacts) claimed by some famous government programs to help unemployed individuals get and keep employment were shown, by evaluations, to be due to general, normal job-hunting behavior and therefore were not in any way affected by program participation (Gueron, 2005).[11]

For a more in-depth example, let's return to CEO. In 2004, CEO was selected to be part of a U.S. Department of Health and Human Services multisite national study of programs that serve "hard-to-employ" populations—which certainly is true for prisoners reentering society. The research was conducted by MDRC, a highly recognized evaluation organization. CEO was required, as part of this evaluation, to participate in a randomized control trial (RCT) in which potential program participants were selected randomly from eligible individuals (New York State prisoners being released) and then compared with those who had not been selected—a method that eliminates most nonprogram factors as explanations for why outcomes are achieved. Two years after discharge from the program, CEO's graduates (the intervention group) showed a statistically significant reduction in criminal convictions and incarceration for a new crime—better at a statistically significant level of confidence than the outcomes for those evaluation study participants who did not participate in the program (the control group). *These long-term outcomes thus are legitimately recognized as the impact of CEO's programming*—and indeed are very important and unusual. (And the report indicates that preliminary data show these impacts holding for the third year.) On the other hand, even though CEO focuses on and monitors employment readiness and fully expects employment to be a long-term impact, the MDRC study showed that employment in fact is not a long-term program impact of CEO programming—that is, participants were no more likely to be employed than were members of the control group after 3 years (Redcross, Bloom, Azurdia, Zweig, & Pindus, 2009).

Using the concepts discussed in this section, we now move to considering some basic issues that must be looked at when evaluating organizational impact.

Preconditions for Driving to Organizational Impact

There are numerous preconditions for organizational success in driving to impact. These include having the following:

- Strong, inspiring, and decisive leadership committed to achieving results
- Management that knows how to nurture and get the best out of staff
- Dedicated staff who work relentlessly and with high intentionality to achieve good results in each and every case
- An organizational culture that is results- and data-focused, values transparency, and supports messengers who bring up evidence of "bad news" that allows the organization to make essential adjustments
- Appropriate organizational depth, competencies (e.g., ongoing efforts to monitor the contexts within which the agency works, anticipate strategic threats, and make adjustments as indicated, and also the tenacity to continue to drive for results even when major obstacles emerge in the day-to-day work), and capacities
- The right mix of resources (e.g., growth revenues, operational revenues) that will support strategic plans

These have been discussed by many analysts concerned with organizational performance, including this author. Here we will focus on two further preconditions for organizational impact: a strong strategy and a robust theory of change.

Strategy

It is never easy to change the course of events or even just shift the course of likely developments—be it for nations, populations, groups, families, or individuals. It requires a clear vision of what one is trying to accomplish, the organizational capacities and resources to do what is necessary, and the tenacity to keep on course even when the going is rough. In other words, an organization that intends to produce impacts must have a strategy for doing so, and the commitment to stick with it. With its origins in military thinking, a strategy requires an organization to have the following:

1. **A clear mission** that articulates the domain within which it will work and the results it wants to achieve and why (this is often referred to as an organization's value proposition by social entrepreneurs and funders using what has broadly been termed a "venture philanthropy" approach)
2. **A plan for succeeding** with well-developed **goals** and **measurable objectives**

In the absence of a strategy, then, it is unlikely that an organization will know how to focus on what it is working to achieve, nor will it have a collective commitment to getting key results. However, by definition, strategy is a big-picture concept—much like the view one has while flying across the United States and looking down on major topographical features. To get to strategic success, one also needs a framework for making it real and doable (operational) and successful down on the ground—here the "small picture" is immediate, must be dealt with as it changes, and requires constant focus, concentration, and intentionality of effort. Such a framework is provided by what often is called a theory of change—a conceptual structure that bridges from strategy to operations and keeps operations dedicated to and aligned with strategic priorities and success.

Theory of Change

As just noted, a theory of change is really best thought of as an organization's blueprint for success. It is

> ...the guide whereby the organization structures its daily activities to achieve its strategic goals and objectives. It also provides the framework within which each organization can examine what works and what does not work within its own programming, and manage performance for continuous improvement. (Hunter, 2006a. p. 183)

To develop its theory of change—both for the organization as a whole and for each of its programs and services—it is essential that the organization answer the following three sets of questions (Hunter, 2006b):

1. **Target population(s)**: Whom are we in business to serve so that we can measurably improve some aspect of their lives? (And the corollary: Whom should we not serve, or serve minimally with no accountability for results?)
2. **Outcomes**: What is the sequence of incremental changes that program participants/service recipients should pass through as they progress toward achieving the ultimate set of outcomes for which the organization or program is holding itself accountable?
3. **Programs/services**: What should our staff (or volunteers) be doing for or with target population members (intended beneficiaries), how much time per day or week is a sufficient amount, how long should the program or service go on, where should services be delivered (e.g., home-based, center-based), and what should be the competencies of those who deliver the programming or services so that we can be confident that target population members indeed will progress through the outcome sequence as intended?

In other words, an organization's theory of change provides the framework with which it will work, learn from its efforts, and make the necessary (timely) organizational and programmatic adjustments needed for it to succeed on the terms laid forth in its mission statement. What makes for a good theory of change? Among other things, it should be (a) meaningful to stakeholders, (b) plausible (conforming to common sense and the opinions of experts), (c) doable within resource constraints, (d) clear in specifying the metrics that will be used to execute it, and (e) a useful framework for managing performance reliably, sustainably, and at high levels of quality and effectiveness.

Absent a theory of change for making its strategy operational, an organization will be unlikely to (a) have effective plans for achieving results, (b) have amassed the resources to support its plans, or (c) be able to organize and manage its efforts to achieve results—reliably, sustainably, effectively, or at high levels of quality. Having a strategy is a necessary condition for achieving social impact as a result of intentional efforts. Both a strategy and a theory of change (blueprint for success) are necessary preconditions for driving to results (managing to outcomes). Without them, it is unlikely that an organization will generate much of anything in the way of meaningful social impact, and evaluating its impact would be a waste of time and money.

Children's Aid Society

As an example, New York's CAS, introduced earlier, had a long and distinguished history of serving the city's children and families, seeking to fill the gaps in supports and opportunities that many needed to improve their immediate lives and future prospects. To do so, it was running dozens of citywide and neighborhood-based programs in areas as diverse as health clinics, foster care services, preschool programs, after-school programs, tutoring, mentoring, a summer camp, employment services, and more—earning appreciation from city government, neighborhood groups, and the families and individuals it served. Yet recently, under its new president and CEO, Richard R. Buery Jr., it came to recognize that it was not living up to its potential. As Buery observed,

> Despite the good CAS does for tens of thousands of families, including the lives CAS has literally saved, we cannot say with certainty that the children who enter CAS programs will—as a result of our work—consistently become adults with the skills and education necessary to escape the poverty into which they were born.

Buery concluded that there were four strategic challenges that needed to be addressed to ensure CAS future success. In his words,

> First, although the breadth and depth of CAS's services are inspiring, many of the services that we provide are short term or limited to a specific aspect of a child's life. This is the result of structuring ourselves to meet the needs of public funders focused on short-term interventions, instead of organizing ourselves around the long-term, complex needs of our clients. Second, although staff will go to extraordinary lengths to assure the safety, health, and happiness of our children, not all of our programs have defined their intended outcomes or can track whether they are achieving them. Third, our organization operates in silos. The benefit of being a comprehensive multi-service agency is the opportunity to meet all of our clients' complex needs. Yet because our services are not fully integrated, it is not always easy for our clients to know what services we provide or how to access them. In addition, a teen who walks into one CAS center might receive a completely different service than he would receive at another site simply because the programs—which might operate in different divisions and with different priorities—do not share a common standard of success. Fourth, like many organizations faced with overwhelming need, CAS has a history of wanting to serve everyone in every way, a

commitment reflected in what had been our mission statement: "The Children's Aid Society provides comprehensive support for children in need, from birth to young adulthood, and for their families, to fill the gaps between what children have and what they need to thrive." As an organization, CAS recognizes that if we want to be more certain of the impact we are having in moving children out of poverty, we need to be more disciplined; client-centered rather than organized around funder mandates; and committed to articulating, measuring, and tracking the outcomes that will help children escape poverty and achieve life-long success. Our children deserve no less.[12]

These are courageous and crucial strategic insights. And they led CAS to ask *four key strategic questions*:

1. *Which children are we here to serve?* (How do we define our target population? Where do they live? What are their demographic characteristics? What are the key risk factors that we look for?)
2. *What outcomes do we want to achieve for the children we serve?* (What measurable and meaningful changes do we want to occur in children as a direct result of our efforts?)
3. *What services will we provide in order to achieve these outcomes?*
4. *How must we change as an organization to achieve those outcomes?* (How will we create the programmatic and organizational structures required to drive consistent program quality and client outcomes?)

Considering these questions in depth, CAS reached the following *strategic decisions*[13]:

1. It adopted a new mission statement: *The CAS helps children in poverty to succeed and thrive. We do this by providing comprehensive supports to children and their families in targeted high-needs New York City neighborhoods.*
2. It clarified and narrowed its focus on poor children, declaring "We are a poverty-fighting organization."
3. It recognized the need to make long-term investments in each child it serves in order to help him or her break out of poverty.
4. It recognized its limitations and decided to work with fewer children (in order to be able to work with them longer and more intensively, and thereby also more effectively). That is, CAS adopted the strategic principle that it would "rather transform the lives of a few than simply serve many."

CAS moved ahead to make the following **theory of change decisions**:

1. **It drew back** from its citywide services, adopting the approach **that it would work with children living or going to school in specifically targeted, low-income, high-risk neighborhoods** in New York City.
2. **It adopted educational attainment as the mechanism to leverage these children out of poverty**, and **hence created "outcome maps" (short-term, intermediate, and long-term outcomes), using educational process, performance, achievement, and attainment metrics to understand success and guide constant reassessment and real-time (tactical) adjustments as indicated**—at the level of each case, program, and division, and also at the organizational level (although here decisions of necessity are more strategic in nature).
3. It decided to **implement uniform performance management practices and data utilization** across the entire agency.
4. And it is currently working hard on a long-term **implementation plan** and **developing a business plan** to allow it to change its operations and practices where they no longer fit with the decisions already described.[14]

PERFORMANCE MANAGEMENT FOR ORGANIZATIONAL IMPACT

As was noted, strategic clarity and a robust blueprint for success are two necessary preconditions for an organization to achieve its intended social impact. But by themselves, these are not sufficient. Organizations that deliver social impact reliably, sustainably, and at a level and scope that are socially meaningful must be able to run their operations with great intentionality to produce the results they have targeted—that is, they must be very adept at performance management.

What is performance management? Late in the 19th century and into the early 20th century, performance management was synonymous with managing *workers*—that is, getting the best available workers with the right attitudes, knowledge, and skills to work in specific settings (such as agriculture, mines, and factories). By the middle of the 20th century, performance management had come to mean the management of *work*, which was seen as a process that needed to be codified into elements and understood in terms of costs—with the intent to keep inputs (resources expended, including money, time, and even the number of workers) down and the creation of outputs (desired activities and products) up. Only in the last three to four decades has performance management come to mean working in such a way as to optimize an organization's ability to produce desired *results* (Penna, 2011).

But moving accountability from the production of outputs, over which an organization has direct control, to the achievement of outcomes, where control is much less direct, continues to be controversial. Why? Because it does away with the long-standing idea that organizations should be accountable only for what they can control absolutely—and that, as the saying goes, when things go wrong it is time to assign blame (Mayne, 1999). Outcomes are inherently constrained by realities that are external to an organization or program and so, often, one finds an institutionalized helplessness regarding accountability for the achievement of outcomes in many a nonprofit sector agency. But things are changing.

The focus on results, as opposed to simply managing work processes and other outputs, received an enormous boost from the passage, in 1993, of the U.S. Government Performance and Results Act. GPRA, as the act came to be known, was elegant in its simplicity (it is only 12 pages long) and was intended to help eliminate waste and inefficiency in government programs, to improve the public confidence in the competence of government and the effectiveness of its programs, and to promote accountability by emphasizing both program quality and the achievement of measurable results—that is, social impact. This means being able to answer the *So what?* question (Hunter, 2006a):

- *So what* if you provide mentors to 100 teenagers a year—what are the results?
- *So what* if you provide 1,000 women a year with mammograms—what are the results?
- *So what* if you print and distribute 10,000 safe-sex pamphlets addressing how to limit the spread of HIV/AIDS—what are the results?
- *So what* if you replicate your after-school program in 50 cities across the country—what are the results?

What does it take in order to manage performance for results? In addition to the elements already discussed as preconditions for organizational impact, key aspects of a performance management system include (a) real-time monitoring of both outputs and outcomes, (b) the use of short feedback loops, and (c) systems and processes for learning from one's efforts and the results they produce—a combination of data from internal databases and external evaluations.

Performance Data and Evaluative Data

As discussed, in the last few decades there has been a great movement toward understanding the results of organizational efforts. Sometimes dubbed the "Outcomes Movement," it was promoted by GPRA, and in the nonprofit sector, it was championed early on by United Way. This movement led to a rush by funders toward demanding that organizations and programs evaluate their work and demonstrate results. Unfortunately, while this reflected a new and welcome skepticism about the often exaggerated claims made by nonprofits and their funders regarding the value of (both government and nonprofit) programs, it also was grounded in a great deal of ignorance about evaluations and what they can and cannot explain and, perhaps even more destructively, led to a devaluation of internally collected performance management data (Hunter, 2006a; 2009).

Let's consider performance data and evaluation data in turn.

Performance Data

Performance data consist of information collected by organizations and programs to understand what they are doing, how well they are doing it, and what they are accomplishing. These data are used to make sure the organization or program is operating as intended and to plan improvements where performance does not meet expectations (Walker & Moore, 2011, p. 5). Typically, performance data will include unduplicated clients (with unique identifiers), client demographics, client service utilization (dosage and duration), information about which clients do not complete a program (premature dropouts) and why, client progress toward achieving short-term and intermediate outcomes, long-term client outcomes, and staff activities (as measured against program design specifications). These data are collected continuously throughout the organization's or program's existence and will be used at all levels of the organization to monitor progress, learn from the work, and make adjustments to improve performance as indicated. High-performing organizations use benchmarks for key measures in order to focus their attention on critical issues (and, of course, adjust these as they learn from experience).

Evaluation Data

Generally, the term evaluation is used to indicate that an outsider (or an internally employed scientific researcher) will be looking at the organization from an unbiased, disinterested perspective. The evaluator may collect data independently or analyze internal performance data using scientifically validated methods. Generally, evaluations involve both kinds of activities, with the former providing rigorous ways of testing the validity and reliability of internally collected data sets.

It is useful to think of evaluations as falling into two major types:

- **Formative evaluations**—these explore the degree to which a program or organization is serving those whom it claims to serve, is indeed doing what it believes it is doing, and is getting the outcomes it thinks it should. Often, these evaluations are termed "implementation evaluations" or "process evaluations," because of their focus on the workings of a program or organization.
- **Summative evaluations**—these focus more intensively on results, in essence answering the question, "What is the program or organization's likely impact and on whom?" Hence, these evaluations often are referred to as "impact evaluations."

TABLE 3.1 Evaluation Data Versus Performance Management Data[15]

Data-Related Activity	Data Sets and Their Use	Performance Management Data	Evaluation Data[16]
Deciding what data to collect	Specifying measurements and metrics Data focus Frequency of data collection Types of data collected	Ongoing, evolving in response to experiences, iterative Broad: tracks all operations and outcomes specified in the theory of change Constant/ongoing Process data and content data: inputs, outputs, outcomes, indicators, benchmark data	Negotiated up front (before the evaluation starts) as indicated by the theory of change and evaluative learning objectives Issue specific Periodic—monthly/quarterly/yearly[17] Process data and content data: inputs, outputs, outcomes, indicators, impacts[18]
Obtaining data	Data production Data orientation Data validity Tools used to collect data	Ongoing, real time Forward looking[19] Presumed for operational purposes Internal performance management data system	Periodic—monthly/quarterly/yearly) Backward looking Must be established as part of the research Internal performance management data system, desk research, public databases, interviews, surveys, and so forth
Using data	Establishing attribution of—or contribution to—causality Organizational learning Tactical data use[20] Strategic data use Users within the organization	Causality presumed for management purposes Real time or ongoing High (real-time flow of data) Low Many (all of the organization's leaders, managers, staff)	The core issue that must be established scientifically Infrequent Low (very slow flow of data, often "stale") High Few (mostly the organization's leaders)

These two kinds of evaluation form a logical sequence.

When programs are young or undergoing significant changes, formative evaluation may be appropriate after program staff members and managers have gone as far as they can in assessing and improving their own performance. Once evaluators are assured that the program is ready for an investigation of its outcomes, then impact evaluations may be conducted—along with an implementation evaluation to explain the findings. (Walker & Moore, 2011, p. 5)

To have organizational impact, clearly both performance data and evaluative data are essential. Table 3.1 compares performance data and evaluation data in relation to deciding what data to collect; how data are obtained; and how data are used.

Methods and Metrics for Understanding the Likelihood of Organizational Impact

There are three steps that an organization must take to be confident about the likelihood that its services are helping clients as intended.

Step 1: Knowing the Evidentiary Basis for Assuming Program Impacts
The first step in determining the likelihood that an organization's programs and services are effective is to be clear about the quality of the evidence that the organization is using to select and implement its program model(s). This amounts to looking at a hierarchy of evidence for program effectiveness, such as shown in Table 3.2. Some researchers will only accept Level 1 as sufficient evidence that a program has impact; others will settle for Level 2. Most practitioners and funders, however, would include Level 3 as sufficiently compelling evidence that a program or organization is having an impact. Another way of saying this is that the organization should know the current state of research regarding what works for the individuals, families, groups, or populations it serves—and, for that matter, also know about what doesn't work—and understand clearly where, on a ladder of increasingly robust knowledge about program effectiveness, its own program(s) fit (Hunter, 2003; Terzian, Moore, Williams-Taylor, & Nguyen, 2009).

Step 2: Clarifying How Evidence-Based Knowledge Is Used to Design and Implement the Organization's Own Programs and Services
The second step for assessing the likelihood that an organization is achieving intended outcomes for service participants is clarifying how closely the services or program elements it has implemented reflect the hierarchy of knowledge regarding program effectiveness presented in Table 3.2. One way of doing so is to use an approach like the one presented in Table 3.3.

Step 3: Knowing How Likely It Is That the Organization Can Deliver Programs and Services With Fidelity to the Codified Model
Finally, it is essential for an organization to be able to deliver its services with fidelity to the program model(s) it has selected. It must do so across personnel (all frontline staff must work within program design specifications) and sites (ditto). It must do so reliably and be able to sustain this over the long haul.

As noted, this requires the organization to have an operational blueprint for program management and service delivery. Such a blueprint should codify the following elements in answer to the questions framed earlier and have performance standards for each:

1. **Characteristics of its target population(s)**—in terms of both demographic and baseline characteristics. A performance standard concerning target population might specify the number and percentage of people enrolled in programming or services who meet the target population definition. The concept of "target population" refers to those individuals, families, groups, or populations that an organization is serving with programs that are intended to produce meaningful changes in their lives and/or prospects. In contrast, a "service population" consists of those people who may participate in programming but for whom the organization does not expect to see anything in the way of meaningful and sustained changes resulting from such activities. Not all human services are intended to produce outcomes. For example, a teen drop-in center may provide high-quality programming that engages young people and gives them opportunities to entertain themselves safely, a valid reason for providing services in and of itself. But a drop-in center alone will not likely change anybody's life unless there are other things that go on there, such as promoting strong relationships with caring and competent adults who communicate high expectations for the young people with whom they interact and who will be there reliably to support them for an extended period of time.

TABLE 3.2 Hierarchy of Evidence for Program Impact

Levels of Confidence That Evaluative Research Can Provide With Regard to Program Effectiveness (From Highest at Level 1 to Lowest at Level 7)	Type	Examples
1. Replicated proof of program impact	Using a series of randomized control trials (RCTs), a given program has been proven again and again to produce specific outcomes for a clearly designated target population.[21] This level of evidence currently is very scarce in the nonprofit sector and tends to be confined to organizations that have national replication strategies.	• The Nurse–Family Partnership[22] • Youth Village's Intercept Program[23]
2. Proof of program impact	An RCT[24] has proven that a given program produces specific outcomes for a clearly designated target population. This level of evidence is beginning to accumulate in the nonprofit sector. Agencies with national replication strategies or plans for very significant local growth tend to engage in RCT evaluation.	• Center for Employment Opportunities[25] • Career Academies[26]
3. Demonstrated evidence for program effectiveness using rigorous quasi-experimental methods[27]	Outcomes for program participants are compared with measured outcomes for groups of nonparticipants who are carefully selected to match a significant number of participant demographic and risk factors. This level is growing in the nonprofit sector and often is used by organizations that have replication or growth strategies but are ethically against the use of randomized selection of program participants or where the technical challenges of RCTs seem too complex or expensive.	• KIPP Academies[28] • Citizen Schools[29]
4. Demonstrated evidence for program effectiveness using less rigorous comparative means	Outcomes for program participants are compared with measured outcomes for groups of nonparticipants who are believed to match a significant number of demographic and risk factors of participants, or are benchmarked against similar groups using public data sets (e.g., high school graduation rates). This level of evidence is becoming common among nonprofit agencies that have a high stake in showing evaluative data that attest to their effectiveness but do not have the resources to undergo more rigorous evaluations.	• First Place for Youth[30] • Promise Academy[31] (charter school of the Harlem Children's Zone)
5. Apparent effectiveness	The organization collects outcome data to understand what it is accomplishing and make adjustments as indicated, but does not compare these data with any external information. This level of data collection is becoming very widespread in the nonprofit sector (in no small part due to the influence of United Way).	Examples are too numerous to list meaningfully.
6. Effectiveness based on practitioners' experiences	Program elements are designed by using available information about what practitioners believe to be best practices or widely accepted standards for high-quality programming. Most direct service organizations seeking to gain credibility from funders in the nonprofit sector achieve this level of evidence.	Examples are too numerous to list meaningfully.

(continued)

TABLE 3.2 Hierarchy of Evidence for Program Impact *(continued)*

Levels of Confidence That Evaluative Research Can Provide With Regard to Program Effectiveness (From Highest at Level 1 to Lowest at Level 7)	Type	Examples
7. Anecdotal effectiveness	Organizations collect and publish stories from current and former program participants. Without disputing the truth of such stories, one cannot help observing that universally, only positive stories are proffered—reflecting either selective inattention to negative results or the common human failing of forgetting. Anecdotal data can be useful for providing nuance and deeper understanding to quantitative data, but when they stand alone (as they do for the vast preponderance of social service agencies, especially those operating at the grassroots level), they are dismissed as virtually meaningless by evaluators and other practitioners interested in understanding social impact.	Examples are too numerous to list meaningfully.

TABLE 3.3 Hierarchy of Using Evidence-Based Knowledge to Implement Social Services or Programming

Levels Regarding the Use of Evidence-Based Knowledge in Program Design and Implementation (From Highest at Level 1 to Lowest at Level 6)	Discussion
1. Full implementation of program model that has been proven to produce impacts in at least two randomized control evaluations.	This means that an organization's programs or services are rigorously designed to implement a codified program model that meets the criteria for "replicated proof of program impact" described in Table 3.2. This level would, all things being equal, provide the highest level of confidence that an organization's programming or services are likely to be very effective.[32]
2. Full implementation of a program model that has been proven to produce impacts in one randomized control evaluation.	This means that an organization's programs or services are rigorously designed to implement a codified program model that meets the criteria for "proof of program impact" described in Table 3.2. This is also a very demanding level that can provide a high degree of confidence regarding an organization's program effectiveness.
3. Implementation of selected elements of a program model that has been proven to produce impacts.	This means that an organization has decided to implement aspects of programming that have proven effective at generating impacts but to modify implementation in some way. This might be by varying the target population for which the program is used; generally this will involve broadening the population to extend program reach.[33] Or it might involve selecting only certain program elements to implement while electing not to implement others. This considerably reduces confidence in an organization's program effectiveness.
4. Design and implementation of internally designed programming or services that reflect an understanding of professionally accepted evidence-based practices for delivering services to the target population.	This requires mastery of the current state of research regarding effective practices, programming, and services intended to help the specific kinds of individuals, families, groups, or populations that the organization serves and a highly developed rationale (often called a logic model) for using this knowledge in designing services to implement. Researchers will be quick to point out that this represents a considerably lower implementation standard and hence that one should be cautious in believing that an organization's programming is effective.
5. Design and implementation of new programming for which there is no directly applicable evidence that it is likely to be effective in achieving results for the people served but for which internal program performance data (specifically target population enrollment, service utilization, and outcome data) show that participants are achieving outcomes as intended at a sufficiently high rate for the organization's purposes.	Currently, a very high premium is being put on "innovative programming."[34] While on the one hand this is good because it encourages creativity in looking for ways to address challenges that have proven refractory to intervention efforts, the risk is notable that, in the end, these new and untested approaches will prove not to work. This represents what economists would call a high opportunity cost—and more urgently, it would mean that intended beneficiaries' trust has been betrayed.[35]

(continued)

41

TABLE 3.3 Hierarchy of Using Evidence-Based Knowledge to Implement Social Services or Programming *(continued)*

Levels Regarding the Use of Evidence-Based Knowledge in Program Design and Implementation (From Highest at Level 1 to Lowest at Level 6)	Discussion
6. Design and implementation of new programming for which there is no directly applicable evidence that it is likely to be effective in achieving results for the people served and for which there are no internal program performance data showing that participants are achieving outcomes as intended at a sufficiently high rate for the organization's purposes.	The comments for the previous level apply here. Unfortunately there is considerable enthusiasm among donors for supporting the replication of programs and services for which not a single shred of evidence exists regarding their effectiveness.[36]

2. **A map of the short-term (immediate), intermediate, and long-term (ultimate) outcomes** that its programs and services are intended to yield. A performance standard concerning outcomes could specify the number and percentage of participants enrolled in outcomes-producing programs and services who are expected to attain the targeted short-term, intermediate, and long-term outcomes. Of course, such outcomes-based performance standards must be appropriate for the characteristics of the target population. Thus, one would expect a work readiness program for recently discharged prisoners to have lower performance expectations regarding new job placements and retention than would a service intended to help people who recently lost employment due to corporation closures or reductions in workforce.

3. **The programs and services that it will deliver as indicated to the target population members** whom it enrolls in its services (Hunter, 2006b). A performance standard might specify that programming must be delivered in conformance with established service quality indicators. At a minimum, a well-codified program will specify (a) what activities will be performed with clients; (b) the competencies that staff or volunteers delivering these activities should have; (c) the dosage program participants should get (e.g., per day, per week); (d) how long someone should participate in programming before it is likely that he or she will benefit as intended; (e) the modalities that will be used to deliver the activities (e.g., workshops, one-on-one coaching or counseling, face-to-face interactions or telephone calls); and (f) the indicators that will be monitored to ensure that services are delivered at uniformly high levels of quality. For example, youth development practitioners recognize that high-quality youth development programming should have the following characteristics (quality indicators):

   a. Physical and psychological safety—including practice that increases safe, and decreases unsafe or confrontational, peer interactions
   b. Appropriate structure—clear and consistent rules with predictable and appropriately firm control
   c. Supportive relationships—warmth, caring, good communication, connectedness, support and guidance, and responsiveness
   d. Ongoing opportunities to belong—meaningful social inclusion regardless of ethnicity, gender, sexual orientation, or disabilities
   e. Positive social norms—rules of behavior, expectations, and obligations for service
   f. Support for efficacy and mattering—youth-based empowering practices that support autonomy, making a real difference in the community and in being taken seriously
   g. Opportunities for skill building—predictable occasions and intentional learning experiences to acquire physical, intellectual, psychological, emotional, and social skills
   h. Integration of family, school, and community efforts—concordance and coordination among activities and values in these diverse venues (Eccles & Gootman, 2002, pp. 7–8). Related to these indicators, there is research evidence for the following indicators (Hair, Moore, Hunter, & Kaye, 2001):
      • Adults interact with participating young people in predictable, stable, and caring ways, and hence care and effort are put into matching adults with youths
      • Effort is devoted to involving participants' nuclear or extended families—or other significant adults—in the program
      • Care is taken in the recruitment, screening, training, and supervising of staff and volunteers using well-developed guidelines
      • Where programs offer standardized services, these are tailored to individual participants' needs, which are assessed systematically; also, one-on-one adult–youth relationships are valued, available, and supported organizationally
      • Young people participate in the program(s) for a minimum of 1 year, and often longer

- Young people have a valued voice in, and can make choices about, how they participate in the program[37]

To summarize, regarding methods for understanding the likelihood of organizational impact: Once these three steps have been taken, an organization will know (a) the evidentiary basis for claims about the effectiveness of the programming it has used to implement its services, (b) how closely its own approach adheres to the models or practices it has implemented, and (c) how well it is able to deliver its programming with fidelity—that is, in conformance with the requirements (codified model, performance standards) of its service approach.

Fidelity of service delivery requires that the organization have a well-developed and well-implemented performance management system. This involves the ability to measure and monitor key performance indicators in the areas of target population enrollment, outcomes achievement, and service delivery as described above. It includes the organizational systems and processes for ensuring good data integrity, that is, accuracy, completeness, and timeliness of data entry (preferably entered and used by frontline staff in real time to manage their work), as well as for supervising staff to drive up quality and effectiveness and for making organizational adjustments as indicated in order to keep the organization on track to meet its mission-driven goals and objectives.

Only when all three elements are firmly established and fully implemented does it make sense for an organization to employ external evaluators to determine how well what it actually does conforms with what it is supposed to be doing (a so-called formative, process, or implementation evaluation). Only after one can have confidence in the level of an organization's implementation of its programming and its ability to operate its services reliably over the long haul (at least several years) does it make sense to consider taking steps that will establish its actual impact—that is, through an externally conducted summative evaluation. It is the latter kind of evaluation that will provide the data necessary to understand how effective an organization actually is in helping people as promised in its mission—that is, the *nature of its organizational impact*.

Metrics for Understanding the Scope of Organizational Impact

But, to calculate organizational impact beyond knowing how effective a program actually is in helping participants achieve outcomes as intended, it is also essential to know how many people are likely to benefit from such services.

As discussed, a frequently used metric is the turnstile count—that is, the number of people served (or "touched") by an organization. It is often assumed that scale of presumed impact can then be assessed simply by counting how many people are receiving some service from a given organization or a group of collaborating organizations. Unfortunately, turnstile counts tell us nothing about the likelihood that service recipients will benefit. To understand how many service recipients are likely to benefit from an organization's efforts, a different, more incisive metric is needed.

My colleagues and I developed such a metric in order to understand the scale of impact that youth development grants were having at the Edna McConnell Clark Foundation (EMCF). We coined the term "active service slots" and, after inviting extensive comments from a blue-ribbon panel of evaluators and other practitioners in the nonprofit sector, adopted the following definition:

By "active service slot," we mean the position in a program occupied by a participant receiving the appropriate type and level of service(s) called for in the program's theory of change. Thus, counting active service slots means counting the number of . . . [service recipients] who are using the program or services as they were designed to be used (Hunter & Koopmans, 2006, p. 188).

We went on to note that

> The use of active service slots quantifies a program's capacity to serve clients at a level of intensity at which effectiveness of service is a reasonable expectation. The value of this approach is that it specifically grounds the notion of service capacity in a program's theory of change and performance standards. (Hunter & Koopmans, 2006, p. 188)

The challenge, of course, is to figure out the right formula for calculating the level of service utilization that a program participant must reach in order to be occupying an active service slot. Defining active service slots for different organizations and program models or service approaches requires detailed knowledge of the evidentiary basis of their design, the clarity of their implementation standards (especially regarding the minimum necessary dosage and duration of service utilization that will produce intended outcomes), and the robustness of their theories of change. The interesting thing is that when we moved to implement this metric at EMCF, the people who tended to be most concerned about the justification of this approach were either other funders or advocates for the youth development sector—the organizations actually doing the work on the ground found that the definition made good sense and reflected how, in fact, they themselves thought about service capacity.

Here is an example of how one such organization defined an active service slot in a mentoring program (Hunter & Koopmans, 2006, p. 189):

1. It must have a one-to-one match between a young person and a mentor
2. The match must be high quality, which is defined as there being at least two face-to-face contacts per month, weekly phone contact, and documentation in monthly reports submitted by mentors
3. It must include only youth who are simultaneously enrolled in two of the other programs the agency operates (e.g., a tutoring program and a mentoring program)
4. It must be limited to participants who attend at least 70% of the sessions of the two programs

It is worth observing that although the organization served about 400 young people in 2005, only 70 were in active service slots as they defined them. So the turnstile count would be 400 participants in a year, but the number of these participants who actually can be expected to benefit from the program—that is, those in active service slots—is only 70. This is an important point because use of this metric results in lower counts for calculating the scale of operations that lead to impact and hence the scale of expected impact. Funders will need to be informed about the reasoning behind such lowered capacity measurements and to validate organizations' adoption of this much more realistic—but less grandiose—metric.

SUMMARY

The nonprofit sector's continued reluctance to collect meaningful performance data, engage in external formative evaluations to understand what is being done and how it seems to be working, utilize summative evaluations to understand impact in rigorous ways, and adopt realistic metrics for understanding scale of impact is a serious obstacle that contributes to the low level of performance one observes across the sector (Hunter, 2010). Both funders and direct service providers need to become more receptive to using such approaches to drive up the competence of nonprofit social service agencies.

This is a moral imperative. The nonprofit sector is essential to our nation's future. It does not need apologists. It needs critical friends. This author counts himself among the latter and hopes that this chapter will contribute to efforts to bring clearheaded and sober thought, predictability of funding streams, and accountability for performance to a sector in which these attributes long have been kept at bay by sentimentality and good intentions. In particular, we need to drive down the enormous cost to society of funding and nursing along organizations that are not high performers and show no potential to become organizations that could be counted on to deliver good social value. The bottom line of concern should not be protecting nonprofit organizations because we like them—it should be promoting and protecting the likelihood that people who need a hand and rely on the nonprofit sector will benefit as promised and thereby improve their lives and prospects.

NOTES

1. Observed by the author. The names of the participating organizations will be kept confidential for reasons that should be obvious.
2. This concern leads to some bizarre thinking among funders. Many foundations have explicit policies limiting the number of years that a grantee can be funded (often three or even fewer) before the foundation cuts its grants to the organization regardless of how well it is performing against the foundation's metrics and how much measurable social value it is generating against objective measures. Why is this done? The usual explanation is "We don't want them to become dependent on us." The officers of foundations using such practices should consider the following question: In assessing their own stock portfolios, would they arbitrarily (say, after three years) take money out of an investment that is achieving three times the return when benchmarked against similar stocks...so that the company "won't become dependent" on them? Not likely. The nonprofit sector, if it ever is to live up to its potential to create social impact reliably and sustainably, must have funders who think like social investors and, as long as an organization is delivering high social value, will continue their support for it or engage strategically with other funders so that even when ending their own support for such an agency, they can ensure the continuity of its funding stream (Hunter, 2009).
3. For stylistic purposes, "service recipients," "program participants," and "intended beneficiaries" are used interchangeably.
4. Practitioners looking for a wealth of information about outcome indicators and measures to use should visit www.childtrends.org.
5. Leaving aside, for the moment, the issue of attribution that is discussed in the following.
6. Youth Villages. "Youth Villages' Programs July 2000 through September 2010," Memphis, TN, Villages performance data published on the website www.youthvillages.org, 2011.
7. The WINGS creed is a series of statements that were developed by participating kids and professional staff that articulate the importance of self-respect, mutual respect, constructive conflict resolution, academic and related kinds of self-efficacy, the importance of setting high goals, and so forth. Kids and staff recite it daily; it can be read on the organization's website: www.wingsforkids.org.
8. *Center for Employment Opportunities*, ceoworks.org
9. This definition of impacts is the one that most evaluators would use. However, it is worth noting that in popular parlance the term often is used to mean something else entirely—namely, the long-term consequences attributable to some degree (even if loosely) to a program, service, or other kind of intervention (see, for example, Penna, 2011, pp. 19–20). In the framework of this chapter, that definition would apply to the concept of long-term outcome or ultimate outcome but not to "impact."

10. *WINGS for Kids* knows this and currently is in the middle of planning a series of external evaluations that ultimately will show whether or not its SEL outcomes are due to its programs—that is, are program impacts.
11. Yes, this means it is fair to suggest that these programs were a waste of money…lots of money!
12. Buery Jr., R. R. (2011). *Keeping the promise: A blueprint for the future of The Children's Aid Society*. New York, NY: internal document; based on Hunter (2011).
13. Buery Jr., R. R. (2011). *Keeping the promise: A blueprint for the future of The Children's Aid Society*. New York, NY: internal document; based on Hunter (2011).
14. Buery Jr., R. R. (2011). *Keeping the promise: A blueprint for the future of The Children's Aid Society*. New York, NY: internal document; based on Hunter (2011).
15. Adapted, with additions, from Steffen Bohni Nielson and Nicolaj Eljer (2006).
16. The nature of the evaluative data will be determined by the learning objectives for the evaluation and by the evaluation design and methods that are implemented.
17. Obviously, this will depend on the evaluation design.
18. When the right kind of summative evaluation is done; see previous discussion of impacts.
19. That is, asking and answering questions such as "What do we need to do better in order to improve the quality or effectiveness or efficiency of our work?"
20. That is, to manage operations on a daily basis.
21. A randomized control trial (RCT) is designed to eliminate all demographic and risk factor distinctions between program participants and a group of nonparticipants (control group) by first selecting all those who will participate in the evaluation study (experiment) and then selecting program participants randomly from the group. There are significant ethical issues that come up with randomization as the basis for selecting program participants, but in cases where there are long waiting lists these concerns are moot.
22. The Nurse–Family Partnership is headquartered in Denver, CO, and is replicating nationally; it has three major RCT evaluations that produced proof of program impacts on first-time pregnant, low-income mothers (reduced stress, reduced child abuse, delayed second pregnancy, quicker entry into the workforce, reduced substance abuse) and on their children (reduced incidence of low birth weight and then 16 years later—when the children were teenagers—improved school attendance and achievement, reduced criminal behavior, and reduced substance abuse; Olds, 2002).
23. Youth Villages is headquartered in Memphis TN, and is replicating in the eastern United States. While it has completed only one RCT of its community-based Intercept program for deinstitutionalized and criminally involved youths, its main intervention method (multisystemic therapy) has had about a dozen RCT evaluations that proved impact. Youth Villages has achieved a success rate of more than 80% with its program participants, in that 2 years after service discharge they are employed or in school and succeeding academically, not substance abusing, and living in stable homes (Mark Vander Weg and other academics, Unpublished research).
24. Randomized control trial: This is a method evaluators use to attribute the outcomes achieved by program participants and eliminate alternative explanations (e.g., selection bias) for why they did so.
25. CEO runs a supported employment program for reentering prisoners in New York State. In a study by MDRC, CEO participants proved, up to three years after discharge, to have significantly lower recidivism rates than did the control group (Redcross et al., 2009).
26. Implemented across the United States, Career Academies is a "school-within-a-school" that fosters rich learning opportunities. According to 10 years of RCT research by MDRC, its programs improve high school outcomes (e.g., on-time graduation) for

students at risk of dropping out (refer to www.mdrc.org/publications/366/over-view.html).

27. Quasi-experimental indicates RCTs that do not use randomizing to create the two groups that will be compared. Rather, the comparison group is carefully designed to match the participant group on a large number of points that are believed to represent the demographic and risk factors thought to be most likely to cause different outcomes for the two groups regardless of program participation.

28. KIPP operates 22 residential charter schools nationally, to which it admits underperforming students. In a study by Mathematica, KIPP students in comparison with similar students who were tracked at other schools show academic gains large enough to reduce race- and income-based achievement gaps (Tuttle, Teh, Nicholls-Barrer, Gill, & Gleason, 2010).

29. Started in Boston, MA, and replicating nationally, Citizen Schools offers enriched after-school programming to middle school students that includes mentorships with representatives of local businesses and focused tutoring for academic improvement. A quasi-experimental evaluation by Policy Studies Associates showed that compared with a tightly matched group, Citizen Schools participants were more than three times as likely to enroll in and complete 4 years at a high school rated as being educationally in the top tier (Arcaira, Vile, & Reisner, 2010).

30. Headquartered in Oakland, CA, but replicating throughout the greater Bay Area, First Place for Youth provides transitional housing, educational support, and employment readiness training to young people aging out of foster care. It has robust outcome data for all participants, benchmarks its data against outcomes for former foster care youths locally and nationally, and is presently undertaking a formative evaluation with Public/Private Ventures as a precursor to an impact evaluation that was scheduled to start in 2012 (S. Cobb, executive director of First Place for youth, personal communication, 2010).

31. Promise Academy is a charter school operated by the Harlem Children's Zone (HCZ) in New York City. It collects rigorous academic outcome data for all students, benchmarks these data against local public school students, and uses its findings to make program adjustments as indicated to drive up performance (Tough, 2008).

32. The obvious example of this level of using evidence-based knowledge would be the Nurse–Family Partnership.

33. Youth Villages has done this broadening of the population for which it has implemented MST in what it calls its Intercept program. However, the organization fully recognizes that it can no longer rest on evidence of MST's effectiveness in other venues; rather, it is embarking on a new evaluation that will test the effectiveness of the Intercept program with the expanded range of participants. And in the meantime, it is tracking its internal outcome data rigorously and making adjustments in the delivery of services as necessary to maintain its high standard for the achievement of long-term outcomes 2 years postservice participation. These include the avoidance of criminal behavior, success in school, and the attainment of a stable living situation.

34. Note, for example, the Obama Administration's Social Innovation Fund, specifically dedicated to investing in and replicating innovative solutions to refractory social problems (refer to the websites of the Corporation for National and Community Service).

35. I believe that most of the "Promise Neighborhood" service continua that are being funded by the government at this time reflect this level of using evidence-based evaluative knowledge in designing and implementing human services. Inspired by the admirable but not yet fully evaluated efforts of the HCZ, most of the current efforts to create these zones in new localities ignore one of the most compelling characteristics of HCZ—namely, that one organization provides, controls, and manages all the services in its continuum. This provides an organizational foundation for managing

the quality of program implementation and ongoing service delivery with associated efforts to keep the quality of services high and their effectiveness constantly improving. It is far from clear that partnerships of social service agencies seeking to work collaboratively to implement Promise Neighborhoods will achieve the unity of governance, the consistency of management, the reliability of staff, the quality of services, and the effectiveness of programming that will ensure that they are sustainable long enough to make significant differences in the lives and life prospects of the people they are intended to help and support.

36. A personal anecdote. Recently, I spoke with three social entrepreneurs fresh out of business school who had spent a year building a couple of schools in Africa—and who had recently been awarded over a million dollars to replicate in India. They had no outcome data for their African schools, and the donors had not requested such data. They wanted my help to develop a system of measurements to manage the replication. I refused, saying that in my view it was utterly irresponsible to replicate before any evaluative data supported the idea that their schools were resulting in students' learning and that I would be interested in helping them design a formative evaluation of the current schools and then, if warranted, an impact evaluation that might or might not show that their model was worth replicating. They let me know that they couldn't be bothered with such fundamentals because their "funders won't wait."

37. Although it's not research based, indicator 14 is held to be important by many youth development practitioners.

REFERENCES

Arcaira, E., Vile, J. D., & Reisner, R. (2010) *Achieving high school graduation: Citizen Schools' youth outcomes in Boston.* Washington, DC: Policy Studies Associates.

Bohni Nielsen, Steffen & Ejler, N. (2006). *Improving performance through evaluation?* Copenhagen, Denmark: Ramboll Management.

Collins, J. (2005). *Good to great and the social sectors* (p. 31). Boulder, CO: Jim Collins.

Eccles, J., & Gootman, J. A. (Eds.). (2002). *Community programs to promote youth development.* Washington, DC: National Academies Press.

Gueron, J. M. (2005). Throwing good money after bad: A common error misleads foundations and policymakers. *Stanford Social Innovation Review, 3*(3), 68–71.

Hair, E. C., Moore, K. A., Hunter, D., & Kaye, J. W. (Eds.). (2001). *The Edna McConnell Clark youth outcomes compendium.* Washington, DC: Child Trends.

Hall, P. D. (2006). A historical overview of philanthropy, voluntary associations, and nonprofit organizations in the United States, 1600–2000. In W. W. Powell & R. Steinberg (Eds.), *The non-profit sector: A research handbook* (pp. 32–65). New Haven, CT: Yale University Press.

Hunter, D. E. K. (2003). Edna McConnell Clark Foundation: Guide to assessing youth development program and effectiveness. *Child Trends, 36.*

Hunter, D. E. K. (2006a). Daniel and the rhinoceros. *Evaluation and Program Planning, 29*(2), 180–185.

Hunter, D. E. K. (2006b). Using a theory of change approach to build organizational strength, capacity and sustainability with not-for-profit organizations in the human services sector. *Evaluation and Program Planning, 29*(2), 193–200.

Hunter, D. E. K. (2009, October). The end of charity: How to fix the nonprofit sector through effective social investing. *Philadelphia Social Innovations Journal.* Retrieved from www.philasocialinnovations.org/site/index.php?option=com_content&id=36:the-end-of-charity-how-to-fix-the-nonprofit-sector-through-effective-social-investing&Itemid=31

Hunter, D. E. K. (2010, May). A means to assess social investment risk—and a plea on behalf of the people who need nonprofit organizations to deliver the value they promise. *Philadelphia Social Innovations Journal, 3.*

Hunter, D. E. K. (2011). *Children's Aid Society of New York City: Blueprint for success with key elements of programmatic and organizational redesign and a framework for performance management.* Unpublished manuscript submitted to the Children's Aid Society.

Hunter, D. E. K., & Koopmans, M. (2006). Calculating program capacity using the concept of active service slot. *Evaluation and Program Planning, 29*(2), 186–192.

Mayne, J. (1999). *Addressing attribution through contribution analysis: Using performance measures sensibly.* Ottawa, Canada: Office of the Auditor General of Canada.

Redcross, C., Bloom, D., Azurdia, G., Zweig, J., & Pindus, N. (2009). *Transitional jobs for ex-prisoners: Implementation, two-year impacts, and costs of the Center for Employment Opportunities (CEO) prisoner reentry program.* New York, NY: MDRC.

Morino, M. (2011). *Leap of reason: Managing to outcomes in an era of scarcity* (Chapter 9). Washington, DC: Venture Philanthropy Partners.

Olds, D. (2002). Prenatal and infancy home visiting by nurses: From randomized trials to community replication. *Prevention Science, 3*(3), 153–172.

Penna, R. M. (2011). *The nonprofit outcomes handbook.* Hoboken, NJ: John Wiley & Sons.

Terzian, M., Moore, K. A., Williams-Taylor, L., & Nguyen, H. (2009). Online resources for identifying evidence-based, out-of-school time programs: A user's guide. *Child Trends, 36.*

Tough, P. (2008). *Whatever it takes—Geoffrey Canada's quest to change Harlem and America.* New York, NY: Mariner Books, Houghton Mifflin Harcourt.

Tuttle, C. C., Teh, B., Nicholls-Barrer, I., B., Gill, B. P., & Gleason, P. (2010). *Student characteristics and achievement in 22 KIPP middle schools.* New York, NY: Mathematica.

Walker, K. E., & Moore, K. A. (2011). Performance management and evaluation: What's the difference? *Child Trends, 2,* 5.

OUTCOMES AS SCALING PLATFORMS

Ken Berger, Lisa R. Kleiner, Jeff Mason, Farrah Parkes, and Robert M. Penna

It seems clear that outcomes are the way that nonprofit sector impact will increasingly be measured as we move forward. The sector has a way to go, however, in learning what outcomes to measure, how to measure them, and the ways they can be used. The first part of this chapter considers the parallel between the emerging nonprofit sector imperative to make outcomes-based decisions in a rational, objective manner and recent changes in professional baseball. The next section provides a practical guide for developing an effective outcome measurement system that will provide valid information upon which programming can be evaluated and donations based. The chapter concludes with a due diligence framework containing key questions, or scaling criteria, that organizations or investors can use to determine capacity before considering large-scale impact.

BILLY BEANE AND OUTCOMES: WHAT CAN BASEBALL TELL THE NONPROFIT WORLD ABOUT MEASURES AND MEASUREMENT?

Although promising examples exist, for the most part, the nonprofit sector is talking about outcomes far more than it is actually utilizing them, and much of the conversation centers on three questions:

1. What is the "value" of outcomes?
2. What do outcomes tell us; why are they (or why should they be) important?
3. Should they be applied to everyone in the sector?

To get to an answer, perhaps the questions should be posed in a different way: *How valid is the "knowledge" upon which individual and organizational donations are traditionally and largely based?*

This is an especially important question for donors because their decisions very often determine which efforts will be implemented and which will survive. Every day, organizations and individuals invest in the work of a given nonprofit. Sometimes they have some reliable information upon which to base their decisions; very often they have little. So how are these decisions being made?

Traditionally, donors have not considered outcomes. But if outcomes truly hold the key to rational decision making, then virtually all other considerations that have been used must be wrong—or at least inadequate. A contemporary and accessible example can be found in, of all places, professional baseball.

Organized professional baseball, as even nonfans generally know, is a game that has compiled a staggering number of statistics throughout its long history. The most prevalent of these are, for hitters, the batting average, and for pitchers, the earned run average (ERA). Both of these measures (along with several others) were established by Henry Chadwick in 1859 and have been used ever since to assess performance, to rank players, and, most crucially, to judge the potential of young hopefuls and to justify an investment in them.

In the social sector, the late 1800s saw the first concerted efforts at collecting programmatic information regarding the effectiveness of the public policies then enacted in the United States. But the effort was unsystematized, and early practitioners lurched from one concept of inherent program value to another with little direction.

By the early 20th century, the sector began to rely heavily upon legislative fiat or executive order. From temperance to health, various efforts sought to establish rules for general behavior rather than seeking to change individual behavior. Programs were designed to address *problems*, not necessarily their causes: Outlaw alcohol, so the thinking went, and all social problems stemming from its abuse will disappear. There also existed, however, a faith in the effectiveness of these programs that required little or no "proof" once the worthiness of the effort had been established (Suchman, 1967). The impacts of social programs, to the extent that anyone actually thought in such terms, were assumed to be readily apparent in the number of people touched by an effort, or the number of dollars expended. Later, concepts like service units and compliance were added to notions of commitment, caring, and effort as the hallmarks of effective programs and organizations. That said, the sector largely continues to count activities rather than assess effectiveness.

So what do baseball and the nonprofit sector have in common when it comes to the respective yardsticks of performance and effectiveness? Only one thing: They have both proven to be decidedly misleading and, very often, wrong.

In his best-selling book *Moneyball*, Michael Lewis chronicles the efforts of Oakland Athletics (A's) general manager Billy Beane to compensate for the team's low payroll when competing for talent with the deep pockets of teams such as the Yankees, Mets, and Red Sox (Lewis, 2004). Beane realized that the reliance of those well-funded teams on traditional measures of player value not only led them to overvalue (and consistently overpay) star players but also blinded them to the true value of overlooked journeymen and minor league players.

But if the traditional formulas, batting averages (or ERAs) combined with "the look" and then filtered through the scouts' sage instincts, were as accurate as everyone supposed, there should have been no bad teams. More to the point, expensive yet bad teams should not exist if high payrolls reflected the best talent available.

Observers might be forgiven for seeing in this parallels to the social sector, where the best minds have sought out the best programs for over 40 years, and yet in the words of one long-time activist, "We've been fighting this 'war on poverty' since Johnson was in the White House. But not only haven't we won it, I'm not sure for all we've spent that we even have anything to show for it." Could it be that our "traditional formulas," like those in baseball, have been simply and irredeemably wrong?

In Lewis's account, Bill James, a rabid fan and complete outsider, was the first to ask, "If we can't tell who the good [players] are from the record books...how *can* we tell?" (Lewis, 2004, p. 69). The answer, James concluded, was by *counting* things. But not the things baseball was already counting, because they told, at best, an incomplete story.

James began with what his eyes told him he was seeing in various players and with what other people said was there in terms of talent and performance. But he then asked himself, "Is any of it true? Can you validate it? Can you measure it?" (Lewis, 2004, p. 75). What he learned was that you could *not* validate the traditional wisdom regarding talent or performance by using baseball's traditional measures. In fact, his new measures proved most conventional wisdom wrong.

The nonprofit sector has also been counting. By 1907, the New York City Bureau of Municipal Research was collecting data on social conditions and helped to launch a broad tradition of counting. Over the years, a staggering number of government and private agencies have counted numbers of children, numbers of residents per dwelling, numbers of people living in poverty, and a host of other things. Yet for all this, for the most part, no one could provide compelling evidence that programmatic efforts were actually working. (In his survey of over 60 years of social science writing, Zimbalist did not find evidence that there existed within early research efforts *any* question about the effectiveness of social work's interventions; as cited in Mullen, 2002.)

Just as James realized that runs batted in was not really an accurate assessment of a player's value, some in the nonprofit sector slowly began to realize that service units and compliance measures were a poor proxy for actual performance and effectiveness.[1,2] The early voices calling for an objective measure of program (and by implication, organizational) effectiveness, however, were lonely and few. For example, in 1955, Knutson argued the importance of defining program objectives more specifically (1955). Ciocco, perhaps mindful of the growing reliance on strict measurement in the corporate field of management theory, followed 5 years later by stressing the importance of using indices of "known reliability and validity" (Ciocco, 1960).

In 1969, the Urban Institute completed an extensive study of the performance evaluation of federally sponsored programs and concluded that such assessments of effectiveness were "almost non existent" (Horst, Nay, Scanlon, & Wholey, 1974). That same year, Suchman observed that "what passes for evaluative research [today] is…a mixed bag at best, and chaos at worst." Looking at program objectives themselves, he concluded that

> far too many [program goals]…are grandiose-but-usually-vague statements of intent and procedure…based upon largely untested or even unsound assumptions whose validity rests primarily upon tradition or "common sense," and not upon proven effectiveness. (Suchman, 1967, p. 16)

If this were true, on what "knowledge" were programs being funded by philanthropy and governments? The answer was a combination of the tried and true measures of head counts and compliance, mixed with the judgment of funding agencies regarding what successful programs (and the organizations that ran them) "looked like." Oddly enough, *just* like baseball.

Beginning with the foundations laid by Donald Campbell, and continuing through the work of Claude Bennett, Joseph Wholey, Martha Taylor Greenway, Williams, Phillips, and Webb, and others, a powerful argument began to form that suggested that measuring performance—outcomes—was a far more accurate way to assess, rank, and (ultimately) fund charities than were the old measures that had been in use for so long. Yet just as James's insights on baseball mostly fell on deaf ears early on, the logically inarguable idea of outcomes met resistance: They were a fine intellectual concept, the critics murmured in staid and profound tones, but could never work in practice. Indeed, many critics still make such arguments, but the consensus is slowly shifting away from such ideas.

In the case of baseball, James's work went largely ignored by the professional estab-lishment until utter and dire necessity forced Beane to look beyond statistics and to try to identify the diamonds in the rough that the wealthier teams had overlooked in their rush to sign superstars. Success called for a new way of thinking; in fact, in Beane's view, the entire game needed to be rethought. He willfully ignored baseball's hallowed devotion to runs scored and focused instead on limiting outs, seeking players who made the fewest (Lewis, 2004).[3]

The situation in the nonprofit sector is not all that different. The days of virtually unlimited funding are long gone. Like Beane, the leaders and managers of today's non-profits are being forced to do more with less. Yet just as the baseball establishment initially put more effort into trying to stymie Beane's success than they did understanding and emulating it, today's nonprofit sector seems to be spending more time discussing the challenges presented by outcomes than actually implementing them.

Lessons for the Nonprofit Sector

1. The conventional wisdom about what a successful program (or organization) looks like is misleading at best and dead wrong at worst. Just like the baseball establishment, the sector has been looking at (and responding to) the wrong things.
2. The measures the sector has used in the past—activity counts and compliance, commit-ment, passion, and even management savvy and financial strength—are inadequate. They tell no more about the contribution an organization or program is making to social change than a hitter's batting average tells about his contribution to a team's victories or a pitcher's ERA tells about the quality of the defense around the bases behind him.
3. Better measures are needed, and outcomes are the best the nonprofit sector is likely to have for a long time. As a guide to individual and institutional giving decisions, sev-eral questions must be asked:
   - Does an organization utilize a program management system that includes measur-able outcome indicators?
   - Does it do so in a systematized way?
   - Do an organization's targeted outcomes have any intrinsic value—that is, are they *meaningful* outcomes?
   - Are outcomes being used to enhance performance? Does the organization change *its* behavior if target outcomes are not achieved?
   - Are the organization's outcome reports available to funders and the public?
4. The sector needs to begin using the outcome-based tools that have already been devel-oped. Tools and formats are now available to practitioner organizations for virtually every stage of programmatic planning, management, and reporting. These tools are only being used by a few organizations; they need to be used across the sector. To make this possible, however, donors need to make an effort to provide the wherewithal that organizations need to learn about, master, and adopt these tools.

For the purposes of informed social investing, the failure of the predictive power of the sector's traditional measures has been evident for a long while. Like Beane, leaders must look elsewhere if they are to intelligently allocate scarce resources.

Yet the question remains, what will the sector do?

The ultimate choice lies with the sector's institutional and individual donors. When they begin demanding better, more reliable information upon which to base their giving decisions, the sector will have no choice but to comply.

For those still reluctant to embrace outcome thinking and its associated practices, the few organizations that have gone down the outcomes path have reaped its rewards. Summer Search, a national leadership development program that helps low-income young people graduate from high school, go to college, have successful careers, and give back to society, is a popular program that had existed for nearly 20 years; it nonetheless had no set curriculum or outcome targets. Instead, there was activity, lots of activity. Recruitment was becoming "a challenge" according to its chief executive officer (CEO), and retention had become an even bigger problem. There was too little the program could point to as a means of attracting new participants or keeping the ones it had.

After a recent move to outcomes, however, not only did the Summer Search students see their highest college acceptance rates ever, but overall enrollment and retention blossomed. Of particular interest is the fact that even in the current economic downturn, when so many charities are seeing funding slashed, Summer Search has sustained its funding. A significant donor recently told the organization that its verifiable outcomes *proved* that they are a "high-impact investment."

Equally inspiring has been the success of the Oakland area's First Place for Youth, an organization mentioned earlier that supports youth in their transition from foster care to successful adulthood by promoting choices and strengthening individual and community resources. After a move to utilize outcomes tracking to illustrate the effectiveness of its model, the organization experienced growth from a $1.7 million budget and staff of 25 to an $8 million budget and a staff of 60. Even more amazing, however, has been the organization's success in helping to grow state dollars in these tough economic times. Partnering with the John Burton Foundation and relying upon the proof of effectiveness its outcome information provided, First Place was able to convince lawmakers in Sacramento to increase from 40% to 100% the state's portion of the Transitional Housing Plus funding stream that supported its work, an increase that translated into an investment that grew from $5 million to $40 million.

Returning to Beane and his A's, how did Beane's shift in thinking work out? Beane abandoned the old school wisdom of the scouts (and his own reliance upon the game's hallowed and traditional measures of potential and success). In their place, he employed a new analysis that led him to a collection of players nobody else wanted. To the stunned amazement of the rest of baseball, and armed only with this collection of castoffs, rejects, and nobodies, he improved the A's third-place standing and 46–36 record on July 1 to first place and an 87–51 record on September 1. People noticed. In October of that year, Mr. John Henry, the new owner of the Red Sox, decided that 86 years of frustration was enough. He was going to emulate Beane. He was going to hire Beane's inspirational sage James to help him do it. In fact, he was going to try to hire Beane himself.

In the end, Beane stayed in Oakland, but his methods were transplanted to Boston. Two years later, the Sox stunned the world by finally shaking off the Curse of the Bambino and winning their first championship since 1918.

A DUE DILIGENCE FRAMEWORK FOR SCALING AND REPLICATING SOCIAL IMPACT

Organizations that have demonstrated social impact, that is, those that have evidence-based social solutions, may want to expand beyond their immediate markets. To scale or replicate successfully, it is important to understand which elements of the program or model must be kept constant (often referred to as fidelity to the model or to the program), to have a strategic action plan, and to ensure that leadership, financial, and organizational capacity exists to execute the plan.

In early 2011, the Social Impact Exchange worked collaboratively with a number of experts and practitioners in the field of scaling and social impact—including members of the Exchange's Market Development Working Group and the Alliance for Effective Social Investing—to design a common due-diligence framework that would provide funders with guidelines on basic due-diligence topics to cover when dealing with scaling initiatives.

This framework is meant to guide funders who are considering scaling investments (serving more people more effectively). By collecting the types of information identified in this framework, funders should be able to make more fruitful investments. The Due Diligence Framework for Scaling Initiatives is equally important to nonprofits that are looking to generate scaled impact because it can serve as a self-assessment guide that will help determine an organization's readiness for growth.

The framework is divided into six sections. The first asks whether an organization has developed a theory based upon well-defined social impact goals and whether it has determined that there are additional markets, both consumer demand and capital investments, into which it can expand. The second category covers an organization's social impact and proof, or level of evidence, that a program or initiative "works." Levels of evidence are defined as self-reported data, third-party evaluations, quasi-experimental studies, and randomized control studies (or trials, RCTs). The third section asks logistical questions about an initiative's well-defined program elements, standardization of elements, training, and quality performance systems. The fourth category deals with organizational strength and capacity to scale, including management, engagement, governance, and operations. The fifth section addresses the organization's or initiative's readiness to scale and probes whether there is a well-defined new organizational structure, scalable process, demand, market entry and ramp-up process, commitment to growth, and organizational brand. The sixth and final category reflects the economic model and sustainability and deals with revenue, expenses, required capital, and national and local economic needs. Table 4.1 to Table 4.6 lay out the questions that need to be asked in each category of the scaling framework.

TABLE 4.1 Scaling Goals and Market Analysis

Social impact goals	1. Are the nonprofit's scaling aspirations (including growth and impact goals) clearly stated?
Industry/field/ ecosystem	1. What are the main strategies being employed in the field to address the problem? Which are the most effective? Which have scaled successfully? How large is the target population? 2. What does the comparative landscape look like, for example, market share or players by geography? 3. How does the funding flow in this field? Are there significant funds available for scaling?

TABLE 4.2 Social Impact and Levels of Evidence

Self-reported data	1. Is the program's theory of change (TOC) based on evidence and/or knowledge that was gathered in the field? 2. Is there a strong system in place to track participants' outputs and outcomes before, during, and after program participation? Are the same data collected consistently from all program sites? 3. How have these data trended over the last 3 years? 4. Are the data compared with baseline data (target population's "outcomes" prior to the intervention)?
Third-party evaluations	1. Were the evaluations well designed and conducted? 2. What were the results regarding program outcomes (immediate, intermediate, and long-term outcomes) and impacts? If outcomes differed substantially among different participant segments, why, and what did the organization do to address this? How do the organization's outcomes correspond to the state-of-the-art knowledge regarding what is most helpful for the group(s) being served? How closely do these outcomes align with the organization's social impact goals, TOC, and core program? 3. Were unintended outcomes considered? 4. Were the program recruitment and selection processes reviewed for skimming and motivational bias? Did the evaluation consider the rate of premature program dropouts? 5. Have program completion rates for various subgroups been analyzed? Are there any relevant groups that are unlikely to complete the program? Have appropriate adjustments been made to increase the likelihood of completion? 6. What difference does the program make (i.e., beyond what would have happened without it)?
Quasi-experimental studies	1. What were the results of any quasi-experimental studies? 2. Are outcomes stronger than they would have been without an intervention? 3. How similar were the comparison groups?
Randomized control trials (RCTs)	1. Is an RCT appropriate for this program? 2. If an RCT was conducted, what increased impact did the program have compared with the control group(s)? 3. What are the limits of what the RCT(s) proved?
Other impact indicators	1. Are there multiple early indicators and/or proxies that provide a strong degree of confidence that the intervention will result in the desired outcomes? 2. How consistent are the outcomes or impacts across program sites? 3. What are the economic savings to society based on program outcomes? 4. Do the reported outcomes reinforce the validity of the organization's theory of change? 5. Is the level of evidence commensurate with the nonprofit's stage of growth and capital request? 6. How does the organization believe its primary constituents see it?

Broader impact	1. What strategies are in place to scale impact beyond the individuals served by the nonprofit itself, for example, policy initiatives, catalyzing a broader movement or coalition, training executives from other nonprofits, creating a market-based solution, forging a public–private partnering model, leveraging systemic change, and implementing a broad-based communication strategy?
	  a. Does the organization have clear goals for these strategies?
	  b. How effective have these strategies been? How does the organization measure their effectiveness?
	2. Does the organization seek to partner or collaborate with others where appropriate? How does it assess and improve its relationships with third parties?

TABLE 4.3 Program

Program elements	1. How much training and expertise are required to deliver the program? How customized is the program to a specific location and population? Will the program be difficult to standardize and therefore present a greater challenge to replicate? 2. Has the program identified key elements that must be held constant to achieve outcomes? 3. Have aspects of the program that lead to outcomes been examined, for example, intensity, dosage, recruitment process, level of participation and completion, quality of materials, experience of staff? 4. Does the nonprofit know which factors lead to poor outcomes and how to improve weak sites? 5. Can the program adapt to local conditions? Is it clear which program elements can be customized as the program enters new communities or targets new populations?
Program standardization	1. Are program processes and elements standardized and documented? 2. Is there a complete and thorough operating manual? Is it suitable for use in scaling efforts? 3. As the organization has scaled up, has it maintained fidelity to the key elements of its program model? Does it have performance data to demonstrate this?
Training	1. What is the quality of initial and ongoing training for staff, management, and site leaders? 2. Are there training tools and curricula that can be rolled out during scaling?
Quality and performance systems	1. Is the organization quality- and performance-driven? Does it have systems and standardized processes in place to ensure consistent outcomes? Is it focused on continuous improvement? 2. Is there a "performance scorecard" in place? Are short- and long-term goals and metrics clear? 3. Are systems and people in place to gather, analyze, and act on the right data in a timely and strategic manner? 4. Has the organization considered how its processes and systems need to evolve as it grows? 5. Does the nonprofit have an ongoing performance management and evaluation strategy with staff and resources dedicated to it?

TABLE 4.4 Organizational Strength and Capacity

Management	1. Has an assessment of the nonprofit's leader been conducted? Have references been checked? How experienced is the leader in raising money, thinking strategically, motivating and directing staff, and cultivating a learning environment? 2. Is there enough management depth to scale at the projected pace? Do managers work well as a team? 3. Does management have the skills and expertise required for scaling?
Board of directors	1. What is the board's level of engagement and strategic competence? Is the board committed to ensuring sufficient operating revenue? What is the board's level of involvement in developing growth capital and revenue? 2. Will the board be a strong asset in the nonprofit's scaling effort?
Governance	1. What is the relationship between the national office and local sites, for example, legal structures, decision rights, agreements governing quality standards, services, fund-raising? 2. Will this governance structure be appropriate during and after the intended scaling? 3. How transparent and accountable is the management team to the board? 4. Does the nonprofit comply with best practices regarding conflict of interest, whistleblower policy, CEO compensation, and so forth?
Operations	1. How strong and scalable are the nonprofit's nonprogram operations, for example, finance, accounting, Internet technology, human resources, knowledge management, public relations, volunteers, government relations, and marketing?

TABLE 4.5 Readiness to Scale

Organizational structure for growth	1. What is the nonprofit's growth structure (e.g., the affiliate model)? How effective has it been to date? 2. What limitations does the nonprofit's chosen structure place on its ability to scale up? 3. Have the trade-offs of different growth structures been considered? 4. Are program sites satisfied with the structure and with the support received from the national office? 5. Do sites have formal input into how the program network is managed? 6. Are there tensions between the sites and the national office that affect program outcomes or fund raising? 7. How is quality ensured if sites have significant autonomy? 8. Are there complications with raising money locally given the existing structure? For example, if local programs are part of a larger local nonprofit, do they receive enough attention?
Scalable process	1. Are there standard requests for proposals and criteria for selecting new sites or expansion partners? 2. Are there standard processes for entering new markets? Are they consistently applied? 3. How are local funders engaged in starting up new sites or programs? 4. Does the organization adequately focus on its resource chain (for example, pool of staff, volunteers) when entering new markets? 5. Is there experience with local scaling, that is, "going deep" in a city once a program is established? If so, what are the successes to date? What lessons have been learned?
Demand	1. What is the market demand for the program? Is there a backlog of requests for the program?
Market entry and ramp up	1. How long does it take to get new sites established? What are the major impediments to site start-up? 2. What are the costs of starting a site and the average budget of maintaining a site? 3. What are the success and failure rates of sites?
Commitment to growth	1. Are the board, management, employees, and other constituents committed to scaling? 2. Do these constituents understand their roles and responsibilities to ensure successful scaling? 3. Do they understand the implications of scaling for the nonprofit, for example, funding, operations, risks?
Brand equity	1. How strong is the nonprofit's brand equity among constituents who are important to successful growth, for example, foundations, donors, public officials, and partners? 2. Are there plans to protect the brand equity during (potential) scaling challenges?
Growth planning	1. Has a high-quality, multiyear growth plan been developed that includes growth and outcomes targets, strategies, interim goals, operational plans, and capital requirements? 2. Is there a prioritization of goals in case resource constraints require scaling back the plans? 3. Has the nonprofit engaged the appropriate partners for scaling? 4. Are projected growth, revenue, and cost targets realistic? Have the main assumptions been tested? 5. Were alternate scenarios evaluated? 6. Have risk factors been identified? Is there a contingency plan? Are sufficient funds being raised?

TABLE 4.6 Economic Model and Sustainability

Financial/expense review	1. What are the major categories of expenses? How are these expected to change with scale?
Financial/revenue stability	1. What percentage of national and local revenue comes from private contributions, fees for service, income, and government funding? What portion of private contributions comes from each of the following: foundations, individuals, and corporations? 2. Is revenue consistent, reliable, and adequately diversified? 3. Does the organization dedicate sufficient resources to revenue generation? 4. Will the revenue model be able to scale in line with the projected growth of the organization? 5. Will scaling require the nonprofit to have additional reserves? 6. What percentage of contributions is unrestricted?
Capital structure	1. Does the organization distinguish between growth capital and operating revenue? 2. Is capital being raised via the growth plan for support of ongoing operations or to support the costs of expanding the operation and establishing the infrastructure to manage at scale? 3. Is the nonprofit investing in its ability to generate increased revenue to support a scaled-up organization?
National office growth and sustainability	1. Is there an achievable plan for sustaining the national office at scale with reliable revenue? 2. Does the nonprofit's plan include earned income to support scaling? If so, does it have a track record of doing so and the capacity to increase its earned income? 3. Has the national office attracted growth capital in the past? Have national funders expressed strong interest in funding increased national office capacity to manage growth?
Local program start-up and sustainability	1. Is there a demonstrated fund-raising model and ability to raise start-up capital for local sites? 2. Is there a track record of local sites' becoming sustainable? Can local sites become sustainable in the future without ongoing fund-raising assistance from the national office? 3. Where does sustainable funding for local office operations and growth come from, for example, philanthropy, earned income, a reliable third-party payer, state government contracts?

Source: © 2012 Growth Philanthropy Network and the Social Impact Exchange. Reprinted by permission.

NOTES

1. James pointed out that a run batted in (RBI) was in fact not a measure of an individual player's prowess because he needed someone else to get on base before him so that he might, through his own hit, allow that person to score. The fallacy of this statistic, James noted, was that a runner who played it too cautiously on third base could rob a hitter of an RBI, just as an audacious one, sprinting from second base and taking a chance on getting home safely, might unduly reward the hitter of a mere blooper single by stretching an expected one-base advance to a two-base score. Either way, the hitter actually had nothing to do with the result. More to the point, James's analysis led to the inescapable conclusion that hitters on teams with poor offense had fewer opportunities to rack up RBIs because their teammates were lousy hitters. The RBI, in other words, was more of a reflection of a team's combined hitting than that of any individual player.
2. Similarly flawed, for that matter, is the National Football League's (NFL) insistence on measuring the value and performance of a quarterback based upon a ratio of

touchdowns to interceptions, the latter of which can be caused by a multiplicity of factors, only some having to do with the quarterback.
3. Beane's calculation was that runs are potentially unlimited but that the out was the game's most precious commodity. Teams are allowed only 27 of the latter, and the faster they accumulate them, the quicker the chance to score runs diminishes. His thinking was that by limiting the number of avoidable outs made during a game, even a team of (less expensive) average hitters would have ample opportunities to score sufficient runs to win—especially if the other side was squandering its outs. He similarly realized that the hallowed batting average was a far less reliable predictor of team scoring success than was a player's on-base percentage, which takes into consideration bases awarded on walks: The patient hitter who draws more walks would usually score more often than the power hitter who also swings at bad pitches and strikes out more frequently.

REFERENCES

Ciocco, A. (1960). On indices for the appraisal of health department activities. *Journal of Chronic Diseases, 11*, 509–522.

Horst, P., Nay, J. N., Scanlon, J. W., & Wholey, J. S. (1974). Program management and the federal evaluator. *Public Administration Reviewer, 34*(4), 300–308.

Knutson, A. (1955). Evaluation program progress. *Public Health Reports, 70*(3), 305–310.

Lewis, M. (2004). *Moneyball.* New York, NY: W. W. Norton.

Mullen, E. J. (2002, July 4–6). *Evidence-based social work—Theory & practice: Historical and reflective perspective.* Fourth International Conference on Evaluation for Practice. University of Tampere, Tampere, Finland. Retrieved from www.uta.fi/laitokset/sospol/eval2002/CampbellContext. PDF

Suchman, E. (1967). *Evaluative research* (Chapter 4). New York, NY: Russell Sage Foundation.

NEXT-GENERATION NONPROFITS

*Michael Clark, Clifford C. David, Jr., Jason Hwang, Nancy Moses,
Suzy Nelson, and Nicholas D. Torres*

There are many reasons to view the finance industry with skepticism. The financial engineering of synthetic products that few people understood, and even fewer knew how to regulate, bears a large part of the blame for the 2008 financial crisis. Exotic financial instruments were created in the name of advancing the personal wealth of a few at the expense of many.

Financial instruments can, however, generate large-scale social good. When the poet Holderlin used the term "saving power," he was referring to what individuals truly value. He implied that danger creates the opportunity for this realization (Seyfettin, 2006). There are pioneers in the emerging field of impact investing who assert that capital markets can be harnessed to generate societal wealth, not just personal gain. They predict that organizations pursuing social outcomes will be able to access a pool of assets totaling more than $500 billion (Bugg-Levine, Brandenburg, Leijonhufvud, O'Donohue, & Saltuk, 2010). They predict that a new social economy will emerge, linking financial and social value. Leaders of the impact investing movement refer to this concept as "blended value creation." Traditionally, organizations have been structured to create either financial or social value; the impact investing industry takes a *both–and* approach (Bugg-Levine & Emerson, 2011, p. 10).

The conversation becomes more interesting when financial value is linked directly to social impact. Through altruistic financial engineering, impact investors will be able to "create markets where there were none" by investing heavily in the most promising social ventures (McKinsey & Company, n.d.). A new social economy may form. Nonprofit, for-profit, and hybrid organizations with the greatest impact in areas such as education, health care, and social service delivery could also create new social industries and spur economic development. Nonprofit organizations would rely on steady cash flows and adopt capital structures appropriate to their missions. The public, private, and nonprofit sectors could all be working together to address society's most intractable problems. A vast amount of the financial assets sitting in foundations and pension funds could be unlocked to generate social impact. In fact, if only 5% of assets sitting in charitable foundations, typically committed to mainstream investments, could be unlocked, an impact investing market the size of the entire U.S. venture capital industry would be created (Bugg-Levine & Emerson, 2011, p. 197). As Lisa Hall from the Calvert Foundation notes, if public-sector pension fund portfolios committed just 1% of their assets to impact investments, it could unlock billions of dollars to improve social outcomes (Clark, 2011). This must serve as an attractive proposition for the public sector. Widespread budget deficits hinder the public sector in addressing social ills; unlocking pension fund assets would allow it to leverage limited resources.

If this sounds like a dream, it is. An industry infrastructure for impact investing does not yet exist. Standard methods of measuring social and financial performance have not yet been adapted, let alone standard methods of linking social and financial performance. Governments have not yet decided how to regulate this emerging industry, and many remain skeptical about the volatility of capital markets in general. Further, impact investing should not be seen as a panacea for social ills or as a replacement for traditional philanthropy and government social programs.

Many concrete and important steps have, however, been taken to make this dream a reality (or at the very least, within reach). Organizations like the Global Impact Investing Network have begun to create the necessary industry infrastructure. In light of severely limited resources, public-sector regulators and politicians have begun to warm to the impact investing industry.

FUNDERS DRIVE BEHAVIOR: ANGEL INVESTING AND SOCIAL IMPACT BONDS (SIBs)

Angel investing blends the heart and the mind in the investment decision-making process. Angel investing entails loaning money to small start-up businesses that have an operational need for capital. It is designed to be the next step in growing a business after what is often referred to as bootstrap financing—using savings, credit cards, and friends and family to launch a business. Angel investors are often the first professional lenders who provide financial support to a growing business. These investors come before a bank or lending institution would incur the risk associated with a start-up. Angel investments are usually small, ranging from as little as $25,000 to up to $250,000. Once a company gets beyond a quarter of a million dollars, larger investors are sought to take the company to the next level.

Impact Investing

Within the angel investment community, there is growing interest in what is called impact or triple bottom line investing. This is the idea that money can be invested where it can have a positive impact.

First, like any good investment, it will produce a return on capital. Impact investing, however, strives for two additional elements: first, a business that produces a positive impact on the environment (solar panels, new techniques for recycling, shared automobiles, etc.) as well as generating returns for investors and second, the treatment of company employees, vendors, suppliers, and related businesses in a healthy, sustainable manner. Angel investors want to see fair working conditions, fair pay, medical benefits, nondiscrimination, and, in general, a place where people want to work.

In Philadelphia, there are a number of angel investment groups (Robin Hood, Delaware Crossing Investor Group, etc.) that meet to evaluate start-up businesses. These groups are made up of qualified investors, as defined by the Internal Revenue Service

(IRS) and by other investment funds, who are looking to finance start-up companies that they believe have a strong chance of success.

Investing in Start-Up Impact Companies

There is no science to determining which companies will succeed and which will fail. As the saying goes, "If I knew that, I would probably be on a tropical island with an umbrella drink in my hand and not writing this chapter." With that said, a great deal of research and thought has gone into evaluating what constitutes a promising social impact company for angel investment. Investor Circle, one of the Philadelphia-based angel investment groups, has developed a questionnaire, mentioned previously, to ensure that critical questions are asked and answered before an investment decision is made.

Angel investors have broken the inquiry process into five major categories:

- Management
- Business model and strategy
- Financial assessment
- Operational assessment
- Research and development

Within each of these categories, there are hundreds of questions that cover everything from "Is the CEO a leader, a manager, or both?" to "Have you considered recent changes in the tax law that affect the company?"

SIBs

One of the most promising financial instruments is the SIB. Launched in the United Kingdom, SIBs raise funds from nongovernment investors, that is, trusts and foundations, high-net-worth individuals, and so forth, to pay for preventive services. If the services make a difference, investors receive "success payments" from the government purse. The size of the payments depends on the success of these services. The mechanism relies on leveraging private capital to ultimately generate a blended return on investment. To properly leverage investments for the greatest impact, system designers proposed the creation of an SIB delivery agency, described later in the chapter. The agency brings investors and public entities together and facilitates a contractual agreement outlining the measurable outcomes to be achieved by a chosen service provider. The public sector then makes payments to investors if these defined outcomes are met within a certain time frame.

Several key ideas, apart from its having both a private- and a public-sector standpoint, set this approach apart. As it stands now, foundations, trusts, and high-net-worth individuals give large amounts to social projects without seeing a direct financial return on investment. The SIB approach not only gives these entities a financial return on their original investment but also encourages further investment in proven solutions. Public-sector entities also benefit from SIBs, which have several advantages over performance (aka outcomes-based) contracts. First, all risk is transferred away from the public sector. Second, the public sector only pays for success, and these payments are proportional to the improvement in social outcomes. The SIB model provides additional, nongovernment financing to improve social outcomes, fund service providers' costs upfront, and facilitate cooperation among multiple service providers (Bolton & Savell, 2010). This strategy, however, can only be successful if public-sector savings can be proven.

Once SIB models are optimized to provide investors greater assurance that social outcomes will be obtained and financial returns realized, investors will be encouraged not only to invest in proven solutions but to invest in those solutions to an even greater degree. This virtuous cycle of investment could generate the financial resources and cross-sector collaboration necessary to scale proven solutions in education, health care, and the criminal justice system.

How This Financial Innovation Works: The First SIB in Peterborough, United Kingdom

Although SIBs have the potential to spur the creation of widespread societal wealth, the reality of SIB implementation will be slow, measured, and fairly complex. The model is intriguing for governments because they only pay for success. In fact, SIBs have been dubbed "pay-for-success bonds" in the United States.

With Social Finance, a UK government agency, as the financial intermediary, the UK Ministry of Justice launched the first SIB. The SIB was to be used to pay for antirecidivism interventions aimed at offenders serving short-term prison sentences at Peterborough prison.

An excerpt from *Lessons Learned From the Planning and Early Implementation of the Social Impact Bond at HMP Peterborough* sheds light on the process:

> The Ministry of Justice has appointed independent assessors from QinetiQ and the University of Leicester to undertake data analysis in order to determine whether offenders who receive interventions on release from Peterborough are reconvicted less than similar "matched" offenders from other prisons who do not have access to SIB-funded intervention. If members of the Peterborough cohort are reconvicted less than offenders in the comparison group in the year following their release from prison, then the SIB will have entailed benefits for the Ministry of Justice and wider society, in the form of improved outcomes for the offenders and for their communities, which experience less crime. In addition, there will be benefit to the government which, in theory, will have saved money through reduced costs of policing, court cases, prison places, and so on. If the independent assessor calculates that reoffending has reduced by at least 10% for each cohort, or 7.5% overall, compared with a matched comparison group, the Ministry of Justice (has committed) to pay a return on investment to investors for this improved outcome...Clearly, while there are other good reasons for seeking to improve outcomes for the target group in this SIB, the SIB model is based on the premise that the interventions funded will deliver cashable savings to government within the period of the bond. The SIB at HMP Peterborough is not likely to result in substantial cashable savings to the Ministry of Justice or other government departments, which can be achieved only through significant reductions in the prison population. (Disley, Rubin, Scraggs, Burrowes, & Culley, 2011, p. 3)

The Peterborough case demonstrates the complexity of establishing control groups and dealing with independent assessors as well as the coordination necessary to implement the SIB model. Additionally, the first SIB will not save the UK government any money, nor will it create broad social change.

Why, then, do SIBs continue to be considered? The answer is potential and dreams. Yes, the Peterborough SIB probably will not lead to government savings, nor will it significantly reduce the prison population. The United Kingdom, however, will take the lessons learned from this pilot to optimize its SIB model to fight recidivism. The more governments learn from SIB experimentation, the closer they get to legitimizing the SIB as a financial instrument and shifting nonprofits from delivery organizations to having social impact.

Social-Sector Winners and Losers in the SIB Model

The sector has much to gain from financial innovations such as these. There will, however, be some losers. Greater levels of funding will be directed to organizations—next-generation nonprofits (next-gens)—that can prove impact and take operations to scale. Nonprofit organizations already compete for a relatively small pool of resources; widening that pool by unleashing capital markets will solve some funding problems, but it will also eliminate some players from the game. SIBs and similar financial innovations will direct funding to proven solutions, not just those organizations that can run effective marketing campaigns.

Of course, parts of the nonprofit sector will continue to operate according to the status quo. Nonprofits will still solicit charitable donations and write countless grant applications. Financial innovations like the SIB, however, will direct funding to organizations that are actually doing good and away from organizations that are only claiming to do good.

Financial innovation in the nonprofit sector is not only about engineering financial products or creating profits; it is ultimately about dealing with people. Knowledge of what motivates people to change current behaviors and empathy for others' circumstances are vital skills in this emerging industry. Linking financial value to social outcomes is predicated on the idea that leaders can drive effective organizations to improve social outcomes. Experienced nonprofit leaders understand that the impact investing industry is not only about dealing with numbers on a spreadsheet but also about people living in an increasingly complex world.

DISRUPTIVE AND SUSTAINABLE INNOVATIONS

The concept of disruption has long evoked negative connotations. A disruptive student keeps the rest of the class from focusing. A detour on the street might disrupt traffic and make drivers late for work. A tropical storm will likely disrupt weekend plans. Disruption in industry, business, and nonprofits, however, can be beneficial to employees and customers. It can mean an improvement has come along that gets the job done more easily, such as a clinic that opened in a local grocery store where people can see a health care worker without an appointment and then finish shopping. Customers appreciate the clinic's convenience and simplicity because it means they do not have to make a doctor's appointment to be seen for a routine issue. Hundreds of these "retail clinics" have opened across the country and are changing how hospitals, primary care physicians, and emergency departments operate. Convenient care clinics (CCCs) are a disruptive innovation.

Speaking an Innovative Language

A disruptive innovation fills a particular gap in the marketplace. Very sophisticated services and goods are often targeted at a relatively small group of people who require an advanced product. That leaves a gap of potential customers who would use the product if it were simpler, more affordable, and easier to access. Christensen (2003) calls these products "good enough." They are affordable and easy to distribute. The competitiveness of these products stems from the fact that they satisfy customers who otherwise would not be able to access them (Christensen, Grossman, & Hwang, 2009). Finally, a disruptive innovation must also be sustainable in the sense that it can survive and continue to grow. This can be difficult in the nonprofit sector, in which so many initiatives rely on outside funding. This is the point where the for-profit and nonprofit worlds start to blend. The for-profit world already has discovered many successful business models that can be adapted to benefit nonprofits. This chapter discusses two very different innovations that are also sustainable business models, the retail-based CCC and the Apple iPad2—one is disruptive while the other is not.

CCCs

Retail-based CCCs are the epitome of disruptive innovation. CCCs are relatively new and have provided patients with a simple, affordable method of receiving health care. Across the country, well-known stores such as CVS, Walgreens, Walmart, and many others are offering this low-cost alternative to seeing a primary care physician. CCCs operate under different names, including Minute Clinic, Redi-Clinic, Take Care Health Systems, and Quick Quality Care. To date, 1,300 CCCs operate in 40 states and the District of Columbia. Trained nurse practitioners meet with patients for approximately 20 minutes to assess and treat common illnesses as well as provide vaccines. Care is governed by a strict protocol that only allows nurses to treat certain conditions, such as strep throat and urinary tract infections, or provide certain services, such as sports physicals. Any patient with an emergency or suffering from a chronic illness such as coronary artery disease will be directed to visit a qualified medical doctor or an emergency department.

Why is this model disruptive? As most people are well aware, physicians are burdened by the consequences of managed care. To meet their monetary needs and patient demand, physicians must pack their daily schedules with five-minute appointments. Quality care, however, cannot be rushed, especially when it concerns complicated and chronic diseases. Thus, doctors usually spend more than the estimated five-minute time frame, becoming later and later for each subsequent appointment. Consequently, patients spend more time in the waiting room and less time with the doctor. This is dangerous, costly, and unfair for a number of reasons. First, doctors burn out quickly, leaving them vulnerable to malpractice suits. It is difficult for any person, no matter how well trained, to succeed when impossible demands are made of them. Second, patients are getting less care for their money while insurance companies reap the rewards of this unfortunate situation. Finally, those with serious conditions do not always get the attention they require, putting them at risk.

The CCCs have shaken up this tired system. These clinics are meant to treat easy-to-care-for patients who do not necessarily need the specialized services of an MD. Doctors' schedules are lighter and they are able to spend more time with each patient, ensuring better care. Patients don't have to wait for hours with conditions like strep throat, and doctors benefit from seeing clients (Christensen, Bohmer, & Kenagy, 2000). An important power shift also occurs when patients make decisions about their own care. Having the choice to drop by a CCC during a lunch break rather than taking the afternoon off from work to sit in the waiting room is empowering. It promotes responsibility on the patient's part, which in turn provides the opportunity to invest in one's own health (Christensen & Hwang, 2009).

CCCs are a sustainable for-profit model. The cost to patients is usually somewhere between $40 and $70, which is less than an emergency department visit, even for an uninsured individual. Many insurance companies cover visits to CCCs, so patients need to pay only their regular copay. Clinics, of course, pay overhead and other associated costs, including staff, equipment, tools, and their own insurance. They maximize business by offering weekend hours and staying open late to serve working patients. As noted, they provide immunizations and sports physicals, which are regular services. Nurse practitioners adhere to a strict protocol, which reduces the incidence of malpractice suits. These practices help make the model financially sustainable and independent (Stine, 2011).

iPad2

As noted, disruptive innovations are sustainable. This is different, however, from the concept of sustaining innovations. Sustaining innovations are improvements or updates made to better a product. Fine-tuning goods and services is a natural part of pleasing customers and keeping them coming back. Sustaining innovations are not always inspired by customer feedback, but that is usually a vital piece.

Spotting a sustaining technology is fairly simple. The features of the iPad2 were noted on Apple's website: "Thinner, lighter, and full of great ideas. Now iPad is even more amazing."[1] The iPad2 was a sustaining technology for Apple because it made a good product that customers were already using even better. While this is an example of an excellent sustaining innovation, it is not really disruptive to the marketplace. Apple's competitors were anticipating the improvements and busy making their own adjustments to keep up. Not all sustaining innovations are dramatic or spectacular. Some are routine updates that still drive the improvement of the product or service (Christensen et al., 2009).

Catalytic Innovation

Catalytic innovations are a subset of disruptive innovations. Like disruptive innovations, catalytic innovations also fill the consumer gap to provide a good enough solution. Instead of selling products to an underserved market, however, these solutions work to reduce large-scale social issues. This is where the social and nonprofit sectors have a special niche. Five key elements comprise a catalytic disruption.

- Social change is induced through scaling and repetition of the disruption. If the public sees a successful program, many will want to try to achieve similar results in their own communities.
- The solutions offered are considered to be good enough, even though more costly and complicated solutions already exist.
- The population served by the disrupter is currently underserved or being served by a complex solution.
- Competitors are often initially uninterested in the disruptive solution because they underestimate the significant resources and capital to be found there.
- Those who are uninterested in the catalytic innovation tend to remove themselves from the market, thereby eliminating more competition (Christensen, Bauman, Ruggles, & Sadtler, 2006).

For the sake of simplicity, the terms catalytic innovation and disruptive innovation will be used interchangeably.

Community Colleges

The community college model is an example of a catalytic disrupter. Community colleges have transformed their reputations from mediocre places to pass the time and get a low-cost education while one waits for acceptance letters from higher-end, more expensive institutions. A degree from a community college used to be something to be wary about including on a resume because of the stereotype that only "slackers" end up there. This is not the case today. Many students choose to attend community colleges for a few years to save money, but with plans to transfer and finish their degrees at their schools of choice. Other students choose to obtain their degrees from community colleges because they are attracted by the improved quality of advanced courses and high job placement rates of these schools. These students were previously underserved because they may have been turned off by community colleges' traditional reputations but could not afford higher-priced institutions. And community colleges offer flexible schedules and easy transfer options.

Surprisingly, traditional universities have helped this catalytic innovation come alive by recommending community college to first-year students, thereby saving themselves precious housing space and allowing professors to focus on teaching advanced courses. A true catalytic innovation, community colleges are successfully educating previously underserved students with a good enough solution that their competitors were not interested in. Certainly, the replication of this model has achieved recognition across the country.

I-LEAD

The cycle of disruptive innovation is endless. Just as the model of community colleges became well known, another innovator dropped in to stir the mix. Philadelphia-based international organization I-LEAD (Leadership, Education, and Development) is gaining attention and praise. I-LEAD attacks the concept that those without the finances, access, or ability to travel to attend community college need to take out loans or, worse, not attend at all. According to founder David Castro, "Rather than ask how we can enable more students to afford higher education, we must shift the question to ask how we can make quality postsecondary education affordable." Castro entered into a partnership with Harcum College. The design of the partnership is one in which tuition is set just above what an average low-income student can leverage in financial aid, education is provided within a community setting (high schools, community-based organizations, faith-based institutions), and a cohort model is used to ensure student support. Within a few years, I-LEAD and Harcum have generated a new student body of over 400 nontraditional students who are participating in the degree program with approximately 90% of their tuition subsidized. In the next few years, that student body is expected to double, which would mean that over half of Harcum's student body will be educated within community sites.

This model is sustainable because I-LEAD is making money to grow on. Harcum College reinvests about one half of tuition into the program and its partners. The students' tuition is almost completely subsidized by financial aid, not loans, because it is based on the amount of aid that an average part-time student receives each year. As communities begin to see successes and local leadership gets stronger, more individuals will be encouraged to take part.

The Disrupter-o-Meter[TM]

The Disrupter-o-Meter (see Figure 5.1) is an excellent, low-cost place to begin determining an innovative idea's feasibility. It is a tool created by the Innosight consulting firm to measure an idea's "innovativeness." It has won the approval of author Clayton Christensen, who defined the schema of disruptive innovation. This tool works in two phases to help professionals determine if their idea is innovative and, if so, how innovative it is and how it can be improved. The first phase requires the user to enter target consumers and describe what the solution might look like from both customers' and competitors' perspectives. These data will help determine what innovation rating this idea might have. In describing the tool, Caroline Ridgway writes, "The exercise pushes aspiring entrepreneurs to ask themselves, 'What would happen if . . . ? What would happen if the target consumer group were smaller, or in a different geographic setting? Or what if the price of the product were cut in half or the main competitor were brought on

Disrupt-o-Meter™

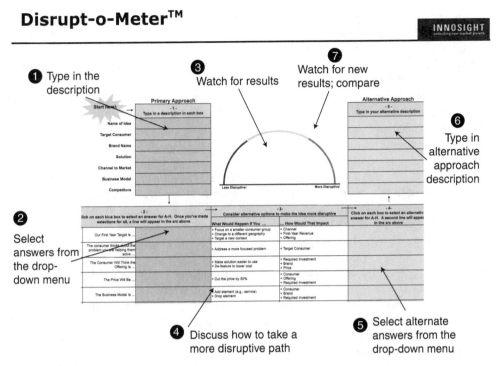

FIGURE 5.1 The Disrupt-o-Meter.

as a partner?'" Such questions breed creativity and allow the innovator to see his or her idea through a new lens.

Phase 2 of the Disrupt-o-Meter pushes the idea's logistics further. Determining effective marketing, associated costs, and other practical details helps to make the idea as tangible as possible. One major challenge for a company or organization considering the implementation of a disruptive or catalytic innovation is that it is much easier for a new venture to be disruptive rather than an existing and successful company. This is because disruptive innovations take attention and competition away from products already on the market. It is often detrimental for an organization to introduce a product that will disrupt its existing product line and put it out of commission. Monetary losses are bound to occur, often dissuading organizations from moving forward.

There is, however, another way to look at this situation. Perhaps it is not always wise to implement a service or product that disrupts your own organization, but you also cannot lose the competitive edge that you worked so hard for. This means more hard work and service improvement. It means constantly measuring, evaluating, and asking clients what can be done better. Not only will this lead your organization to the small adjustments that keep boosting it up the expertise ladder, it also allows the organization to see more clearly when the right disruptors come along.

Measuring an Innovation's Positive Social Impact

Imagine that an innovative idea was tweaked through the use of the Disrupt-o-Meter and the inventor got the go-ahead from management to begin planning the initiative. How will the inventor convince funders and investors that the innovation is worth every dollar spent on it? One method is to create a social return on investment (SROI) formula for the program. SROIs measure a positive effect on an economy, society, or environment. This is a fairly abstract concept, so instead picture a giant piggy bank. On the outside of the pig, imagine writing "SROI" in big letters and then hold onto the image of the piggy bank while looking at a concrete example.

Remember I-LEAD, the associate's degree program designed to reach nontraditional students right in their communities? The masterminds behind this initiative have a few choices when it comes to choosing SROI metrics. One is to examine how I-LEAD impacts the environment. I-LEAD takes place in community centers and schools that are being used regularly. No new classrooms had to be built, so money and construction materials were saved. Picture all the dollars that were not spent on paying a construction crew, installing plumbing, lights, and parking, and buying furniture. Now picture all the wood, metal, chemicals, fabrics, and land that were not needed. It's time for the fun part: Imagine being surrounded by all that money and materials and start dumping it into the SROI piggy bank. That full piggy bank represents what and how much I-LEAD saved the environment by choosing not to construct new buildings.

The formula is not yet complete. Although I-LEAD should be recognized for its environmental savings, adjustment needs to be made for the amount of money and materials being used to operate the community spaces as classrooms. Many of these spaces are underutilized, but running a program will inevitably bring expenses. Lights are left on longer, more water will be used, and so forth. Professors' salaries, insurance premiums, advisors, and cleaning staff must all be paid. That means reaching into the giant piggy bank and pulling out the money and materials to pay for it all. Even after the added costs of providing services in the community, I-LEAD can officially boast that its innovative program has a positive return on investment while avoiding a negative impact on the environment.

How to Create an SROI Formula

At this point, you may be skeptical about measuring the work that your nonprofit performs. How can the human impact of serving a meal to hungry people or teaching adults to read possibly be measured? Although it is admittedly difficult and imperfect, this type of measurement is possible with a little creativity. To help spark such creativity, two very different SROI formulas with realistic calculations are discussed step by step.

The Common Market, a Philadelphia-based nonprofit, attacks the cycle that keeps independent farmers from earning a fair living selling their produce. The Common Market does this by paying farmers a higher price for the food, which can result in increased wages for farmers and farm employees, and then directly selling it to institutions with a high demand, such as restaurants. This two-step process cuts out all of the middlemen, including shippers, distributors, and brokers. Liz McKenna (provides the following formula:

SROI = Benefits to individual + Benefits to society − Investment costs.

Totaling the farmers' income and subtracting from it their costs calculates individual benefits. Societal benefit was found by estimating how much each farm employee earned minus the amount he or she spent back in the economy. Investment costs are the money originally put in to start the venture, plus any extra that was needed for growth. McKenna calculated the Common Market's SROI to be $2,131,650 over 3 years.

If an organization provides a service that is less measurable, such as educational experiences or issue awareness, creativity is needed. For example, the Free Library of Philadelphia (FLP) is a well-known, well-loved, and often-visited location in Philadelphia.

Yet its impact is a challenge to measure. Count how many books children read? How often seniors utilize the social spaces?

Anna King took a different approach. She looked closely at the population of children younger than 5 in Philadelphia, an age group toward which the library targets many of its educational programs. Some children younger than 5 may already be involved in a Head Start or early intervention program, but many children do not have such an opportunity. King realized that the library's services might be filling in this gap. She began to create her formula by utilizing the library's data that about 10% of its patrons were younger than 5 years old. She estimated that about 25% of Philadelphia prekindergarten children had the educational preparation to begin school. "Acknowledging that the FLP is not a prekindergarten program, a 75% 'discount rate' from the national impact can be taken. This means that the FLP might have 25% of the impact that a pre-K program would have" (King, 2011, p. 5). Next, King multiplied the number of unprepared, younger-than-5-year-old patrons by 25%, the impact rate noted above. She researched what happens to children who are not reading at grade level when they enter school. It turns out that this factor is associated with a continued pattern of below-grade-level academics and low graduation rates. Her last step was to examine the societal costs associated with not graduating from high school or not obtaining employment. She then took into account factors such as insurance and unemployment costs and ended up with this SROI formula (King, 2011, p. 5):

> SROI = [Cost–benefit and lack of diploma attainment or job attainment
>   (government unemployment/health insurance, etc.)
>   × [Assumed number of children entering FLP who are not
>   adequately prepared for school]
>   × [Assumed FLP impact percentage]

When the corresponding numbers were entered, suddenly the library could be proud of its positive impact on Philadelphia's prekindergartners. It should be noted that there is an assumption that by providing disadvantaged children access to books, the FLP is increasing the likelihood that they will enter school reading at grade level.

Individuals should examine the data about the populations they work with and, based on the research, see where individuals would be without the program's services. Does the research indicate that the target population would most likely be eating fresh food less than once a week, or dropping out of GED programs, or having medical issues undiagnosed? If one or more of these types of problems would be worse without intervention, then the program is most likely making a significant social impact. If research indicates that the target population appears to be stable without assistance, the program may not be as needed as was initially suspected.

The Art of Sustaining Quality Innovations

Most good products and services that are currently being improved will already be sustainable. Think back to the iPad2: Using the innovation criteria, it was noted that the iPad2 was a sustaining but not disruptive innovation. This does not mean, however, that it does not have value. In fact, many customers practically salivated over the thought of buying their own updated versions. This is because the first iPad was well received as a quality product worth investing in. The second version was expected to be of the same quality but with some exciting new features. Best of all, any kinks or problems in the first one were expected to be nonexistent in the second one. In fact, many customers held out specifically for the second-generation version so they could invest their money in a cool product once without any of the initial issues.

The financial situation looks a bit different for those on the production side. They need to keep investing money to continue measuring and improving the product. This concept is the same in the nonprofit sector as it is in the business world. With proper support, a good human services program has the capacity to become a great one. David Hunter describes the process funders can use when making the decision to invest their money:

- Use rigorous selection criteria to choose which nonprofits to support
- Structure investments to strengthen organizations to enhance their ability to provide effective, sustainable, high-quality services
- Track performance and provide nonfinancial supports as indicated, thereby helping agencies become more effective in helping the people they serve to measurably improve their lives and life prospects
- Diminish transaction costs to help organizations stay focused on achieving their respective missions
- Help nonprofits build reliable revenue streams that will sustain them at the appropriate scale before terminating the investment (Hunter, 2009)

This information is also useful for the employees who actually perform the nonprofit organization's services. In fact, these bullets can be used as talking points when opportunities to speak with funders arise.

When a Product or Service Is No Longer Innovative

No matter how amazing, useful, interesting, or helpful a disruptive product or service is, at some point, it will no longer be innovative. The nonprofit sector, just like the business marketplace, is constantly changing. In the *Innovator's Prescription*, Christensen et al. state, "Stuff just happens to customers. Jobs arise in their lives that they need to do, and they hire products or services to do those jobs" (2009, p. 11). In the nonprofit sector, clients also hire services to do jobs in their lives. The difference is that the jobs nonprofit clients need filled often put clients in a state of crisis. Health care is a huge job. Quality education on a low budget is another. CCCs and the I-LEAD model are disruptive innovators that were successfully "hired" to fill these jobs.

Sometimes the services being offered to fill a client's job do not seem to be working. This feels like a frustrating mystery: "The community said they wanted a free health clinic, but hardly anyone uses it." Asking the right questions of consumers will help to fit the product to the job. Christensen et al. (2009) would immediately ask what job that community health clinic is doing for patients.

If a health clinic, after-school program, or support group has low numbers, ask clients why they come and what else the organization can provide that would keep them showing up. What job is the program filling in their lives? How can the organization expand services to better fill that job for others? Maybe the hours need to be altered or the receptionist is grouchy. Perhaps the building is too hard to find or clients do not have bus fare to get home. Once the organization gets some feedback, test it out. Peter Brinckerhoff (2010), the author of *Mission-Based Marketing*, suggests using client and investor feedback to try changing 1% every day. One hundred days later, there should be results. Small change is easier than large change, even for those who want it.

CHARACTERISTICS OF NEXT-GENS

Next-gens tackle an old issue with a new approach or model, providing simple but effective solutions to social problems or issues that affect consumers, thereby creating value not only for consumers but for society as a whole.

1. Next-gens are led by management teams with strong analytical, political, and strategic skills.
2. Next-gens have the potential to foster ongoing relationships with donors, customers, communities, political leaders, the media, peers, and even competitors.
3. Next-gens forge strategic, mutually beneficial partnerships with compatible organizations to help extend their impact.
4. Next-gens are especially adept at the entire panoply of social marketing and media, using it to expand their reach, promote their causes, raise funds, and even deliver on their missions.
5. Next-gens are financially sustainable because they blend missions with profits. They create related enterprises because they realize that dollars earned afford greater control than dollars raised, which often come with red tape.
6. Next-gens are metrics-driven toward social impact; they collect and use data to drive management decisions, measure progress, foster transparency, and increase social impact.

DISRUPTIVE AND SOCIAL INNOVATIONS

Management Teams

The nonprofit world was previously where second-rate talent was paid third-rate salaries. No more. Today, nonprofit management jobs are prized, despite the lower salaries. Not only do they allow for the work–life balance that many prize, they also provide important intangible rewards. Nonprofit employees spend every day with people who share their passion for a cause.

Relationships With Donors

Nonprofits are surrounded by a large cast of characters: board members, clients, competitors, community leaders, funders, regulators, the media, and all kinds of donors. These individuals and others comprise stakeholders. They are friends and foes, bedfellows, allies, and adversaries. Navigating through and around them is what stakeholder relations are all about. Larry Wiseman, former CEO of the American Forest Foundation, defines a stakeholder as anyone who can affect an organization's success or failure, saying "They're everywhere, sometimes where you least expect them."
Wiseman says,

> When I began the job, the environmental movement was bipolar and extraordinarily contentious. But, beginning in early 2000, people began to realize the problem with forests was not saving the biggest tree on earth but protecting forests against development. This was an issue that crossed the lines between people who support conservation and those who depend on forests for the livelihoods (personal communication, April 2003).

Driving this sort of paradigm shift in thinking about natural resources is difficult, and for the next-gen executive, even risky. More than time and energy, change of this magnitude demands the will to overcome resistance even among one's closest allies. At American Forest Foundation, many board members held onto the conventional wisdom that there were friends and enemies and they were locked in a zero-sum game. According to Wiseman, "Somebody would win, and somebody would lose. The notion that we could find a win–win solution didn't resonate, and board members let me hear about it" (personal communication, April 2003).

Equally challenging were the foundation's efforts to create a public climate in which this kind of change would even be possible. Wiseman says, "We recognized that most people learned about environmental issues from headlines, and maybe the first few words of a news story." By 1995, the organization decided that to move the issue of forest conservation forward, it had to help create opportunities for journalists to learn more about the environment itself—to understand the context in which these kinds of stories unfold and, in Wiseman's words, "to touch it, feel it, smell it, and live it." In partnership with the University of Montana's school of journalism, American Forest Foundation cofounded the Institutes for Journalism and Natural Resources, which sponsors week-long learning expeditions for reporters and editors, immersing them in issues ranging from ocean biology to forest economics in locales from Alaska's Tongass National Forest to Maine's Acadian Coast. The Institutes for Journalism and Natural Resources continues today as an independent nonprofit. More than 200 newsrooms, including all major dailies and broadcast outlets, have been represented on its study tours (Larry Wiseman, personal communication, April 2003).

Strategic Partnerships

Funders of all kinds, but especially foundations, have long encouraged nonprofits to work together as a way of increasing their programs without adding administrative costs. Now, organizations are cooperating on a number of fronts: theater groups share marketing lists and cross-promote to audiences; charities jointly purchase and occupy buildings; and community development organizations and providers of education and health and wellness services work together to bring essential services to clients. These collaborations work best if organizations have similar values, complementary missions, and compatible markets.

Social Marketing and Media

Nonprofits always look for ways to stretch their marketing dollars. That is why many have been quick to master the web and social media as vehicles for fund raising, friend raising, promotion, and content distribution. The most advanced ones are moving beyond, experimenting with online initiatives that blur the lines among all of these to gain a unique presence on the web.

ArtBabble is doing just this for the Indianapolis Museum of Art. ArtBabble is a cloud-based online portal for video about art: not just art at the Indianapolis Museum of Art but even art from thousands of miles away. On any given day, ArtBabble visitors can see videos from 34 institutions ranging from the Prado in Spain and Museo Tamayo in Mexico City to the J. Paul Getty Museum in Los Angeles, the Asian Art Museum of San Francisco, the Art Institute of Chicago, the New York Metropolitan Museum of Art, three of the Smithsonian Institution's art museums, and two or three public television producers. ArtBabble's goal is to become the go-to site for videos about art, and it is well on its way.[2]

ArtBabble was a partnership between the new media and software development teams of the Indianapolis Museum of Art. They were seeking a way to connect with young people—not always the easiest market to get into museums—and at the same time gain a single presence. The Indianapolis Museum of Art was already on YouTube and iTunes U.

To go to the next step, the team decided to build a video-specific site that could grow over time into a premiere destination for art content.

ArtBabble offerings, all of which are free, include videos about artists, art handlers, curators, and even museum guards. They also include themed tours of museum holdings, live demonstrations of glass making, lectures, and video art exhibitions. But users of the site get more. Embedded in the content of the videos are "Notes," small pieces of enhanced web content that connect users to other videos, references in the museum collections, and other websites. The notes provide content producers with the ability to add extended descriptive content that can be indexed as keywords by search engines. This allows users to use the videos as a point of departure to pursue their own interests. It also creates its own content by combining art from a number of institutions.

A robust legal infrastructure undergirds ArtBabble, providing copyright and content licensing protection to partner institutions as well as the Indianapolis Museum of Art. An ArtBabble advisory team governs the site, which is managed on a daily basis by the Indianapolis Museum of Art. It uses Amazon Web Services cloud computing tools and infrastructure. Since funding comes from the museum and the grants it gets, efforts are made to control costs while improving user access and high-resolution digital quality.

ArtBabble is a powerful tool for the Indianapolis Museum of Art, placing it at the cutting edge where art meets technology. It builds allegiance from young users, carries the museum's brand throughout the world, and demonstrates the value of interactivity. ArtBabble is not only about art; it is also about connectivity, collaboration, and community.

Financial Sustainability

The nonprofit business model is fraught with illogicalities. The most valuable and skilled employee, the CEO, spends most of the time on the least creative assignment: fundraising. Philanthropic grants and gifts will pay the direct costs for a program but not for general operating costs, which can leave organizations with the dollars to launch a worthy initiative but without the funds to pay the electric bill. It is more efficient to cultivate a few large funding sources than it is to pursue a large number of smaller ones. But if any of the large ones slash their giving or eliminate it altogether, nonprofits find themselves forced to reduce or eliminate the critical services they are in business to provide.

How do nonprofits beat these odds? By diversifying revenue and building up earned income. Next-gen leaders seek to replace the "tin cup" model of philanthropy with the entrepreneurial approach of the business world. They strive to control their organizations' destinies, which means controlling their revenues. Whenever possible, they cultivate many different philanthropic sources so the organizations can survive the loss of one. Of great importance, they create profitable businesses.

Diversifying philanthropic sources and creating profitable businesses in a nonprofit organization is never easy, but it is possible, even in the most unlikely of organizations. At the Atwater Kent Museum of Philadelphia History, where former executive director Nancy Moses entered the picture, earned income accounted for only 15% of the budget. Another 30% came from the City of Philadelphia, but at the time the City was facing bankruptcy. That meant 55 cents on every dollar had to be found somewhere else. Many museums have endowments that fill the gap—the Atwater Kent did not. It was essentially a cash business with an out-of-date product, a limited customer base, and no cash reserves.

Working with the staff and the board of directors, Moses used market research to build a menu of topics the public wanted. These included an exhibit by and for schoolchildren; a Norman Rockwell display to draw tourists; and a show of political memorabilia that opened during the Republican National Convention, serving as the perfect venue for receptions and fund-raising events.

To build the customer base, the museum sponsored VIP tours for tour guides, hotel concierges, and taxi drivers so they would drive traffic to its doors. Fifteen percent of the tiny budget was invested in advertising, direct mail, sponsorships, media promotions, and a new marketing director with an oversized Rolodex of media contacts.

As an agency of Philadelphia's city government, the museum was entitled to city services—as long as it could find the service and successfully lobby for it. A staff member was assigned to this task. Over time, telephone service, mail service, all utilities, and minor repairs were provided by the city, allowing the museum to reassign dollars to product development and promotion.

Earned income was not only the most challenging but also the most essential, because so much of the funding was earmarked for specific programs. The museum became a cultural entrepreneur. With a foundation grant, a tent was purchased for the garden and rented, along with the facility, for social events. The staff dramatically expanded the summer camp, launched a marketing campaign to increase school visits, and developed fee-based in-service classes for teachers. The museum produced appealing events: summer concerts, an annual tribute to local businesses, trolley and brewery tours, and a mother–daughter–grandmother tea party. An exhibition business was set up to supply history exhibits to public agencies and corporations. An expert assessed the small museum shop, upgraded the merchandise, and extended the hours. Over time, the percentage of earned income gradually increased until it represented over one third of revenue.

Metrics as the Driver

Boards and donors have long pressed nonprofits for hard data that demonstrate the differences they make. Next-gens are now responding by employing empirically based logic model theory as well as metrics from corporate America to track operational effectiveness and impact.

Take, for example, the Philadelphia Zoological Society under the leadership of president and CEO Vikram Dewan, a Wharton School of Business graduate and former bank president. He began introducing measurement early in his tenure, and now it drives the entire operation. Quantitative data are collected on expenditures, website visits, attendance, and visitor satisfaction. Qualitative data are tracked on such institutional objectives as teamwork and attitudinal change. These data are analyzed, compiled into a dashboard, and distributed monthly to all zoo staff and board members. Sharing the numbers fosters transparency, another trait of next-gen nonprofits.

Management by measurement seems to be making a difference. Between 2005 and 2011, zoo attendance grew by over 25% to 1.3 million. This gain may be enough to satisfy a corporate board but not a nonprofit. To be truly effective, nonprofits must also measure how well they are advancing their mission.

Although mission measurement is a challenge, the Philadelphia Zoo embraced it. The zoo's mission is to advance discovery, understanding, and stewardship of the natural world through compelling exhibition and interpretation of living animals and plants. Dewan explains,

> In relation to the mission, we have two objectives. One speaks to education: changing perceptions. For this, we can conduct longitudinal studies, following children for a couple of years. Measuring the conservation mission is much more difficult. We can give you the metrics: we invest well over $100,000 each year, plus hundreds

of hours of staff time, in 12 conservation organizations that preserve animal species and habitats. The zoo itself conducts amphibian conservation on frogs around the world and in our backyard. But it's tough to connect these investments with changes in attitudes toward conservation.

At the suggestion of its teacher advisory council, the zoo joined with area school districts and independent charter schools in piloting a new service-learning program in which students will learn about conservation by doing conservation—restoring habitat areas and saving migratory birds. The experiment in service learning is also an experiment in measuring the mission. If the program proves successful, every year a fresh cadre of young people will exhibit measurable levels of attitude and behavioral change. They will not only talk the conservation talk but also walk the walk.

If they do not, then the Philadelphia Zoo will figure out something else, because there really is no choice. The greatest difference between a bank and a zoo is that, at the end of the day, the measure of success is not how much money is made but how far the mission is taken.

NOTES

1. Apple Online Store. (2011) www.apple.com/ipad/features
2. www.artbabble.org

REFERENCES

Bolton, E., & Savell, L. (2010). *Towards a new social economy: Blended value creation through social impact bonds*. London, UK: Social Finance Ltd.

Brinckerhoff, P. C. (2010). *Mission-based marketing: Positioning your not-for-profit in an increasingly competitive world*. Hoboken, NJ: Wiley & Sons, Inc.

Bugg-Levine, A., Brandenburg, M., Leijonhufvud, C., O'Donohue, N., & Saltuk, Y. (2010). *Impact investments: An emerging asset class*. New York, NY: The Rockefeller Foundation & J. P. Morgan Investment Bank.

Bugg-Levine, A., & Emerson, J. (2011). *Impact investing*. Hoboken, NJ: Jossey-Bass.

Christensen, C. M. (2003). *The innovator's dilemma*. New York, NY: HarperCollins.

Christensen, C. M., Bauman, H., Ruggles, R., & Sadtler, T. M. (2006, December). Disruptive innovation for social change. *Harvard Business Review, 84*(12), 94–101.

Christensen, C. M., Bohmer, R., & Kenagy, J. (2000, September–October). Will disruptive innovations cure health care? *Harvard Business Review, 78*(5), 102–112.

Christensen, C. M., Grossman, J. H., & Hwang, J. (2009). *The innovator's prescription*. New York, NY: McGraw Hill.

Christensen, C. M., & Hwang, J. (2009, October 5). Power to the patients. *The Atlantic*. Retrieved from www.theatlantic.com/magazine/archive/2009/10/power-to-the-patients/7727

Clark, C. (2011, August 2). *Building an impact economy* [Web log post]. Retrieved from http://blogs.fuqua.duke.edu/casenotes/2011/08/02/building-an-impact-economy

Disley, E., Rubin, J., Scraggs, E., Burrowes, N., & Culley, D. (2011). *Lessons learned from the planning and early implementation of the social impact bond at HMP Peterborough*. London: UK Ministry of Justice. Retrieved from www.justice.gov.uk/downloads/publications/research-and-analysis/moj-research/social-impact-bond-hmp-peterborough.pdf

Hunter, D. E. K. (2009, October). The end of charity: How to fix the nonprofit sector through effective social investing. *Philadelphia Social Innovations Journal*. Retrieved from www.philasocialinnovations.org/site/index.php?option=com_content&id=36:The-end-of-charity-how-to-fix-the-nonprofit-sector-through-effective-social-investing&Itemid=31

King, A. (2011, April). Books are just the beginning: On the road to innovation with the Free Library of Philadelphia. *Philadelphia Social Innovations Journal.* Retrieved from www. philasocialinnovations.org/site/index.php?option=com_content&view=article&id=26 7%3Abooks-are-just-the-beginning-on-the-road-to-innovation-with-the-free-library-of- philadelphia&catid=21%3Afeatured-social-innovations&Itemid=35&limitstart=4

McKenna, L. (2011). Common market: Smart, sustainable sustenance. *Philadelphia Social Innovations Journal.* Retrieved from www.philasocialinnovations.org/site/index.php?option=com_content &id=376%3Acommon-market-smart-sustainable-sustenance&Itemid=30&showall=1

McKinsey & Company. (n.d.). *New ways to fund social innovation* [Web log post]. Retrieved from http://voices.mckinseyonsociety.com/new-ways-to-fund-social-innovation

Seyfettin. (2006, August 10). *The travelogues of a traveler* [Web log post]. Retrieved from http://wasa- laam.wordpress.com/2006/08/10/the-danger-of-human-evolution

Stine, T. (2011). Convenient care clinics: An innovative business model that broadens primary care accessibility. *Philadelphia Social Innovations Journal.* Retrieved from www.philasocialinnovations. org/site/index.php?option=com_content&id=352%3Aconvenient-care-clinics-an-innovative- business-model-that-broadens-primary-care-accessibility-&Itemid=35&showall=1

CONVENING, LEADING, AND SUPPORTING THE SOCIAL SECTOR: BEST AND NEXT PRACTICES

Richard Cohen, Liz Dow, Tine Hansen-Turton, and R. Andrew Swinney

> Effective leadership is putting first things first. Effective management is discipline, carrying it out.
> —Stephen Covey[1]

Today, all sectors—not just the nonprofit sector—are redefining themselves. A well-functioning nonprofit sector is an essential third leg to the three-legged stool that is a vital community. This chapter explores the need for nonprofits to have leadership, particularly board membership that will help them to weather the current economic times and come out on firm footing for the future. It considers how government, business, and foundations can play an important role in building nonprofit capacity.

SUPPORTING THE SOCIAL SECTOR: BEST AND NEXT PRACTICES

For too long, society has taken for granted that the nonprofit sector will be there to serve. Imagine, though, what life might be like without its services—without schools, colleges, and universities, hospitals, museums, theaters, and parks. While many individuals may be fortunate enough not to need direct service from homeless shelters and food banks, communities as a whole benefit from the nonprofits that ensure that such basic needs are met. Consider the strain on government budgets if these safety nets were to evaporate. Undeniably, much is at stake in how nonprofits are led and operated. It is time for communities around the country to be bold in how that is done.

Today, all sectors—not just the nonprofit sectors—are redefining themselves. Millionaires and billionaires are tackling social change through "giving while living" philanthropy. Businesses know it is not enough to satisfy their customers and shareholders;

they also need to be perceived as having a triple bottom line through which they actively contribute to the communities in which they operate. Likewise, governments can no longer afford to be the sole providers of human service stability and social cohesion; they rely heavily on nonprofit partners to assist in that effort. Rahul Bhardwaj, president and chief executive officer (CEO) of the Toronto Community Foundation, may have said it best in an address in Brazil to the Sao Paulo Foundations Association:

> We need to stop thinking of our sectors as walls but rather as bridges. If we can find ways to align our interests, to start by finding what we share rather than what we don't, business will prosper all the more, the social sector will better serve more people, and government will improve the lives of its citizens. (Bhardwaj, 2011)

Perhaps the nonprofit sector needs to be renamed the community benefit sector?

Larger foundations, such as community foundations, straddle all three realms. Community foundations link those with financial resources with those who serve societal needs, thereby working with both the business world and the nonprofit sector. Community foundations also invest the dollars provided to them, and from the resulting revenue they provide long-term funding for a wide range of programs—many of which government does not have the ability to support or is not yet ready to invest in.

Today's Social Sector

A 2010 study of the nonprofit sector by the Philadelphia Foundation (TPF) concluded that the financial fragility of nonprofits is often rooted in the business models under which they operate (2010b). The study suggested that too many nonprofits make operational decisions based on insufficient financial data. They need to, as Peter Drucker suggests, determine what business they are really in. In so doing, they will realize that focusing disproportionately on their missions, rather than on long-term market viability as organizations seeking to fulfill those missions, is not the best approach. Similar to a corporate board, it is the responsibility of nonprofit boards as well as funders to correct this imbalance if the nonprofits they most care about are to survive.

Nonprofits' problems usually develop because the market forces that provide feedback in the business world generally do not do so for them. In economic downturns, businesses adjust production, pricing, marketing, and staffing based on demand for their products. Businesses also use research and development to improve efficiency, product quality, and competitiveness. Their shareholders have a financial interest in ensuring that necessary adjustments are made. By contrast, a nonprofit's revenue, much of which is restricted, comes mainly from the voluntary contributions of individuals, foundations, and government, not from a customer buying a product or service, and shareholders are the clients they serve.

During economic downturns, demand for nonprofit "products"—especially in the case of social service organizations serving the most vulnerable—tends to increase even as funding diminishes. Nonprofits' decisions about programs, staffing, and sustainability are generally not based on research about comparative effectiveness or viable alternatives because they cannot afford it, and funders rarely want to underwrite such evaluations. Moreover, nonprofit "shareholders," that is, the community at large as well as those who serve on nonprofit boards, are not necessarily direct investors and may therefore lack a direct financial stake in ensuring that necessary adjustments are made. Nevertheless, in a weak economy, nonprofits' survival becomes even more dependent on their ability to appeal to supporters who are committed to carrying out the mission. While these dedicated backers make valuable monetary contributions, when they restrict the use of those contributions, they limit a nonprofit's ability to be flexible and function as a healthy organization.

So, as counterintuitive as it may seem, nonprofits must focus now—in the economically depressed short term—on their long-term fiscal health. It is important that nonprofit leaders have frank discussions with donors about the value of capitalization, and about avoiding slow starvation through a lack of investment in infrastructure and overhead. Nonprofits also must tell their supporters that they need unrestricted dollars as well as general operating support to fund day-to-day activities. Further, they need to get the word out that an established funding pipeline through planned giving programs is needed just as much as—if not more than—the underwriting of new endeavors to build the reserves that protect the future health of the organization.

Nonprofits whose revenue comes mostly through government contracts—under which the rates paid for services are negotiated without regard to true cost, supply, demand, and quality—face a much more complicated challenge. In these cases, data from "research and development" need to be liberally shared with legislators, government officials, and the public at large with the goal of achieving more realistic allocations. This process needs to include open dialogue about the actual costs of running vital nonprofits and, especially, the resulting societal savings through the essential services these nonprofits provide.

Nonprofits: The New Economic Driver

With the growth of nonprofits, especially those in the social and human services, and their financial fragility, there needs to be a new outlook on the nonprofit sector. Take for instance Philadelphia, one of the largest cities in the country, where a study showed that in 2007 the region's nonprofits generated revenue of $36 billion and total assets of $64 billion, employed 242,200 people, and provided $11 billion in wages (TPF, 2010b). When education and health care nonprofits were excluded, nonprofits still had more than 87,000 employees earning about $3 billion in wages. This made the nonprofit community Philadelphia's third largest sector and a major economic driver. The study indicated that the region's nonprofit sector grew 40% from 2000 to 2008.

The nonprofit sector comprises a large part of the economy in many U.S. cities, and it has grown tremendously. In 2009, nonprofits employed 13.5 million individuals, or approximately 10% of the country's workforce. More people work in the nonprofit sector than in the entire finance industry, including insurance and real estate. The sector paid $668 billion in wages and benefits to its employees, while nonprofit employees received 9% of wages paid in the United States in 2009.[2] Given these facts, the demand for nonprofits to think like businesses is increasing.

Building Capacity for the Future

While the nonprofit sector currently provides the kinds of services government has traditionally performed, most nonprofits have not grown their infrastructures or changed the way they operate. Indeed, they are still treated as charities. Nonprofit leadership has traditionally used boards of directors for fund-raising purposes, but they now need to look to them for fiscal oversight and operational expertise as well. It is going to take a commitment from the business sector and foundations to change things for the better.

The private sector understands the need to build capacity to grow and prosper. It is part of the business model of any new business, and investors are usually willing to support it with the idea that it will yield a return on investment. The nonprofit sector is another story. Both institutional and individual funders like to direct their money to specific projects, programs, or services rather than infrastructure or capacity building. Company stocks are influenced by how well Wall Street considers a company's leadership team to be functioning. For nonprofits to truly build capacity, grow, and prosper as organizations, the same rules apply: Nonprofits must also put systems in place to use their funds effectively.

Unlike charitable organizations in other countries, the U.S. nonprofit sector is one leg of a three-legged stool that comprises American communities. The stool can only be used if all three legs (nonprofit, government, and the private sector) work collaboratively. Given the growth of the nonprofit sector, the government and business sectors have a vested interest in ensuring that the communities in which they operate are safe, thriving, diverse, and strengthened by a dynamic and robust nonprofit sector. In most communities, it is the nonprofits that educate the community about issues, inspire, protect health and natural resources, and assist those most in need.

Nonprofits constitute the very fabric of each and every community they serve, yet they always tend to be the weakest part of the three-legged stool. So what can be done to strengthen the nonprofit sector?

Tough economic times have imperiled many vital nonprofits. Innovation and support must come from the very top—from the boards that govern nonprofits. When boards include leadership from business and funders (often represented by foundation leaders), they can play a critical role in supporting and strengthening the infrastructure of nonprofits. A regional study of Philadelphia nonprofits, however, found that these organizations need support in recruiting and training effective board members as well as in evaluating existing board governance models (TPF, 2010a). The study framed several key questions that must be explored by communities throughout the United States:

- How should the challenge of recruiting, training, and supporting nonprofit board members be addressed?
- How should the quality and effectiveness of the current governing bodies of nonprofits be addressed to ensure appropriate, consistent, and ongoing training?
- How should the established governance structures used by nonprofits be evaluated and, if needed, improved?
- How should nonprofits be supported not just in weathering the current economic crisis but also in putting themselves on firm footing for the future?

The study examined nonprofit board leadership in the contexts of strength, capacity, and renewal. In a metropolitan region like Philadelphia, which has more than 1,500 nonprofits, filling the boards, with an average of 10 members per board who might serve up to 6 or 7 years, presents a daunting recruitment challenge. There are tens of thousands of new board seats to be filled every year and, given how financially vulnerable the nonprofit sector has become, getting the right people on boards and ensuring that they are trained are key.

The question communities need to ask themselves is how they incent and reward service so that serving on nonprofit boards is recognized as a civic responsibility and a point of pride. Communities also have to ask themselves how they get corporations that have business expertise to maintain a culture of civic responsibility, helping to build the infrastructure of the nonprofit sector. Equally challenging is the task of ensuring that nonprofit board members are informed, properly trained, and engaged about the responsibilities of their roles in protecting the public good. This is an opportunity to create a more consistent approach to training—one that is specifically geared to the unique challenges faced by the nonprofit sector.

In sum, communities across the United States need to recommit to effective nonprofit governance leadership. It starts with considering whether the traditional path—one that frequently begins in the ranks of dedicated volunteers and key supporters who have a passion for the nonprofit's mission—is the most appropriate arena for board recruitment. Given their sustainability challenges and infrastructure weaknesses, nonprofits will be better served by actively recruiting a wide range of board members who can apply their professional and business expertise, as well as analytic strategic practices, to the work they do.

CASE STUDY: LEADERSHIP PHILADELPHIA, MOBILIZING THE PRIVATE SECTOR TO SERVE THE COMMUNITY

Context: Leading LEADERSHIP

While the background, values, and leadership style of the CEO always drive the culture of an organization, the impact is more immediate in a small entrepreneurial organization. In order to put this program in context, it makes sense to give the reader a sense of this writer's background.

LEADERSHIP Philadelphia was founded in 1959 to mobilize and connect the talent of the private sector to serve the community. It was the first of over 400 similar community leadership organizations throughout the United States. I am only the third leader in its long history. The organization was started at the University of Pennsylvania's Fels Institute of Government with a class of a dozen banking executives. It has been independent for over 30 years and now serves about 150 client executives annually. LEADERSHIP enhances participants' civic knowledge and awareness and enriches their leadership skills through a series of intensive seminars. Participants receive nonprofit board training, and board placement is offered to all interested participants and graduates. I went through the program in 1986, with about 30 classmates, when I was a director at Coopers and Lybrand (now PWC).

Seven years later, a headhunter called to tell me that LEADERSHIP was in dire financial straits. The CEO had resigned, and if someone didn't step in to quickly turn it around, this beloved Philadelphia institution would go under. The search committee was led by the CEO of PECO, the local utility company. It comprised corporate executives who were looking for someone who understood finance, had good contacts in Philadelphia, and had the passion and guts to do whatever it would take to turn around LEADERSHIP's financial performance.

I received the call as I was commuting from Wilmington to Austin, Texas, to address some serious customer service challenges. As senior vice president with an entrepreneurial credit card bank, I was accustomed to solving complex operating and human resource challenges. Equipped with a Wharton MBA and years of consulting experience with the Hay Group, I was managing the job while raising two young children. I was, however, feeling increasingly torn by guilt over the toll that the unrelenting travel and the demands of constantly playing hardball was taking on my family life. As I stepped into the company's Lear jet, I found myself thinking, "I am living the Wharton dream, but it's not *my* dream." When the call came, I was ready to listen.

Two competencies kicked in at this point: Understand your values (because social entrepreneurs perform best when their values and mission align) and be willing to sacrifice and take risks for the privilege of making a difference. With the prospect of applying my corporate skills to reviving a dying and beloved institution, I decided to go for this job with a fury, even though it meant serious financial reversals, changing my lifestyle, and the prospect of losing the option to go back to a lucrative corporate job if this opportunity did not pan out. The search committee worried that I was too senior for the job and the financial sacrifice was too great, but its chair was later quoted as saying that I was the best hire he ever made.

In the first year, I used my corporate competencies to negotiate out of an expensive lease and into 2 years of free space (thanks to a banking connection). I reduced the head count and did not take a salary for the first 6 months in order to make payroll. I talked the chair into cosigning a large loan with me to cover the costs of our considerable debt. We ran focus groups to learn what the clients wanted but were not getting. I held some of the classes at my home to save money. After 2 years of cost cutting, extensive client cultivation, and program redesign, LEADERSHIP was back on its feet, offering the region's premier leadership development and civic affairs program. The organization now boasts participants and alumni ranging from the mayor to the CEO of PECO to a network of corporate and civic leaders who work together to move Philadelphia forward.

How Has LEADERSHIP Thrived?

LEADERSHIP Philadelphia puts 150 executives through civic affairs and leadership training programs each year. The outcomes range from a cadre of informed, inspired, and engaged corporate executives who serve the community as volunteers, to a group of nonprofit leaders whose confidence, contacts, and boards of directors are strengthened, to government employees who feel both appreciated by classmates' reactions to their work and empowered by the network they have joined to make things happen in the city. The process that mobilizes them has been carefully crafted to achieve results. The model is composed of program elements, critical experiences, and a focus on building relationships. The cumulative effect has been to create a brand that stands for trusted, connected community leadership that serves the common good.

Practice Fundamentals

In order to transform business executives into socially responsible leaders, you must first earn their respect. They need to know that their time is well spent, that what they are learning is practical, and that they will benefit by being socially responsible.

While LEADERSHIP is a nonprofit organization, everyone on the staff comes from the corporate sector. They understand the importance of professional protocols, explaining why things are done, never cutting corners, and observing common corporate courtesies like starting and ending meetings on time and providing goals, objectives, and agendas at each meeting. Customer service is the top priority, so that staff members routinely bend over backward to do favors for clients and to provide top-notch experiences at every turn. Clients are asked to evaluate every speaker, every class session, and the program as a whole. Goals and roles are clearly stated up front so there is never confusion about program intent. Quality standards demand that speakers who do not score at least six on a scale of seven are not invited back. A summary evaluation is shared with the board of directors at the conclusion of each program.

LEADERSHIP's back-office operations also reflect businesslike discipline. The board is led with transparency, with clearly stated and signed annual objectives for each member. Prior to the first meeting of every year, small lunch meetings are held to share expectations and gather feedback and input around improving the next year's performance. The CEO has specific operating goals that are reviewed annually and that incorporate elements of the annually reviewed strategic plan. Budgets are prepared on time and reviewed monthly internally and quarterly with the board in order to ensure that the organization always operates with a financial surplus. The organization knows who its stakeholders are and makes a conscious effort to cultivate them. Year-end board evaluations invariably include the phrase, "You run a tight ship," which is high praise from individuals who have high standards and know the level of effort required to earn this high mark. Without this obvious and intentional level of discipline behind the scenes, no matter how compelling individual programs or speakers might be, business executives would be less receptive to the extra effort required to become socially responsible leaders. Strong infrastructure and deliberate service are at least as important as good intentions.

The good intentions that this program cultivates in its clients must be modeled by the staff and speakers. Senior staff members are active in the community as volunteers. They demonstrate the principles that the program teaches: from clarifying goals and roles to treating everyone with respect to small things like returning e-mails promptly and pleasantly and sending thank-you notes. Speakers for LEADERSHIP's programs are selected for their integrity as well as their impact. No matter what position you hold, if your behavior does not reflect LEADERSHIP's values around trust, commitment, and impact, you will not be invited to speak. This is all because clients, particularly early on, are alert for signs that this group of socially responsible executives is a club they want to belong to.

Show and Tell

Knowledge is a key ingredient in creating civic engagement. LEADERSHIP's programs cover education, economic development, safety and justice, marketing, infrastructure, health care, media, the arts, and a variety of current civic topics. It is important for clients not only to know the basics about their community but also to hear unvarnished views of what is going on behind the scenes. This means that the participants learn about the complexity and level of effort behind what might seem like a simple issue. Furthermore, by hearing the off-the-record "inside scoop," they start to feel like insiders and gain a sense that they are part of a cast of leaders who really know how this city works.

While the facts are learned in classroom settings at various sites around the city, adding an experiential element makes the process more fun and engaging. Participants are invited to do police ride-alongs to observe the work of the police up close. Invariably, after watching officers face routine danger and seeing the level of dedication and risk taking involved in their job, participants become staunch supporters of the police. After one alumna was robbed, she went to the precinct to report the offense. Observing the poor condition of the building prompted her to start a campaign to upgrade their space. This program made a social issue tangible so that this alumna could use what she learned in class to take productive action—not your standard response to a robbery.

On the day that the class focuses on education, the school district CEO speaks, as do a university professor who specializes in policy, a charter school head, and a college president who talks about universities as economic development engines. This class is held at the public High School for the Creative and Performing Arts. To engage participants' hearts and minds, the program shows and tells. In the afternoon, the dance students put on an energetic and poignant dance rehearsal. The chorus then lines up on the steps in the magnificent old center hall and sings powerfully and beautifully. This is a day when grown men cry. Observing these talented students perform so well and with such great heart, the participants feel the impact of good teachers. They feel the joy of observing children from all parts of the city find their voices in song. The facts explain the issues. Observing the children in action makes the issues matter.

Level the Playing Field

Leaders must understand how groups work in order to lead them. We begin teaching this by dividing the core class of 110 people into 11 diverse teams of 10 members. The teams are chosen carefully to give participants the opportunity to meet people whom they would not meet under normal circumstances. These teams remain intact for the entire program, leading to lifelong friendships and connections that come in handy later.

Business executives are accustomed to factoring rank into their behavior. LEADERSHIP intentionally levels the playing field during the first two sessions of the core program in two ways. First, each person stands and briefly describes a character-building moment on opening day. These touching stories open the participants' empathy for one another, which makes it hard to judge each other on surface-level indicators going forward. On the second day, Outward Bound puts each team through a series of outdoor problem-solving challenges. It becomes clear to participants that they may be leaders at some point in the process and followers at another. They see that each person has something to contribute. In order for the team to succeed, each person's individual strength is required. Class members begin to see each other for their strengths and as allies. Their rank outside of the classroom becomes irrelevant.

Once the class understands that the room is a level playing field, they settle down and are receptive to learning not only from the speakers but from one another. The teams are intact throughout the program so that individuals can get comfortable having conversations that count. When learning about emotional intelligence, for example, they become capable of having direct but diplomatic conversations about their own and each others' strengths and weaknesses. They can have unguarded conversations about issues around race, opportunity, and justice that would not be possible without the trust they built on that first day, through Outward Bound exercises and through an ongoing team structure.

Concrete Assessments and Feedback

Business executives relate to hard data, so in order to improve their self-awareness competency, they are given online assessments with objective, written feedback that they discuss with team members. Each participant receives an Individual Development Plan at the end of the year, which incorporates these hard data, team feedback, and their own baseline skills assessments. This concrete action plan provides a road map for continuing to improve their performance as leaders at work and in the community.

The most recent lesson incorporated into the curriculum is the value of specific positive feedback in improving performance and building bonds. Participants are asked to share specific positive feedback with their teammates in a series of exercises. They are given "Regarding Leadership" correspondence cards on which to write notes that provide specific positive feedback to leaders in the community, at their workplaces, or in their families. Business executives are required to have strong critical thinking skills. Turning their attention to the power of seeing what is right about something or someone, as opposed to what is wrong, gives them a tool to connect with their followers more effectively.

Outcomes: Initiating Action

Each team is required to do a community service project prior to graduation. These "Pay It Forward" projects range from renovating rooms in social service organizations to planting community gardens to making career-coaching presentations. They see firsthand that they can make a difference.

Once these executives have gone through the experiences explained earlier, they care more about the community and the people around them. In an environment of economic and political uncertainty, and lives full of demands at work and at home, this process creates space for them to breathe and to feel more positive about their communities, themselves, and their ability to make a difference. They are taught to use this space to think through the legacy they want to leave behind—in their communities, at their workplaces, and in their families. They have been allowed and gently forced to take their lives more seriously and, as a result, they step up and serve.

The program offers access to board service through an agency fair, where 50 nonprofits are available to talk to participants in a setting much like a job or career fair. LEADERSHIP's placement officer has relationships with over 100 area nonprofits who are seeking qualified and committed board members. Participants have an opportunity to observe board meetings and to select boards that might interest them. Matches are made and alumni not only serve on over 500 area boards but often end up as members of executive committees or as board chairs. The class training on governance, board strategy, financial responsibility and ethics, and fund raising serves these boards well.

The outcome of this transformational program is best described by its graduates. They describe why and how it works below. Their words explain how to get businesses involved with nonprofits one leader at a time:

> LEADERSHIP Philadelphia plays a key role in creating ambassadors to serve the city. I am proud to be an alumnus of this program, which raises awareness, connects, and issues a call to action to the region's emerging leaders.
>
> Mayor Michael Nutter (1989), City of Philadelphia

> LEADERSHIP Philadelphia encouraged me to think big, to never take no for an answer, and to realize that through hard work, collaboration, and creativity much can be accomplished. LEADERSHIP makes Philadelphia a place where leading means giving and giving means making tangible changes occur.
>
> Jane Golden (1996), *City of Philadelphia Mural Arts Program*

Participation in LEADERSHIP Philadelphia 2011 provided an excellent learning opportunity for me, which allowed me to grow exponentially in my networking and leadership skills. It helped me and my employer connect to corporations, community partners, politicians, and educators across the city. I can honestly say that I can pick up a phone and connect with another leader in the city to get questions answered or things accomplished quickly. This was the single most valuable thing I have ever done for my professional career and it will be beneficial to the Fox School, Temple University, and the city for the next two decades (or more!).

Through the program, I learned more about my own style of leading, how to work with diverse teams to accomplish goals, how to grow my personal network, and how to build strong partnerships with organizations across the city based on the kind of cooperation that allows all to benefit and accomplish more. Partnerships that can leverage what each organization excels at move everyone forward and benefit the city as a whole. Because of my participation in LEADERSHIP, I am more in tune with what is happening within the city and where my personal skills can be utilized to help others who are striving to make things better. I have learned that I can find time to work with community organizations where there is a strong fit between my personal values and the organization's mission. I have joined the boards of Urban Tree Connection and Cardinal Bevilacqua Community Center, both connections that I made because of my participation in the LEADERSHIP Philadelphia Core Program.

> Debbie Campbell (2011), *Fox School of Business and Management,*
> *Temple University*

LEADERSHIP Philadelphia connected me with the City of Philadelphia in ways I never could have imagined. It was a phenomenal experience—like getting an MBA in City of Brotherly Love studies. More than the knowledge I gained, though, was the experience of becoming connected to others committed to making a difference in this region. It takes the concept of six degrees of separation to an art form. No matter what I need to accomplish in my professional or personal life, I know there are 110 other LEADERSHIP fellows I could contact who would help me. That's pretty powerful.

> Donna Farrell (2011), Archdiocese of Philadelphia

The fifth-largest city in the nation is in reality a small town filled with talented, committed, and community-oriented professionals. LEADERSHIP affords you the opportunity to connect and collaborate with these gifted people to achieve results beyond what you can alone imagine. When you are surrounded by extraordinary people on a mission, ideas quickly take shape and materialize into projects that are rapidly accomplished with energy and results that exceed expectations. Does that sound like a blueprint for success in your organization? Imagine an opportunity to spend a year interacting with the city's best and the brightest, learning what makes Philadelphia (and yourself) truly exceptional, while simultaneously enhancing the lives of the less fortunate in your community, and you have just imagined LEADERSHIP Philadelphia.

> Mike Fortunato (2011), *Rubin, Fortunato, and Harbison, PC*

So much changed because of this program. I am absolutely thrilled to have had the opportunity to participate:

Ten great new friends

Dozens of new contacts

I learned more about Philadelphia in 9 months than I did in 31 years growing up here.

I learned new things about myself,

I developed my leadership skills,

And realized the importance of civic involvement.

I will lead a more balanced, fulfilled life from here on out…Thank you, LEADERSHIP staff—you changed my life!

Scott M. Miller (2008), *CB Richard Ellis, Inc.*

Through LEADERSHIP, I came to understand the geometric power of making connections—from the large ones to the little ones—especially when driven by a "pay it forward" mentality. By pooling our resources and our talents and leaving our egos behind, our capacities to make a difference for our community, our workplaces, and, as a consequence, ourselves, have no real limitations. Congratulations to Liz Dow and her team at LEADERSHIP for creating a reality-based yet irrepressible crucible for positive change.

Stella Tsai (2008), *Archer & Greiner, P.C.*

LEADERSHIP is an investment with the highest possible return: It changes lives. For those of us who went through the program, each month was a gift, packed with energy, inspiration, and insight. For those whom we now lead, and for the city we now serve, our focus is clearer and our passion is deeper. Every year, LEADERSHIP Philadelphia turns out 110 connected, committed leaders whose impact on the lives and city around them is forever changed. As a nonprofit leader, I'm a better teacher, influencer, and motivator. As a citizen, I have stronger civic connections that will serve a lifetime. As an individual, I have a deeper sense of place and a forum through board service to stretch beyond our organization and be part of LEADER-SHIP's legacy to this region. Thank you.

Tom Kaiden (2007), *Greater Philadelphia Cultural Alliance*

CASE STUDY: TPF'S CAPACITY-BUILDING STRATEGY—TWO SUCCESS STORIES

CONTEXT

TPF

TPF is a community foundation that pools hundreds of charitable funds and endowments established by caring people to support nonprofit causes. The foundation, which awards millions of dollars a year to thousands of area organizations, is Southeastern Pennsylvania's leading center for giving back to the community and is committed to improving the quality of life in Bucks, Chester, Delaware, Montgomery, and Philadelphia counties.

TPF's Capacity-Building Grant-Making Strategy

In 2007, TPF changed its grant-making strategy and became one of a few foundations focused on building the capacity and improving the organizational effectiveness of nonprofit organizations. Through its capacity-building grant-making strategy, TPF seeks to help high-performing organizations better meet their mission in the five-county Philadelphia region. TPF defines capacity building as "any service that enhances the organization's internal effectiveness at achieving its mission sustainably—in other words, services which strengthen the foundation or 'engine' of the organization, not its specific programs."

TPF's capacity-building grant-making strategy addresses the foundation's commitment to contributing to the betterment of the community by improving nonprofits' effectiveness through investments in their business and management practices, enabling them to better meet their missions.

These grants strengthen and improve nonprofits' business and operational practices. As in business, these practices are critical to the success of nonprofits' efforts to *adapt, lead, manage,* and *use technology* effectively. These core competencies are critical to nonprofits' effective delivery of services, employment of best practices, use of data to drive decision making, ability to adapt to new demands and risks, and avail themselves of opportunities.

Capacity Building at Educating Communities for Parenting

Educating Communities for Parenting (ECP) is a private nonprofit organization that has provided high-quality youth development and parenting education programs throughout the Philadelphia area for over a quarter of a century. By using the healthy parent–child relationship as the role model for all relationships, the mission of ECP is to provide services that cultivate independence and responsibility in young people and families, break the cycle of child abuse and interpersonal violence, and build stronger communities. In order to achieve this mission, ECP provides a variety of services for young parents, youths in the juvenile justice and foster care systems, and other at-risk populations, providing the knowledge and tools necessary to nurture the self and others.

November 2007

A TPF capacity-building grant of $48,000 to ECP was approved to help them to develop and implement a plan for program evaluation and to update their information technology. ECP's capacity-building project was designed using the results of the TPF Core Capacity Assessment, with which ECP evaluated its organizational effectiveness. With the TPF funds, ECP developed a mechanism to evaluate its programs on an ongoing basis and updated its information management system to support these enhanced program evaluation efforts. The specific results of the project were that:

- ECP contracted with Owens Consulting, a youth development consulting firm, to
  - Develop program evaluation tools
    - Power to Parent Survey
    - Empowerment Zone/Youth Development Survey
  - Develop evaluation data collection systems
  - Develop an internal client database
  - Evaluate program outcomes
- ECP contracted with NPower PA, a respected organization with experience supporting nonprofit clients' technology needs, to
  - Conduct an information technology (IT) audit
  - Purchase hardware including network server, external backup drives, and two additional workstations
  - Purchase new and/or upgraded software to support the program
  - Enhance its website to provide online course registration and enable clients to complete program registration and evaluations online

August 2009

An additional TPF capacity-building grant of $28,000 to ECP was approved for a data management implementation project. ECP maintains extensive records about each youth it serves but until 2009, most of its files were paper based or in scattered sites on staff computers. ECP did not have a centralized database to manage their client information. This created barriers to growing the organization in an effective manner. Key tasks, such as timely and accurate reports to funders, clear understanding of programmatic strengths and weaknesses supported by data, and gap analysis, became overwhelming.

To identify, purchase, and implement a client data-tracking tool, the ECP executive director worked with NPower consultants to complete the following:

- Research and identify a web-based client management database, Salesforce
- Purchase and install the database
- Hire temporary staff to input existing data located through the organization
- Train staff to use the new tool
- Test the accuracy of data

It soon became clear that in order to fully utilize Salesforce, ECP would have to enhance its website to provide for a secure site, online student registration, and far greater interactivity between the agency and its clients. Because of this, ECP also engaged the services of a web designer and accessed and/or purchased additional software and services such as Twitter, Google Analytics, Druple upgrades, enhanced export capabilities, and vertical responses for sending out mass e-mail messages and class and workshop reminders.

Impact of the 2007 and 2009 Capacity-Building Grants

The support from TPF for technology upgrades and data management has improved ECP's ability to monitor, analyze, and evaluate program services. Until this point, ECP was entering all client data into the Department of Health and Human Services (DHHS) database. Although student data were required to be put in, ECP was greatly restricted in the types of reports they could take out. Demographic data, attendance, retention, student evaluation results, populations served, trends, and so forth—none of this was available to the organization.

Because of its enhanced capabilities in entering and exporting data internally, ECP is now able to generate a variety of reports that allow the organization to monitor course and student benchmarks, review evaluation data, track attendance and retention, and note both positive and negative trends at much earlier stages. These reports allow ECP to examine all aspects of program and service delivery, note what is working and what is not, and make necessary adjustments and changes when required. Additionally, the reports provide ECP with valuable information that can be shared with current and potential funders.

ECP's increased data management capacity has led to program enhancement and expansion. In 2010, the funding environment for the organization changed. The DHHS support for parenting education, the primary funding for these services, was changed so that ECP was funded to work with pregnant and parenting teens for only 12 weeks. ECP used the data they had collected in their new database to establish a narrative about the impact of these limits and the importance of more hours of programming for the success of their young clients as parents. This information contributed to successful grant requests for two new projects to allow extended services. In the first project, ECP collaborated with a health center and an antiviolence organization to develop the Partnering with Parents program, which received funding from the Pennsylvania Children's Trust Fund. The program will take place at the health center, where the organizations will collaborate to provide young parents with parenting classes and ongoing support sessions.

May 2011

A $50,000 grant to ECP for its Imagine Project was approved by the Fund for Children—Strategic Investment in Youth. The Imagine Project was developed in an effort to improve long-term educational and parenting outcomes and has the goal of building on and enhancing the strong connections that ECP develops with youth who participate in and successfully complete its 12-week Power to Parent courses.

From its long history working with youth, ECP understands that the issues of abuse, violence, and unplanned pregnancy develop into cycles that span generations and affect entire families and communities. Research shows that the programs that are most effective at addressing these issues take place over a long period of time within the context of strong and trusting relationships between providers and constituents. In an effort to improve long-term educational and parenting outcomes, the goal of the Imagine Project is to build on and enhance these strong connections. The Imagine Project will provide teen parents with opportunities to continue developing their healthy parenting practices; set and work toward goals for themselves and their children; practice and enhance decision-making skills; engage in projects and opportunities with community partners; and increase their self-esteem.

One of the major goals of this project is to actively engage youth in all aspects of ECP's parenting programs from planning and implementation to marketing and advocacy. The first step in this process will be the selection of five teens to serve on the advisory committee. Students recruited to fill these positions will have successfully completed all requirements for the Power to Parent course; demonstrated leadership qualities; and expressed interest in continuing their parenting education.

The teens will work side by side with the other advisory committee members on all aspects of the project including program planning and design, site location, staffing, curriculum development, implementation, and evaluation. These youth committee members will also be actively involved in recruitment and retention for the Imagine Project. While serving on the committee, the teens will not only be assisting ECP in developing a program that meets the needs of its students, they will be learning invaluable life, interpersonal, and leadership skills that will prepare them to successfully meet the challenges and opportunities they face as young adults and parents. Upon completion of the pilot project, the young members of the advisory committee will be invited to join in establishing and serving on the very first ECP youth board, which will work in conjunction with the board of trustees.

Capacity Building at Depaul USA

After establishing operations in 2008, Depaul USA opened Depaul House in Philadelphia's Germantown neighborhood in April of 2009. Depaul House is a shelter that provides housing and supportive services for men experiencing homelessness, with the goal of moving residents from homelessness to employment, permanent housing, and a savings account within one year. Depaul House serves men between the ages of 20 and 65. Approximately 85% of the residents are African American, 30% have a mental health diagnosis, 60% have substance abuse issues, 16% have co-occurring disorders, 40% have a criminal background, and 20% have not completed high school. Men who come to Depaul House are referred from the City Office of Supportive Housing and Project HOME, the funder and the leading nonprofit provider of services for the homeless in Philadelphia.

Each Depaul House resident lives in a single occupancy room and is afforded the maximum privacy possible. Three balanced meals per day and emergency supplies are provided. Counselors and staff provide case management, goal development, education, and employment support. Depaul also offers GED and adult basic education classes on site 1 day per week and provides drug and alcohol treatment, mental health therapy (twice a week), and medical treatment in partnership with Northwestern Human Services. Of current residents, 79% are employed either full or part time within 90 days after entry into DePaul House. The average length of stay is 7 months, during which time residents save an average of $700. Depaul House evaluates the success of its programming by calculating how many men become employed, move to independent living, and reintegrate into the community.

Since its doors opened in 2009, 68 men have been discharged from the program. Of these, 79% moved to permanent housing, 23% reintegrated with family and friends, 56% rented their own market-rate or subsidized housing, and 71% were employed on their departure from Depaul House. Sixty percent of these men had full-time employment.

March 2011

A TPF capacity-building grant of $30,000 to Depaul USA was approved to help them complete a new site feasibility and development process and corresponding staff development to support new program delivery. After completing a community assessment, Depaul USA found that the needs of homeless individuals facing complex medical issues were not being adequately addressed. However, Depaul staff lacked the skills necessary to develop programs to address the needs of this medically fragile and underserved population in Philadelphia.

Depaul identified Community Ventures, a nonprofit developer of affordable housing in Philadelphia, to assist the organization in training staff on the real estate development process, including site selection, creation of a development team, assembling financing, bidding out projects, and managing contracts, while doing site feasibility and developing a planning process around the new project and proposals for funding. In partnership with Community Ventures, Depaul developed a project to provide residences for 10 to 20 individuals as well as a small number of beds for hospice and palliative care. Medical care and other services were to be provided on site. The specific results of the project were that:

- An appropriate site for the project was identified.
- A plan to obtain community support for the project was developed.
- An appropriate architectural firm for the project was identified.

- A development team for the project was assembled.
- Budgets for Department of Housing and Urban Development (HUD) and Federal Home Loan Bank funding were developed.
- A financing plan for the project was created.

Impact of the 2011 Capacity-Building Grant

As a result of TPF's investment, Depaul USA staff not only acquired the skills necessary for producing real estate development proposals but also increased its capacity to design and implement new projects. Depaul USA submitted a formal project proposal to the City of Philadelphia in the spring/summer of 2011 for inclusion in the city's funding request to HUD's McKinney-Vento Homeless Assistance Program. Depaul's proposal was the project rated the highest in the cycle and was included in the submission to HUD. Final grant determination from HUD was expected in early 2012.

Without the capacity-building support provided by TPF, these two organizations would likely not have been able to succeed in developing and finding funding for these projects that will help them accomplish their missions.

CASE STUDY: THE INS AND OUTS: *INNOVATING THROUGH OUTSOURCING*

The old saying goes, "The closest exit may be behind you." If this saying is applied to thinking through solutions, individuals need to look in all directions, including behind them. Sometimes, in seeking the best way to innovate, individuals can learn from the effective models that came before and adapt them to move individuals ahead.

The Issue

Public Health Management Corporation (PHMC) was created from the then-groundbreaking notion that nonprofits could partner with governments to help them work more efficiently. That was more than 40 years ago; PHMC came on the scene in 1972 as Philadelphia Health Management Corporation. From that moment until about 10 years ago, the model experienced growth in Philadelphia. Over that time, city, county, state, and federal government entities invited PHMC and other nonprofits to collaborate on myriad programs.

As PHMC consistently showed that this approach made the delivery of government services more rapid and flexible, with dramatically lower overhead (the combined administrative rate across all programs and affiliates is under 7%), Philadelphia became a national leader. About 10 to 15 years ago, what PHMC had been perfecting for a quarter of a century caught on across the country. At the same time, however, the state government began to question the approach. Locally, these partnerships became much more difficult to structure and maintain.

Fast forward to 2012: Government hunkers down to try to hold on to public jobs, and with less funding available, it now costs more for government to do the same work that had been achieved cooperatively, let alone to develop new responses to address emerging issues. What can help meet Philadelphia's growing needs with today's severe economic constraints?

The Solution

Imagine developing a government-sponsored health service that will require a new director and other staff, real estate to house these people, access to and experience with a broad range of other health and human service programs across the region, and an infrastructure of community-based operations. How long might it take government to put all this together on its own, and how much of the initial budget would get eaten up in doing so? On the other hand, what if there were a nonprofit partner that already collaborated on a range of such programs with government, had the infrastructure and real estate in place, and could put qualified people on the project immediately? Does it not make sense to build further on this existing, proven relationship by bringing the new program under its umbrella?

Think of it this way. If there are two televisions in your home, will you use a different content carrier for each, just to avoid the appearance of excess loyalty to one over the other, or will you choose the single carrier that can give you the best combination of programming at the most affordable rate?

Now consider a government program funded annually from a state budget allocation. The program was developed and planned as a multiyear program, but after the first year the state funding disappeared and the government was unable to find other resources to keep it going. Consider what it would cost government simply to end the program, from exiting real estate agreements to providing employee severance. With the program outsourced to a nonprofit partner, however, that real estate and those employees are not government's concern. Government remains free of those costs.

Ego-free expert services. That sounds ominously like a slogan, but it is really just a simple answer to the problem of helping government resources do more while keeping government programs more flexible. It is about putting aside a focus on appearances with the understanding that maintaining a high standard of ethics does not preclude constructive relationships but instead makes government a responsible custodian of the public trust and pocketbook.

The New Approach

If PHMC first pioneered this model four decades ago, what is so innovative about it now? With the increasing complexity of government challenges and the parallel constraints on spending, an ongoing relationship with a partner with which to house and manage programs—rather than incurring the time and expense of sourcing and launching a never-ending series of new transactions—shifts the outsourcing model to answer today's requirements. It is now, after 40 years of testing relationships and establishing where the expertise lies, that government is best positioned to know exactly where to place the public's trust for such ongoing contracts.

Another emerging element also makes this an opportune time to identify such partners for government. PHMC has seen dramatic growth in mergers and acquisitions among nonprofits, with large organizations attracting smaller nonprofits that seek fiscal strength and expert management capabilities. Thus, some of the nonprofits most effective at providing outsourced services not only are becoming more easily identified through this sector consolidation but also are expanding to further achieve the economies of scale that will make them still more valuable as government partners. Governments should look first at these entities when seeking their long-term management partners.

The Impact

Innovating through outsourcing to ongoing partners, particularly those with proven nonprofit sector leaders in a period of mergers and acquisitions, will positively impact the delivery of government programs. This is especially true as governments operate under tighter constraints, face public needs that demand more rapid responses, and must adjust on a dime to funding shifts. A model that gets programs online faster and responsibly places the burden outside of government—for hiring and housing staff, building infrastructure, managing services, and even dismantling at the program's end—better serves the needs of the community.

NOTES

1. www.brainyquote.com/quotes/quotes/s/stephencov100553.html
2. The Urban Institute, National Center for Charitable Statistics, www.nccs.urban.org/

REFERENCES

Bhardwaj, R. (2011, October 12). *Stand up for Toronto, Bhardwaj urges in Vital Signs address* [Web log post]. Retrieved from http://canadasvitalsigns.wordpress.com/tag/rahul-bhardwaj

The Philadelphia Foundation (TPF). (2010a). *Governance: Bench strength, capacity, renewal*. Retrieved from https://www.philafound.org/Portals/0/Uploads/Documents/Public/Governance_White_Paper_March_2010_web.pdf

The Philadelphia Foundation (TPF). (2010b). *The Philadelphia Foundation: Nonprofit study*. Retrieved from https://www.philafound.org/Portals/0/Uploads/Documents/Public/TPFNonprofitStudy.pdf

GENERATIONAL LEADERSHIP IN LEADING SOCIAL INNOVATIONS AND IMPACT

Mark Carnesi, David Castro, Tine Hansen-Turton, Erin N. Hillman, Jeff Klein, R. Andrew Swinney, Independent Sector—the 2010 American Express NGen Fellows, convened by Independent Sector[1,2]

Leadership and learning are indispensable to each other.
—John F. Kennedy

As we look ahead into the next century, leaders will be those who empower others.
—Bill Gates

The spark from one fire lights another fire, and there is a wind that blows down the path of history.
—John W. Gardner

SOCIAL SECTOR LEADERSHIP DEVELOPMENT

Context

The question of how to develop leadership for the social sector is of paramount importance. The challenges facing a global society are complex and interconnected, and the premise of this book should certainly be on the minds of educators and practitioners in every sector. Influential leaders from each of the sectors—public, private, and nonprofit—in every region of the world have issued a call for leadership within and across sector boundaries, boundaries that have inhibited economic and social wealth creation in times of great need.

The United Nations has worked to identify critical areas of focus and investment: extreme poverty and hunger; primary education; gender equality and female empowerment; child mortality; maternal health; eradication of HIV/AIDs, malaria, and other diseases; environmental sustainability; and global partnerships for development (see Table 7.1). Not only are these issues deeply interconnected, they cannot be resolved

TABLE 7.1 The Wharton leadership development framework.

1. Be a student of leadership.
2. Join learning communities comprised of peers, mentors, and coaches.
3. Seek and accept stretch experiences.

without active and sustained leadership from each of the sectors. Put more bluntly, social sector challenges do not reside solely within the social sector, and nonprofits and nongovernmental organizations (NGOs) cannot hope to achieve sustainable change without the active investment, participation, and support of the public and private sectors.

The Wharton School at the University of Pennsylvania aspires to be the best business school in the world and for the world. Through the strategic pillars of innovation, global presence, and social impact, it recognizes the profound impact that scholarly research has when it is translated into applied frameworks that can be implemented by businesses, governments, and nonprofits to propel these organizations toward their objectives.

Leadership Is Personal

Wharton assumes that leadership is personal. At its core, leadership is about personal decisions made at specific moments. The progression of theoretical frameworks for leadership has been well documented. The "Great Man" theory of leadership has its roots in the heroic stories of the past, where the success of armies, nations, and religions relied upon great men (and, yes, the use of the gender-specific descriptor "man" is deliberate...the stories of "Great Women" are much fewer and farther between). Leadership theory next evolved into trait theory as scholars attempted to identify the combinations of traits that predicted and undergirded leaders. Situational leadership then focused more on context, attributing the emergence of leaders to sets of conditions present in their given situations, while contingency theory began to link sets of traits and styles to specific situations.

Michael Useem's work introduced the concept of "the leadership moment" (Useem, 1998). Within every context, a given set of actions is available to each individual, and leadership is reduced to a specific action within a specific context. Ronald Heifetz further reinforces the point, defining leadership as an activity (Heifetz, 1994). Finally, Kenwyn Smith amplifies the definition as action with an emerging framework to evaluate actions for their leadership impact (K. Smith, personal communication, January 2010). This structure for leadership provides a unique vantage point from which to consider the influences, complexity, and impacts of individual actions in specific moments. In aggregate, the level of analysis becomes the leadership action in the leadership moment.

The Wharton Leadership Development Framework

Be a Student of Leadership

Just as Wharton strives to be the best business school in and for the world, the Wharton Leadership Program holds itself accountable to a specific, developmentally focused mission: To develop leaders who act with a deeper understanding of themselves, their organizations, and their communities and contribute positively to the growth of each. To achieve this mission, faculty have adopted a three-pronged approach to leadership development that connects theory to practice and traditional education to experiential learning (Useem, 2011).

The Wharton Leadership Program's development framework consists of three distinct calls to action. First, it implores students to become "students of leadership." In practice, faculty want students to expose themselves to new ideas and to develop a shared vocabulary. The Wharton framework has three main objectives for students who deliberately pursue leadership: (a) develop a conceptual leadership framework; (b) receive exposure to new research and theories; and (c) build a shared vocabulary with which to discuss and reflect on personal leadership experiences.

Join Learning Communities Comprising Peers, Mentors, and Coaches

The second facet of the Wharton framework is that every student joins multiple learning communities. The shapes and sizes of these communities vary, although every student is part of a learning team. In addition, students join fellowship programs, clubs, conference teams, and elective teams. The framework identifies three important features of a learning community: (a) members of the community are engaged in similar work through similar roles (e.g., MBA students in a peer environment); (b) members of the community are willing and active in providing feedback to their peers; and (c) members of the community are aware of—and hold each other accountable to—the learning goals established by each student. Faculty then augment these learning communities by serving as coaches and mentors who work one on one with students on their leadership development plans.

Seek and Accept Stretching Experiences

The third aspect of the leadership development approach—and the factor believed to be most important to individual leadership development—is encouraging students to seek and accept stretch experiences at Wharton and beyond. The Wharton Leadership Program has developed nine major programs that include stretch experiences, such as the Learning Team experience, the Learning Team Retreat, and the Feedback and Coaching Network. These programs feature a highly experiential pedagogical design, placing students in new situations in which they join new teams and apply new skills in pursuit of a common goal. The setting and context of the stretch experiences vary widely, from joining a local nonprofit board to high-altitude mountaineering, from facilitating a face-to-face 360° feedback session for a learning team to evaluating organizations addressing social sector issues in innovative and impactful ways.

Of course, stretch experiences presented and completed in isolation do not promote learning. After all, individuals make many choices and engage in many actions in the course of any given day without learning from them. Using experiential models developed by David Kolb and adapted by Wharton staff and partners at Earth Treks, NOLS, and Vertical, S.A., faculty design programs that incorporate individual and group reflection, develop context-specific lessons, and transfer those lessons to different (though related) contexts (Kolb, 1984). Learning is framed in transferable terms, for instance: What needs to be learned about a new environment? What is important in the formation of a new team, and how is it accomplished? What kind of support is necessary to successfully acquire a new set of skills or be successful in a new team?

Skill Development

Ultimately, then, we at Wharton take the view that leadership resides in the actions individuals and groups take in support of a common goal. Specifically, a leadership action is

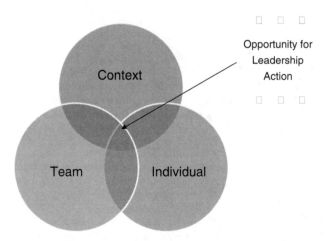

FIGURE 7.1 The leadership action framework.
Adapted from Jordan and Garay (2011).

any act that, once taken, moves the group closer to its shared objective. The impact of a leadership action is most clearly observed among the followers and affected stakeholders (Figure 7.1).

No blueprint exists or can be developed that can predefine the actions necessary in a given situation. Principles for action and specific behaviors can be identified as impactful and appropriate (more on this later), but the application of these actions is dependent on three important factors: the context, the team, and the individual (Jordan & Garay, 2011). With an understanding of the current conditions, interests, and goals embedded in these factors—and recognizing that each of the factors is, by itself, a constantly changing construct—the set of available opportunities for leadership actions can be identified, evaluated, and prioritized.

This leadership action framework is a first-stage diagnostic tool. When team members are unsure of next steps, they are encouraged to assess their own self-awareness, their perceptions of the team and its evolutionary stage, and the context or environment in which the team is operating. The links among the individual, the team, and the context provide the set of available choices and a means by which they can be analyzed and prioritized.

Context is especially important. The context shared by students is the social sector. Remember, however, that the sector of origin is a major influence on the conditions that teams and individuals find themselves muddling through. One of the more interesting questions—and one that this book tackles head on—is the extent to which the locations and roles of nonprofits demand a certain kind of leadership. Certainly, factors such as personality traits and behavioral styles play a role in defining the set of available leadership actions, and these factors would theoretically remain (mostly) static regardless of sector. The nature and work of the team and the context of the organization, its mission, and its strategy also play major roles.

The Wharton Dimensions of Leadership

Like many large organizations—public, private, and not-for-profit—Wharton has developed a set of seven leadership competencies to which it devotes significant resources and programs. The seven competencies that constitute the Wharton dimensions of leadership are influence, emotional intelligence, teamwork, communication, decision making, diplomacy, and organizational awareness. These can be construed both as actions and as skills that provide for greater awareness and evaluation of available actions.

Influence

Wharton conceives of influence in a broad manner, covering both the designated team leader who creates a shared vision and communicates it to the team and the peer leader who has the ability to work within and across boundaries—usually with ambiguous authority—to help shape the needs of others and the goals of the team. Specifically, influence is the ability to draw on your own personality traits, the needs and strengths of others, and the context in which you are situated in order to inspire, motivate, stimulate, and empower others.

Emotional Intelligence

Simply put, emotional intelligence is the ability to identify, use, understand, and manage emotions effectively. Each of these four components is important, and Wharton uses the framework developed within the Mayer–Salovey–Caruso Emotional Intelligence Test (MSCEIT), based on the work of John Mayer, Peter Salovey, and David Caruso, to think about emotional intelligence and broaden students' ability to communicate and understand macro/micro expressions, tone, and nonverbal behaviors.

Teamwork

Teamwork consists of the ability to build trust, assess team dynamics, and improve team performance. Students skilled in the teamwork dimension show a strong ability to create and promote a culture of team success while influencing the composition and structure of a team.

Communication

Communication, as the saying goes, is a two-way street. It includes the ability to both convey information effectively for maximum understanding and listen carefully and encourage the input of others. In addition, Wharton defines communication as also encompassing a student's ability to conduct difficult conversations about positive impacts and to engage in coaching conversations as appropriate.

Decision Making

Within this framework, Wharton defines decision making from a group perspective. It includes understanding the interdependence and interconnection among group members as well as the knowledge of and ability to manage group decision-making biases. Additionally, it features the ability to improve information sharing and minority influence within a group while encouraging innovative thinking.

Diplomacy

The features of diplomacy highlighted in the Wharton framework include the ability to act with integrity and to focus on shared understandings and mutual interests. Diplomacy also features the ability to foster collaboration and solicit cooperation among parties as well as the ability to mediate agreements and negotiate disputes equitably.

Organizational Awareness

Finally, organizational awareness focuses on the context in which the team and the individual operate and includes an understanding of organizational culture. Beyond understanding, though, it also includes the ability to create and shape organizational culture and the ability to maintain long-term focus and create new solutions during change or crisis.

LOOKING TO THE FUTURE

As baby boomers begin to retire, leaving many leadership positions vacant, there have been discussions taking place across the country regarding succession planning and leadership development. Philadelphia has been very active in conducting such discussions and often includes the role of diversity in succession planning and leadership development conversations. Organizations that have held intergenerational focus groups include Independent Sector American Express NGen Fellows and National Urban Fellows. Conversations around succession planning are pertinent for nonprofit-, public- and private-sector entities; however, the focus here is on succession planning and leadership development in the nonprofit sector.

The United States is fortunate that young people continue to want to join the nonprofit and philanthropic worlds with the passion and drive to make a difference. Young people must continue to be provided with the tools to ensure that their drive and passion can be effectively channeled to advance the important work that is being done by the many varied organizations that define our nation's quality of life. All are in a long-distance race. The challenges that nonprofits address and the solutions they apply are not those of quick fixes. It is important to ensure that when the current team is ready to pass the baton, the next set of runners is fit and in condition to take up their leg of the race.

To develop a thriving future nonprofit sector, it is essential to look at leadership. In these crisis-centered times, the focus is often on the moment. Keeping up with what is directly in front of managers can be all consuming. As difficult as it is to step off the typical daily treadmill, if the nonprofit sector is ever to advance beyond the crisis du jour, its future also needs attention. Each community needs to ask itself:

- Where is the next leadership cohort coming from?
- What is being done to advance the next generation of those who will manage the organizations that will teach future workers, heal illnesses, uplift and entertain, support natural areas, and care for the people who fall through the cracks in the nation's frequently overburdened social safety net?

As the baby boom generation begins to retire, the need to identify and equip future leaders becomes critical. Pathfinder Solutions, Inc., a Colorado-based organization that specializes in providing research to foundations, has estimated that as many as 70% to 80% of senior nonprofit leaders may exit the sector in the next decade, resulting in the need for 640,000 new leaders.[2]

Although the 2008 economic recession slowed the executive exodus as individuals deferred their retirements, the large number of those approaching retirement age, combined with the significant role nonprofits play as employers, strongly indicates the need for a proactive approach to preparing for the inevitable vacancies. The nonprofit sector has to ask itself:

- Is it, as a sector, ready?
- Is it doing all that it can to not only identify but also equip future leaders with the tools that are so essential to success in the fast-changing world in which it operates?

The nonprofit sector is diverse in both mission/purpose and size. While it might seem that this diversity would create many options and opportunities for those who wish to develop leadership skills, that diversity is instead cited by some observers as the reason there is no established career path for the next generation of leaders to follow. The nonprofit sector encompasses too much, that line of thinking goes, to provide a universal track of progression for key management positions. Many of those who come to the sector initially stumble upon their roles, it is argued, and they are driven more by passion for a particular cause than by a commitment to or an understanding of the field as a sector unto itself.

Recently, Emerging Practitioners in Philanthropy (EPIP) held its annual conference in Philadelphia. This organization works to attract young professionals in the philanthropic sector who want to seek guidance and mentoring for their own careers. It effectively provides hands-on opportunities for young professionals to hone their own management skills by helping them develop their own agendas by structuring presentations and applying the lessons learned from the feedback they receive. EPIP encourages nonprofit organizations to ask themselves the following about their agencies:

- Does the agency provide such opportunities within its own organization?
- Does the agency intentionally look at new hires as future leaders?
- Does the agency identify opportunities through which these hires can grow and develop a broad set of skills that will allow them to advance?

When young people enter the nonprofit sector, many assume their career paths could include going to larger institutions, but there is no identifiable way to get to them. For many young employees, nonprofits appear to be silos unto themselves, and advancement seems to depend on someone above retiring or on the ability to uncover upcoming openings outside of their organizations through networking. Even today, it is common to hear about people who seek to advance by moving to another organization only to be told that their particular experience does not qualify them for the role. The nonprofit sector seems to typecast individuals early on as "youth organization manager" or "arts leader," rather than seeing that these positions share a skill set. While each nonprofit certainly has its particular area of expertise, such functions as fund-raising, personnel management, and nonprofit business acumen, to name a few, apply across the board and are, in fact, highly portable skill sets. Rather than being insular in its thinking and limiting candidates for executive management to the usual suspects in any specific field, the sector might be better served by embracing the out-of-the-box approaches a nontraditional management candidate might bring.

The nonprofit sector must become more focused on providing a clearer path for advancement for nonprofit leaders, a path that transcends these self-imposed barriers. To get there, the sector must also come to agreement on the necessary skills for young professionals and provide a progression of opportunities through which they can learn and apply these common proficiencies. The alternative is a lack of intentionality that will further damage the nonprofit sector by discouraging the next generation of leaders.

CASE STUDY: SUCCESSFUL SUCCESSION PLANNING THROUGH LEADERSHIP DEVELOPMENT

National studies and daily experience demonstrate the importance of succession planning in the nonprofit sector (Bell, Moyers, & Wolfred, 2006). Yet the status quo persists: succession planning by accident. The 2010 American Express Independent Sector NGen Fellows, young leaders aged 30 to 40 and convened by Independent Sector, defines this problem and offers an alternative through summarized research and findings from four focus groups of diverse professionals in the nonprofit sector.

The Problem: Succession Planning by Accident

Over the past 50 years, the nonprofit sector has become a strong force for solving social problems. While the sector has professionalized, constrained resources have limited investments in organizational development. Generally, nonprofits decide to devote their limited resources to activities that are directly linked with their programmatic missions at the expense of building a pool of strong, young leaders, not to mention the risk of a leadership vacuum as founders of nonprofits begin to retire. If an organization has developed a succession plan, it typically only addresses the position of executive director/chief executive officer (CEO).

Today, most nonprofit leaders are made by chance, stepping up to new responsibilities in a crisis or learning quickly on the job when a tenured staff person leaves suddenly. This pattern puts organizations, and their missions, at risk. Moreover, without intentional succession planning, eager young talent often leaves the organization and even the sector.

Succession planning through leadership development is an alternative to the status quo. For the purposes of this project, succession planning through leadership development is defined as building cohorts of engaged, emerging leaders in an organization's leadership pipeline and systematically developing and advancing these employees. Instead of expecting new leaders to rise to the occasion, this report proposes that when leadership opportunities arise, organizations dedicate resources, both human and financial, to developing the talent pipeline and proactively discussing succession plans at all levels of leadership, not only at the top of the C-chain.

Report Background and Methodology

The 2010 NGen Fellows chose to design their project to build on the efforts of the 2009 NGen Fellows, the inaugural cohort. The 2009 Fellows conducted a survey of more than 2,000 individuals and identified issues of particular concern for next-generation leaders. One of the major findings was the need for stronger formal and informal leadership development within the nonprofit sector. The Fellows found that the sector needs and wants new leaders to address some of the nation's most pressing problems, a challenge that has intensified in recent years as governments have cut spending and services, nonprofits' caseloads have grown, and financial resources have shrunk. The need for strong, creative leadership in the sector has never been greater.

Fellows found the need to be compelling and were troubled by the lack of leadership development opportunities reported by survey respondents. The incongruity between the need for talented leaders and the dearth of talent development opportunities is a critical issue for the sector. As a result, NGen Fellows focused their efforts here. They describe the heart of this challenge as "succession planning through leadership development." This type of planning ensures the availability of experienced and capable employees who are both strengthening their skills to add responsibilities to their current roles and preparing for promotion.

To better understand the challenges and opportunities surrounding succession planning, NGen Fellows reviewed relevant literature, interviewed key thought leaders, and conducted intergenerational focus groups. (A description of the methodology can be found in Appendix A.) The conclusions of the project are organized along four themes that emerged from the research:

1. Generational differences are real but may not be the most relevant lenses for leadership development.
2. Mentoring is a critical aspect of leadership development.
3. Successful organizations make leadership development an intentional part of their cultures.
4. Nonprofit organizations have unique challenges and need external supports to advance sector-wide leadership development.

Based on research and reflections, the Fellows believe that organizations that focus on succession planning through leadership development are able to:

• Create future leaders with stronger skills who are better prepared for leadership
• Utilize strong performers more fully, keeping them more engaged, challenged, and likely to stay

- Involve employees with different generational perspectives in setting organizational direction and helping the organization evolve with changing times
- Ensure that the workplace is fulfilling and challenging for employees of all generations
- Maintain a diverse work force that is competitive in a global society
- Better fulfill the missions of their organization

Succession planning through leadership development matters if nonprofits are to invest in a healthy and vibrant nonprofit sector. It matters to individuals pursuing careers in the nonprofit sector, to nonprofit organizations seeking growth and sustainability, and to the nonprofit sector's ability to make an impact on society.

Conclusion 1: Generational Differences Are Real but May Not Be the Most Relevant Lenses for Leadership Development

The initial assumption for this work was that generational differences were of paramount significance. Early conversations on succession planning were largely couched in generational terms, and sometimes even focused on generational conflict. The NGen Fellows' research disabused them of this notion early in the process.

Generational cohorts are an easy lens through which to view the workplace because they are readily observed and constitute one stereotype that generally does not offend. While differences in age are cited as a source of workplace conflict and stress, staff also found connections in similar backgrounds that transcended age. Experts have argued that once individuals are in a workplace, there are not many differences between generations. Rather, conflict most commonly surfaces around issues of authority, for example, who is in charge and who thinks they should be in charge.

Individuals in similar circumstances have more in common with one another than with their generational peers who are in different phases of life. For example, work–life balance is a significant concern across generations, but a single 25-year-old has more in common with a single 45-year-old than with a 25-year-old married person with a child. Professional development, therefore, should be tailored to where employees are and where they want to go rather than generational status.

Intergenerational focus groups affirmed this thesis. While participants acknowledged some differences across generational lines in orientations and expectations, participants of all ages agreed on basic principles of what constitutes effective leadership development. What is often overlooked, however, is how an organization encourages leadership in action instead of by position.

That said, the NGen Fellows also found that participants truly enjoyed the intergenerational conversations. For most, it was a novelty to discuss organizational development issues with people of varying ages and in different career phases. Thus, while generational differences may not be the primary lens, it is nonetheless a useful lens. Ensuring diversity in generational perspectives when addressing issues of leadership development will help to create policy and practice that work across an organization's entire pipeline.

Conclusion 2: Mentoring Is a Critical Aspect of Leadership Development

Throughout the research process, one thing was clear: Mentorship is a critical aspect of leadership development. Younger staff may be very promising and proficient in their roles, but they "don't know what they don't know," especially regarding staff supervision and management. Developing younger staff for leadership requires that more senior employees step up, share their knowledge, and support the development of new leaders.

Most focus group participants were able to describe a mentorship experience that had a significant positive impact on their careers. Participants identified multiple benefits of mentoring, including the following:

- Individuals who had strong mentors had a better sense of their organizations' current status and future direction. This provided perspective that helped mentees be more effective in their roles.

- Mentors were valuable as people to consult as trusted advisors on issues. Mentors both inside and out of the mentees' organizations helped mentees consider issues in a larger context, outside of the politics of their situations.
- Mentees gained exposure to senior staff who provided insight into effective leadership and built confidence in their mentees to take the mantles themselves. Many participants emphasized the value of simply being in the room, hearing conversations, and observing dynamics as valuable development opportunities.

Participants also made it clear that the value of mentorship does not accrue only to the mentee:

- People at the top of organizations benefit from mentoring as much as anyone. Some participants referred to this as "reverse mentoring." It becomes harder to ask simple questions in senior leadership positions. Leaders become isolated and less effective when they are not able to continuously learn from younger colleagues.
- Many participants who have been in their fields for long periods, or who were pioneers in their fields, considered mentoring and encouraging others to mentor to be a satisfying experience and a natural extension of their own career development.

Participants cited chance opportunities more frequently than formalized programs as factors in their own leadership development. Opinion was split about whether mentorship programs must be formal to be effective. There was strong consensus, however, that more mentorship opportunities are needed to build the talent required in the nonprofit sector.

While supervisors can and should be effective mentors, there is a need for others to provide mentoring opportunities both inside and outside of organizations. Finding a mentor other than the person who appraises a mentee's performance is important for full candor and trust.

To move the field forward, participants recommended that the nonprofit sector create more mentorship opportunities, both within the sector and across the government and private sectors. Some participants suggested specializing in different aspects of the nonprofit sector according to issue area (e.g., housing, civil rights, education) or job function (e.g., development, advocacy, executive leadership, finance). All agreed that collaborative ventures are required to take fuller advantage of the benefits that good mentoring can bring to the sector.

While participants strongly encouraged organization-level and sector-level action to encourage mentorship, they acknowledged that the success of any mentoring effort requires individual initiative and commitment. Across the board, individuals need to take responsibility for their own career trajectories, be assertive, ask for help, and fulfill their needs for professional development.

Conclusion 3: Successful Organizations Make Leadership Development an Intentional Part of Their Cultures

Organizations play a critical role in fostering leadership development. Oftentimes, nonprofit leaders—and organization founders in particular—feel they must choose between achieving the mission of the organization and focusing on organizational development. This is a false choice. Nonprofit missions can only be accomplished through effective organizations and the development of people. Organizations must make learning opportunities and the coaching required to create effective leaders a priority.

A dominant theme throughout the research was that doing leadership development well is not about programs or policies; successful organizations make leadership development an intentional part of their cultures. When a culture of feedback and professional development is fostered openly and intentionally among all staff, the organization better develops leaders and inspires staff to stay engaged. Participants noted three characteristics that are true of organizations that make leadership development part of their cultures:

1. *Successful organizations make the development of people an explicit principle and value.* Organizations that develop leaders well give staff true ownership of the mission. Participants believed that talent development has to be at the mission/values level to create the culture required

for success. This means not just viewing employees in terms of whether or not they complete their job responsibilities but truly understanding, and then capitalizing on, the potential of each employee.

2. *Successful organizations create a learning culture.* Successful nonprofits do not just put policies in place; they focus on creating a learning culture that supports autonomy and provides opportunities for employees to innovate and grow. They place great emphasis on internal communications, including meaningful feedback loops. As a result, the organization is strengthened and employees want to stay.

3. *Successful organizations spend time and resources training effective managers.* Many respondents noted both good and bad experiences with managers and the impact those experiences had had on their own overall personal growth and development. Further, participants noted that organizations that invested resources into growing leaders had smoother leadership transitions. Paying for certificate programs, graduate school programs, or a variety of skill-type training demonstrated that organizations were interested in the futures of their employees and their continued growth.

Participants identified a number of obstacles to effective leadership development. First and foremost, nonprofit staff members have traditionally been overloaded with responsibilities. The pace of work is rapid, and it can be difficult to turn away from the tasks of achieving the organization's mission and prioritize leadership development. The passion of nonprofit leaders and, in particular, founders can be a double-edged sword. Too often, nonprofit leaders feel as if they are the only ones who can do the job, and they are so committed that they feel there is no time to prepare others to step up to new levels of leadership.

One way to overcome these challenges is to engage the board in the planning process. The opportunity to engage the board in identifying and implementing a plan that develops staff potential can be very positive. It raises the visibility and importance of talent management and helps the board focus on long-term organizational health. To fully realize the promise of the nonprofit sector, nonprofit leaders have to avoid a myopic focus on mission to ensure that they are developing the talent required for long-term organizational success. This requires raising the development of people as an explicit value, creating a learning culture, and investing in the training of effective managers.

Conclusion 4: Nonprofit Organizations Have Unique Challenges and Need External Support to Advance the Sectorwide Development of People

Leadership development and succession planning is an issue across all three sectors, nonprofit, for-profit, and government. While some respondents felt that the for-profit sector was much better at leadership development than its nonprofit counterpart, others felt this view was skewed by the strong talent management of large corporations.

Both experts and focus group participants felt that size mattered. Larger organizations have greater resources and more robust human resources functions to support strong talent management regardless of sector. Experts also suggested that organizational age correlated with the strength of talent management. Approximately 80% to 90% of all nonprofits were founded after 1965 (Data360, 2011). These newer organizations are less likely to have strong succession practices and more likely to be heavily influenced by a founder. Across all sectors, organization founders tend to focus on building and innovation versus strategically planning for succession.

That said, there are some meaningful sector differences that transcend organizational size and age. Nonprofit organizations have unique challenges and need external support to advance the sectorwide development of their people. For example:

- Private-sector businesses are often able to provide more significant financial incentives and rewards for their employees and to invest more in human resources support and training than are nonprofits.
- For-profit organizations also have competitive threats in the market that lead them to focus more on performance measurement and management. There is strong incentive for managers to remove poor performers and build the capacity of high performers.

- As noted, the intense focus on mission within the nonprofit sector can inhibit focus on organizational development issues, both because organizational leaders are likely to undervalue these issues and, significantly, because funders are attracted to programmatic work and less likely to fund organizational capacity building. For-profit organizations can choose to invest their revenues however they believe is best for the organization, but nonprofits often have their hands tied by fund-raising.

Funders who focus narrowly on overhead ratios may be doing the sector a disservice if they are not encouraging nonprofits to invest in their own organizational health. Having to choose between investment in direct, mission-related programming or leadership development opportunities for staff is counterproductive. The nonprofit sector must realize that investments in human capital will pay significant dividends in achieving mission.

Focus group participants saw a need for sectorwide strategies to support leadership development because:

- The nonprofit sector work force is highly mobile. One disincentive for individual organizations to invest heavily in developing young talent is the likelihood that employees will leave. Cross-sector initiatives can work to keep talent in the sector so that it can benefit.
- The difficulty of raising individual funds for capacity building suggests a great need for collaborative efforts. Research can help funders see the value of leadership development work that will increase the impact of all nonprofit organizations.
- The fact that the nonprofit sector is not characterized by competition in the way that the private sector is should be used to its advantage. Cross-organization leadership programs help to spread good ideas and strong talent across the entire nonprofit sector, to the ultimate benefit of the communities it serves.

Recommendations: A Call to Action

The NGen Fellows began this project believing that leadership development and succession planning were critical issues for next-generation leaders: They concluded that they are critical issues for *everyone* in the nonprofit sector. There is tremendous opportunity to make important changes in the sector by supporting the development of leaders, especially if the sector can come together to do so. Based on the insights from reading, interviews, and focus groups, the Fellows offer the following recommendations:

For individuals:

- Find a mentor/Be a mentor. Building the leaders of tomorrow requires individual initiative and individual generosity.
- Encourage organizations to make leadership development a priority. It is easy to NOT focus on leadership development in the pursuit of mission. Remind leaders that it is worth slowing down for the sake of their organizations.

For organizations:

- Make the development of people an intentional part of organizational culture. Developing the talent essential to long-term success requires raising people development as an explicit value, creating a learning culture, and investing in the training of effective managers.
- Provide opportunities for intentional development and time to reflect. The most cost-effective leadership development strategy is one of the most successful: Give staff members stretch opportunities and the range to reflect on and learn from success and failure.
- Encourage formal and informal mentorship. Learning from others is critical to developing future leaders.
- Engage the board. Getting boards involved in leadership development elevates this issue to the strategic priority it should be.

For funders:

- Invest in the capacity of grantees. For the long-term organizational health of grantees, capacity building, including leadership development, is essential.

- Invest in capacity-building intermediaries. Support intermediaries that do effective capacity-building work and/or create opportunities for cross-organizational leadership development.
- Ask potential grantees about succession planning. Make sure supported organizations are thinking strategically about leadership development.

For the sector:

- Create sector-wide training programs to develop leaders and keep them in the nonprofit sector. There is a significant opportunity for effective nonprofit intermediaries to provide the essential training and support that most individual organizations are not providing.
- Provide more intentional mentorship opportunities. Cross-organizational mentorships are valuable for spreading good ideas and strengthening leaders for the benefit of the entire sector.

The nonprofit sector has a crucial role to play in addressing society's most pressing issues. Action must be taken now to build a work force that can lead today's nonprofits successfully into tomorrow.

CASE STUDY: ASHOKA: INNOVATORS FOR THE PUBLIC

The Ashoka Fellowship Program was founded by William Drayton, a pioneer in the development and dissemination of the concept of social entrepreneurship. In Drayton's view, social entrepreneurs are individuals who develop innovative solutions to society's most pressing problems. These innovators do not simply solve problems; they transform systems. In Drayton's words, "Social entrepreneurs are not content just to give a fish or teach how to fish. They will not rest until they have revolutionized the fishing industry." Drayton received a MacArthur Fellowship for his leadership and creativity in the arena of social entrepreneurship, particularly through the organization and development of Ashoka. In the past three decades, Ashoka's work has stimulated and reinforced the development of the global citizen sector as a third force in human progress, surpassing the roles of government and for-profit businesses in societal change. Beginning with the first Fellows elected in India in 1981, Ashoka has grown to an association of over 2,000 Fellows in over 60 countries on the world's five main continents. Ashoka operates with a broad base of private support and without religious or political affiliation. Within Ashoka, the phrase social entrepreneur describes an individual who conceives and doggedly pursues a new idea designed to solve societal problems through fundamental systems change. Per Drayton,

> The job of a social entrepreneur is to recognize when a part of society is stuck and to provide new ways to get it unstuck. He or she finds what is not working and solves the problem by changing the system, spreading the solution, and persuading entire societies to take new leaps.

Ashoka's vision of social entrepreneurship is more targeted than the broader concept of social enterprise that relies on earned revenue to support a philanthropic mission such as a hospital or school. To be a social entrepreneur in Ashoka's parlance requires more than founding a new organization or developing an innovative way of sustaining philanthropic work. Social entrepreneurship describes citizen-sector initiatives that lead to broad-based societal transformation.

In selecting Fellows, Ashoka employs five criteria:

1. A New Idea

Ashoka will not elect someone to the Fellowship unless he or she is possessed by a new idea—a new solution or approach to a social problem—that will change the pattern in a field, be it human rights, the environment, or any other. Ashoka evaluates the Fellow's idea historically and against its contemporaries in the field, looking for innovation and real change potential.

2. Creativity

Successful social entrepreneurs demonstrate creativity both as goal-setting visionaries and as problem solvers capable of engineering their visions into reality. Ashoka believes that creativity is not a quality that suddenly appears in a candidate's life. It almost always appears early in youth and persists.

3. Entrepreneurial Quality

Ashoka Fellows have demonstrated entrepreneurial abilities. They are leaders who see opportunities for change and innovation and devote themselves entirely to making that change happen. They generally have little interest in anything beyond their mission, and they are willing to spend the next 10 to 15 years making history. Ashoka Fellows are fully committed to their life's mission and work.

4. Social Impact of the Idea

This criterion focuses on the Fellow's idea rather than the Fellow. Ashoka is only interested in ideas that it believes will change the field significantly and that will trigger nationwide impact or, for smaller countries, broader regional change. For example, Ashoka will not support the launch of a new school or clinic unless it is part of a broader strategy to reform the education or health system at the national level and beyond.

5. Ethical Fiber

Social entrepreneurs working toward major system changes make major demands on those around them. For this reason, the entrepreneur must inspire trust and confidence, living up to the highest standards of ethical integrity.

Ashoka's selection process is rigorous. Applications are welcome from anyone, but Ashoka's nominators—a global network of experts in their respective fields—play a critical role in identifying candidates who meet the selection criteria. After nomination, Ashoka conducts an investigation of the candidate involving independent reference and background checks, site visits, and multiple interviews. Once a candidate has been recommended, he or she proceeds to an intensive second interview by an Ashoka board member or senior professional. If the second opinion concurs with the first, the candidate is then interviewed by a selection panel of social entrepreneurs, led by a board member or representative from another continent. This panel decides whether the candidate is likely to become a truly first-rate, large-scale social entrepreneur. The final step entails board approval by Ashoka's international board of directors to ensure worldwide standards and consistency in the application of the selection criteria.

During the first 3 years after election, Ashoka supports its Fellows with significant cash awards. These vary across regions and organizations, but the goal is to allow the Fellow to be devoted full time, while enhancing impact and accelerating development. Ashoka also provides ongoing support and technical assistance to its Fellows through access to a potent worldwide network of social entrepreneurs and supporters. This technical support continues beyond the initial 3-year period of financial support.

To measure the impact of social entrepreneurs, Ashoka employs an instrument called the "Measuring Effectiveness Survey," a self-assessment tool that is combined with the in-depth personal interviews to engage a cross-section of Fellows. Social entrepreneurs create complex changes in their societies, often working from multiple angles and on several levels to solve a problem. The diversity of the work of individual entrepreneurs makes it difficult to design a standardized tool for measuring impact.

The survey, conducted 5 years and 10 years post-fellowship, relies on a number of proxy indicators that serve as measures of Ashoka's successes in strengthening civil society by supporting social entrepreneurs, their ideas, and institutions. These indicators include the following:

• Does the Fellow's idea persist and has it spread?
• Is the Fellow still working toward his or her original vision?
• Have others replicated the original idea?
• Has the Fellow impacted public policy?
• Has an institution been created or expanded?
• What position does the institution currently hold in the field?

As a further evaluation tool, in-depth interviews supplement the surveys and provide a basis for understanding Fellows' work and the impact of the Fellowship experience. From these interviews, Ashoka staff develop case studies to introduce some of the narrative specificity lost by quantitative and multiple-choice responses alone. All of these measures suggest Ashoka's significant impact, demonstrating persistence (over 90%) and project replication (over 80%), as well as policy influence and leadership in the field (over 50%).

Following are some illustrative examples of projects reproduced from Ashoka's descriptions of its Fellows:

Gerald Chertavian

Fellow Gerald Chertavian is the founder of Year Up, a model for work force development that offers marketable technical and professional skills and apprenticeships in top companies. The program focuses on the "ABCs" of professional skills—attitude, behavior, and communications—and encourages teachers, mentors, advisors, and a growing network of supporters to show young people consistent respect, something they have often never received. Companies praise Year Up as a source of prescreened, pretrained employees. Chertavian got the idea for Year Up while serving as a Big Brother after college. While spending time in the housing project where his Little Brother grew up, Chertavian met many disconnected young adults. "We as a society waste a tremendous amount of human capital," says Chertavian. He wrote his entrance essay to Harvard Business School on this social challenge and discovered that there are a disproportionate number of disconnected 18- to 24-year-old young adults (those who have not progressed beyond a high school diploma and are neither employed nor enrolled in postsecondary education) who are trapped in urban low-income communities and generally regarded as unredeemable or simply forgotten as contributors to society. Chertavian graduated with honors and continued to mentor youth while he built a $20 million communications company. In 1999, at the age of 34, he sold the firm to pursue his purpose in life. In 2000, he started Year Up with the mission of providing the skills, experience, and support needed to empower young adults to reach their potential and succeed in professional careers and higher education. Year Up focuses on marketable skills, including customer service, help desk support, business communications, and investment management and operations. "Teaching the skills is not that difficult," he says.

> We are good at teaching the technology needed in professional settings. What's harder is helping a young adult from a disadvantaged background to gain the communications skills and confidence needed to succeed in a prestigious workplace. It's said that employers hire for skills and fire for behavior. We have high expectations for our participants and we never lower the bar.

In 7 years, the program has served more than 1,300 young adults, with 87% of graduates being hired for jobs that pay on average $30,000 a year.

Mary Gordon

Fellow Mary Gordon is the founder of Roots of Empathy, an award-winning charitable organization that offers empathy-based programming for children. The program's vision is to change the world child by child. Roots of Empathy is considered a model of social innovation and has two programs: the flagship program of the same name for children in elementary school (Roots of Empathy) and Seeds of Empathy, its "younger sibling"—a program for children aged 3 to 5 in early childhood settings. Both programs have demonstrated dramatic reductions in children's levels of aggression while raising their social and emotional competence and increasing empathy. Mary Gordon created Roots of Empathy in Toronto, Canada, in 1996, and it became a charitable not-for-profit organization in 2000. To date, the program has reached an astounding 450,000 children worldwide. Roots of Empathy is delivered to schoolchildren from kindergarten to Grade 8 across Canada, in English and in French, and in rural, urban, and remote communities. It also reaches children in the United States (in Seattle, Washington), New Zealand, the Isle of Man, Northern Ireland, the Republic of Ireland, and Scotland. The program has been called "Canada's olive branch to the world." In 2008, the Canadian Assembly of First Nations passed a resolution to endorse Roots of Empathy and Seeds of Empathy, calling both programs "compatible with traditional First Nations teachings and worldviews." Both programs are offered in a growing number of First Nations communities, including urban and rural aboriginal children across Canada, and the organization works in partnership with indigenous people globally.

Wendy Kopp

In 1990, as a 21-year-old, Fellow Wendy Kopp founded Teach For America with the mission of enlisting the nation's most promising future leaders in addressing educational inequity. Kopp believes it is possible to ensure that all children, irrespective of their circumstances, attain an excellent education. Teach For America has had unprecedented success across the United States since its founding and has come to be recognized as one of the premier organizations that provides the education field with new ideas and exceptional talent each year. Kopp aims to fundamentally restructure America's educational system by working at multiple levels, including in classrooms, in school and district administration departments, and ultimately at the level of local, state, and national planning and policy making. She instigates this broad-based change by recruiting top college graduates of all academic majors and career interests to commit at least 2 years to teaching in urban and rural public schools. In the short run, these individuals provide a critical source of talent and go above and beyond traditional expectations to help their students achieve academic success. As alumni, they bring strong leadership to every level of the school system and across all fields, working to minimize the challenges facing children growing up in low-income communities, build the capacity of schools and school systems, and change prevailing ideology through their examples and advocacy. Kopp's ultimate vision is that one day, all children in the United States will have the opportunity to attain an excellent education.

Kopp's most immediate challenge in the initial stages was to recruit nontraditional teachers who would bring new ideas and fresh energy into America's struggling classrooms. She knew the talent and motivation were there because she watched so many of her bright friends take high-paying, high-profile jobs upon graduation despite their desires to find meaningful work. But Kopp witnessed firsthand how few public service opportunities were available for new college graduates seeking work that was ambitious and challenging and that offered the possibility of achieving nationwide change on a critical social issue. From this recognition, Kopp's high-profile recruiting program was born. Teach For America has subsequently succeeded in attracting top-notch and nontraditional talent, with college graduates signing on from all over the country with all varieties of degrees and experience. In the first year alone, over 2,500 graduates from the country's top colleges and universities applied to fill nearly 500 two-year teaching positions. In 2009, over 35,000 applicants competed for about 4,000 new Teach For America positions.

While these numbers reflect a notable accomplishment, recruiting a large and expanding pool of unconventional teaching talent each year is only part of the challenge Kopp perceives. The necessary second step is to ensure that these teachers lead their students to significant academic achievement. Therefore, the program invests in the training and professional development necessary to ensure its teachers' success. A growing number of independent studies show that Kopp's teachers have a greater impact on their student's achievement than do even the veteran and traditionally certified teachers in their schools. In succeeding with their students, these teachers gain the added conviction that educational inequity is a solvable problem in addition to a grounded understanding of how to solve it. The more than 14,000 alumni of the program have proven to be an unparalleled force of leaders who are driving change in public education—as principals of the nation's top-performing urban and rural schools, state and national teachers of the year, and reform-oriented superintendents, policy makers, and social entrepreneurs.

CASE STUDY: EISENHOWER FELLOWSHIPS (EF)

Since its inception almost 60 years ago, EF has identified over 1,900 men and women from over 100 countries around the globe as emerging leaders well on their way to positions of regional and national leadership and provided them with opportunities for professional, intellectual, and personal growth. The organization was founded in October 1953 as a birthday present to President Eisenhower during his first year in office, and 10 years later he described it as "possibly the most splendid birthday present I have ever received." EF was established as and remains a nonprofit, nonpartisan, nongovernment organization. This independence from government and party has been a key characteristic of the organization from the onset. Its first chairman, Thomas B. McCabe, although a Republican and former chairman of the Federal Reserve Board, had close affiliations with two Democratic presidential administrations and was CEO of the Scott Paper Company when he and several other prominent citizens, including Walter Annenberg and Ward Wheelock, constituted the original board of trustees, which included the journalist Edward R. Murrow, Thomas Watson of IBM, and other business and civic leaders.

McCabe was a pivotal figure not only in founding EF but also in its growth; among other things, in 1957 he donated the building in Philadelphia that became EF headquarters for 50 years until space constraints required a recent move to a larger building. Another point worth noting: The board of trustees has been a veritable who's who from the start—two former U.S. presidents and two former U.S. secretaries of state have served in the role of chairman, with General (retired) Colin L. Powell serving in this capacity since 2006. The current board is large for an organization of its size, with 71 members in total, 56 based in the United States and 15 overseas. An ongoing effort has been underway in recent years to diversify board membership by increasing the number of women and foreign trustees.

The EF mission statement is as follows:

> Eisenhower Fellowships engages emerging leaders from around the world to enhance their professional capabilities, broaden their contacts, deepen their perspectives, and unite them in a diverse, global community—a network in which dialogue, understanding, and collaboration lead to a more prosperous, just, and peaceful world.

Although the format and length of the Fellowship experience have changed dramatically over the years to reflect changes in societies and communities, professional fields and endeavors, and resources and technologies, the organization has remained true to its founding vision and core values.

At the time of its founding, EF differed from existing international exchange programs in that Fellows from overseas and the United States were not students but midcareer emerging leaders with proven track records and the potential for even greater impact and influence. It also differed in the degree of individual attention given to each Fellow—no two Fellowships were alike. This remains the case to this day, with program officers working closely with Fellows months in advance to develop customized, unique travel itineraries consisting of meetings, site visits, seminars, conferences, and other activities aimed at promoting dialogue, strengthening professional knowledge and contacts, enhancing leadership skills, and fostering global awareness. Over the years, four alumni Fellows have become heads of state, over 100 have achieved cabinet ranks in governments, and hundreds more have served as CEOs of leading corporations, heads of major nonprofits, university presidents, legislators, diplomats, journalists, and thought leaders, among other endeavors.

EF programs and operations are financed through ongoing fund raising aimed at soliciting donations from corporate, foundation, and private donors; an annual draw on the organization's private endowment; and interest on a federal trust fund established by Congress in 1990 to honor the centennial of President Eisenhower's birth. This last piece covers about 5% of the organization's operating budget; therefore, the vast majority of funding comes from private sources.

In February 2004, EF commissioned the OMG Center for Collaborative Learning to conduct an in-depth evaluation of EF and its programs and impact. This study included a comprehensive survey disseminated to all living alumni as well as case studies of 15 alumni Fellows.

Nominations and Selections

In its report of January 2005, OMG states,

> The EF theory of change hinges upon the notion that the program identifies individuals from around the world who will be influential in the future, and intensifies or strengthens their potential impact through the Fellowship experience and via access to the EF network and relationships.

This statement speaks to a key piece of the puzzle: identifying the right candidates for the Fellowship. The nomination and selection processes are crucial to the success of EF in achieving its mission. The criteria for consideration for both the international and U.S. programs are:

• Five to 10 years of exemplary leadership with a preferred age range of 32 to 45
• Demonstrated impact in the individual's professional field
• Active leadership in broader professional/community activities
• Integrity, energy, and motivation to make a difference
• Breadth of perspective and enthusiasm for continued learning
• Likelihood of contributing to the EF network
• Demonstrated potential for advanced leadership and societal impact

Also given great attention is the diversity of candidates by profession, gender, and geography to encourage interaction across borders and professional sectors. Identifying candidates is the responsibility of local nominating committees in 48 countries around the globe, plus four regional hubs (Philadelphia, New England, Research Triangle [North Carolina], and St. Louis) and nationwide recruitment focused on agriculture in the United States. These nominating committees comprise alumni Fellows and other prominent individuals from government, business, social services, science and technology, academia, and the arts. The participation of nonalumni committee members helps ensure transparency and the casting of the widest net possible in identifying potential candidates.

Programs

The Multi-Nation Program (MNP) is the flagship EF program and dates back to 1954. At that time, Fellows came to the United States for almost a year. Today, the MNP provides intensive 7-week Fellowship experiences each spring for individuals from 20 to 25 countries. In the fall, EF conducts one of several program options. Single Nation/Single Region Programs provide Fellowships for approximately 20 Fellows representing a range of professions from a single country or region. These allow EF to take great strides toward a critical mass of Fellows who can collaborate on making an immediate and measurable impact within their countries or regions. First launched in 2007, the Common Interest Program combines the stimulating geographic diversity of the MNP with an intense focus on a common theme.

In all of the programs, the primary selection criterion is demonstrated excellence. Once selected, international Fellows work in conjunction with experienced program officers to develop individually tailored programs that take them to six to eight cities around the United States for anywhere from 60 to 80 meetings, site visits, and other activities. In addition, the Fellows participate as a group in opening and closing seminars in Philadelphia and in a midprogram retreat at the Grand Canyon. These activities provide an opportunity for the exchange of ideas among Fellows and are critical in developing a sense of camaraderie, trust, and group identity.

Candidates in the four regional hubs and the agriculture program complete a rigorous application and interview process hosted by a local steering committee. EF sends 8 to 12 U.S. Fellows abroad annually to spend 4 to 5 weeks in a country or countries of their choosing, selected from a list of approximately 30 possible destinations. While abroad, these Fellows pursue customized programs in their fields of interest. They develop their programs in close coordination with EF staff and alumni Fellows, with logistical support provided by a professional program coordinator in the country or countries visited. The key difference between the United States and international programs is that the U.S. Fellows do not travel at the same time and/or to the same country as other U.S. Fellows and therefore do not have quite the same cohort experience.

The international and U.S. programs are two facets of an integrated whole and both are needed to support a vibrant global network. EF brings together international and U.S. Fellows during the course of their Fellowships and during their lifelong experiences as EF alumni. U.S. Fellows participate in opening and closing seminars in Philadelphia and play an invaluable role in hosting international Fellows and arranging meetings and other activities for them around the country. Similarly, hosting U.S. Fellows has grown into an important element of EF's efforts to stimulate overseas network activity and engagement. This has proven to be such a successful tool for energizing international alumni that EF has recently expanded the number of destination countries, targeting those nations where alumni Fellows can support and benefit from visiting U.S. Fellows. Another key component in ensuring the highest caliber Fellowship experiences is the engagement of trustees and sponsors in the programming process, inasmuch as they can often use their networks and contacts to obtain high-level meetings for Fellows in the United States and abroad.

Alumni Network

A Fellow's travel program is simply the beginning of his or her participation in the lifelong EF experience. The EF alumni network is an active and robust network of over 1,700 living Fellows who interact regularly within their countries and across borders with alumni from around the world. They often collaborate on projects with one another, with EF trustees and corporate sponsors, and with people and organizations they visited on their Fellowship travels. In so doing, they build lasting relationships and develop international linkages that benefit them, their organizations, and their societies.

It is worth noting there are numerous EF alumni from the 1950s who are still very active. The individuals selected each year as Eisenhower Fellows join an active network that has an ongoing impact on local, regional, national, and global issues. This is perhaps more important now than ever before—in an increasingly interdependent world, participation in the network enables alumni to learn from one another's best practices and provides them with a lifelong vehicle for meaningful collaboration. Although there were regional conferences prior to it, the first international alumni conference was held in San Francisco in 1976. Today, regional and international conferences are held regularly in different locations around the globe.

A very positive recent trend is the formal incorporation of alumni associations in the United States and abroad, now numbering over 30 chapters. In addition, beginning in 2008, alumni Fellows around the globe plan for and participate in an Eisenhower Day of Fellowship on or around October 14 as a way to commemorate the spirit of the Fellowship experience. In many cases, these events include activities designed to benefit the community or society at large. In Sri Lanka, for example, the alumni chapter holds a national essay contest on the topic of leadership that provides college scholarships to underprivileged youth.

This speaks to another positive recent trend: EF now challenges Fellows to identify specific, concrete projects they will undertake on completion of their Fellowship travels, often in collaboration with other Eisenhower Fellows, and to remain engaged with EF throughout their lifetimes.

Another important though less tangible aspect of the alumni experience is the trust that exists between and among Fellows. This word is mentioned often by alumni both in informal settings and in formal assessments and evaluations, including the aforementioned study conducted by OMG. A symbolic but important practice, which dates back to the 1950s, is that every Eisenhower Fellow is given a key to the headquarters building which is theirs to keep, the idea being that "EF House" is their home in Philadelphia and will remain so for the rest of their lives.

EF staff members in Philadelphia communicate with alumni Fellows by a variety of means, including mass and individual e-mails, e-newsletters, announcements, and updates posted on www.efworld.org, and more recently via social media including Facebook and Twitter.

Finally, EF has an Alumni Advisory Council that consists of representatives from over 40 countries and meets annually. At a recent meeting held in Istanbul in September 2011, the council decided to rename and reconfigure itself as the Alumni Council and will focus on collaborative projects and consequential outcomes rather than just serving in an advisory capacity.

Impact and Outcomes

In its study of the organization, OMG focused on three categories of outcomes, individual, organizational, and societal, and reported in February 2005 that, "All evaluation findings show that Eisenhower Fellowships is a powerful experience that has positive effects on Fellows' personal and professional lives."

The report goes on to state that:

Eighty-one (81) percent of respondents said that the program had a moderate to strong effect on *all* of the following: their professional knowledge, international perspective, understanding of the U.S. (or country visited), ideas and plans for their work, personal and professional goals, self-confidence, their ideas about leadership, and their perception of themselves as a leader.

In addition,

Fifty-seven (57) percent of the Fellows also reported organizational-level outcomes as a result of their Fellowship experience. In particular, these respondents said that EF had led to improvements in their organizations or institutions. Societal-level outcomes were difficult to attribute solely or directly to the program, but about half (51%) of the survey respondents said that EF had led to new programs, policies, organizations or institutions, which were often a result of strategic collaborations.

Examples of societal-level outcomes include a cross-strait effort initiated by the alumni Fellows from China and the Republic of China (Taiwan). The Eisenhower Fellows Association (EFA) head-quartered in Taipei sponsored 40 students on a 3-week long "2010 Cross-Strait Youth Leadership Camp" that included university students from Beijing, Shanghai, and Taipei and was designed to enhance relationships and understanding across political boundaries. Another prominent example resulted from strong personal ties that developed between a Fellow from the Republic of Ireland and one from Northern Ireland during an Irish regional program in 1989. Almost 10 years later, these two individuals were key participants in the multiparty negotiations that led to the historic Good Friday accord of April 1998, and they have continued to collaborate in the ensuing years. Although these are two of the more prominent, there are many other examples of personal and institutional collaborations that have developed among alumni Fellows around the globe and that are beneficial in myriad ways.

In its report, OMG recommended that EF continue to evaluate its programs and impact using 1-year and 5-year postfellowship surveys. The results of these surveys, which have been conducted annually since 2005, have been consistent with OMG's results and, in some areas, marginally higher. In the narrative sections of these 1-year and 5-year surveys, and in evaluations completed by Fellows before returning home at the end of their Fellowship travels, another key benefit has been frequently mentioned, namely, the benefit of being able to step back, take time away from their day-to-day routines and responsibilities, and reflect on what they have accomplished to date and hope to accomplish in the future. Fellows comment that this is a unique opportunity in today's fast-paced world that pays great dividends, including a renewed sense of energy, commitment, and desire to create change for the better. As one Fellow put it, "...the Fellowship allowed me to create possibilities for success that never existed before."

Recent Enhancements and Ongoing Challenges

As previously mentioned, in recent years EF has placed greater emphasis on concrete outcomes and collaborative projects. Additionally, the organization has placed greater emphasis on leadership and, more precisely, leading and managing change, by incorporating these issues into group activities such as the opening and closing seminars in Philadelphia and the midprogram retreat at the Grand Canyon as well as the individual itineraries for each Fellow. Additionally, mentoring programs both within the alumni network among Fellows and externally to targeted communities in various countries have proven to be very beneficial.

Another recent enhancement is the implementation of an "at-large" process designed to make the selection process more competitive, which has led to even higher-caliber candidates than in the past. Considering the importance of selecting the best possible candidates for the program, this is an important change. Another enhancement is increased emphasis on collaboration with like-minded organizations. In some cases, this has taken the form of collaboration with other Fellowship programs, such as Nuffield, Loeb, and Kellogg, while in other cases the collaboration is country- or region-specific, such as a recent collaboration on behalf of Fellows from China and Taiwan with the prestigious Committee of 100.

Like any vibrant organization, EF must address ongoing challenges if it is to grow and improve. One of these ongoing challenges has been the visibility of the organization and its programs and attempts to create an "EF brand." Considering the prominence of the organization, its trustees, and many of its alumni Fellows, EF is not as well-known as it should or could be. And although progress has certainly been made in this regard, the process of engaging alumni Fellows in more meaningful ways remains an area of emphasis. Finally, with its 60th anniversary in 2013, the organization's trustees, staff, and alumni Fellows must consider how EF should grow and change if it is to become an even more robust and impactful organization in the years to come.

NOTES

1. The 2010 NGen Fellows are a diverse group of young nonprofit leaders who represent different geographies, backgrounds, and types of organizations in the nonprofit sector. Independent Sector (IS), a leading coalition of nonprofits, foundations, and corporate giving programs committed to advancing the common good in America, introduced the American Express NGen Fellows Program in 2009 to honor and connect 12 younger-than-40-years leaders at IS member organizations.
2. Collaborating authors include Mikaela Seligman and Andrea Affeltranger of IS.

REFERENCES

Bell, J., Moyers, R., & Wolfred, T. (2006). *Daring to lead 2006*: A national study of nonprofit executive leadership. San Francisco, CA: CompassPoint Nonprofit Services & The Meyer Foundation.

Data360. (2011, May 25). *501c organizations in the United States*. Retrieved from www.data360.org/dsg.aspx?Data_Set_Group_Id=471

Heifetz, R. (1994). *Leadership without easy answers*. Cambridge, MA: Belknap Press.

Jordan, R., & Garay, M. (2011). *Liderazgo real: De los fundamentors a la practica*. Santiago, Chile: Pearson Educación de Chile Ltda.

Kolb, D. (1984). *Experiential learning: Experiences as the source of learning and development*. Englewood Cliffs, NJ: Prentice-Hall, Inc.

Useem, M. (1998). *The leadership moment: Nine true stories of triumph and disaster and their lessons for all of us*. New York, NY: Crown Business.

Useem, M. (2011). *The leader's checklist*. Philadelphia, PA: Wharton Digital Press.

THE DEATH OF PLANNING—THE BIRTH OF STRATEGIC ACTION PLANS

Sara Brenner, Fernando Chang-Muy, Paul Connolly,
Jeremy Christopher Kohomban, Nicholas D. Torres, and Peter York

> If you don't like the way the world is, you change it. You have an obligation to
> change it. You just do it one step at a time.
> —Marian Wright Edelman

Planning is a complex subject in which different experts use different terms to discuss the work at hand. This chapter identifies a shift from the traditional strategic planning process to strategic action processes. The first section discusses the who, why, what, and how of a strategic action planning process. The second section addresses a broader business planning process that focuses on identifying market-based, sustainable, and value-added solutions. It also addresses the use of consultants. Several tools are discussed, including the Core Capacity Assessment Tool (CCAT; for more information, see Appendix B), used to determine an organization's readiness to plan and capacity to execute. Finally, there is a case study of an agency that transformed as a result of decisions made about its primary goal.

STRATEGIC ACTIONS PLANS: THE DEATH OF PLANNING?

Revenues are declining. Endowments are shrinking. Funders are reconsidering their commitments. Wherever one looks, there are more demands and fewer resources. Then someone says that organizations need new plans for today's economy. What, however, is innovative about strategic planning? In fact, the word is that strategic planning is on its last legs. Some gurus say that planning should be confined to a 1-day exercise; others posit the environment is changing so fast that planning becomes obsolete almost immediately after it is done and that focusing on issues such as fund raising and market development is more likely to produce results.

There is validity in all of these arguments. Certainly, it has been a while since 10-year strategic forecasting was in vogue or even made sense; 5 years is a stretch these days, and 3 years is a hopeful guesstimate. Planning, however, is far from obsolete. A strong argument can be made for nonprofits' committing to strategic assessments of their opportunities based on the best available evidence and making decisions accordingly. Organizations that do so are much more likely to keep going during difficult times and, moreover, to have the tools to take their efforts to scale.

While most nonprofits are passionate about their missions, they are equally averse to sticking to long-range plans, partly because they lack the critical data to set goals and partly because past planning efforts were not aligned with the changing realities of the organizations. Good planning helps organizations understand what is core to their missions and how to define success and allows them to recognize the conditions for which they will hold themselves accountable.

The best planning processes for today's environment are those that meet organizations where they are, create a framework for dealing with change, and build structures through which decision makers are able to access information to measure impact and respond to evolving realities. Planning should not have defined beginning and end dates. An open-ended process that is constantly referenced and open to amendment as circumstances dictate is much more useful and likely to permeate an organization's culture than a stand-alone activity. When organizations combine this type of planning with passionate and decisive leadership, they create successful models that will empower effective organizational development practices. To paraphrase Mark Twain, reports of the death of planning have been greatly exaggerated.

STRATEGY DEVELOPMENT

Cynthia is the head of a large unit with 30 employees in a nonprofit. At a recent staff meeting, the executive director announced that the organization was going to initiate strategic planning. Although Cynthia has a master's in social work and is knowledgeable about serving clients, she is not sure what to do. What is covered in a strategic plan—only discussion of programs? Who is involved in strategic planning—only management staff like Cynthia? What is the process for talking about the organization? How is the conversation started? Do staff plan by themselves? Should they hire a facilitator? How long will the process take? Is there anything to be done before the planning, or do staff sit around the table and start talking about programs?

Why Plan

Some organizations engage in strategic planning because funders will not make grants without a plan. Others plan because they have added programs or services over time and they wish to stop, reflect, and analyze whether or not the programs or services meet community needs, whether the programs came about only because money was available, or whether the programs are working. Other organizations engage in planning because they anticipate that current funds may be unavailable in the future, and they want to analyze what they can provide given the funding available. Whatever the reason, an organization should begin by asking, "Why do we want to plan at this time?"

Who Should Plan?

After the organization takes stock of why it wants to engage in planning, an equally important question remains: "Are we ready to plan?" The organization is not ready to plan if board and staff members are not motivated. These stakeholders presumably know the ins and outs of the organization and should want to set aside time to take stock and analyze the organization's effectiveness. If the board but not the staff—or vice versa—wants to take the time, the organization may not be ready to plan.

In addition to boards and staff, other useful planning participants can include the organization's clients, funders, community residents, other nonprofit partners, policy makers, and others who may have a stake in the organization. Although they may not participate directly in planning meetings, their perceptions of how well the organization is doing and what it can accomplish can still be gleaned.

What Should Be Covered

Exactly what makes an organization effective in impacting the communities it serves? The following framework provides a useful list of areas to cover in the planning process:

- Programs: Do the organization's programs adapt to the needs of the community? Are programs data driven? Evaluated? Innovative? Do the vision, values, and mission resonate? Are they clear, compelling, easy to articulate?
- Board membership and leadership: Is the board composed of the right people? Are there systems in place to recruit, nominate, orient, mentor, and evaluate board members? Are there term limits? Is there a can-do culture? Is there trust, teamwork, communication, respect?
- Staff and volunteers: Is there teamwork with the right people? Are there systems in place to recruit, hire, orient, mentor, and evaluate staff? Is there a can-do culture? Is there trust, teamwork, communication, respect?
- Operations: Do operations focus on the clients served? Are there systems in place to ensure effective operations, such as staff support, professional development, resource development, facilities, financial management, marketing, communications, and technology?

Process for Planning

Environmental Analysis

Before planning, an organization needs to "plan to plan" and conduct an analysis of the environment in which it operates. This involves accounting for trends in the environment—political, economic, demographic, and philanthropic—and the trends specific to that nonprofit and analyzing how these trends could impact the organization and its opportunities. Such market analysis could be done via scenario planning or trend analysis, but rarely do scenarios predict what actually happens in the market. They can, however, help inform decision making.

Another way to account for environmental trends is to survey stakeholders about their perceptions of the organization. Questions can include: What is the organization's strongest program? Weakest program? What are the perceptions regarding board leadership? Management practices? Stakeholders can be surveyed electronically, through focus groups, or individually. Whatever the process, as with scenario planning, perceptions from diverse individuals help inform decision making, but they do not constitute a crystal ball.

Planning Framework

Once the environmental analysis is complete, the organization is ready to plan. A useful starting framework is to get consensus on: Who is our target? Who are we trying to serve? For each target, what is the desired outcome? Finally, what are the programs and services that would affect this outcome? After agreeing on targets, outcomes, and programs, participants should come to consensus on the organization's vision, values, and mission. Vision is aspirational ("End hunger") and values are emotional/spiritual ("We believe that all people are equal"), but mission is more technical. The mission statement should state why the organization exists, what it does, how it does it, and who is served and where. It can incorporate aspects of the organization's vision and values as well as make reference to its target population.

Program Analysis

Having reached consensus on target, outcomes, programs, vision, values, and mission (or at least agreed that after the planning process is over, the organization needs to tweak and improve the current vision, values, and mission statement), planning can turn to program analysis. A simple but useful lens for talking about programs is the combination of marketing and cost–benefit analysis. The framework in Table 8.1 can be applied to each program.

Strategic planning participants must fully understand current programs, client access prices (which may or may not be monetary), location of the program, how it is promoted, what it costs the organization, the benefit to clients who participate, who the organization partners with to offer the program, its competitors, and how the program is evaluated. After a thorough discussion of these topics, also taking into account the environmental analysis, stakeholders can recommend modifications to the program that can include growing it, keeping it at the same level, or closing it down.

The MacMillan Matrix and strengths/weaknesses/opportunities/threats (SWOT) analysis (see Tables 8.2 and 8.3) are useful tools:

SWOT consists of an analysis of the strengths, weaknesses, opportunities, and threats to the organization, its people, and its operations. People includes board and management, while operations includes facilities, resource development, financial management, marketing, and technology. A simple framework is provided below, but an organization can take a much more in-depth approach to organizational analysis using the CCAT, discussed later in the chapter.

Strategy development, as just described, points the organization in the right direction but does not provide a roadmap to execution. Strategic action plans increase the probability of successful execution and blend traditional strategy sessions with business principles to develop detailed roadmaps.

TABLE 8.1 Cost–Benefit Analysis

Program Description	Price	Location	Promotion	Cost	Benefit	Partners	Competitors	Evaluation	Innovation
Program 1									
Program 2									

TABLE 8.2 MacMillan Matrix

		High Program Attractiveness: "Easy" Program		Low Program Attractiveness: "Difficult" Program	
Fit	Competitive position	Alternative coverage	Alternative coverage	Alternative coverage	Alternative coverage
		High	Low	High	Low
Good fit	Strong competitive position	1. Aggressive competition	2. Aggressive growth	5. Build up the best competitor	6. "Soul of the agency"
	Weak competitive position	3. Aggressive divestment	4. Build strength or get out	7. Orderly divestment	8. "Foreign aid" or joint venture
Poor fit		9. Aggressive divestment		10. Orderly divestment	

TABLE 8.3 SWOT Framework

	Strength	Weakness	Opportunity	Threat	When Done	Who	How Much
Board							
Human resources							
Facilities							
Resource development							
Financial management							
Marketing							
Technology							

SWOT, strengths/weaknesses/opportunities/threats.

A BUSINESS PLANNING PROCESS

A nonprofit executive eloquently expressed the importance of business planning:

> I was very skeptical when we began our business planning process…My senior team was stretched thin and had no "extra" time, but we committed to it and worked it into our senior leadership meetings. Three years later, we are more focused and more in control of our time and achieving our goals. It's not that it was easy, but it has transformed how we do business and how we solve social problems. It's funny. I had another executive director of an organization in our network ask me if they could use our business plan. I explained that even though our missions are similar and it was working for us, you can't just take a plan from one context and place it into another. It is the process that matters. They used it anyway, and today they are out of business. We, however, are stronger than ever.

Simply put, the client was right: The process is what matters. With dwindling resources, nonprofit executives must derive a greater return on time spent on any activity. Business planning is no different. It should yield greater clarity of focus and mission, increased social impact, improved financial sustainability, greater team cohesion, and greater efficiency. If someone promised an organization these outcomes, most would participate in the initiative. Leaders must recognize that outcomes are things they can accomplish for their organizations and partners, but they cannot get them from "borrowing" from others, as the astute client noted. They come from difficult but informed decisions and, most importantly, from the conversations that yield those decisions. A business plan is a series of conversations with key stakeholders that yield decisions and, like a symphony, build on each other so that, when played in unison, they produce a more beautiful world.

There are many business plan templates available. Community Wealth Partners has developed very in-depth templates with 15 pages of detailed questions that have guided hundreds of nonprofit organizations, foundations, and governments through the process of building and growing a social enterprise. This section, however, offers the *CliffsNotes* version, outlining the most important decisions and corollary questions for discussion with colleagues and partners.

The Most Important Decisions in Business Planning

The most important decisions entail marrying a bold vision with a relevant solution tailored to the market and a financial model that will sustain that work.

Vision

Nonprofit leaders are passionate about their missions (how their work gets done). Reexamining the vision (a specific articulation of how the world will be different as a result of that work), however, is an important place to begin planning. Organizations that get the most out of business planning ask themselves hard questions. Why do we exist? How will the world look different when we have succeeded? How do we define success? How do we know if we are making progress?

It is not easy to stand up and say, "We don't want to exist in 50 years" or "We are working ourselves out of a job," especially during hard economic times. Community Wealth Partners has worked with many courageous leaders who make this kind of statement. One client began its work several decades ago to ensure that the homeless had food, a very noble cause, and one that all agree has merit. The organization quickly realized, however, that it wanted to do more for its clients. It began work force development programs and provided access to health services. Although the rate of homelessness has not dropped in its city, the organization receives national attention for its work. In a conversation with the executive director, he recognized that the organization's approach lacked something to end the cycle of homelessness. He understood that as a leader, the most important thing he could do was to change the organization's mental model before jumping to markets and solutions. He set a bold goal: "We are going to end homelessness among children in our city." He admits it would have been easier to keep up existing programs, but the process of planning allowed him and his stakeholders to do something different.

Leaders who redefine their organizations as movements are the most effective at changing behavior and achieve better outcomes. A bold vision—one that is realistic with visible results—is a critical place to begin the planning process. Ending homelessness in the United States is a daunting prospect, but ending homelessness for children in a specific county or city is perhaps attainable. To know if an organization is successful, stakeholders need to crystallize the meaning of words like "end," "children," and "homelessness." Does "end" mean cease to exist? Do "children" mean those younger than 18 or 21 years? Does "homeless" refer to those without housing today or without housing over a period of time?

The importance of creating momentum and early wins in achieving vision and ultimate success cannot be overstressed. It is the responsibility of leaders to know how they will communicate early wins, both within and outside of the organization. Early wins, however, do not preclude mistakes and learning. In fact, failing fast in the beginning, learning, and redirecting often happen in parallel with early wins—and both are necessary for success.

Before moving on, it is critical to point out that the above steps do not occur in linear fashion. After determining the vision, planning requires drawing on market data to define success.

Markets Defined by Value-Added Propositions and Solutions

Building the vision is about creating a common language that those inside and outside of the organization can understand. An organization's vision and solutions must be shaped by those affected by the problem, by those who receive services and those who pay (assuming they are different)—call them constituents. All too often, statements like "We know," "We heard," and "We understand" the issues prevent real listening. To build effective solutions, constituents must be engaged in the planning process in a manner that suits the organization. There are various opportunities for engagement including but not limited to input on how solutions are working, offering perspectives on gaps in services, and participating in shaping a new vision.

Ultimately, the questions to be answered are as follows: What specific constituency will be served? What is the pressing need among those constituents that the organization is uniquely positioned to address? Where are gaps in existing services? In sum, what solutions is the organization uniquely positioned to offer?

At the core, the purpose of business planning is to identify market-based, sustainable, and value-added solutions. This takes traditional environmental analysis to a deeper level (typically funded by a third party like government or foundations) and tests its value added with the direct consumer. To do this,

- **Define Target Constituencies**. The groups receiving services as well as the groups paying for services. The best planning processes help organizations clearly define these groups using multiple criteria like psychographics, demographics, and geography. The organization should be able to communicate to service recipients and service funders a clear picture as well as the differences among varied segments of the populations served. This happens not only by listening to these individuals during the planning process, but also by getting their input as new solutions/services are delivered.
- **Understand Needs and Gaps in Services Clients Are Currently Receiving**. The most successful business planning processes help organizations understand the needs of all constituents in a highly nuanced manner. Organizations should start by asking clients broad questions and engaging them in one-on-one conversations to understand these individuals and their needs, desires, hopes, and challenges beyond a specific program. This methodology also applies to funders. The best business planning processes determine how to add value for funders as well as for those receiving services. From these broad conversations, the organization should refine the characteristics of its target constituencies and develop hypotheses about their needs; from there, any gaps in services and solutions to address those needs can be filled. These hypotheses should be tested through surveys with target constituencies.

- **Understand the Unique Positioning of All Players in the Market: Understand Why People Choose What They Choose.** If business planners develop solutions based on gaps in services, they should create innovative and novel solutions. At the same time, it is critical to understand the other options that constituents have available to them. This is about stepping into clients' shoes and asking, "What are their choices?" For example, in the case of the homeless, they may choose not to seek services, or when they have a health care need, they may turn to a family member for support rather than going to a support group. If board members and staff ask why, they may learn to develop better, more innovative services, such as support groups with family members as leaders or education to help family members handle support needs. In addition, it is essential to understand the unique value that people receive from each option—including nothing. While tangible services are important, when individuals have options, they often make choices based on intangible elements. For example, individuals may feel unwanted or that services are not always genuine.
- **Learn and Experiment While Planning.** Once the client organization's leaders solidify the concepts behind their service solutions, they begin to test them. The most successful organizations pilot ideas, value mistakes and learning, and refine solutions. Through this process, strategy and solutions take practical shape.

Planning for Sustainability and Scale at the Outset

Once the concept for the solution or service is developed, business planning focuses on understanding the economics behind the delivery of the solution. The goal is to identify a sustainable financial model during planning, not during the first year of business or later. A financially sustainable model provides a reliable revenue stream while building a sense of control over the future. It allows for planning costs and revenue by evaluating the number of individuals who will be served and the services that will be offered. It also provides information on fixed costs as well as an understanding of the impact of fewer or more individuals served, services offered, revenue secured, and costs realized.

Business Planners Must Understand the Cost to Deliver One Unit of Service
One unit of service may be one meal delivered, one individual housed, or one support group begun. Costs must include not only the direct costs (like staff time or equipment) that go into delivery of service but also some allocated portion of the indirect costs, also known as overhead (rent, utilities, management). This is often the most difficult part of planning, but it is critical to ensuring sustainability.

Once Costs Are Identified, Business Planners Set Surplus Targets
Surpluses allow organizations to reinvest in programs and achieve scale. With these types of monies, technology can be upgraded, staff can be hired to expand programs, and new programs can be launched without new foundation grants. Surplus targets are set at unit level, so if a unit of service costs $50.00, a 10% surplus would bring the total value of the unit to $55 dollars. This allows for reinvestment while also providing cushion for organizations that will inevitably face unpredictable changes.

Business Planners Evaluate Types and Sources of Revenue
In the market phase, business planners identify value. It is now time to understand who has the ability to pay and how much they will pay for the value created. There is much debate about whether it is better for organizations to be diversified (i.e., to secure different

revenue types—foundation, government, individual donors, fee for service, etc.) or to have a large number of revenue sources within a revenue type (many different government contracts).

What matters most is creating long-term value for those with the ability to pay at a price point that affords the organization sufficient surplus to create a healthy organization. Thus, it is important to understand the need and value drivers of the payers. For foundations, this may be impact. For individuals, it may be services. For corporate donors, it may be more customers or increasing employee retention. For government contracts, it may be impact or delivery of services agreed upon. Once the competencies to understand value, communicate, and build relationships around delivering value and ensure that services provide that value are in place, the funds will come.

This philosophy means not accepting funding that does not cover costs unless subsidies are available from other sources. It also means raising money for an organization's plan, vision, and outcomes—and not accepting funding that requires the organization to deviate from that plan. To achieve this, planners research and test actual pricing and grant amounts throughout the planning process. This requires honest conversations with payers and means having payers try out the service and offering value and price points. Many organizations leave money on the table by overlooking opportunities to charge for some services and produce surpluses that can help fund other areas of work. When the payer is not the service recipient, the organization must understand and collect input on how much the funder values the impact created.

Business Planners Develop Financial Models to Forecast the Future

Once revenue types and sources are identified, estimates are created over time. Leaders develop financial models that enable them to forecast their futures and understand the impact of changes on revenues and costs. It also allows leaders to plan based on changes in revenues or costs. These models, unlike budgets, become actual management tools that leaders can use to analyze conditions throughout the process of implementation and managing toward scale.

Making Progress: How Do We Know?

Business planning is successful if it has defined a vision, a target market, and a sustainable set of solutions and if it helps leaders manage toward success. Measurable objectives and targets are only important, however, if they are used to learn, change behaviors, and improve outcomes. Business planning should help an organization establish a few early milestones that help leaders judge whether they are successful and how to make changes. These milestones should lead to setting important social and financial objectives but should not be confused with an organization's social impact (i.e., client outcomes), goals, or objectives. Milestones include securing a first funder who will encourage other funders to support the organization, launch the new service, and serve a pilot constituency. In addition to engaging key stakeholders, these milestones build momentum and excitement. They help to create visible wins and serve as important opportunities to communicate—a necessary element for long-term sustainability and impact. Through these milestones, leaders and stakeholders can tell if they are building value.

The business plan will also identify major social and financial objectives at 1, 3, and 5 years. While these measures are important, they are not useful if you only look at the data at one point in time but fail to understand what is behind the numbers. Simplifying the number of measures is one of the most important elements in ensuring that the objectives are actually measured and used. Five or fewer annual objectives are a useful starting point. Both social and financial objectives are necessary for measuring impact.

Consultants: What to Expect

If an organization uses a consultant, as with any partnership, there must be an alignment between beliefs and behaviors. Consultants often function as extensions of an organization's staff and should thus have the right set of values for the organization.

Consultants should help fill a void in organizational capacity and help build an organization's capacity to fill that void in the future. The best consultants not only offer advice and strategy but also work with the organization as partners who transfer knowledge, skills, and know-how so that the organization is better equipped to achieve its mission. In the course of working together with organizations, the best consultants help leaders to see their work differently. Leaders and their organizations should grow not necessarily in revenue or in services delivered, but in how the organizations think about and execute their work.

In the nonprofit sector, clients value strategic guidance paired with flexible execution support over strategy alone. Leaders value not only new but also practical ways of bringing about change. The best consultants:

- Offer a fresh perspective and should help leaders see their work in a new context or an entirely new way
- Offer not only a clear direction but also flexibility to change as circumstances warrant
- Help leaders become unstuck by offering a process for affecting change and identifying correct first steps
- Serve as a confidential and objective third party who is useful for facilitating brainstorming/input at meetings with key stakeholders as well as provide general advice
- Provide data, frameworks, and key messages to help rally stakeholders around tough decisions
- Bring the benefit of seeing work like that of the client organization succeed and fail across many contexts and find the right solutions for the client's situation
- Do not just work on an organization or its leader's behalf but supports both every step of the way
- Work as partners with organizations to increase their knowledge and build lasting systems in finance, operations, or staffing

ASSESSING AN ORGANIZATION'S CAPACITY TO EXECUTE

Strategic action plans are only plans in the absence of the organizational and leadership capacity to execute. There are tools that can assess an organization's core capacity and likelihood of success. The CCAT is one example.[1] (Please see Appendix B.)

CASE STUDY: THE CHILDREN'S VILLAGE (TCV)

TCV, formerly the New York Juvenile Asylum (NYJA), was founded in 1851 by a group of prominent citizens concerned about the growing vagrancy problem among New York City's indigent youth. The founding trustees counted inventor and industrialist Peter Cooper among their members, and his early influence had a profound impact on the organization and its noble mission. The NYJA was conceived to house, educate, reform, and find placement for the multitude of homeless and runaway children arrested every year on the streets of New York. Intended to provide a nonpunitive alternative to the House of Refuge—the preexisting destination for most arrested teens—the NYJA was to also serve as a suitable place for children removed from unfit homes or those surrendered willingly by unfit guardians. The founders established and trumpeted the NYJA's goal: "To care for, train, and morally uplift a mixed group of the City's poor children" (NYJA, n.d.).

Children who came to the NYJA's 400-bed residential campus on Manhattan's Lower East Side received six hours of schooling a day as well as moral, religious, and vocational training. In the early years, many children were placed with families across the Midwest via the Orphan Train Movement. The NYJA maintained a permanent agent position in Illinois to assist with these transfers. Emboldened by the organization's resounding success, prominent supporters soon orchestrated a move to a sprawling 29-acre, 1,200-bed campus in Washington Heights. It was here, in 1860, that the trustees first integrated the dorms; early on, the organization was well ahead of the curve when it came to dealing with issues of race. By the end of the century, the burgeoning NYJA had become the gold standard for organizations of its kind nationwide. In 1901, with New York City's population booming, it was once again time to expand. The NYJA relocated 14 miles north to a 330-acre campus in Dobbs Ferry and was officially renamed TCV.

Teens arrived at TCV and lived on campus for 6 to 12 months before returning to a family member or being placed with a foster family. Many went on to not only successfully reintegrate into society but to flourish, building robust lives, families, and careers. Despite all of this success, however, the organization's institutional model was not without its critics. Some posited that "[i]nstitutional life provided an artificial environment and was poor preparation for life in the normal world," while others rebuked the NYJA (and later TCV) for placing "virtuous" children from broken homes with "vicious" children arrested for petty crimes who should rightly be incarcerated (Harris, 2010). Unfazed, TCV continued the residential care mission that had proven effective for generations.

The 1970s saw a significant shift in the racial demographic at TCV. African American teens now made up an increasing majority of the referrals. This trend only became more pronounced in the 1980s, as the influx of crack cocaine and the HIV epidemic ravaged low-income New York City neighborhoods. TCV saw the median age of its inhabitants drop to just 12 years old, and individual lengths of stay increased concomitantly. It was now common for children to stay on campus for several years.

By the late 1990s, the main criticism being leveled at TCV centered on what researchers termed the "aging out" of institutionalized teenagers. Residential organizations were being castigated for purportedly sending teens out into the world ill-prepared to properly care for themselves. "For most of their lives, a government agency has made every important decision for them. Suddenly they are entirely alone, with no one to count on." Many considered these accusations unfair, yet the negative opinion of residential care continued to gain traction and affected government support for TCV; coupled with reduced donor numbers, this spelled financial trouble. Reimbursements had fallen so sharply that TCV, while still highly regarded as a residential program, had suffered multiyear deficits and was using its endowment funds to stay alive (Stangler & Shirk, 2004).

The swelling tide of opposition forced many residential organizations to close nationwide. TCV was faced with a decision: transform or shut down. More resolute than ever, the board's choice was clear: TCV committed to finding a solution to the aging-out crisis and continuing its storied tradition of ardent service to at-risk New York communities by determining and instituting a set of meaningful changes.

The residential model needed to be overhauled. Far too many children were becoming permanently estranged from their biological families or having trouble adjusting to foster families after long-term stays at TCV. After a research and planning process, the goal for the organization became stabilization as a means of preparing for reintegration. With the repositioning of the program to target children's emotional and behavioral problems—placing the emphasis on ameliorating these issues through counseling and a focus on interpersonal relationships—the hope was that the children would eventually be in a position to successfully return to their families, to their communities, or to stable foster homes. The program moved away from focusing on what behaviors or circumstances had brought the child to campus and instead put the emphasis on what could be done to engage both the child and his or her family to avoid the need for long-term institutionalization going forward.

The transition—by no means an easy one—had to start from the inside out. Staff members were issued a challenge: to reevaluate their mind-sets, assumptions, and practices and to implement the new approach's methodology in all of their dealings with the children and their families.

Embracing these fundamental changes, the staff transformed the organizational culture. More and more children were being successfully reintegrated into family life, and even older teens who had largely given up on being a part of a family were coming around to the idea, as an increasing number of foster families began expressing a willingness to take on older children.

The manifest improvements to the institutional paradigm garnered a resoundingly positive reception among donors and members of the press. The state took notice as well, providing funding that allowed TCV to increase its community-based initiatives by over 500%. In the first year of the transformation, the multiyear deficit was wiped out. Over the next 4 years, the number of children assisted annually rose from 5,000 to 10,000. This rise was accompanied by an influx of more than $20 million in additional services. The organization expanded to Long Island and across the state.

One hundred sixty years after its inception, TCV once again stands at the forefront of child and family advocacy. Just as the founders challenged themselves to transcend prevailing racial practices through desegregation, so too the current leadership challenges itself to adapt the organization to the ever-shifting social landscape. Learning from past mistakes and striving for continued success, TCV endeavors to instill hope in every child who comes through its doors: the hope that it is never too late to have a meaningful connection with a family; that it is never too late to feel loved, accepted, and cared for.

NOTE

1. www.tccgrp.com

REFERENCES

Harris, T. L. (2010). *Juvenile depravity and crime in our city*. Farmington Hills, MI: Gale Publishing Company.

New York Juvenile Asylum (NYJA). (n.d.). *New York Juvenile Asylum records (Children's Village), 1853–1954*. New York, NY: New York Juvenile Asylum. Retrieved from www.columbia.edu/cu/lweb/archival/collections/ldpd_6909466/index.html

Stangler, G., & Shirk, M. (2004). *On their own: What happens to kids when they age out of the foster care system*. Boulder, CO: Westview Press.

COMPLEX ORGANIZATIONS
IN THE NONPROFIT SOCIAL SECTOR

Richard Cohen, Maria Cristalli, Undraye Howard, and Tine Hansen-Turton

In recent decades, a number of large, complex human services and public health organizations have developed, which are becoming known as the Fourth Sector. These organizations generally offer direct services to the public but also have sophisticated financial, human resource, and information technology (IT) capabilities that allow them to offer management support to high-quality but low-cost nonprofit, for-profit, and government programs. The roots of this type of management services organization are usually in the nonprofit sector; however, the principles that guide them cut across business, nonprofit, and government organizations. This chapter defines and explores the Fourth Sector, and its large, complex, nonprofit organizations, many of them members of the Alliance for Children and Families. A case study provides in-depth information about this organization and the work of the Alliance to support the complex organizations among their members.

THE BIRTH OF THE FOURTH SECTOR: COMPLEX NONPROFITS

Throughout the nation, there is a growing movement of larger nonprofits leveraging their high-performance and efficient management services to assist the government, private business, and nonprofit sectors. First and foremost, management services help ensure the proliferation of high-performing, efficient, and effective nonprofit organizations. At the same time, these businesslike functions help generate revenue for the organizations that provide them, revenue that is reinvested in the organization's programs and services.

These nonprofits are differentiated from traditional nonprofits by a business model that blends management and direct services. These organizations have developed sophisticated financial, human resource, research, and IT capabilities that render them high functioning, attractive to funders, and positioned to support other agencies. Taken as a whole, this new group of business-function-oriented nonprofits is called virtual management services organizations, here to be titled the Fourth Sector.

The principles that guide Fourth Sector nonprofits cut across business, nonprofit, and government organizations and include:

• Relationships matter
• Vision and mission are important, but the goals of building business or attaining funding must also be sustained
• Money can be leveraged to build new businesses, programs, and services
• Services can and should be connected
• Strong business infrastructure serves to improve performance in all sectors
• Continual organizational assessment and self-correction are vital to success
• Data, research, and information technology can serve as the basis for service and program integration

Fourth Sector organizations come to be known as the go-to organizations that get the work done in their regions, fields, or sectors. The missions of these agencies are deliberately broad, allowing the sector to be entrepreneurial and opportunistic. Some of the chief executive officers (CEOs) who run Fourth Sector nonprofits will argue that while a focused mission is important, mission does not create money or equity.

The Fourth Sector has grown and prospered because of the will and vision of its leaders to think and act like business sector executives. As a result, the Fourth Sector acts like the business sector in many ways. It prides itself on following sound business practices, such as maintaining high return on investment and generating revenue in excess of expenses. It relies on managing quality programs and services. As with any business, it understands that only happy and satisfied customers return; in the nonprofit world, the customers are the funders—government, corporate, and private—that supply the revenue stream. Thus, the Fourth Sector often invests in both evaluation and IT infrastructure to monitor the impact and outcomes of the programs and services it manages. The Fourth Sector also realizes that a highly skilled workforce is key to a healthy community; many therefore offer a wide variety of educational and professional development opportunities to their staff as well as other specialized professionals in their service regions. Finally, communications, both internal and external, play a significant role in the success of the Fourth Sector.

More descriptive research is needed to fully understand all of the complexities of Fourth Sector organizations and to entirely maximize the potential of this undertapped sector. In a time of economic challenge, more than ever there is a need for the Fourth Sector, which can step in to support the nonprofit, government, and business environments.

The downward-spiraling economy has already negatively impacted the service-driven nonprofit community. Nonprofits should think about effective ways to affiliate with the Fourth Sector, while they are still able to do so. Governments, too, are facing cuts and should view the Fourth Sector as a potential partner through which to gain efficiencies by outsourcing staff and programs where feasible. The same is true for the private sector. The efficiency and effectiveness by which the Fourth Sector operates make it an ideal partner in tough times—and a smart way to do business when the economy rebounds.

While the renewed efforts of nonprofit leaders to promote social change through theories will continue to put pressure on the existing mission-driven nonprofit service industry to effect greater social impact, as the Fourth Sector connects, facilitates, and supports the government, business, and nonprofit sectors, it can offer a business context in which this is possible.

Some may criticize Fourth Sector organizations as being scattered, unclear, unfocused, and nonmission driven. Others will suggest that these organizations were "lucky" and grew organically from being pulled in multiple directions. Criticism will also come from those unwilling to be accountable for constituencies and results. Regardless, it is critical to understand that fundamentally, these organizations have the capability and credibility to serve all three sectors in the United States, often better, less expensively, more efficiently, and with positive outcomes.

In conclusion, the Fourth Sector presents a unique partnership opportunity for government and must be viewed as a resource, strategic management partner, and operations entity at the state, regional, and national levels. The Fourth Sector is, in many respects, an example of what new government leadership suggests in its plan to create a mechanism to develop the capacity and effectiveness of the nonprofit sector. These leaders need look no further than these management services organizations. In this win–win model, everyone comes out stronger, including the communities, families, and individuals who need the services—services that in many cases are vital to their survival in these economically challenging times.

CASE STUDY: THE ALLIANCE FOR CHILDREN AND FAMILIES COMPLEX ORGANIZATION AFFINITY GROUP

The Alliance for Children and Families is a membership association that provides a variety of services to private nonprofit human service organizations throughout the United States and Canada. Alliance members are human-serving organizations dedicated to serving children, families, and adults. The Alliance's mission is to strengthen the capacities of high-impact nonprofit human service organizations. The Alliance's network contributes to decreasing the number of people living in poverty; increasing the number of people living safe and healthy lives; and putting more people onto pathways for educational and employment success.

Among the many pathways the Alliance takes to meet its mission are its Center on Leadership cohort as well as affinity and learning groups, which encourage resource sharing, increasing dialogue, and networking. This is done so that members can plan better, implement more effectively, and bring various initiatives and venues to scale to serve families and children within their communities. One such group that has come together around these elements is the complex organization group.

Typically, these agencies possess one or more of the following characteristics:

- They are large, with a multitude of program services.
- They have overall operating budgets that typically exceed $20 million.
- They have a CEO who has multiple reporting relationships to various boards within the organization.
- They have a for-profit arm attached to the nonprofit that generates over $1 million through its operations.
- They are facing and addressing complexities related to sustainability and functioning.

Although this list is not exhaustive, it gives a feel for the types of organizations that fit the complex organization description.

The complex organization group creates and offers a mechanism for executives and their senior leaders to stay connected to peers; provide support for each other; create knowledge; share resources; and be challenged to continually develop their intellectual capacities for leading high-performing organizations.

Succession planning is another issue examined by the group. Developing and/or finding the right future leaders with the required breadth of talent and experience is one of the most important challenges facing the management and boards of nonprofits, particularly in complex organizations, where doing so is critical for sustainability.

Among other projects, the group has examined how complex organizations deal with culture and culture change. The Alliance organizations were challenged to understand why their cultures needed to change. In addition, the organizations discussed the approaches utilized when culture change was initiated. Finally, they were challenged to consider some of the biggest challenges in culture change, the effects on their organizations today. In the end, the Alliance's complex organizations are working to render themselves more sustainable and impactful within their communities. These organizations can provide powerful resources to the world beyond their current scopes, work as key strategic management partners with other sectors, and ultimately move ahead an agenda that truly can change the landscape in eradicating some of the world's most tragic social ills. The bottom line to all of this is our drive to create high-impact human-serving organizations with a focus on helping nonprofits become high performers that achieve impact against their missions by promoting mastery and proficiency across their commitments:

- Partnering for impact
- Achieving influence
- Driving innovation

CASE STUDY: HILLSIDE FAMILY OF AGENCIES (HFA): USING STRATEGY TO INNOVATE, GROW, AND PARTNER

HFA, a New York-based umbrella organization, provides services to families and youth from birth to age 26. In addition to providing assistance to families, HFA houses administrative services such as marketing, human resources, finance, strategic planning, and quality assurance. Throughout its history, HFA has undergone organizational transformations and changes that have enhanced service delivery and improved outcomes for youth and families. The transformations that have taken place in the strategy domain have been quite effective in both decreasing overhead costs and integrating a once-fragmented system.

One tool that was adopted by HFA to help the organization achieve their strategic intent and meet other goals was the balanced scorecard (BSC). This tool has enabled HFA to plan for the future by being a strategy-focused organization while improving existing services for youth and families. As a strategy-focused organization, HFA has been able to "mobilize change through executive leadership, translate strategy into operational terms, align the organization with strategy, motivate to make strategy everyone's job, and make strategy a continual process"—all of which are key areas defined by Kaplan and Norton in 2001.

By improving strategy and linking it to the organization's operations, HFA has been able to improve outcomes. For example, in 2010, 92% of families responding to surveys reported being either satisfied or very satisfied with services at discharge. Additionally, at 6 months postdischarge, 100% of youth reported no psychiatric hospitalization, and 80% of youth were living with their families at discharge. These are just a few of the improvements that are in part related to using strategy to transform organizations to better serve youth and families.

Because Hillside has made significant progress in implementing an integrated system of care, the organization is now positioned for a new direction: becoming the leader in translating research into effective practice solutions to improve service outcomes in partnership with youth and families.

History

Founded as an orphanage in 1837, the Rochester, New York-based HFA is now an umbrella organization that provides administrative and business support to seven affiliates, four of which offer services to families and youth from birth to age 26, two of which provide investment and fund-raising support, and one of which provides shared services. HFA offers 150 services across 34 counties through more than 45 sites across New York State and Prince George's County in Maryland, with approximately 2,300 staff and an annual budget of $140 million. All administrative services, such as marketing, human resources, finance, strategic planning, and quality assurance, are centralized at the parent corporation and provided to the affiliate corporations, which are 501(c)(3) nonprofit organizations.

HFA provides children and their families with family-focused, community-based, and culturally competent foster care, counseling, case management, behavior management, parent and family support, and a variety of other mental health, developmental disability, and social services. With a mission to *provide individualized health, education, and human services in partnership with children, youth, adults, and their families through an integrated system of care*, Hillside's guiding principle is to ensure that families with children experiencing behavioral, emotional, developmental, and other life challenges have access to a cohesive array of supports designed for their specific needs. The youth and families themselves are participants in the planning and delivery of services and help to build their own goals.

In late 1994, Dennis M. Richardson, the newly appointed president and CEO, had spent 3 months assessing the state of the organization, then known as Hillside Children's Center (HCC). Following this thorough assessment, he concluded that it would need a transformational effort to achieve real change, a breakthrough change that would be required in order to achieve a high level of sustained success for years to come. The reengineering literature suggests that a "fundamental rethinking and radical redesign of business processes" will "achieve dramatic improvements in critical…measures of performance" (Collins & Porras, 1996). In part, a targeted goal for redesigning the new business processes was to address the fragmented nature of the service-delivery system for children and families. Families needed to go to multiple agencies to obtain services, dealing with a different social worker from each agency, each one with different goals. In effect, families had to coordinate their own services and navigate the administrative bureaucracies that deliver, regulate, and fund those services. While each program functioned in the best interests of the children and families it served, the resultant inefficiency and conflicts in the overall system generated less than optimal outcomes (The New York State Coalition for Children's Mental Health Services, 2003).

Building for the future takes vision, commitment, and discipline. Hillside's management team and board worked together to build a vision and strategic intent in the context of Hillside's mission while recognizing the current and future needs of families and children and identifying key gaps in the service delivery system. Until this time, Hillside had worked to develop a system of care that coordinated services for families and had purposely attempted to collaboratively build service delivery systems with other organizations. Most of these collaborations, while well intentioned, were costly, inefficient, and not particularly effective. Organizational structure, process, and territorial issues interfered with mutually integrated success; compromises that benefited youth and families were far too infrequent.

In order to overcome these systemic barriers, obstacles, and shortcomings, Hillside adopted the strategic intent to be the nationally recognized leader and preferred provider of an integrated system of care for youth and their families. Hillside based its guiding principles for an integrated system of care on the widely accepted Children and Adolescents Support Services Program's (CASSP) principles. The CASSP guiding principles support the following in a system of care: a comprehensive and culturally competent array of services that are integrated, coordinated, and managed, and that are provided in an individualized way while keeping children in the least restrictive environment possible (American Academy of Child and Adolescent Psychiatry [AACAP], 1998). Under these guiding principles, family members should be fully involved in all aspects of the system.

Strategic intent is meant to provide a clear, focused, long-term goal for the future (Hamel & Prahalad, 2005). The shift in Hillside's strategic plan required significant organizational changes. To begin with, a change from a fragmented to a fluent, systematized service delivery system was needed. Furthermore, a shift from decentralized, nonstandard business support processes to centralized administrative functions was necessary to create economies of scale and support a larger organization. This strategy required commitment and alignment across the organization. It was necessary to achieve agreement on the strategic intent and include relevant constituents in the process: staff and executives, board members, parents, children, and the community. As opposed to strategic decisions exercised only by the executive staff, Hillside wanted to gather an in-depth understanding of what stakeholders thought might be helpful for achieving improvement in service delivery and organizational functions.

With improvement and the goal of breakthrough change across the system of care in mind, a new parent organization, Hillside Behavioral Health System (HBHS), was formed in 1996. The goal was to standardize administrative services more efficiently and effectively and to position Hillside as an attractive partner for mergers and acquisitions.

In the beginning, HCC and Hillside Children's Foundation (HCF) served as affiliates of the new parent corporation. The Hillside model is similar to the parent/subsidiary partnership model defined in La Piana's Partnership Matrix, in which the affiliate organizations are able to continue their identities and maintain their nonprofit status as 501(c)(3) organizations (La Piana, 2010). Under this model, Hillside's affiliate structure functions very well, positioning Hillside for mergers and acquisitions that most not-for-profit organizations find uncomfortable or unfamiliar. At the same time, the Hillside affiliate structure creates greater efficiencies and produces an overall reduction in administrative and overhead costs. Hillside's administrative overhead fees for the affiliates are 9% of the operating budget. Under this structure, affiliates no longer need their own chief financial officers (CFOs) or marketing or human resource directors; rather, they are customers of Hillside's shared services and are therefore provided with those administrative functions.

Hillside Work-Scholarship Connection (HW-SC), the first affiliate that Hillside engaged, was a strong match with Hillside's strategic intent. It is a youth development service that Hillside had long aspired to deliver. In 1999, Crestwood Children's Center (CCC) and Crestwood Children's Foundation (CCF) were added to HBHS as affiliates. Founded in 1887 as the Infant Summer Hospital of Charlotte, Crestwood had a long and substantial history in the greater Rochester community. Crestwood's specific mission is to provide comprehensive mental health services to culturally diverse children and adolescents who have serious emotional, behavioral, or mental disorders. While such acquisitions would later prove valuable and beneficial, one regulatory agency was initially apprehensive about Hillside's plans to acquire other agencies and share management resources. When Crestwood became an affiliate, the regulatory agency was concerned that overhead costs would rise. An audit later showed that Crestwood's administrative overhead costs had been reduced and services had been improved as a result of being part of Hillside.

HFA was adopted as the parent organization name in December 2000. This better represented the diversity of services provided by each affiliate. In the years that followed, HFA continued to develop through inorganic and organic growth in pursuit of its strategy to build an integrated system of care for youth and their families.

Implementing the BSC

As growth continued, HFA needed an organizing methodology or framework to help align the affiliate organizations to strategic intent. HFA executives believed that they needed to become better strategists and thereby allow the organization to become much more active in decision and policy making. Instead of simply being reactive to government policies and decisions, HFA wanted to help shape those policies. To accomplish this, a tool was needed to articulate the strategy and monitor the execution of the plan. HFA selected the BSC to articulate and execute the strategy.

The BSC is a framework that helps organizations translate strategy into operational objectives that drive behavior and performance. It was developed at Harvard Business School by Drs. Robert S. Kaplan and David P. Norton and first introduced in 1992 (Kaplan & Norton, 2008). The BSC provides a holistic measurement system tied to the organization's strategic intent. It is based on cause-and-effect relationships between performance drivers (e.g., leading indicators) and outcomes (e.g., lagging indicators) across four perspectives, with financial measures supported by customers, internal work processes, and learning and growth. The process involves a formal performance measurement reporting system that allows executives to view an organization through multiple perspectives simultaneously (Alliance for Children and Families, 2010).

HFA attempted to implement the BSC on its own, with a BSC developed by the planning department, but after a year and a half, significant shortcomings became evident. Leadership and staff had not been integrated into the development process. This approach failed to create the buy-in and alignment that were necessary for successful execution. Therefore, HFA sought consulting help from the Balanced Scorecard Collaborative and built a renewed BSC using the six-step process developed by Kaplan and Norton (2008). Through consultation and support from the Balanced Scorecard Collaborative, changes were made to the HFA BSC that resulted in substantial improvement.

HFA began the BSC renewal effort in March 2002 and added a fifth perspective to the scorecard, the stakeholder perspective. This perspective was critical to connecting HFA's strategic objectives to the communities it serves. The primary objective was to create a sense of ownership in each community so HFA would be perceived as a valuable partner that positively and substantially impacted the lives of children and their families. HFA implemented the new enterprise BSC in July 2002. The two foundations, CCF and HCF, subsequently became the first affiliates to build their own BSCs. The BSC planning process helped them integrate staff and reduce unnecessary overhead. The service affiliates then began to create their own BSCs. The BSCs helped the affiliates to establish a diverse and well-coordinated array of services, community resources, and informal supports tailored to the needs of children and their families by building linkages among services and reducing cycle time from referral to service enrollment.

In 2004, HFA aligned the entire organization with the corporate scorecard. All strategic business units (SBU; service affiliates and foundation affiliates) and all shared services units (SSU; support departments) implemented BSCs. HFA's executive team completed personal and team alignment to the strategy. Each team member has a personal scorecard, which is either the SBU or the SSU scorecard of the unit he or she represents. Personal BSCs were added to the annual performance appraisal process.

Key Results: 2003 to 2006

Growth
HFA's focus on strategic expansion continued. In May 2004, this path of growth led to HFA's signing an affiliation agreement with Snell Farm Children's Center, a rural campus outside of Bath, New York, that provides specialized residential treatment for male youth with sexually harmful behaviors. In October 2004, HCC finalized a merger with The Adoption Resource Network, Inc., which enhanced the goal of expanding Hillside's organizational capabilities in domestic, international, and special needs adoption services. At the end of the year, HCC acquired the former Seneca Woods Youth Residential Treatment Center in Varick, New York, and began operations there in December 2004. This presented an opportunity to create high-intensity, low-incidence residential services for youth with severe emotional challenges and high-need behaviors. Family Resource Centers of Rochester (FRCR) became part of CCC in 2005. The purchase of FRCR assets allowed CCC to expand its preventive programs. FRCR services utilize an array of comprehensive, evidence-based parenting programs and treatment services that support and enhance child and family development. Figure 9.1 provides a visual timeline of HFA mergers and acquisitions over time.

Outcomes
As a result of implementing the BSC, HFA has achieved significant outcomes. One objective in the learning and growth perspective was "Youth and families are included as partners in the development of the organization and staff." To measure this objective, each affiliate recorded the number of identified parent and/or youth seats filled on specified work groups, teams, or boards of directors. Over 2 fiscal years (2003 and 2004), HFA doubled the percentage of identified seats filled, which markedly increased the achievement of this objective from 43% to 83%. The parent and youth voice became a critical and integral part of the organizational fabric of Hillside.

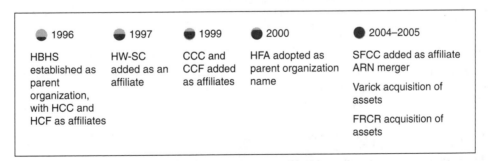

FIGURE 9.1 Hillside Family of Agencies corporate timeline: Mergers and acquisitions.

A second objective focused on access to services. The "manage access to services" objective sought to decrease the length of time from the initial referral to specific services within affiliates to the actual start of service delivery. The average length of time elapsed from referral to service initiation decreased 56% over the first 2 years of BSC implementation, which represents a decrease from an average of 6.2 weeks to 2.7 weeks. HFA was able to sustain this achievement and replicate the lessons learned across services. The cycle-time improvements impacted Hillside's ability to serve more children and families. From 2002 to 2007, the number of families served increased by 37% (from 5,804 to 7,950 families). Finally, at the close of the 2006 fiscal year, HFA's 3-year revenue growth had exceeded the target for eight consecutive quarters.

On September 22, 2005, the Balanced Scorecard Collaborative, a Palladium Group, Inc. company, inducted HFA into the Balanced Scorecard Hall of Fame for Executing Strategy™. HFA was recognized for achieving breakthrough performance results using the BSC (Koch, 2005).

HFA's Execution Premium and Data-Driven Outcomes

According to Kaplan and Norton (2008), HFA has "earned the execution premium" and has flourished dramatically in the areas of revenue growth, numbers of families served, and graduation rates for youth served by HW-SC. HFA also provides a greater return on investment, decreased the duration between referral and service, and diminished the rates of safety holds. The specific execution premium that was listed in Kaplan and Norton (2008, p. 83) is illustrated in Table 9.1.

In addition to improving the above factors, to continually monitor and improve service delivery, HFA also collects and utilizes data-driven outcomes such as family satisfaction, discharge living situations, and postdischarge stability. Outcomes from FY2009–2010 are listed in Table 9.2.

TABLE 9.1 Execution Premium From Kaplan and Norton

"Hillside has exceeded its 3-year revenue growth target for 11 consecutive quarters (2004–2007)."

"From 2002–2007, the number of families served increased 37%, from 5,804 to 7,950."

"Hillside Work-Scholarship Connection continues to graduate high school students at significantly higher rates than among comparison sample students not exposed to the program."

"Hillside Work-Scholarship Connection provides an economic return on investment of $2,263,646 per 100 program participants (to age 30)."

"The average length of time elapsed from referral to service initiation has decreased 50% over 2 years, falling from an average of 6.2 to 2.7 weeks."

"Positive Behavioral Interventions and Supports (PBIS) implementation has resulted in a significant decrease in the number of safety holds and support room referrals in Residential and Day Treatment programs."

TABLE 9.2 Hillside Family of Agencies at a Glance (FY2009–2010)

Family satisfaction	At discharge, 92% of families reported being either satisfied or very satisfied with services.
Discharge living situation	At discharge from service, 80% of youth were living with their families.
Postdischarge stability	At 6 months postdischarge, 100% of youth respondents reported no psychiatric hospitalizations.
	At 6 months postdischarge, 97% of youth respondents had avoided detention or incarceration.
	At 6 months postdischarge, 95% of youth respondents were enrolled in school or employed.

From www.hillside.com/datadrivenoutcomes.aspx

Strategy-Focused Organizations

As a follow-up to the BSC, Kaplan and Norton published *The Strategy Focused Organization* in 2008. In their research, they found that 90% of organizations failed to implement their strategies because of organizational barriers. The follow-up work was meant to provide guidance on the principles of successful strategy implementation. Successful implementation requires all parts of an organization to be aligned and linked to the strategy, while the strategy itself must become a continual process in which everyone is involved. The five principles that are common among strategy-focused organization are (a) mobilize change through executive leadership, (b) translate the strategy to operational terms, (c) align the organization to the strategy, (d) make strategy everyone's everyday job, and (e) make strategy a continual process.

Mobilize Change Through Executive Leadership

The support of executive leadership is a critical component in mobilizing change (Kaplan & Norton, 2008). Led by the president and CEO of HFA, Dennis Richardson, the executive team developed a case for change and communicated the need for an integrated system of care across the entire organization. Children and families deserve an excellent system of coordinated services. The team offered concrete examples from families on the challenges of uncoordinated services that resonated with HFA staff.

Richardson clearly articulated his support for the strategic intent and the BSC to measure progress toward achieving goals. HFA established clear roles and expectations for everyone across the organization. The executive team had responsibility for strategy as team members at the enterprise level and as process owners for their respective organization or support departments. HFA's strategic planning and quality assurance department oversees the strategic management process and provides in-house BSC consulting services. Additionally, each affiliate put together a core team, a cross-section of staff members, to build their initial scorecard. They worked with HFA's in-house BSC consultants over a six-month period. The core team presented each affiliate's new BSC to the executive team; it was an iterative process. Often the team would be asked to go back and rework their BSC to clarify their contribution to the strategy.

Translate the Strategy to Operational Terms

A strategy map is the framework for translating organizational strategy into objectives that are linked by cause-and-effect relationships (Kaplan & Norton, 2008). In HFA's experience, the concept of organizational alignment was a key component of successful implementation. Hillside followed the strategy translation process model prescribed by Kaplan and Norton in *The Execution Premium* (2008). First, the executive team agreed on three strategic themes—*partnerships*, *innovation*, and *operational excellence*—that represent a group of strategic objectives that are linked across perspectives and provide value to the customer. Partnerships represented HFA's partnerships with youth, families, and funders. System of care innovation represented HFA's ability to develop an innovative system tailored to youth's and families' needs that offers solutions that a payer is willing to buy. Operational efficiency represented the discipline of scaling and replacing solutions in different geographic locations for a variety of customers.

Next, the strategic objectives had to be translated into measures and targets that were linked to Hillside's organizational performance management system. The executive team had to agree on the best measures to track progress on each objective followed with an agreement on the level of performance needed and with annual and long-term targets for each measure. The final step was to select strategic initiatives to drive performance across the BSC themes and perspectives. Project proposals were evaluated by the executive team to determine strategic fit, cost to implement, and impact on strategic objectives and/or themes.

Align the Organization to the Strategy

Six business units and six shared service units were aligned to the HFA BSC. HFA created a hybrid model that consisted of some shared objectives and measures. Dennis Richardson defined these nonnegotiable objectives and measures for SBU and SSU scorecards. Each SBU or SSU leader then worked with the designated core team to define his or her unique contribution to strategic intent. Core teams facilitated each process, and BSCs were presented to the executive team for final approval. Executive team members and staff responsible for measures and initiatives met regularly to discuss performance strengths and challenges in implementing the theme. Highlights from these discussions were then shared at the quarterly executive team meetings.

Motivate to Make Strategy Everyone's Job

The BSC provides each employee with line of sight between his or her everyday work and its contribution to HFA's strategic goals. It is important to remember that HFA's strategic intent is achieved through strategy, and the strategy's success depends on execution throughout the organization.

A comprehensive communication and education plan was developed to build awareness and align staff to the strategic intent and the BSC. HFA's Learning Institute and strategic planning staff designed training for all staff focused on the following learning outcomes: understand the system of care values and give examples of behaviors linked to the values; understand HFA's structure, services, and locations; anticipate system of care competencies and give examples of how to demonstrate them; and understand the relationship between the system of care and the BSC.

The marketing department designed a communication plan with a variety of tactics to appeal to diverse target audiences. These audiences included middle management, board members, staff, youth, families, and strategic partners. Diverse vehicles were used, such as the internal newsletter; HFA's annual staff development conference; quarterly PowerPoint presentations highlighting results; quarterly green, yellow, and red status posters; internal website pop-up results for quarterly reports; and one-page descriptions of strategic measure and initiative milestone updates. Leaders used these vehicles to communicate progress at their monthly roundtable meetings.

Make Strategy a Continual Process

The strategy execution has become the focus of HFA's executive team meeting agenda. BSC quarterly reports and implications are discussed and shared with HFA's board of governors. There are two key objectives in these meetings: to monitor performance and to learn about successes and barriers to strategy execution. The affiliate organizations have replicated this process in their respective management team meetings and boards of directors.

HFA holds an annual strategic refresh process. The goal of the refresh is to test and adapt the strategy, based on analyses of environmental conditions, customer feedback, competition, and evaluation of strategic performance. These analyses, followed by leadership discussions, drive changes in the BSCs. Finally, budgeting is linked to the process in order to optimize the use of resources and ensure that strategy is connected to the operational objectives of the organization.

A formal approach to strategy management is critical. Strategy management is different from managing operational functional areas in that strategic management requires cross-functional processes that span the organization. In 2003, HFA established a strategic planning and quality assurance department to oversee strategy development and management processes across the organization. The chief strategy and quality officer (CSQO) leads this department, reporting directly to the CEO. The CSQO has three key functions: (a) the architect, who designs and executes performance management processes; (b) the process owner of organizational planning; and (c) the integrator, who coordinates and aligns key processes to the strategy (e.g., budgeting, human resources; Kaplan & Norton, 2008).

Setting a New Organizational Direction

By 2006, HFA had made significant progress in implementing an integrated system of care. In addition, it had influenced its strategic partners and other human service organizations to systematize services.

The executive team considered the future and how to create a greater impact on the field that would dramatically change the way services are provided to youth and families. The result was a new strategic intent for Hillside: To become *the leader in translating research into effective practice solutions.* This strategic goal is aimed at connecting research and best practices to benefit the lives of children and families and disseminating these solutions to the human service field. This ambitious goal offers benefits to youth and families. For example, on average, there is a 17-year gap between the development of new interventions and the integration into practice settings (National Institute on Drug Abuse, 2007). This goal should help to reduce this gap, and the most effective treatments will be made available more quickly. The application of the most effective treatments and measurement of outcomes to inform ongoing practice should result in improved youth and family outcomes. Hillside is uniquely positioned, given its scope and access to a range of families, to increase national research capacity by integrating research into its organizational activities in ways valuable to strategic partners.

In January 2009, a collaborative research partnership was established between the HFA and the Buffalo Center for Social Research (BCSR) at the University at Buffalo to implement a strategically focused research competency within HFA to achieve strategic intent. A 5-year contract was signed to implement a collaborative research partnership between BCSR and HFA, with an overarching goal for BCSR to assist HFA in establishing and implementing a strategically focused research program that built on the strengths of both partners. The HUB research model was designed to combine the practice expertise and research participant access of HFA with the BCSR research expertise and resources to collaboratively develop a research partnership based on CBPR principles to support HFA's strategic intent. The purpose was not to develop a research department within HFA but instead to build together an evolving research partnership that took advantage of the strengths and assets of both partners to realize a true research to practice and practice to research agenda.

This partnership is designed to decrease the 17-year gap between research and practice, which in turn facilitates HFA's strategic intent (Dulmus & Cristalli, in press). Additionally, potential benefits to clients may include providing more effective and efficient treatments, while outcomes can be identified and measured (resulting in building an information feedback loop to improve services). Not only does the partnership have the potential to benefit the clients of HFA, it may also prove highly valuable to the development of a strong evaluation infrastructure within the organization. For the HUB outcome goals, see Table 9.3.

TABLE 9.3 HUB Outcome Goals

HUB Year 1 Outcome Goals

Formulate relationships with HFA staff and relevant board members and affiliates.

Conduct an environmental scan to assess HFA's existing research capacities and infrastructure needs.

Develop and, where appropriate, begin implementing a training plan to assist HFA staff in understanding and supporting the partnership's research-to-practice and practice-to-research priorities.

Develop a collaborative research department including systems, policies, and procedures.

Collaboratively develop a vision statement of what the partnership will look like in five years.

Begin a strategic planning process that will achieve the agreed-upon vision.

Develop a mutually agreed-upon process to identify HFA research priorities and implement same.

Pending the completion of the strategic planning process, develop and implement an interim systematic research plan and identify necessary resources to support same.

Provide expert guidance on research to HFA staff and board members.

Match BCSR and national experts to HFA's research needs.

Begin to establish a regional and national HFA partnership research presence.

Participate in the development of research grant proposals to secure federal and private funding for research studies.

Design and execute an HFA longitudinal study to follow children postdischarge.

Establish the HFA Speaker Series as a mechanism to engage external experts.

(continued)

TABLE 9.3 HUB Outcome Goals (*continued*)

HUB Year 2 Outcome Goals
Direct a research partnership.
Complete the strategic planning process.
Implement the strategic plan.
Continue to provide expert guidance on research to HFA staff and board members.
Serve as consultant to HFA leadership.
Continue building a regional and national HFA partnership research presence.
Begin to establish an international HFA partnership research presence.
Partner with senior management to appoint a research advisory council.
Participate in the development of research grant proposals to secure federal and private funding for research studies.

HUB Years 3 to 5 Outcome Goals
Direct the research partnership.
Implement the strategic plan.
Continue to provide expert guidance on research to HFA staff and board members.
Continue building a regional, national, and international HFA partnership research presence.
Participate in the development of research grant proposals to secure federal and private funding for research studies.

Conclusions

Although some of the obvious benefits of developing a strong strategic intent and infrastructure for evaluation are evident from an organizational standpoint, above all, these changes are intended to provide the most beneficial services to youth and families and to integrate services so that families can navigate throughout the system of care with ease. HFA strives to improve every aspect of the organization, from business, financial, and human resources to service delivery to youth and families. Through the evolution, changes, and implementation of the strategic intent and data-driven outcomes to inform practice, services are improved on a continual basis.

REFERENCES

Alliance for Children and Families. (2010). Learning to act instead of react. *Nonprofit Director, 1*(1), 24–26.

American Academy of Child and Adolescent Psychiatry (AACAP). (1998). *Best principles for measuring outcomes in managed care Medicaid programs.* Washington, DC: AACAP Work Group on Community Systems of Care. Retrieved from www.aacap.org/cs/root/member_information/practice_information/best_principles_for_measuring_outcomes_in_managed_care_medicaid_programs#authors

Collins, J. C., & Porras, J. I. (1996). Building your company's vision. *Harvard Business Review, 8,* 13.

Dulmus, C., & Cristalli, M. (2012). A university-community partnership to advance research in practice settings: The HUB model. *Research on Social Work Practice, 2*(2), pp. 195–202. doi: 10.1177/1049731511423026

Hamel, G., & Prahalad, C. K. (2005). Strategic intent. *Harvard Business Review, 7*, 15.

Kaplan, R. S., & Norton, D. P. (2001). *The strategy-focused organization: How balanced scorecard companies thrive in the new business environment.* Boston, MA: Harvard Business School Press.

Kaplan, R. S., & Norton, D. P. (2008). *The execution premium: Linking strategy to operations for competitive advantage.* Boston, MA: Harvard Business School Press.

Koch, J. (2005). Transformation of a nonprofit: Hillside's BSC-enabled innovations. *Harvard Business Review, 7*, 1–16.

La Piana, D. (2010, Spring). Merging wisely. *Stanford Social Innovation Review*, 28–33.

National Institute on Drug Abuse. (2007). *NIDA's blending initiative: Accelerating research-based treatments into practice.* Rockville, MD. Retrieved from http://drugabuse.gov/tib/initiative.html

The New York State Coalition for Children's Mental Health Services. (2003). *A children's mental health system of care blueprint.* Albany, NY: Comstock, C., & Schimmer, R.

FINDING YOUR FUNDING MODEL: A PRACTICAL APPROACH TO NONPROFIT SUSTAINABILITY[1]

Peter Kim, Gail Perreault, William Foster, and Meg Rayford

> Having a great program wasn't enough to achieve our mission, especially with all of the uncertainty in the economy. We weren't being very strategic about raising funds, which was leading to a good deal of angst and ambiguity about what we could realistically commit to accomplishing. We needed a funding model that could provide a level of stability and produce the revenue required to grow and deliver our programs at scale. Now that we have developed, tested, and refined our funding model, we are growing more than ever before— even while the recession lingers on.
> —Dr. Tiffany Cooper Gueye, CEO of BELL (Building Educated Leaders for Life)

It is a paradox. Most nonprofit leaders spend an enormous amount of time fund raising but typically have little idea how they will secure the money they need over the next 5 years. Their vision for how the organization's programs will evolve over that time, however, is usually clear. The rub is that a well-thought-out approach to raising revenue is essential to that vision and its impact.

When they are small, nonprofits can often meet their budgets by inspiring a handful of donors, seizing unanticipated funding opportunities, or cobbling together a mixture of funding sources. Charismatic leaders are often the key to swaying prospective funders; however, as nonprofits get bigger, personal relationships and a catch-as-catch-can attitude are rarely enough to sustain larger scale fund-raising needs.

What is required is a funding model, defined as a methodical and institutionalized approach to building a reliable revenue base that will support an organization's core programs and services. As Dr. Gueye describes, adopting and organizing around one such funding model put Building Educated Leaders for Life (BELL), now worth $17 million, on the path to financial sustainability and growth.

A funding model has three defining characteristics:

1. **Type of funding:** The model typically revolves around a single type of funding, such as government or individual, that constitutes the majority of the organization's revenue and that the organization invests disproportionately in developing.
2. **Funding decision makers:** Within the principal source of funding, the model focuses on a particular set of people who dictate the flow of funds, perhaps government administrators or a few wealthy individuals.
3. **Funder motivation:** A funding model takes advantage of the natural matches that exist between funder motivations and a nonprofit's mission and beneficiaries. These motivations range from altruism to self-interest.

For BELL's model, the primary type of funding was government, specifically Title I funding through the No Child Left Behind Act (NCLBA). The funding decision makers BELL targeted were the administrators of Title I funding. For example, for the supplemental educational services (SES) provision of NCLB, BELL reached out first to principals to secure access to their schools and then to parents to enroll students. BELL appealed to the motivations of those decision makers by operating effective programs that satisfied the SES criteria, delivering strong results for principals and meeting the needs of families.

UNDERLYING PRINCIPLES OF NONPROFIT FUNDING

This guide builds on two previous publications by The Bridgespan Group. The first was "How Nonprofits Get Really Big," which was based on research on nonprofits that had been founded since 1970 and had reached $50 million in annual revenue by 2004. The vast majority grew big not by diversifying their funding sources but by raising most of their money from a single type of funding (such as corporate or government) that was a natural match for their mission. Moreover, they created professional organizations tailored to the needs of that type of funding.

That article was followed up with "Ten Nonprofit Funding Models," which catalogued distinct types of funding strategies that exist among large nonprofits. The Bridgespan Group identified 10 nonprofit funding models—defined by their main type(s) of funding, funding decision makers, and funder motivations—further confirming that the paths to growth are not idiosyncratic but strategic.

GUIDE TO NONPROFIT FUND-RAISING

Step 1: Analyze the organization's current approach to funding. Assess the reliability of existing sources of funds, crystallize why current funders support the organization's efforts, and evaluate its fund-raising capabilities. This diagnostic will help identify the strengths a future funding model could build on as well as weaknesses that may put certain funding models out of reach or signal the need for specific investments. This knowledge will help fund raisers home in on funding approaches that may be a good fit for the organization going forward. Table 10.1 shows a possible output from the completion of Step 1.

Step 2: Learn from the funding approaches of peer organizations. Float ideas to be investigated for the organization. Fund raisers will also explore how any differences

TABLE 10.1 Sample Output From Step 1 (Analyze the Current Approach to Funding)

Funding Source	Subcategory	Specific Source	Year 1	Year 2	Year 3	Year 4	Year 5	Total (1–5)
Individual	Major gift	Alan Anderson	250,000	250,000	250,000	500,000	500,000	1,750,000
Individual	Major gift	Brian Blocker	500,000					500,000
Individual	Small gift	Caroline Callahan	500	500	500	500	500	2,500
Individual	Small gift	Don Devine	25	50	50	100	250	475
Individual	Small gift	Emma Eng	50			100	100	250
Foundations	National	Big Foundation A		300,000	300,000	300,000		900,000
Foundations	Community	Community Foundation B	50,000	50,000	50,000	50,000	50,000	250,000
Corporations	Corporate giving	Local Company A			10,000	10,000	10,000	30,000
Corporations	Sponsorship	Local Company A	10,000				15,000	25,000
Government	National	Federal TRIO Program	75,000	75,000	75,000	75,000	75,000	375,000
Government	State	NJ DOE	50,000	50,000	50,000	50,000	50,000	250,000
Government	Local	Newark Source A	150,000	150,000	150,000	100,000	100,000	650,000
Government	Local	Newark Source B			250,000	200,000	200,000	650,000
Earned income	Licensing	Proprietary web based tool	10,000	10,000	10,000	10,000	10,000	50,000
Total			**1,095,575**	**885,550**	**1,145,550**	**1,295,700**	**1,010,850**	**5,433,225**

Totals by Funding Source

Funding Source	Subcategory	Specific Source	Year 1	Year 2	Year 3	Year 4	Year 5	Total (1–5)
Individual			750,575	250,550	250,550	500,700	500,850	2,253,225
Foundations			50,000	350,000	350,000	350,000	50,000	1,150,000
Corporations			10,000		10,000	10,000	25,000	55,000
Government			275,000	275,000	525,000	425,000	425,000	1,925,000
Earned Income			10,000	10,000	10,000	10,000	10,000	50,000
Total			**1,095,575**	**885,550**	**1,145,550**	**1,295,700**	**1,010,850**	**5,433,225**

147

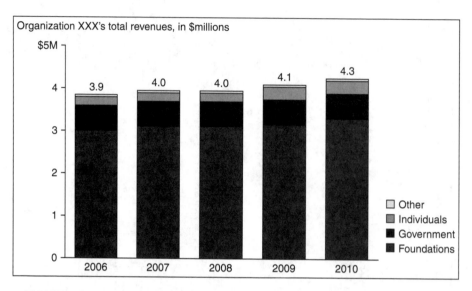

FIGURE 10.1 Sample output from Step 2 (learn from the funding approaches of peer organizations).

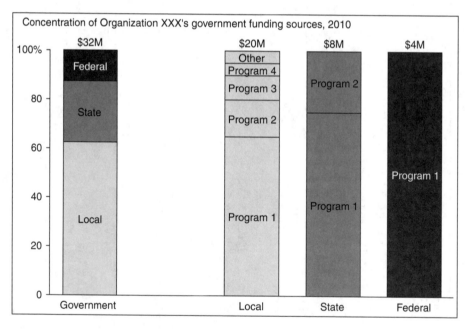

FIGURE 10.2 Sample output from Step 2.

between peer organizations and their own might affect the relevance of their approaches. Figure 10.1 shows what your output might be from your research on peer funding approaches. Figures 10.2 and 10.3 also show sample outputs from this step.

Step 3: Identify and narrow the range of funding model options. Fund raisers will be screening for peer funding approaches that are both sustainable and replicable and thus rise to the level of a funding model. In addition, they will make initial assessments of how

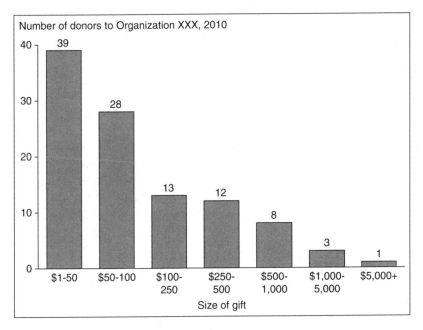

FIGURE 10.3 Sample output from Step 2.

feasible these models are for the organization with the goal of selecting the two to four most applicable models.

Step 4: Evaluate the revenue potential and costs of those short-list funding models. Fund raisers will develop an understanding of the funding available for each model and how much of that funding the organization could reasonably expect to secure given the competitive environment and the organization's relative strengths and weaknesses. They will also estimate the investments (e.g., expanding into new program areas, adding staff, upgrading information technology [IT] systems) the organization would need to make. This knowledge will put fund raisers in a good position to make an informed decision about which funding model(s) to pursue.

Step 5: Select funding models to implement. Fund raisers will draw on all they have learned in Steps 1 through 4 and commit to pursuing one or two of the models on the short list.

Step 6: Develop an implementation plan that will make the funding model plans actionable. The plan will describe in detail the investments the organization will need to make. It will also lay out a timeline for making those investments and implementing the funding model, assigning accountability to appropriate team members, and specifying milestones and a learning agenda that will make it easier to gauge progress and correct the course as necessary.

Why Bother?

Completing this six-step process will require a considerable investment of time and attention from colleagues and the board. Fund raisers are unlikely to see a sudden influx of dollars when they complete Step 6. Funding models are not opportunities to get rich quick; they generally require considerable time and investment to take hold. It took BELL 4 years of concerted effort to cover 70% of its site costs with government funds. There is also no guarantee that even the best-fit model will meet a nonprofit's funding aspirations. Why, then, does Bridgespan advise many organizations to invest in developing a funding model?

Simply put, Bridgespan believes that having clarity about how a nonprofit will fund its mission is as important as having clarity about how it will deliver its programmatic impact. Almost every nonprofit has two jobs, each with its own set of external stakeholders. One is to identify beneficiaries and make a difference for them with programs. Beneficiaries, however, rarely pay the tab—or at least not all of it. Hence, the second job: cultivating a distinct set of funders. Building and scaling sustainable financial support is as complicated and important as figuring out the programmatic dimensions.

Is Your Organization Ready?

At this point, fund raisers may be saying to themselves, "A funding model equals more money. Perfect! That's just what we need!" Well, maybe—but maybe not. Many nonprofits are simply not ready to develop a funding model. Here are some specific questions to help fund raisers assess whether their organizations are ready:

- **Is the organization free of immediate financial distress?** You need to be able to focus on developing a long-term funding strategy. If you and your staff are finding yourselves consumed by efforts to keep the doors open, chances are the time is not right. In contrast, if your organization is humming along relatively steadily but fund raisers just cannot see a way to the next level of growth, now may just be the time to find a funding model.
- **Does your organization have annual revenue of at least $3 million?** The Bridgespan Group generally considers that mark to be the threshold for developing a funding model. As indicated at the outset of this guide, nonprofits below that threshold—particularly those without significant growth ambitions—can often get by with idiosyncratic fund-raising methods. There is no need to get overly strategic until doing so is necessary.
- **Does your organization have clear programmatic goals?** If not, it may not be ready to start this process since strong funding models complement an organization's program model. They take advantage of natural matches between various funding sources and specific types of programs, services, or beneficiaries. Without program clarity, narrowing the search for the right funding model will be exceedingly difficult.
- **Is your organization willing to make the investments—in staff, IT systems, and other areas—required to fully implement the selected funding model?** The Bridgespan Group would only advise this process for organizations that are ready to commit to implementing a funding model. Otherwise, it is bound to feel like a fruitless hypothetical research project.

If you answered "yes" to the four questions above and you are leading a nonprofit with a funding approach that cannot keep up with its programmatic ambitions—be it a $5 million organization that is contemplating developing its first funding model or a $20 million nonprofit that is seeking a new one—read on. By investing time and energy in reading this guide and thinking through its implications for your organization, you will be taking an important step in elevating your organization's funding strategy to the level

---

EXHIBIT 10.1 In Review: Key Questions to Consider When Getting Started

- Why are you interested in learning more about prospective funding models? What is the ultimate goal for this process?
- What are your organization's short-term and long-term goals? What revenue will the organization need to meet those goals?
- Where is there disagreement or lack of clarity in the organization around those goals? How might the organization address these issues before kicking off the funding model work?
- Is your organization clear on the roles and responsibilities staff will play in the effort to establish a funding model? Are these individuals able to commit the time and energy to complete the process within the desired timeframe?

---

of importance it deserves. And Exhibit 10.1 offers some additional questions that you will want to reflect on as you begin the process.

WHAT ABOUT SMALLER ORGANIZATIONS?

Even though a funding model is typically not warranted until an organization reaches at least $3 million in annual revenues, some of the associated concepts can provide helpful guidance to nonprofits below this size. Practices likely to pay off include focusing on types of funding that are natural matches for your non-profit's work, clarifying who the main decision makers are behind those types of funding, and then understanding why those decision makers choose to support the organizations they do. Despite the natural temptation to cover all the bases by pursuing a wide variety of funding types, even at a smaller scale, identifying the most promising ones and investing in them fully is critically important. Sprinkling development efforts across several bases is a recipe for underinvesting in them all—and then not really knowing what could have panned out. Keeping these practices in mind will make it easier to develop a funding model if and when the time is right.

Considering a small set of options that could enhance a smaller organization's development work is also helpful so the organization is not overly reliant on one individual's personal relationships or capabilities. Examples include hiring a chief operating officer (COO) to free the CEO for fund-raising activities, bringing in new development staff, etc.

Getting Started

Before embarking on this process, you will want to spend some time setting yourself up for success. This preparatory work consists of clearly defining what success will look like and how you will organize your resources to deliver on that goal. Considering both of these facets before plunging headfirst into the process will provide invaluable guardrails as you march ahead.

> ## TIPS FOR GETTING STARTED
>
> - Engage key stakeholders early and often. Include the board, staff, and current funders. If a given individual could put the funding model plans on hold by making objections in the future, you should cultivate that person's buy-in.
> - Be realistic about programmatic goals. Fund raisers must recognize that they cannot do it all. Though your organizations might want to expand to 10 new cities and double current sites in size, you may have to choose between those growth options.

Clarify Goals

What do you want to achieve with your organization's funding model? Becoming more financially secure while remaining at roughly the same scale? Propelling rapid growth? Expanding into a new program area? This knowledge will help fund raisers focus on the options that will best support their ambitions.

Start by developing a clear and focused list of the organization's goals. An existing strategic plan may serve as a helpful starting point. Consider your organization's growth and programmatic and financial ambitions.

For Rare, an international conservation nonprofit that set out to develop a funding model in 2010, the primary reason for creating a model was to fuel growth. The $12 million organization had developed an effective program model for operating social marketing campaigns to support conservation efforts, which it had tested with encouraging results in numerous countries. Rare's senior management team was ready to scale up the organization's efforts and expand to new countries. Rare's journey is followed throughout this chapter.

Organize Resources

Navigating the six steps will require a considerable investment of time and energy from individuals across an organization. To help coordinate this undertaking, a project work plan is necessary.

The Team

Start by identifying a project lead (typically a senior staff member, such as the director of development). This individual will be accountable for managing the overall process. The lead should then determine which person or team will tackle each of the six steps. Some steps, such as the analysis of the current approach to funding (Step 1), will require more senior contributors. Others, such as peer research (Step 2) may lend themselves to involving more junior members of the organization (or a summer MBA intern). Throughout the process, the organization's CEO or executive director (ED) will play a critical role in supporting the project lead's efforts.

The Timeline

Once the roles are set, estimate how long each step will take and develop an overall project timeline. Consider using the sample work plan as a starting point for the estimates. The entire process should require no more than four months of sustained effort. If it stretches significantly longer, staff are likely to lose momentum and have a harder time staying on

	Timing (weeks)	Staff support required (in addition to project lead)	Steering committee role
1	2	• ED • Development team • Finance team	• **Understand** current funding approach
2	3-4	• Junior staff (secondary research and Excel support) • Development team (advisory role)	• **Review** peer research findings (optional meeting)
3	2	• ED • Director of Development • Junior staff who worked on Step 2	• **Approve** subset of funding models to evaluate further
4	3-4	• Junior staff (secondary research) • Development team (advisory role) • Finance team (advisory role)	• **Review** research (can be combined with Step 5 meeting)
5	2	• ED • Director of Development • Senior leadership (programs, operations)	• **Approve** one or two funding models to pilot
6	3-4	• Development team • Finance team • Program staff (if program changes required)	• **Approve** implementation and investment plan

FIGURE 10.4 A sample work plan.

track. Figure 10.4 shows a sample work plan for doing the work to narrow down your list of two to four models for further exploration.

The Steering Committee

Most organizations also find it helpful to create a steering committee comprising senior staff from all parts of the organization and perhaps key board members. While some members may be more involved than others, this advisory group will review, provide feedback on, and approve the work done for each step in the process. Schedule periodic committee meetings (ideally one toward the end of each of the six steps) as soon as the timeline is established. Doing so will not only ensure that ample time is blocked off on members' calendars but also serve to establish internal deadlines that will help keep the project on track.

Step 1: Analyze the Current Approach to Funding

With funding models, the way forward starts with a look back. Adopting a new funding model will undoubtedly require new capabilities—in fund raising, performance measurement, reporting, and sometimes even program design and delivery. If these new capabilities are too far from current ones, however, the odds of success may be lower. While external research can reveal which funding models are most promising in the abstract, only an indepth understanding of your own organization can illuminate which could work for it.

There is also the danger that some of what an organization believes about its current funding strategy is wrong. Consider the experience of Love Learning, an education nonprofit that thought tours of its diagnostic learning clinics were key to getting individuals to fund the organization. The group was so convinced of the power of site visits that it spent a disproportionate amount of time arranging tours. It also planned to build more clinics, in part to enhance its ability to raise funds. When the group examined the share of total funding that came from donors who were motivated by clinic visits, however, it learned that it was a startlingly low percentage. With this knowledge, the group abandoned its plans to build more clinics and refocused its fund development efforts on the aspects of its work that were truly driving donors to give.

Use this opportunity to take a deliberate look at your organization's funding approach with a critical eye. By the end of this step, you should be able to:

- Articulate which sources make up the revenue base and have an understanding of how reliable those sources are
- Understand who the key funding decision makers are and what motivates them
- Summarize the strengths and weaknesses of your organization's fund-raising capabilities

You may find (as many nonprofit fund raisers do) that your organization does not have a particularly strategic approach to funding. Perhaps you run after funding opportunities as they arise. Maybe funding is idiosyncratic, varying considerably from year to year. These funding self-assessment results are fairly common and a fine place to start. Knowing where your current funding approach is vulnerable will aid in selecting a model that improves on those weaknesses.

Analyze Historical Financials

Gather the organization's historical funding data. Examining 5 years of data will allow the identification of trends in an organization's approach to funding. With this information, you will be able to articulate clearly—to board, staff, and future funders—what your current revenue streams are. This knowledge will serve as a basis for describing how you may want those revenue streams to change in the future.

One way to go about this is to develop an Excel spreadsheet as follows:

- Collect detailed funding data for the past 5 years, using one row of the spreadsheet for each grant, donation, or fee-for-service category.
- Categorize each line by type of funding (e.g., individual contributions, foundation grants, corporate donations, government funding, earned income). Try to refine the categories even more—for example, by separating individual contributions into small versus large donors, or by distinguishing among federal, state, and local government funding.
- Sort the list by type of funding. You will then see all corporate donations together, all foundation grants, and so on.
- Using Excel's chart function, translate the analysis into a simple visual so trends can be seen more easily.

Consider the following questions, which will help clarify the reliability of the current funding approach and spark some ideas for building on it in the future:

What percentage of ongoing costs is covered by renewable funding sources? In general, a renewable source is one that staff believe, with a high level of confidence, will continue for at least the next 3 to 5 years. This could be a government contract that has been secured for multiple years, with no signs that the funding agency plans to change its decision-making criteria. Or perhaps it is an individual donor, with a deep personal commitment to an organization's work, who has been writing $10,000 checks annually for the last 7 years. In contrast, a foundation grant for a specific initiative that is slated to end in 2 years would land squarely outside of this category. Some sources will likely fall in more of a gray area, so staff will need to make some judgment calls. An organization is generally considered to be in a relatively strong position if at least 70% of its revenue is renewable.

Across how many funders are funding sources spread? Identify major funders—big individual donors, foundations, government agencies, and the like. How many does your organization have today? How many do you expect to have 3 to 5 years from now, assuming you maintain your current funding approach? Ideally, your organization garners revenue from three or more major funders, thereby giving it a good chance of weathering the loss of one.

THE SKINNY ON DIVERSIFICATION

Conventional wisdom has long held that diversifying an organization's funding mix by tapping several types of funding (e.g., government, corporate) is the best way to achieve financial sustainability. Bridgespan's research has not found this to be the case. Very large nonprofits raise most of their money from one type of funding. Fast growing midsized nonprofits rely heavily on one type of funding and strategically tap one or sometimes two others.

What explains this departure from conventional wisdom? Natural matches between a nonprofit's work and funder interests are simply too hard to come by. It is very hard to imagine the same program appealing deeply to government funders, corporations, foundations, small donors, and high-net-worth individuals, given the varied motivations behind their funding decisions. Pursuing the scattershot approach of trying to cultivate all of these groups typically translates to underinvesting in each, making it incredibly difficult to discern which ones are most promising—never mind taking advantage of their full potential.

The case for broad diversification within a single type of funding—say, by accessing several different government funding streams or tapping multiple segments of individual donors—is much more compelling. Diversification brings the desired risk-management benefits while still allowing nonprofits to build and leverage expertise in raising a particular type of funding.

What percentage of funding is restricted to noncore operations and programs? A good indicator of an organization's financial health is its historical success in securing funds that are not restricted to programs and operations tangential to its impact goals (i.e., noncore activities).

As a general rule of thumb, an organization is defined as being in a relatively strong position if no more than 30% of funds are restricted to noncore activities.

When Rare undertook this historical funding analysis, it confirmed that funding was primarily driven by a few high-net-worth individuals who were either on the board or closely connected to board members. Securing or failing to secure a gift from any one of these people had the potential to swing Rare's financial picture quite a bit; in fact, the organization's revenue had been choppy for the past few years. Happily, these loyal funders had been consistent supporters for years and did not place significant restrictions on their donations. More of Rare's other funding, including government and foundation, had grown in recent years but remained at relatively modest levels.

Understand the Motivation of Current Funders

Knowing which funders are likely to give in the future starts with understanding why current funders give. Identify the characteristics of your organization that motivate its most loyal donors. Speaking directly with funders is often helpful here. Does your proven track record drive them? Or does the specific population with whom you work? Create a list of key characteristics that seem to be driving significant, sustainable dollars to the organization.

Based on that list of donor motivations, articulate clearly what differentiates your organization in the eyes of these funders. By getting really specific here, you will be better able to evaluate whether an organization's current positioning will appeal to potential future donors or whether it will need to alter that positioning to attract the level of targeted funding.

Consider, for example, the motivations behind the donors of Susan G. Komen for the Cure, a leader in the breast cancer movement. This organization realized early on that the bedrock of its funding was a group of small individual donors who had been affected by breast cancer, either directly or through a loved one, and who wanted to help combat the disease. Knowing its donors' motivations, Susan G. Komen for the Cure organizes local cancer walks in myriad communities, thereby creating tangible, local opportunities to contribute.

In contrast, Rare's main source of funding was a small group of affluent environmentalists who were impressed by the organization's focus on community-level conservation and its track record of proven environmental outcomes. While Rare believed there was an opportunity to increase the number of individual donors in the coming years, the leadership team worried that the organization might hit a "funding ceiling" with this donor segment.

Understand the Organization's Current Fund-Raising Capabilities

There are undoubtedly certain fund-raising activities that an organization is quite good at, and other areas where it has had less experience or even made some missteps. Maybe appeals to wealthy individual donors often have borne fruit but efforts to win (never mind manage) government contracts have fallen flat. Crystallizing this knowledge will help staff to be honest about what funding sources the organization can realistically hope to secure and what organizational investments will be necessary in order to do so.

The following questions can help evaluate an organization's fund-raising capabilities:

Does a single individual (such as the CEO, ED, or a board member) generate most of the organization's revenue, or is fund raising more institutionalized? Think about how fund-raising responsibilities historically have been spread. An organization that has raised most of its funds through a charismatic leader may need to consider the broader set of staff capabilities needed to access new and larger pools of funding.

What is the development team's current capacity? Getting a sense of your development team's skills will help you select funding models that build on their existing capabilities. Different funding sources may require different skill sets. Someone who is successful at cultivating major donors may not be well suited to writing complicated government grant proposals. Workload is another important consideration. If development staff are flat-out pursuing the organization's current approach to funding (as is so often the case), adopting a new funding model likely will require reallocating staff time or hiring additional staff.

This sort of reflection proved powerful to the Rare team. They recognized that President and CEO Brett Jenks was spending an increasing amount of his time cultivating and managing donor relationships as the number of key funders grew—an unsustainable trend. To support the organization's desired growth, they knew that senior program leaders and the development team would need to assume greater fund-raising responsibilities. Rare also observed that development staff were primarily set up to work with high-net-worth individuals and did not have deep expertise in raising other types of funds, such as government grants.

Share What Has Been Learned With Key Internal Stakeholders
Now that a clear picture of your organization's approach to funding has been developed, consider how widely it is understood throughout the organization. Can board members and staff accurately describe the approach? If not, take the time to familiarize them with what has been learned. In order for there to be productive conversations about the future and to ultimately gain support for the future funding model, all parties need to know where funding stands now.

Determine Which Funding Sources Are Most Attractive to Explore Further
Building on the clearer sense of your organization's current approach to funding, take some time to brainstorm which funding sources may be good fits going forward. Be expansive in thinking; subsequent steps of this guide will provide ample opportunity to pressure-test ideas.

Rare's management team came up with a number of ideas at this stage. Maybe Rare could grow by identifying several more large donors by focusing on cities where it did not have a fund-raising presence or by targeting different profiles of individual donors, such as those who make small gifts. All of these options made the brainstorming list. What about government funding? Rare had a small amount of it but the team knew that other organizations in its space were getting more. Though Rare did not have much experience landing and managing government contracts, this idea made the list. Given the team's past experience with foundation and corporate funding, they decided to keep these options on the table for the time being as well.

Step 2: Learn From the Funding Approaches of Peer Organizations

Now it is time to look at the funding approaches of peer organizations, ideally, peers who have been more successful at securing funds. This research, combined with the ideas that grew out of the Step 1 diagnostic, will ultimately help identify an initial set of funding models for consideration.

Some may be thinking, "My organization is unusual, maybe even unique. What if we require a unique funding model?" That reasoning is in fact why many nonprofit leaders balk at peer research. It is true that nothing that exists before it has happened for the first time, but true first times do not happen nearly as often as many would like. So while creating a never-before-seen funding model is sometimes possible, the truth is that doing so is generally far more difficult and less certain. It is hard to bet mission success on such things.

You may also ask yourself whether a peer's funding approach is worth emulating. Who is to say, after all, that it is any better than your own? Selecting organizations that exhibit some signs of success, such as recent growth or endorsements from your contacts in the field, is definitely a good idea. Rest assured, however, that in Step 3 there will be a good deal of pressure testing and homing in on only those that are sustainable and replicable.

By the end of this step, you should be able to:

- List specific organizations that may serve as potential funding strategy role models
- Describe the essential characteristics of their approaches to funding
- Understand how differences among these organizations and your own affect the relevance of your peers' funding strategies

Identify a Small Group of Peer Organizations

When thinking about your organization's peer group, your mind probably first goes to organizations that are similar to your own in terms of issue focus (e.g., disease eradication, college access) and size (as measured by revenue). These aspects are in fact two of the most important to consider. Issue area is a primary determinant of the types of funders that will support a given organization. Likewise, size matters. But that is not to say that you should only look to organizations that are roughly the same size as your own. If growth is a desired goal, the funding approaches used by organizations of the target size will likely be more informative. Regardless of growth ambitions, choosing larger peers also tends to reveal more organizations that are more successful at fund raising.

Consider the experience of Rare. Because growth was the goal, Rare immediately started with the largest and best-known international conservation organizations, including the Nature Conservancy and Conservation International. Next, Rare added peer organizations that were comparable in size, such as the Rainforest Alliance and the African Wildlife Foundation. To round out this group, it included a few well-known environmental organizations that addressed issues beyond conservation, such as the Natural Resources Defense Council (NRDC).

SOURCES FOR RESEARCHING PEER ORGANIZATIONS

When developing a list of peer organizations, start by mining personal knowledge and brainstorming with staff, board members, and funders. Then reach out to local experts, foundations, and associations that focus on your organization's issue area. A quick literature scan can also be productive and is often a good way to get beyond the usual suspects. Articles in broad-based publications like *The Chronicle of Philanthropy* or domain-specific ones such as *Youth Today* may point to peers on the national scene. Searching Guidestar.org or CharityNavigator.org by field, budget size, and location may also yield possibilities. Case studies on nonprofit organizations are another option, with sources including business school publications as well as Bridgespan's website (www.bridgespan.org).

Once the peer group is identified and your organization is ready to learn about their funding approaches, start by checking the organizations' websites and annual reports (if available). The odds are good that there will be at least some basic financial information, and sometimes much more than that—perhaps press releases describing each major gift. These organizations' websites may also give a sense for which donors they are targeting. For example, a peer that taps corporate funds may have corporate volunteer information on its website. One that relies on large individual donations may have guidance about charitable bequests. If an organization comes up short with these sources, the organization's 990 forms will provide funding information at a high level (i.e., public revenue, private contributions, and earned revenue). Foundationcenter.org and Guidestar both enable searches of 990 forms free of charge.

After mining these public sources, you will likely want to speak with people at the peer organizations themselves. Having direct or indirect connections with these folks are ideal, but cold calls can work as well—particularly when you're reaching out to nonprofits with which you would not compete directly for funds (e.g., a nonprofit that provides a similar service but in a different location, or one that taps similar types of funding but in pursuit of a different issue area). For some practical tips for conducting these conversations, see the sidebar on page 161, "Best Practices for Peer Benchmarking Interviews."

The first pass at identifying a peer group will likely result in a list of organizations with which you are quite familiar. Looking beyond the usual suspects can often bring fresh ideas, however. Strive to include at least two or three organizations that you do not know well. These organizations are often ones with which there is some common bond but also some significant differences. Perhaps these organizations work on different issues but cultivate the same type of funding (e.g., high-net-worth individuals), or pursue a similar programmatic approach to achieving the mission (e.g., advocacy, direct service, lobbying), or focus on similar target beneficiaries of services, or serve a similar geography (e.g., a specific city or state, a similarly sized city, a rural area). If these organizations focus on a unique program niche, there may be fewer "natural" peers to study. If that is the case, you may need to select more nontraditional peers.

WHAT IF AN ORGANIZATION HAS FEW DIRECT PEERS?

If your organization focuses on an uncommon program niche, there may be few (if any) natural peers—heightening the need to get creative in identifying nonprofits from which you can learn.

This was the case for HopeLab, which develops fun, effective technologies to drive positive health behavior in chronically ill young people. An example is its Re-Mission video game, designed to give young cancer patients a sense of power and control over their disease by allowing them to "blast away" at cancer cells and scientifically proven to improve treatment adherence. HopeLab's leaders identified only one direct peer—Benetech, which incubates sustainable technology solutions and relies heavily on government support. They knew they would need to look more broadly for inspiration.

HopeLab's leaders began their search by hypothesizing which types of funding could one day be at the heart of the organization's funding model. They then identified nonprofits known to specialize in cultivating those sources. For example, they researched KaBOOM! (which helps communities build playgrounds) for insight on raising corporate funds, Harvard EdLabs (which conducts education research and development focused on closing the achievement gap) for foundation support, and the Make-A-Wish Foundation (which grants wishes for children with life-threatening medical conditions) for individual donations.

After learning about the keys to these organizations' successful development efforts and comparing them with HopeLab's development capabilities and vision for impact, HopeLab found a closer fit with the approaches for raising government and foundation funds and decided to research their applicability in more depth.

For Rare, branching out meant focusing on organizations that excelled in raising funds from high-net-worth individuals. In addition to its environmental peers, Rare also included education nonprofit Teach For America and international microfinance leader Opportunity International in its benchmark set. Both organizations were known to have developed exceptionally strong individual fund-raising approaches.

Determine the Essential Characteristics of Peer Approaches to Funding

For each peer, first identify the types of funding on which the organization relies. Then, for its top *one* or *two* types of funding, probe deeper to learn more about specific funding sources and tactics. Focusing on the leading sources is often a productive way to guide work, given that most funding models hinge on a single type of funding.

Understand Peers' Overall Funding Mix

Aim to find the last 5 years of total revenue, broken down by each type of funding (i.e., government, foundation, individual, corporate, and earned revenue). Keep in mind, however, that historical revenues may be difficult to find, and data may come in less detail than is ideal. (See the sidebar, "The Art and Science of Benchmarking.") Be sure to understand what the organization's top one or two types of funding are. Even if staff are unable to build a detailed breakout of all the organization's funding, try to develop at least a directional sense (e.g., 70%–80% of funds come from government sources, with the rest mainly from individuals and foundations). If you end up relying heavily on estimates, aim to consult more than one source and cross-check what you learn from each one.

BEST PRACTICES FOR PEER BENCHMARKING INTERVIEWS

- Identify the right contact point: Keep in mind that the most senior person is not necessarily the most knowledgeable. Often, a member of the development team is a better bet.
- Be upfront: Never misrepresent yourself or the reason for the call. Introduce yourself and the organization and tell contacts why your organization needs their help for an important project.
- Make connections: If your organization and its contacts have never worked together with the peer organization before, mention how you found them. Whether the connection was through a mutual friend or staff admired a recently launched program, letting contacts know will help put everyone at ease.
- Make it a two-way street: If your staff are ready and willing to share information about your organization's own development efforts and discuss common challenges, chances are peers will be more open.
- Share results: Contacts may appreciate hearing the results of your organization's benchmarking analysis when it is complete. Just be sure to clarify up front with everyone interviewed the degree of confidentially they can expect.

Respect their time: Before calling, make sure the information being asked for is not displayed on the front page of the organization's website or readily available through other public sources. Know exactly what you would like to get out of the call to avoid having to go back for more information.

Probe Deeper Into the Leading Types of Funding

Now it is time to really understand those top types of funding. The goal here is to develop a sense of the individual funding streams involved—specifically, how many discrete sources the peer organization taps, what those sources are, and what tactics it uses to cultivate them. This knowledge will provide insight into key characteristics of the organization's funding approach—namely, who its main funding decision makers are and, given that generally speaking more sources translate into greater reliability, how reliable its funding base is.

Consider the following probing questions for the peer organization, depending on which type of funding is being investigated (Exhibit 10.2 highlights the primary ones):

- *Government*: What is the organization's mix of federal, state, and local funding? Which grants, contracts, earmarks, and/or government agencies does it tap?
- *Individual*: Do the organization's funds come largely from a handful of wealthy philanthropists or do they consist of many small donations from the general public? (One quick way to figure this out is to determine what percentage of funds comes from the top five donors.) If small donations are key, are they mainly coming from direct mail, special events, online giving, or some combination of these?
- *Foundation*: Does the organization rely on one or two foundations for the majority of its revenue or does it draw revenue more evenly from a larger set of foundations? Do these funds come largely from standard grants or from growth capital grants?
- *Corporate*: Does the majority of the organization's corporate funds originate from one or two companies or does it tap a broad set of businesses? Are the funds in the form of in-kind giving, employee matching programs, or sponsorship and cobranding initiatives? Is philanthropy or corporate goals the primary motivation behind the funds?
- *Earned revenue*: Do these revenues take the form of fees for service or membership fees? If fees for service, does the organization rely on a few key contracts or a broader base? If membership fees, what is its membership base?

THE ART AND SCIENCE OF BENCHMARKING

In an ideal world, you would be able to follow the directions in this section step by step, gathering precise and detailed information from peer organizations. In reality, though, much of this information can be relatively hard to come by. Do not feel discouraged if staff are not able to get all the pieces of information in as much detail as suggested in this guide. When quantitative data are not available, consider using qualitative information to form estimates. Focus on understanding the underlying themes and information and be flexible in considering alternative outputs to those offered as samples here.

Soon after starting the peer research process, Rare confirmed what it had known anecdotally—that many international conservation organizations relied on both individual and government funding. Upon reviewing the African Wildlife Foundation's historical financials, for example, Rare noticed that the organization had both a consistent individual funding base with a number of large individual donors and steadily growing

---

EXHIBIT 10.2 In Review: Key Questions to Consider When Learning From the Funding Approaches of Peer Organizations

- What are the main types of funding on which the peer organizations rely?
- Who are the main entities these organizations need to convince to support their work? What appears to motivate those donors to give?
- What differences between your organization and its peers may limit your ability to pursue their funding approaches?

government funding streams from a variety of sources, including the U.S. Agency for International Development (USAID) and European governments.

Identify Key Programmatic, Financial, and Governance Differences

By now, you should have a fairly good understanding of each peer organization's funding approach. Next comes figuring out how applicable those approaches are to your organization. Identify any key differences between these peer organizations and your organization that could limit your ability to follow in their footsteps. Staff are after points of difference that contribute to peers' funding success.

The attributes used during the scan for peer organizations—such as issue focus, programmatic approach, target beneficiaries, and location—are relevant here, given that they are all things that could factor into why a given funder would support one of the peer organizations but not your own. For example, Rare recognized that funders that were likely to support international conservation were different from funders that supported Opportunity International, which focuses on poverty alleviation. Nevertheless, Rare was able to glean some important lessons about how Opportunity International helped its U.S.-based funders develop a strong sense of affiliation with communities that were thousands of miles away.

Delving deeper, here are a few additional areas in which to probe peers for differences:

- *Organizational structure*: Is the organization configured as a stand-alone entity, as a network unto itself, or as part of a broader network? Within networks, how independently run is each location? A national network may be in a strong position to tap both local and national funding with combined fund-raising efforts on the part of the national office and its affiliates. An organization that is part of a larger network may have fund-raising support from the central office.
- *Age and/or brand recognition*: When was the organization established? How well known is its brand? A more established and better known organization may have an easier time attracting some types of donors, particularly individuals and corporations. Government funders also tend to favor the relative safety of established organizations when awarding grants and contracts.
- *Magnitude of development resources*: What is the organization's budget for development? How many employees and volunteers does it engage in fund-raising activities? This information will give a sense of the resources needed to implement the peer's funding approach at a similar scale. Some funding approaches may require more investment than your organization is willing to make.
- *Results*: Does the organization share its outcome data? Has it tested its results through formal trials by an evaluation expert? Are any of its current funders known for setting a high bar for results? Greater rigor in outcome data can help differentiate an organization from others, giving it an advantage in fund raising. This goes beyond measuring outputs (e.g., number of kids served) to documenting results (e.g., number of kids who graduate from high school). Some funders, including many foundations and government agencies, strongly favor organizations with sophisticated systems for tracking results.
- *Size and prominence of board*: How many members make up the organization's board? How prominent are they? Does a separate advisory board provide additional support? How much are board members expected to contribute and/or raise annually? Board members account for a large percentage of overall revenue at some organizations. Without a complete overhaul of your own board, it could be hard to replicate the peer's approach.

As this information is collected, start forming hypotheses on the extent to which the differences uncovered represent either a fund-raising advantage or a disadvantage relative to your own organization, just as Rare did when considering the applicability of Opportunity International's approach. Note that coming up with this information may very well be a challenge, especially if you are limited to secondary sources. Your staff will likely need to be flexible and a bit creative in creating a profile for each organization.

Step 3: Identify and Narrow the Range of Funding Model Options

By now, staff have likely learned a great deal about how peer organizations get their money. "But which among all these possibilities," you may be asking, "are funding models?" Exactly. Your next step is to identify any funding models your organization might want to replicate. As you will recall, a funding model is defined as a methodical and institutionalized approach to building a reliable revenue base.

Chances are that some of the organizations in the peer group will have clear funding models. Some will be more idiosyncratic in their approaches. The ones with funding models are the gems here, because their funding approaches, by definition, are sustainable and replicable—just what you're after.

By the end of this step, you should be able to:

- List the funding models used by peer organizations
- Decide which of those models are most applicable to your organization

Identify the Funding Models in Use Within the Peer Group

So how can you tell which peers have funding models and which do not? Consider the three defining characteristics of a funding model noted earlier: type of funding, funding decision makers, and funder motivation. Answer the following questions for each peer researched:

- *Type of funding*: What are the organization's major types of funding?
- *Funding decision makers*: For each major type of funding, who determines how much funding is allocated to the organization?
- *Funder motivation*: Why do those decision makers choose to allocate funding to the organization?

If answers to these questions are fuzzy, it is very likely that the peer does not in fact have a funding model. If, however, they are sharp and clear, the chances are good that it does—in which case you will want to figure out which funding model it is. See if the three attributes match any documented nonprofit funding models or if they constitute a new one. "Documented" refers to 10 nonprofit models identified in past research on very large organizations. These 10 are certainly not the only funding models in existence, but they are a good place to start. Descriptions of these models, complete with their funding type, decision makers, and motivations are included in Table 10.2.

After studying its peers, Rare recognized that some did have clear funding models. For example, Conservation International's approach corresponded to the Big Bettor funding model. The organization's ability to identify locations around the world where protecting an area of land could have a significant effect on preserving global biodiversity helps it attract a small number of donors willing to contribute large amounts of money. The African Wildlife Foundation, which manages extensive USAID contracts, matched the description of the Public Provider funding model. NRDC, with its sophisticated small gifts marketing program, fit the Heartfelt Connector mold.

TABLE 10.2 Descriptions of Funding Models

Funding Model	Description	Categorization	Tactical Tools	Example Organizations
Heartfelt Connector	• Mission has broad appeal • Benefits often touch the lives of the funder's family and friends	• Type: Individuals • Decision maker: Many individuals • Motivation: Altruism	• Special events • Direct mail • Corporate sponsorship	• Medical research (Susan G. Komen Foundation) • Environment (NRDC)
Beneficiary Builder	• Mission initially attracts individuals pursuing, and paying for, specific individual benefits • Mission creates a strong individual connection through the delivery of the benefit	• Type: Individuals • Decision maker: Many individuals • Motivation: Self-interest followed by altruism	• Earned income or fees • Major gifts	• Universities (Princeton University) • Hospitals (Cleveland Clinic)
Member Motivator	• Most benefits have a group orientation, creating an inherent community for fund raising	• Type: Individuals • Decision maker: Many individuals • Motivation: Collective interest	• Membership • Fees • Special events • Major gifts • Direct mail	• Religious congregations (Saddleback Church) • Environment and conservation (National Wild Turkey Federation)
Big Bettor	• Majority of support comes from a few individuals or family foundations • Mission may be fulfilled within a limited number of decades	• Type: Individuals/foundations • Decision maker: Few individuals • Motivation: Altruism	• Major gifts	• Medical research (The Stanley Medical Research Institute) • Environment (Conservation International)
Beneficiary Broker	• Individual beneficiaries decide how to spend the government benefit (e.g., charter school vouchers)	• Type: Government • Decision maker: Many individuals • Motivation: Self-interest	• Government reimbursement	• Health (E. Boston Neighborhood Health Center) • Housing (Metro. Boston Housing Partnership) • Employment (Peckham Vocational Industries)
Public Provider	• Services that are perceived as a core government responsibility are provided	• Type: Government • Decision maker: Administrators • Motivation: Collective interest	• Government contracts	• Human services (TMC) • International (Family Health International)

(continued)

TABLE 10.2 Descriptions of Funding Models *(continued)*

Funding Model	Description	Categorization	Tactical Tools	Example Organizations
Policy Innovator	• Government funds are secured for a significant new approach to addressing a problem not currently viewed as a core government responsibility	• Type: Government • Decision maker: Policymakers • Motivation: Collective interest	• Legislative appropriation or earmark • Executive earmark • Government pilot program	• Human services (Youth Villages) • Education (Communities in Schools)
Resource Recycler	• The nonprofit uses goods created in the market economy where there are surpluses (e.g., food) or where marginal costs to produce a product are low (e.g., pharmaceuticals)	• Type: Corporations • Decision maker: Few individuals • Motivation: Self-interest	• In-kind giving	• Food (Oregon Food Bank) • International (AmeriCares Foundation)
Market Maker	• A funder with some degree of self-interest and the ability to pay exists (e.g., a health system buying blood)	• Type: Mixed • Decision maker: Many individuals (one side), few individuals (other side) • Motivation: Altruism (one side), self-interest (other side)	• Earned income or fees • Major gifts (corporate or individual)	• Health (American Kidney Fund) • Environment or conservation (The Trust for Public Land)
Local Nationalizer	• An issue that is a top local priority is addressed • That issue is common enough to exist in many localities nationwide	• Type: Mixed • Decision maker: Few individuals • Motivation: Altruism	• Major gifts • Special events	• Youth development (Big Brothers Big Sisters of America) • Education (Teach For America)

Some peer organizations embody more than one or two of these models. In fact, non-profit leaders frequently describe efforts to pursue three, four, or even more models. While this is theoretically not impossible, the odds of pulling off such a scattershot approach (i.e., making that many successful matches with donor motivations, developing the necessary capabilities to cultivate that many different types of funding well) are incredibly low. In prior research on large organizations, the vast majority had one dominant funding model, a few had two, and none had three or more. Accordingly, it is far more likely that what is being observed is an idiosyncratic grab bag of funding approaches rather than a collection of viable funding models. Tip-offs here include volatility in the organization's revenue mix or total amount of revenue over the 5-year period studied in Step 2.

Bear in mind that the list of 10 funding models is not comprehensive, given that it is derived from studying organizations that have reached $50 million in annual revenue. A wider array of funding models applies for smaller nonprofits. So even though there is not yet a match, an organization *may* still be dealing with a viable funding model.

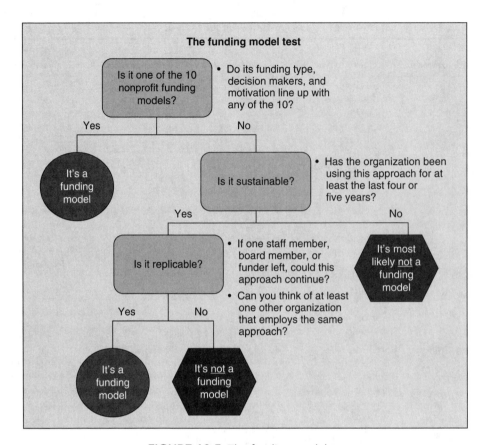

FIGURE 10.5 The funding model test.

For example, Rare observed that some peer organizations seemed to depend on support from a *network* of high-net-worth individuals. This approach did not meet the criteria for the Big Bettor model, with its traditional reliance on a *small number* of ultra-high-net-worth individuals. While it matched the Local Nationalizer model on the network dimension, a key point of departure existed: While the peers' funders supported overseas issues, Local Nationalizer funders focused on issues in their own communities. Nevertheless, out of Rare's research and internal knowledge emerged a clear donor profile for individuals who funded international conservation efforts. So they kept this approach on the list even though it was not one of the 10 established funding models.

More generally, staff need to determine if the peer's funding approach is sustainable and replicable—the hallmarks of a funding model (see Figure 10.5). Start by assessing its sustainability. How long has the organization been following the funding approach in question? If it is 2 years or fewer, its approach could very well be short term or opportunistic.

As for replicability, make sure that the organization's funding success is not inextricably tied to a unique asset—such as a specific leader or board member or an unmatched set of resources or capabilities. Additionally, take some time to see if there are any other organizations that use this model; if your organization cannot, there is likely a reason.

Consider, for example, the Council of Chief State School Officers (CCSSO), a national membership organization of public officials who head departments of elementary and secondary education. CCSSO provides leadership, advocacy, and technical assistance on major educational issues. Most of its revenue comes from foundations, but it does not fit the mold of the aforementioned foundation-driven (or wealthy-individual-driven) Big Bettor model. CCSSO's decision makers include many foundation program officers who contract with CCSSO for specific projects, compared with the Big Bettor model, in which a small number of individuals provide grants altruistically to help the organization wipe out a societal problem within a foreseeable time frame.

Does CCSSO's approach constitute a funding model? The organization's revenue and revenue mix have been relatively stable at just under $25 million per year with consistent sources, making for a "yes" on sustainability. Because the foundations that contract with CCSSO do so primarily on the basis of the organization's expertise (rather than personal relationships or some other hard to match attribute), it is reasonable to assume that a similarly skilled organization could replicate its approach. In fact, nonprofit consulting organizations, such as The Bridgespan Group, and advocacy organizations, such as the Center for Law and Social Policy, also use this funding model, which is akin to a business-to-business model.

Determine Which Peer Funding Models May Be Feasible

Now it is time to do an initial assessment to narrow down the list of peer funding models to those that seem as if they could apply to your organization—ideally just two to four models. Doing so will allow you to focus on in-depth assessments of their pluses and minuses.

For each funding model on the short list, consider your organization's fit along the following dimensions:

The three defining characteristics of the model—type of funding, funder decision makers, and funder motivations: For the model's primary type(s) of funding, would the program model allow staff to appeal successfully to the relevant decision makers, tapping into the same motivations that lay behind their funding of peer organizations? To do so, would staff need to make any changes to the program model, such as adjusting existing programs, adding new ones, serving different beneficiaries, or expanding to new locations? Would they be willing to make those changes?

Fund development capabilities: Does your organization have the capabilities required to access the relevant sources of funds? For example, could it cultivate wealthy individual donors or manage the complexities of government contracting? If not, could it realistically develop those capabilities? Does the organization have the appetite for doing so?

Funding model goals: Will the funding model support the goals staff laid out while working on the "getting ready" section of this guide? For example, can it get your organization to the size staff aspire to achieve? (If the peers that use the model are smaller than your target, it is quite possible that the funding model would not get you to the desired size.)

See Table 10.3 for some more detailed questions tailored to the 10 funding models that are common in large organizations.

Two funding models were particularly prevalent in Rare's peer group: the Public Provider funding model and the previously mentioned model (Table 10.3) that revolved around networks of high-net-worth individuals. Both warranted further investigation.

Two other funding models—Big Bettor and Heartfelt Connector—were also represented in Rare's peer group, but with less frequency. Given this difference, Rare looked at them with an even more critical eye. Rare's social marketing was not the sort of approach that could eradicate a given environmental conservation issue in a relatively small number of years—the time frame and results Big Bettor donors look for—but rather was geared toward continual progress over several years. Similarly, its science-based marketing efforts did not tend to evoke the emotional response in small individual donors that

TABLE 10.3 Key Questions to Assess the Feasibility of a Funding Model

Funding Model	Key Questions to Assess the Feasibility of a Funding Model
Heartfelt Connector	• Has a large cross-section of people already shown that they will fund causes in this domain? • Can you communicate what is compelling about your nonprofit in a simple and concise way? • Does a natural avenue exist to attract and involve large numbers of volunteers? • Do you have or can you develop the capabilities to attempt broad outreach in even one geographic area?
Beneficiary Builder	• Does your mission create an individual benefit that is also perceived as an important social good? • Do individuals develop a deep loyalty to your organization in the course of receiving its individual benefit? • Do you have the infrastructure to reach out to beneficiaries in a scalable fashion?
Member Motivator	• Will your members feel that the actions of the organization are directly benefiting them, even if the benefit is shared collectively? • Do you have the ability to involve and manage your members in fund-raising activities? • Can you commit to staying in tune with, and faithful to, your core membership even if it means turning down funding opportunities and not pursuing activities that fail to resonate with your members?
Big Bettor	• Can you create a tangible and lasting solution to a major problem in a foreseeable time frame? • Can you clearly articulate how you will use large-scale funding to achieve your goals? • Are any of the wealthiest individuals or foundations interested in your issue and approach?
Beneficiary Broker	• Can you demonstrate to the government your superior ability to connect benefit or voucher holders with benefits, such as successful placement rates and customer satisfaction feedback? • Can you develop supplemental services that maximize the value of the benefit? • Can you attract enough clients/customers? • Can you master the government regulations and requirements needed to provide these benefits? • Can you find ways to raise money to supplement the fees you receive from the benefits program?
Public Provider	• Is your organization a natural match with one or more large, preexisting government programs? • Can you demonstrate that your organization will do a better job than your competitors? • Are you willing to take the time to secure contract renewals on a regular basis?
Policy Innovator	• Do you provide an innovative approach that surpasses the status quo (in impact and cost) and is compelling enough to attract government funders, which tend to gravitate toward traditional solutions? • Can you provide government funders with evidence that your program works? • Are you willing and able to cultivate strong relationships with government decision makers who will advocate change? • At this time, are there sufficient pressures on government to overturn the status quo?
Resource Recycler	• Are the products that you distribute likely to be donated on an ongoing basis? • Can you develop the expertise to stay abreast of trends in the industries that donate products to you, so you can prepare for fluctuations in donations? • Do you have a strategy for attracting the cash you'll need to fund operations and overhead?
Market Maker	• Is there a group of funders with a financial interest in supporting your work? • Are there legal or ethical reasons why having a nonprofit deliver the services would be more appropriate? • Do you already have a trusted program and brand name?

(continued)

TABLE 10.3 Key Questions to Assess the Feasibility of a Funding Model *(continued)*

Funding Model	Key Questions to Assess the Feasibility of a Funding Model
Local Nationalizer	• Does your cause address an issue that local leaders consider a high priority, and is this issue compelling in communities across the country? • Does expanding your organization into other communities fulfill your mission? • Can you replicate your model in other communities? • Are you committed to identifying and empowering high-performing leaders to run local branches of your organization in other communities?

is characteristic of the Heartfelt Connector model. Rare decided to cross both of these models off its list. Rare's senior vice president of strategy and growth, Martha Piper, saw great value in this step, noting that, "One of the most helpful exercises was eliminating models we didn't want to pursue. We no longer needed to talk about mass mailings or other similar marketing tactics."

In Review: Key Questions to Consider When Identifying and Narrowing the Range of Funding Model Options

• What is the range of funding models among the peer group?
• What is your organization's appetite for change from the way things are done today?
• What are the main benefits of moving to the funding model in consideration? What might be lost?

Step 4: Evaluate Revenue Potential and Costs of Short-List Funding Models

Now that a short list of potential funding models has been developed, staff will take an in-depth look at how realistic those options are from a cost–benefit perspective, building on the initial assessment in Step 3. Here, staff will get a directional sense for both how much revenue they can reasonably expect to access through each model and what investments in your organization's programs, staff, and systems would be required. This knowledge will put you and your staff in a good position to make an informed decision about which funding model(s) to pursue.

By the end of this step, staff should be able to:

• Understand the funding available for each funding model on the short list, as well as the competitive environment for that money
• Describe how likely the organization is to secure significant dollars through each model
• Estimate the investments the organization would need to make to pursue each model

Understand the Funding Available
There is a wealth of readily available information that can help staff understand the revenue potential of a given funding model. With the options now down to just a few models, staff can conduct research in a targeted way. For each of the funding models on the short list, focus on the leading type(s) of funding on which the funding model is built, using the following questions to guide efforts:

Which funding sources should your organization prioritize? It is important to get specific here. Perhaps your priority is the few dozen high-net-worth donors with an affinity for your organization's issue area, or a particular federal funding stream that aligns well with your services and target beneficiaries. If peers have been particularly successful with a source, chances are you will want to pay close attention to it, too.

How many total dollars are awarded annually through each of the prioritized funding sources? This information will allow staff to see if the dollars associated with the funding model match the scale of your organization's size aspirations. If, for example, staff hope to secure $10 million annually from foundations, but total foundation giving to the organization's area only averages $20 million each year, chances are staff will be hard-pressed to hit their fund-raising target.

"FALSE POSITIVES" ON GOVERNMENT FUNDING WEBSITES

Early scans of government websites often turn up long lists of potentially promising grants and contracts. The reality is that closer examination will undoubtedly reveal that the majority are not in fact relevant. Digging into their requirements is essential to getting a true read on prospects for government funding.

How competitive is the environment for these funding sources? Understand which other organizations are going after the same funding sources. This will help staff gauge how difficult securing funding would be—and thus how much of it your organization could reasonably expect to access. Would it be one of the first organizations to access a source of funding? Is it competing with many similar nonprofits? Another important indicator is the average grant or contribution size relative to the total dollars awarded; the more concentrated the opportunities, the more pressure on the organization to stack up favorably against competing organizations.

Beyond mining previous peer benchmarking work, website research and expert interviews can both be effective approaches here. With government funding, for example, staff may want to start by canvassing websites such as Grants.gov and those of relevant state government departments and then filling in any important knowledge gaps by interviewing relevant public officials. For foundation funding, staff will likely want to spend some time on the Foundation Center's online database, which will allow them to determine total foundation giving to your organization's issue area and to pinpoint foundations that seem to be a good fit based on their giving history. (For more detail on how to research the funding available for various funding models, please see Appendix C.)

By way of example, consider Rare's experience exploring the potential of the Public Provider funding model. One of the public funding sources Rare's management team researched was USAID, having noted that several peer organizations received USAID contract funding. Canvassing USAID.gov gave them a detailed understanding of how much USAID funding had gone to international conservation over the past several years in the countries where Rare had (or was planning to establish) programs. They then interviewed contacts at peer organizations and USAID to gauge how much funding an organization like Rare could reasonably expect to access. USAID emerged as a promising funding source that could help Rare achieve its growth goals.

Rare also sought to understand the market for high-net-worth individuals who give to environmental issues. They referenced the Center on Philanthropy's "Million Dollar List," a list of individuals who have made gifts of more than $1 million, segmented by issue area. They complemented these data by interviewing contacts at a number of peer organizations. Through this research, Rare identified promising pockets of high-net-worth individuals living in a handful of urban areas beyond the small geographic area where Rare's current donors were clustered.

Determine the Strength of an Organization's Fit

Beyond the competitive environment for funds, another big variable is how well your organization fits with that funding model. Chances are the fit is at least pretty good, given that the model has made the short list. The better the fit, however, the further you are likely to get.

Consider three factors:

Funding motivation: How well does your organization's work align with the motivations behind the key funding decision makers associated with the funding model?

Requirements to access funding: Could your organization realistically satisfy the eligibility rules, programmatic requirements, and necessary processes to qualify for this funding source?

Peer funding recipients: How is your organization similar (or dissimilar) to other nonprofits that have been particularly successful in securing this funding source in the past? (The peer research from Step 2 will be helpful here.)

When Rare's management team evaluated the organization's fit with USAID funding, for example, they reasoned that Rare possessed the same qualifications that made its peer organizations successful at accessing the funding—conservation programs with proven results in countries where USAID invested in biodiversity. The team confirmed that Rare would be a viable candidate by interviewing peers and researching the qualification criteria for USAID's funding outlined on USAID's website.

Estimate the Required Investments

Staff now have a good handle on the upside associated with the funding models on the short list. But as the old adage goes, "nothing in life is free." Adopting a new funding model often requires investments in programs, staff, IT systems, and communication materials, with some funding models requiring higher levels of investment than others. That level of investment is an important consideration when deciding which model to pick, not the least because things that are harder to do often bring a higher risk of failure. In addition to the sidebar on the following page, Exhibit 10.3 offers a few other questions you will want to consider from the financial/investment angle.

EXHIBIT 10.3 In Review: Key Questions to Consider When Evaluating the Revenue Potential and Costs of Short-List Funding Models

- How many dollars can your organization realistically capture, given how many others provide services similar to yours and given your ability to distinguish yourself?
- How might you need to adapt your programs, staff, IT systems, and communications to meet the requirements of a particular funding model? What are you not willing to change?
- Do the benefits of this funding model outweigh its costs?

Programs

Program investments may be essential for some funding sources, particularly in the government realm. Sometimes these changes take the form of adapting existing programs to meet the funding source's standards (say by extending the length of time your organization works with a given program recipient). You may even need to introduce an entirely new program or serve a different group of beneficiaries.

QUESTIONS TO GAUGE THE REQUIRED INVESTMENT

The following questions can help staff wrap their heads around the investments required to adopt a given funding model. Peer research can come in handy again, illuminating some of the likely areas of investment.

Programs

- Would you need to adapt current programs in a major way (e.g., offer additional services, modify existing services)?
- Would your organization need to introduce new programs?
- Would you need to target different beneficiaries?

Personnel

- Would your organization need to create and fill new roles (e.g., hiring a government relations expert for the first time)?
- Would the CEO's role need to evolve? How would you need to support that evolution (e.g., bringing in a COO to free up the CEO's time to lead priority development efforts)?
- Would you need to rehire for existing roles (e.g., if a current program director lacks the skills to adapt to the new funding strategy)?
- Would you need to hire more staff to give it sufficient resources to pursue additional funding?
- Would you need to provide staff with additional training?

IT Systems

- Would your organization need to enhance data management systems to support performance management and reporting efforts?
- Would you need to improve your donor management system?

Communication Materials

- Would you need to develop new marketing materials?
- Would you need to engage outside specialists to improve your grant applications?

Tread carefully when exploring program investments, though. The strongest organizations tend to be the ones that remain focused on what they do best. Any changes staff decide to make to your program offering should improve *both* the likelihood of securing funding and, more importantly, the organization's ability to make progress on the issue it cares about. BELL, the after-school and summertime learning organization discussed in the introduction, had to make several hard decisions involving program investments. Accessing Title I SES funding would require it to make only modest changes to its programming. In contrast, several other funding streams that targeted related but different program outcomes, such as early child advocacy, would have required much more substantive changes—changes BELL elected not to pursue for fear that doing so would compromise the organization's mission.

In the case of Rare, research on USAID and other public funding opportunities revealed a sufficient number of contracts that aligned with Rare's existing approach, so it did not have to pursue program modifications. It would forego the opportunities that were beyond the organization's current program focus and target countries.

Personnel

New capabilities and more staff time are often required to source and manage the funds associated with a new model. Staff may find that they need to create and fill new roles, evolve the CEO's role in development, replace existing staff who lack the skills the new funding model demands, add more staff in areas where capacity is constrained, and/or provide additional training. These personnel investments may not all fall directly into the development arm of your organization.

For example, staff may need to:

- Add marketing staff if your organization plans to pursue an individual funding strategy
- Enhance your organization's performance measurement capabilities if new funders require increased reporting
- Develop new skills among program staff if your organization is planning to make significant programmatic changes
- Allocate significant ED time if the organization intends to cultivate relationships with new foundations

Rare spent a fair bit of time figuring out the personnel implications of pursuing public funding, given that its development team was built around individual fundraising. Through interviews with peers and public funding contracts, Rare learned that organizations that successfully accessed key sources of public funding had a number of key development staff who specialized in cultivating those sources. While Rare had some government funding, it realized from its work in Step 1 that the team was not well equipped to deal with public funding contracts at any meaningful level of scale. Rare recognized that hiring development staff with these skills would be a necessary investment but decided that the potential funding available outweighed the cost of bringing on new staff.

IT Systems

New funding models often place greater demands on IT systems, particularly related to performance measurement. Existing data management systems may not be sufficient to support the reporting requirements of new funders and/or to provide your organization with the information needed to manage a growing organization effectively. Additionally, stepped-up efforts to cultivate individual donors could require an enhanced online donor management system.

Rare had learned from its public funding research that organizations with demonstrable results had the advantage. Fortunately, Rare had already invested in a performance monitoring system that would support the associated reporting requirements.

Communication Materials

New funding models may make it more important to have top-notch communication materials to support external relations and marketing. Perhaps a more compelling annual report will be important in cultivating individual donors. Or maybe your grant applications need more depth if your organization is to win new government contracts or foundation grants.

Rare learned that the NRDC's small-gifts marketing campaigns were more successful when its mailings included clear visuals of "charismatic" animals like polar bears and details of how contributions would support efforts to protect them. While Rare did not believe that it should go after the same type of donors that NRDC generally sought, learning about NRDC's communications strategy led Rare to consider how it might need to invest in this area.

Step 5: Select Funding Models to Implement

Now it is time to select one or two funding models to implement, considering the questions summarized in Exhibit 10.4. There is no math formula or complex decision rule to dictate the answer here. Staff just have to draw upon all their hard work from Steps 1 through 4, use best judgment, and make the call.

DO NOT THROW THE BABY OUT WITH THE BATH WATER

Developing a funding model does not mean that an organization should relinquish existing funding sources that do not fit with the new model. In fact, those sources often play complementary roles on a sustained basis by, for example, advancing a particular program or organizational objective for which the new model is not well suited or providing a buffer against funding volatility.

For example, while Susan G. Komen for the Cure derives the bulk of its revenue from small, individual donations, corporate sponsorships for its breast cancer walks constitute a healthy secondary source. One of Rare's important secondary sources was foundation support; beyond financial contributions, foundations provided the organization with highly valuable thought partnership on programs and also played a critical role in validating Rare's program for other donors. Rather than abandoning efforts to cultivate existing sources, pursuing a funding model involves focusing the next set of investments of time and staff on funding sources that are closely aligned with the model. The new sources will become the growth engines for the future, while revenues from current sources may remain roughly steady and thus represent a declining share of the organization's growing funding base.

You may be wondering why you should choose only one or two models. Why not pursue all options that seem promising? In short, implementing more than two carries a high risk of overtaxing management and development staff. Succeeding with a funding model

---

EXHIBIT 10.4 In Review: Key Questions to Consider When Selecting Funding Models to Implement

- What funding model options are most likely to help you achieve the goals that the organization set for itself at the onset of the process?
- Would the board and other stakeholders support the investments required to develop this funding model over time?

---

hinges on getting really good at cultivating its characteristic funding sources, so splitting staff in too many directions is bound to undermine these efforts. When none of the models shows the hoped-for results (as will likely be the case), staff will be hard pressed to discern which failed due to poor fit versus underinvestment. On the flip side, you may be wondering why you should consider implementing two instead of just one. After all, Bridgespan's research has shown that large nonprofits tend to have only one funding model. The issue here is uncertainty. Despite all the research, at this stage it may still be difficult to really know which model will work best for a given organization. If so, before fully committing to one, consider trying out the two most promising options to see which has the most success.

Have one or two strong front-runners already emerged as staff have navigated Steps 1 through 4? If so, reach out to key stakeholders on the board and staff to make sure they would support the decision to pursue and invest in building them.

Do three or more funding models still seem appealing? Well, then it is time to make some tough choices to further narrow down the list. Compare each model that remains on the list across the dimensions investigated in Step 4—the amount of funding available, your organization's ability to access that funding, and the investments required to do so. Staff may want to go as far as to develop a simple scorecard that the steering committee could use to rate each funding model option on these three dimensions.

When Rare decided to pick a funding model or two to implement, its management team remained confident that a funding strategy anchored around public funders had high potential. The team also recognized that the organization was not yet positioned to maximize those funding streams because it did not have the right development staff in place. Accordingly, Rare's leadership team and board decided that over the next 3 years the organization would strengthen its longtime individual giving strategy while also pursuing the Public Provider funding model. By investing in both its current capabilities and its long-term funding aspirations, Rare's leadership had a plan to strengthen the organization's short- and long-term outlooks. There was a great deal of energy and enthusiasm behind these decisions, with Senior Vice President Piper noting that, "Doing the analysis and using the data enabled us to make choices with confidence." (See Figures 10.6 and 10.7, which show the model implementation overview and milestones that Rare's team established after completing the process.)

Step 6: Develop an Implementation Plan

Congratulations on making it to the sixth and final step. The goal now is to make the funding model plans actionable by developing an implementation strategy.

As noted at the outset of this guide, creating a funding model will not happen overnight, or even in 6 months for that matter. Building the right capabilities, finding the right people, and forging the right relationships take time. Funding models typically require 2 to 3 years to take hold. A good implementation plan is an invaluable resource as your organization navigates that journey.

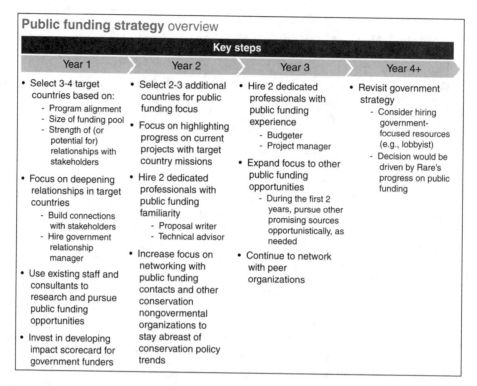

FIGURE 10.6 Rare's public funding model plan.

Public funding strategy milestones

Milestone	FY10	FY11	FY12	FY13+
Determine short list of public funding priority countries	X			
Schedule introductory conversations with stakeholders in potential priority countries	X			
Establish 3-4 priority countries	X			
Hire relationship manager	X			
Commit additional investment into impact assessment	X	X		
Cultivate relationships with other missions and public funding sources		X		
Identify additional priority countries		X		
Commit to regular presence with peer organizations on funding trends		X		
Hire proposal writer		X		
Hire technical advisor		X		
Hire budgeter			X	
Hire project manager			X	
Revisit need for DC lobbyist				X

FIGURE 10.7 Rare's public funding model milestones.

The implementation plan will give staff and board a shared vision of where the organization is heading. It will spell out the intermediate steps required to get from the current funding approach to the desired funding model(s), thereby helping to coordinate staff efforts and increasing the odds that efforts will be successful. It will also establish clear milestones and a learning agenda, making it easier to track progress and make course corrections.

Exhibit 10.5 summarizes the questions you'll want to answer as you develop your plan. By the end of this step, you should be able to:

- Describe in detail the investments your organization will need to make
- Create a step-by-step plan for making those investments and implementing the funding model
- Understand the communication and monitoring commitments required to keep implementation efforts on track

COMMUNICATE, COMMUNICATE, COMMUNICATE

Even the best-laid implementation plan will go nowhere if the individuals required to make it happen are not onboard. That means committing deeply to communicating at every step of the way. At any given time, are key stakeholders clear on the plan? Are they aware of the priority investments required to bring the plan to fruition? Are they clear on their roles in making that happen? Are they aware of the progress that has been made and of the roadblocks encountered? Consider these questions periodically, and double down communication activities if the answers are "no" or "I'm not sure."

There are a lot of stakeholders to keep in mind here—the senior team, the development team, staff in general, the board, and key funders. Be thoughtful about the information needs of each (frequency, level of detail, format) and tailor communications accordingly. For example, perhaps the full development team will need weekly live check-ins and the board will require monthly memos and quarterly advisory discussions.

EXHIBIT 10.5 In Review: Key Questions to Consider When Developing an Implementation Plan

- Are key stakeholders—including board and current staff—on board with the plan?
- Of the many potential changes and investments your organization could make to increase its success, which will have the most impact for the least cost?
- How will your organization make sure that it is successfully implementing the chosen funding model(s)? How will you hold staff accountable for this success?
- Does your organization have a clear learning agenda that will help keep it on track?
- Is your organization making appropriate progress toward its ultimate goal? If not, how can you recalibrate so that you meet the goals you set at the start of this process?

Crystallize Priority Investments

In Step 4, staff identified the key program, personnel, IT system, and communications investments required to pursue the chosen funding model(s). Now it is time to revisit that list and make it much more specific. Maybe staff will need to determine how many more hours of programming each service recipient will need, or which personnel will shift into new roles and how they will get the necessary training to transition successfully, the detailed requirements of the new IT system or the marketing materials that need to be developed.

Staff will also want to revisit their initial takes on whether the potential benefits of the investments outweigh the costs. Make extra certain that they do. If not, cross them off the to-do list. Is the current system good enough for funders, or would incremental improvements make the difference between getting and not getting money?

There may very well be many changes worth making—more than staff could possibly undertake at once. As with the rest of this process, be focused and disciplined in selecting the few changes that will have the highest impact in setting your organization up for funding success.

During Step 4, Rare recognized that the organization would need to make investments in personnel. Once it decided to move forward, the team researched in greater depth what it would take to build a high-performing development team that could cultivate public funding successfully. Additional interviews with peers and public funding contacts indicated that the organization would eventually need to fill a small set of specific, specialized roles. Rare also learned that applying for the contracts would require some support from program staff as well and factored that knowledge into its planning and budgeting. Senior Vice President Piper underscored how useful this research was, sharing that, "This analysis helped me really understand the different types of fund-raising professionals I needed to hire."

Lay Out Specific Steps and Milestones

Once priority investments have been decided on, staff will be ready to detail a plan for implementing them, complete with specific milestones to target. Consider the following tactics that have been found to work well:

- *Break broad to-dos down into smaller, more actionable steps.* For example, "Develop new marketing materials for high-net-worth donors" might become: (a) Identify the key characteristics of high-net-worth donors; (b) prepare a list of key messages to highlight; (c) prepare draft materials, based on key messages; and (d) revise draft materials with team feedback.
- *Get as detailed as need be for the to-dos to truly feel actionable.* For example, staff may find that "Identify the key characteristics of high-net-worth donors" is too vague to marshal the team's efforts and that crystallizing the individual steps (e.g., interviewing potential donors, speaking with colleagues at peer organizations, and researching the typical behavior of high-net-worth donors) is a better level of detail for the work plan.
- *Assign clear accountability.* Each broad to-do should have an overall point person, and each substep should belong to a specific staff member (who may or may not be the same as the overall point person). Set deadlines against each to-do to clearly understand if things are on track.
- *Set milestones that focus on results rather than pure process.* Doing so will help to track whether progress on the to-dos is translating to progress on implementing the chosen funding model. A well-developed set of milestones is one that leads, in logical steps, to the ambitious goals that have been set. For marketing materials, these might read

"By 6 months, distribute marketing materials to 12 high-net-worth individuals. By 12 months, secure donations from at least three of those individuals."

* *Keep in mind any other major initiatives within the organization that will draw on the team's time and energy.* Make sure the plan is realistic in that context. If it is too much too fast, adjust the timeline or sequence initiatives or otherwise scale back ambitions.

Prepare to Learn and Adjust

The more explicit the staff are about what they hope to learn as they try to implement their chosen funding model(s), the more likely they are to learn it—and to learn it quickly. This is where setting a formal learning agenda can be invaluable. What key assumptions were made when staff decided to implement a given funding model? How will your organization understand whether those assumptions were correct or not? Having a learning agenda will make it far easier to see if the beliefs on which staff based their choice of funding model are bearing out.

The Rare team, for example, flagged some important areas of uncertainty related to the intricate workings of public funding. It charted a path to clarify them over time, with the development staff lining up discussions with funders, development consultants, and counterparts at peer organizations—so it could ask more specific questions about the rules of public funding and opportunities. Having a clear learning agenda helped the Rare team gather the information it needed to fine-tune the government funding strategy in accordance with the most promising opportunities.

Like Rare, your organization will want to keep its eyes wide open to indications that course corrections are necessary. If you find that you are not hitting multiple milestones and you are debunking key assumptions underlying your choice of funding model, it may be time to reevaluate your approach ; Exhibit 10.6 highlights some questions you and your staff will want to answer as you examine it. This is not unusual. As an organization moves forward in implementation, it is bound to learn more about both internal and external factors that will influence its approach. The most successful organizations are those that are willing to use real-time lessons to reshape and refocus their efforts when appropriate. Of course, it is not wise to change course drastically at every little setback, but missed milestones should urge careful reflection on what your organization can do to improve.

EXHIBIT 10.6 In Review: Key Questions to Consider When Analyzing Your Current Funding Approach

* What are the biggest limitations of your current funding approach? Which of these are the highest priorities to address with the new funding model?
* What inspires the most loyal funders to support your organization?
* What are your organization's strengths and weaknesses when it comes to revenue generation? Which of these can be easily addressed (e.g., hiring one new development person if the team is stretched too thin)? Which are harder to change (e.g., building an entirely new skill set in development staff)?
* Can key stakeholders—such as the board and senior management—clearly articulate your funding approach? If not, what steps can be taken to provide greater clarity *before* discussing future funding model options?
* Which funding sources is the organization interested in researching further? Why do staff think each source may be promising?

CLOSING THOUGHTS

The funding paths that nonprofits take will vary. Some will find models that support large-scale programs, while others will not. All can benefit, however, from greater clarity about how they can sustainably fund their critically important contributions to society.

As a result of its search and its effective implementation of a funding model, BELL can now predictably cover 70% of its costs in any locality. With this model in place, BELL has been able to expand much more rapidly than leadership originally envisioned. In 2004, when its funding model first took shape, BELL was reaching 1,500 students. Today, it is reaching 15,000.

Rare, while not quite as far along in the journey, is allocating staff time and making key investments to fortify its individual donor-based funding model and to develop a new funding model rooted in government funding. Along the way, the organization is building essential knowledge and experience about how these funding models will work in practice.

With individual funding, Rare has succeeded in spreading fund-raising efforts beyond President and CEO Brett Jenks's hiring three additional individual fund raisers. Each covers a specific region of the United States where individuals who support international conservation are clustered, and each has a team of existing major donors and board members providing support.

Rare has also made progress in pursuing funding. For example, it recently won a $2 million contract from the German development group Deutsche Gesellschaft fur Internationale Zusammenarbeit (GIZ) and is working with U.S.-based government contractor Chemonics on a USAID project. Through its implementation efforts, Rare has learned a lot, and the management team is adapting its plans accordingly. Most notably, the organization has shifted its public funding focus to cultivate the sources that showed the most promise during the first 12 months of piloting the Public Provider model.

There have also been important investments in communications. As Rare has expanded its fund-raising staff and programs, its management team has found that it has needed to get really clear on its messaging so that staff can represent the organization's efforts in a consistent way. To that end, Rare is in the middle of a rebranding project.

Reflecting on this journey, Jenks noted,

> Clarity is king when running a nonprofit. Picking a sensible revenue model was one of the most liberating and clarifying things we've done to date. I empathize with leaders who constantly wonder (or are constantly asked), why not membership, what about online giving, how about government grants, or fee or service? Taking "maybe" out of the process has already boosted our bottom line.

NOTE

1. This chapter is based on an article by the authors that appeared in *Stanford Social Innovation Review*, "Finding Your Funding Model" (2011, Fall).

MARKETING AND COMMUNICATION

Dina Wolfman Baker and Theodore Search

The art of communication is the language of leadership.
—James Humes

You can have brilliant ideas, but if you can't get them across, your ideas won't
get you anywhere.
—Lee Iacocca

Communication with both external and internal communities is essential to organizations'
success in achieving their missions. Effective marketing requires an integrated approach
and a structure to carry out its planning and implementation. The first part of this chapter
discusses the importance of integrating marketing with an organization's mission and
goals and describes the structural levels that can produce a cost-effective marketing strategy with messaging as its centerpiece. The second section examines cause marketing,
which can serve as a link between corporate support and societal needs as well as a means
to engage individual consumers in the support of an initiative. The third portion explores
the global phenomenon of social media, which is quickly becoming a major form of communication. Three aspects of social media are discussed: the generation factor, the power
of social marketing within niche networks, and the power of a connected organization.
Examples from Public Health Management Corporation (PHMC), A Drink for Tomorrow
(ADFT), and the niche social networking provider Skipta are included.

A STRATEGIC APPROACH TO COST-EFFECTIVE
MARKETING FOR NONPROFITS

In response to the economic downturn, many nonprofits are taking a renewed look at their
marketing and communication efforts in an effort to get more for less. If they were already
executing a well-developed strategic plan, however, they probably would have been achieving an excellent return on their marketing investment (the definition of getting more for

less). In addition, they would be well positioned to determine where they could further cut their investment without destroying their returns. If, on the other hand, they were taking a scattershot or reactive approach to their marketing and communication efforts, it is unlikely they would have been getting a sufficient return on their investment of time, money, and creativity. No matter what the economy, this dynamic should be unacceptable.

Integration

The key to building *cost*-effective marketing and communication is no different from the key to building *effective* marketing and communication. It depends on building an effective strategy, and the first key to that is integration.

Marketing is not simply about good, creative ideas. A good idea that fails to integrate with the rest of a campaign, message, mission, or any other organizational or marketing goals will not yield sufficient return on investment (ROI). When everything is integrated, each element helps the others perform better. Think of it this way: A thumb is a great idea, but the opposable digit does not give much return without a hand to oppose it...and that works best with an arm to connect it...and so on right to the brain function that maps it all out to work together.

In 2008, PHMC developed and executed a comprehensive rebranding strategy. The initial indicators of success were impressive. PHMC's average number of monthly media stories increased nearly 28% in the year after the hard launch of the new brand, and more than 45% if one outlier month is excluded (when a PHMC program made national news just before the launch). Apart from that outlier period, in the 1-month period immediately following the hard launch, PHMC experienced its highest ever number of media impressions. The day PHMC sent its initial e-vite to the launch event, web visits jumped from 192 per day to 760 per day and remained high, with an average of 465 per day for the month. Key reporters stated that the rebranding effort and associated media activities helped them to understand the depth and breadth of PHMC as a news resource, and there have been various anecdotal stories of the brand campaign's success.

What is more, PHMC maintained these positive results, as measured against a series of rebranding objectives in comprehensive stakeholder research conducted in fall 2009, 1 year after the hard launch (Table 11.1). The objectives reflect areas in which PHMC had identified deficits prior to the rebranding and had thus designed the rebranding components, launch, and ongoing dissemination to help address them.

The campaign involved many elements—renaming the organization, developing a new logo and colors, issuing news releases, pitching related business stories, planning an event, developing a brochure, and much more. This is what is crucial to understand: Many of the very same tactics could have been executed, yet the campaign could still have failed without full integration. For example, sending the news release would have been far less effective—and possibly even harmful—had we not prepared PHMC employees by training them to understand, live, and communicate the brand and purpose.

So, rule number one is integration. It is generally believed in marketing circles that it takes five to seven impressions to be remembered. Make that five to seven integrated, strategically related impressions.

Structure

If integration is rule number one, then it is important to understand how to achieve integration. That comes from rule number two: structure.

TABLE 11.1 Public Health Management Corporation Rebranding

Objective	Result
Brand awareness: Develop brand awareness with a regional reach (beyond Philadelphia); communicate that PHMC is a nonprofit public health institute.	Most of the community demonstrated awareness of the rebranding, with the majority favoring it; it reached as far as Bucks County with 83.5% awareness. Nearly 83% of respondents understood that "a nonprofit public health institute" was part of the PHMC identity.
Cohesion: Help build cohesion across the organization.	More than 50% of employees were aware of the relationship among the parent organization, its programs, and its affiliates, and more than 80% were moderately aware or higher; more than 80% correctly identified PHMC's mission. Among management of the affiliates, more than 88% felt valued by PHMC. Approximately 75% of all employees rated the personal level of intraorganizational relations to be at least somewhat strong, suggesting that the previous internal perception of the organization as "too big" and "too cold" was being dispelled.
Management: Highlight the value and strength of the organization's management role and capabilities; communicate PHMC's ability to leverage funds and connect services; impress upon stakeholders the value and rigor of PHMC's business model.	Nearly all stakeholder groups responded very positively regarding PHMC's responsiveness, its professionalism, and its business model's effect on its ability to manage funds, provide health outreach, and partner with other organizations. Ratings were also above average for resource allocations, experience, cost effectiveness, efficiency, and innovation. Respondents believed PHMC was committed to helping all populations obtain health care and very committed to helping at-risk populations do so.
Impact: Communicate the quality of PHMC's services and that the organization is improving the health and vitality of the community.	Clients, funders, and the health care provider community believed that PHMC offered high-quality services. PHMC, its affiliate clients, and its government partners rated highly PHMC's ability to improve the health and vitality of the community.

Structure leads the organization through the development of strategy and helps ensure integration. It dictates both how to go through the strategic process and how to write the strategic plan. PHMC uses a structure that contains six levels:

1. Background/context
2. Audiences/stakeholders
3. Key messages/messaging architecture
4. Objectives
5. Strategies
6. Tactics

With these six steps, the organization will move from the high level to execution—and the strategic plan will develop a logical flow. The tactics will reflect the strategies, which will assist in meeting objectives, which will serve the audiences, all of which will support the organizational context and strategy. The key messages fall in the middle—as something of a centerpiece—and appear here, rather than just before or after the tactics in which they will be incorporated, for reasons that will be discussed later.

A manager in the organization cannot develop these six elements entirely alone. Plan a facilitated strategy discussion—with an outside facilitator who will both lead the discussion and use the findings from it to draft the comprehensive plan to focus on the context, identify the audience, and discuss the marketing objectives. The facilitator should be an expert in marketing and communications strategy development. Attendees should include key stakeholder representatives—some staff and board members—a member or two from the marketing or communications committee if there is one, and a funder or some client representation if it is available. Although it is good to have broad stakeholder representation, it is also important to have a manageable group size of only five to eight people. This strategy session will focus almost entirely on Levels 1 and 2. The facilitator will use what he or she learns to build Levels 3 to 6 and then reflect it back to the group for further refinement.

Level 1: Background/Context

The strategy session will begin with a discussion that reveals the organizational context for marketing and communications. In this step, the group will go through a situational analysis that encompasses the organization-level mission and goals and the positive position of the organization as well as its challenges, its aspirations (a marketing strategy should help the organization get to where it wants to be, so it has an aspirational aspect), and the market context (the competition and how you stand up to it). This analysis will be used as the basis for accruing further information and insight during the facilitated session. The facilitator may also gather information from independent research. The first part of the strategic plan document will capture these findings in a background/context section.

Level 2: Audiences/Stakeholders

Based on the context developed in Level 1, the group will identify all of the organization's audiences and stakeholders. Depending on time limitations and the readiness of the group, the facilitator may wish to begin audience segmentation with the group and refine it later, or the facilitator may handle the segmentation independently. The example in Exhibit 11.1 is an audience segmentation for which the group brainstormed to develop

---

EXHIBIT 11.1 Results of a Strategic Audience Segmentation

- Customers: Funding streams and partnerships
  - Government entities
  - Foundations
  - Individual funders (existing and potential)
  - Corporate funders (existing and potential)
  - Consulting clients and potential clients
- Communication/marketing channels
  - Policy makers
  - Media
  - Professional organizations with which the organization has relationships
  - Internal audiences
    - Board members
    - Senior staff
    - Employees
- Opportunities for direct impact
  - Direct service clients
  - Other nonprofit organizations in the region, as interested parties

the list of audiences, and the facilitator—based on knowledge gained before and during the session—added the segmentation later. The results of this discussion will form the basis for the second section of the strategic plan document.

Level 3: Key Messages

As stated earlier, the messaging forms the centerpiece of the strategy. The discussion and information from the group session inform the messages, but the facilitator develops them independently while drafting the strategy. It is critical that he or she craft the messages after drafting only the context and audience sections of the document. This is because the messages should be based in that context and directed to those audiences but be otherwise unfettered by the proposed marketing approach. The messages should offer a thorough set of building blocks for communication, rather than be reactive to—and thus limited by—how they might be used, as defined by the objectives, strategies, and tactics. Putting it another way, the messages are about the organization, not about the marketing plan. In this way, they will serve not only the marketing plan but also many other possible applications, such as internal and external speeches, funding proposals, and so forth, ensuring cohesion and consistency among all communication.

There are many formats for key messages, from bulleted lists to the summary statements popularly known as "elevator speeches." The PHMC preference is a set of statements that the communicator can mix and match (it is nonlinear) and tailor to the situation. The central point is the overarching message, a statement *with which anyone can agree* and that gets at the heart of the organization in a very broad way. This offers the communicator a starting point for engagement or a place to go to reengage…a common ground. Although the set of PHMC statements is nonlinear, it can be depicted in a linear—or narrative—fashion. Alternatively, it can be depicted as a mind map. Examples of both are offered in Table 11.2 and Figure 11.1. Table 11.2 presents a segment of the key messages in a narrative format. Figure 11.1 presents the key messages as a mind map.

The key messages offer a range of content, from mission to vision to hard facts and data. Different communicators will find themselves more comfortable with different aspects, and they will use what works for them, in their situations, with their audiences, for their purposes. They also will embellish. The key messages do not include the heartwarming anecdotes. They provide a superstructure, and the communicator will build on them. They will keep everyone on message and consistent but not sounding like automatons. There is room for individual expression, and that will make the messages hit home; this is a level of flexibility and personalization that traditional elevator speeches cannot easily provide. The best stories combine data that tell why (establish the need), stories that tell how (evoke emotion), and outcomes that prove results (show value). The key messages should provide much of what is required for the first and last of these; for the middle one—the emotion—the communicators need an always-refreshed armory of stories that they can connect to the key messages to give them firing power. Either they draw from their own stories in their own day-to-day work or, if the resources are available, an ongoing project can separately be initiated to build and disseminate the anecdotal stories so the communication troops are always well supplied with new ammunition.

Once the messages appear in the plan, they require ongoing stewardship in two critical respects. First, they require dissemination to key communicators—usually employees, volunteers, and board members—through training, role playing, and modeling. Second, they require vigilant updating to ensure that the statistics and any other changing facts remain accurate.

TABLE 11.2 Public Health Management Corporation Key Messages Effective January 2011

Overarching message: The health of our community is critical to its vitality and to its future.

Proof point: PHMC makes a difference in the community through our unwavering commitment to developing access for all to the full array of public health services.

Supporting message:
We make a real and measurable impact on the lives of people in our region, with programs and services that are effectively aligned with the needs of the people and communities we serve.

Proof points:
We bring health services to more than 123,000 people per year in locations throughout the region.
Our effectiveness comes not only from our skill, knowledge, focus on workforce development, and capacity to serve, but most fundamentally from our heartfelt concern for the well-being of the individuals, families, and communities we touch.
We build capacity by helping to ensure that our affiliate nonprofits continue to provide vital services by taking on their accounting, human resources, information systems, administration, training, communications, and marketing functions.
We consult with external nonprofits to help them reach more people more effectively and cost efficiently.
PHMC conducts the Household Health Survey, one of the largest regional health surveys in the country and the data source for our Community Health Data Base. This yields a rich fund of intelligence from which to develop the right programs and services in the right locations to effectively target current and emerging needs.
PHMC's Research and Evaluation Group enhances health and human services programs at PHMC and throughout the region through a broad range of services in all phases of assessment, evaluation, and program implementation.
With unwavering commitment to our accountability, we identify and implement the metrics to assess the quality and effectiveness of the programs and services we provide.

Supporting message:
We are connectors—bringing people and communities the health care they need, bridging across our own programs and many others, linking clients to a broad array of services, leveraging across the spectrum of government, foundations, academic institutions, businesses, and community-based organizations—to meet public health challenges and lead in the identification of and response to existing and emerging public health issues

Proof points:
We leverage funds, connect services, and collaborate with hundreds of organizations.
We have more than 200 programs, spanning behavioral health and recovery, community-based and culturally relevant health promotion, smoking cessation, obesity prevention, early intervention, HIV/AIDS, violence intervention, homeless health services, and much more, plus the research and evaluation that allow us to assess and target health issues effectively.

Our sound infrastructure and financial stability allow us to maintain critical capabilities and establish new programs, services, and affiliations to meet the public health needs of the community.

Supporting message:
Our management practices save more than $14 million per year, which we can reinvest in services.

Proof point: With a $180 million budget, we have administrative costs under 7%, compared with a norm of about 15% among nonprofits.

Supporting message:
Our vital infrastructure supports PHMC's programs and affiliates in their daily work to create and sustain healthier communities.

Proof points:
PHMC benefits from robust in-house, professional teams in the full scope of key infrastructure requirements: fiscal control, human resources, information systems, administration, marketing, and communications.
Nonprofits across the region recognize the value of our infrastructure capabilities and benefit from them through our consulting practice, Targeted Solutions, a key element in PHMC's capacity-building work. Each year, more than 100 organizations seek out PHMC's expertise.

(continued)

TABLE 11.2 Public Health Management Corporation Key Messages Effective January 2011 (*continued*)

PHMC actively helps to ensure the future of public health and social services.

Supporting message:
PHMC provides high-level, innovative professional and leadership development that builds a knowledgeable, capable, and vigorous workforce.

Proof points:
PHMC's in-house training and professional development team offers career pathways programs at multiple stages and a comprehensive program in the foundations of leadership.
PHMC partners with major area universities to offer its qualified emerging leaders customized executive master's degree programs in public health and social work.

Supporting message:
PHMC disseminates public health information and promotes public health issues to help educate our communities and reinforce a positive image for public health approaches.

Proof points:
PHMC is active in public health communications, including social marketing and media relations activities that help inform the public.
PHMC's Community Health Data Base provides open access to its data to members of the media and policy makers, and offers a broad range of information on its public website, as a means to bring key community health information to the public.

Level 4: Objectives

Quite simply, the objectives state *what* the marketing and communications are meant *to achieve for the organization*. There is no consideration at this stage of how to meet the objectives. It is critical that every objective make sense for the context that has been established and can reach at least one of the identified audiences. For example, some objectives might read as follows:

- Communicate that we are a nonprofit that does ___, and the benefit that this brings.
- Highlight the strength and value of our management role and capabilities.
- Build cohesion across the organization (remember that if you have internal audiences, you need to market/communicate to them as well).

There may be some discussion in the strategy session about the group's goals, but the facilitator will not simply recount them in this section of the plan. He or she will draw from the context and audiences to establish the most appropriate objectives.

Level 5: Strategies

The strategies state *how* the marketing and communication are to be used *to meet the objectives*. The flow remains critical—you should be able explicitly to trace every strategy as a means to achieve at least one objective for at least one audience (preferably more). Examples of strategies might be the following:

- Develop visual representations that aid in communicating our messages to prospective funders.
- Engage the workforce as organizational advocates.

Level 6: Tactics

This is where the plan states the specific tactics to implement in order to operationalize the strategy. Every tactic must serve as a tool to achieve at least one strategy, in support

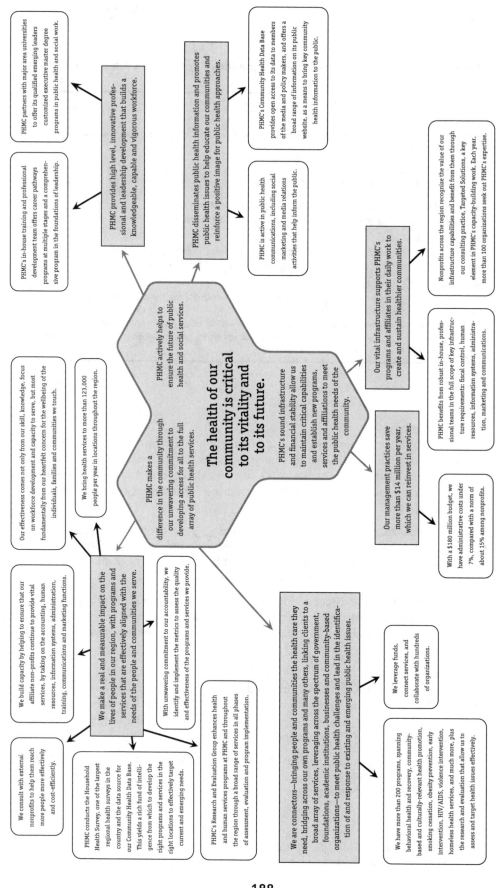

FIGURE 11.1 PHMC's key messages mind map.

TABLE 11.3 Relationships to Objectives and Audiences, Timelines, and Responsible Parties

Tactic	Strategies Primarily Served	Objectives Primarily Served	Audiences Primarily Served	Time Frame	Responsible Parties	Cost
Develop an interactive website, directed at funders, that guides them visually through the story of the organization's services and benefits as a valuable funder investment.	# 3, 5	#1, 2	Funders	March to May	Internal: Communications manager, development manager, development coordinator External: Interactive designer	$7,500

of at least one objective, for at least one audience (preferably more). But beyond this, the tactics must reflect *all* constraints. The context, audiences, objectives, and strategies are among the constraints, and so are the budget and available internal and external personnel. All are valid, and the challenge to overcome—with the help of the facilitator—is identifying the integrated group of tactics that allows the organization to work within all of its constraints.

You may find it helpful to view the tactics in a table in which you can demonstrate the relationship to objectives and audiences as well as the timelines and responsible parties. Table 11.3 offers an example. This visual device serves several purposes:

1. It ensures that the tactics fully reflect the parameters set out in the audience, objective, and strategy sections of the plan while conforming to the budget and personnel resource constraints.
2. It provides a clear picture of the plan to help present it to key decision makers.
3. It establishes a blueprint for moving forward, avoiding missteps, saving time and money, and keeping the team on track. Many people say they have difficulty implementing their marketing plans because they are not concrete enough. With this blueprint, you should be able to overcome that obstacle.
4. When parameters change—a funding gap, a new priority that steals away a key resource for 3 months—the plan can help determine how best to adjust without leaving behind any of the goals or audiences.

Conclusion

If an organization wants its marketing and communication to achieve the greatest effect, it needs an integrated strategy. If you worry about limited resources, you need an integrated strategy. If you want to make the case for marketing to decision makers, you need an integrated strategy. The good news is that it is not as difficult as some fear. You need a marketing and communication strategy expert to facilitate your strategy session and draft your plan, a group of stakeholders who will give several hours of their time, and an organizational dedication to follow through once the blueprint is in place.

CAUSE MARKETING: AN INNOVATIVE FUND-RAISING MODEL

Sustaining the work of nonprofit organizations requires continued funding, and most nonprofits rely heavily on membership and donor-based models to support their work.

However, as individual giving has declined, especially in the present economic climate, nonprofits are looking for other fund-raising approaches, and many are exploring the potential of cause marketing. Cause marketing provides the missing link between corporate support and societal needs, but the real power of cause marketing lies in its ability to engage individual consumers in the support of an initiative.

Cause marketing is defined by Cone Communications as "a business strategy that helps an organization stand for a social issue to gain significant bottom line and social impacts while making an emotional and relevant connection to stakeholders" (Cone Communications, 2007). Cause marketing involves the sale of a product or service with a percentage of profits designated for a specific cause or nonprofit organization. Successfully utilized by the Susan G. Komen Breast Cancer Foundation and the Product Red Campaign, cause marketing creates a mutually beneficial relationship between an organization and the business supporting it.

Cause marketing expenditure has increased steadily over the last several years, with an approximate market spend of $1.50 billion in 2008, according to the IEG Sponsorship Report.[1] According to a 2007 survey of 1,000 adults conducted by Cone, more than 66% of Americans consider a company's business practices when deciding what to buy, 92% have a more positive image of a company that supports a cause they care about, and 87% are likely to switch from one brand to another if quality and pricing are the same but the other brand is associated with a good cause (Cone Communications, 2007). As consumers become increasingly alert to the social and environmental impact of their purchases, more corporations are responding by exploring their own cause marketing opportunities.

By pairing their products or services with a nonprofit organization, businesses can increase sales, improve brand image, generate positive public relations, and help save lives. Likewise, cause marketing benefits nonprofits by generating greater awareness of their causes and by raising money to fund their work. This approach allows businesses to engage in important social issues while giving the public an easy way to help by simply choosing one product over another.

CASE STUDY: A DRINK FOR TOMORROW

A Drink for Tomorrow (ADFT) provides an example of the cause marketing fund-raising model. Founded by Stephanie Weaver of Moorestown, New Jersey, ADFT uses cause marketing to raise funds and awareness for the global water crisis. Currently, 1.2 billion people suffer because they lack access to clean, safe drinking water. This translates to one in every eight people globally who live without access to a basic need. Although the water crisis presents immense social problems, it is not insurmountable.

The technology needed to provide clean water is readily available. Water projects are one of the most effective ways to save lives and one of the most cost-effective investments in disease prevention. The World Health Organization (WHO) estimates that every $1 invested in water and sanitation yields between $3 and $34 in reduced medical costs and increased productivity. Therefore, funds raised for the cause can make a huge difference in the lives of those in water-poor countries.

ADFT's first campaign, "Turn Wine into Water," creates partnerships with members of the wine industry through promotions at businesses and restaurants. Through these partnerships, ADFT mobilizes the for-profit sector to advance support for a social cause, as has been done previously with funding and awareness for both AIDS and breast cancer. A crucial element of ADFT's strategy is that it involves both the support of the partnering business and the involvement of the public. Through the purchase of items designated to donate a percentage of profits to the water crisis cause, consumers have the opportunity to make a financial contribution by simply selecting a partnering business's brand. In the face of a problem as potentially overwhelming as the global water crisis, it is important to provide individuals with an easy and direct way to contribute to a solution.

ADFT has partnered with both wine stores and restaurants through Turn Wine into Water. Partnerships with local wine stores encourage individuals to buy wine from select stores with a promise that a percentage of their purchase will be donated to the organization. The wine storeowner has the discretion to choose which wines are available and the duration of the promotion. The wine store advertises with in-store flyers using the Turn Wine into Water campaign logo, and ADFT issues a press release to promote the campaign among its supporters. Other means of promotion are inclusion on ADFT's website and blog, additional media relations, and social networking sites. The Wine Cellar in Cinnaminson, New Jersey, is currently a wine store partner, and ADFT hopes to expand this opportunity with additional wine stores in the region.

Restaurants offering a selection of wine also make suitable cause marketing partners in this campaign. ADFT has partnered with Bridget Foy's South Street Grill of Philadelphia to fund clean water projects. Each time a patron orders St. Clement Chardonnay or Baron Phillippe de Rothschild Pinot Noir, Bridget Foy's donates 10% of these wine sales to ADFT. This partnership raises awareness for the global water crisis as well as funds to alleviate the problem. Bridget Foy's and other business partners are allowing their customers to help save lives by simply enjoying a glass of wine. The funds generated from this and other similar partnerships are advancing ADFT's goal of providing clean water to communities across the world.

ADFT recently funded its first clean water project, a well in West Bengal, India, entirely through cause marketing campaigns such as Turn Wine into Water. This young nonprofit hopes to continue engaging businesses and consumers in social change by pairing their products with the water crisis cause.

By promoting their cause through the products of business partners, nonprofits are bringing global social issues to the forefront of public conversation. If citizens are more aware of social problems, and how their money can be used to provide solutions and hope around the world, nonprofits believe, more individuals will join in partnerships to solve global problems.

USING SOCIAL MEDIA TO ENHANCE ORGANIZATIONAL COMMUNICATION

Social media provides the ability to communicate, collaborate, and connect with anyone, anywhere, anytime. Message boards, discussion forums, wikis, virtual whiteboards, and blogs are examples of the various social media frameworks. These reside on a number of communication platforms that make connections possible, such as Facebook, LinkedIn, Skipta, and Twitter. Together, they provide organizations with the opportunity to achieve, attain, and contribute more than could ever have been conceived of by prior generations (Jue, Marr, & Kassotakis, 2010).

The acceptance and use of social media have skyrocketed and, as a result, how we communicate among ourselves has changed forever. We expect feedback, answers, and results instantaneously and, for the first time in history, there is a way to accomplish this. Within organizations, social media can lead to increased organizational learning, enhanced change readiness, and stronger relationships among members. Organization leaders must learn to leverage social media inside their organizations, just as individuals do independently. With this ability, leaders will reduce the time needed to make decisions and drastically enhance their organizations' performance and levels of innovation (Jue et al., 2010).

With this power available, the question becomes, "What is the ROI for the organization and is a social media initiative imperative?" When contemplating this question, it is important to think of how social media can become integral to the fabric of the organization rather than just a tool that can be used for news and/or advertising. Collaboration with others to achieve common goals is key for organization leaders. Social media is the foundation that can facilitate this (Jue et al., 2010). When initiating an organization's social media initiative, the following are essential:

1. Engage in a network in which professional norms and rules can be established.
2. Look for networks that have your target audience.
3. Find a solution that facilitates both external and internal social media campaigns.

All organizations strive to meet objectives to ensure both immediate and future success. Improvements to communication and collaboration efforts within an organization will enhance the overall performance of that organization (Jue et al., 2010). To accomplish this, operational efficiency, member engagement, and innovation are vital. As a result, leaders should embrace the opportunity to make social media a vital and integrated part of their organizations. It is the ideal solution for streamlining the time, capital, and resources required to communicate and collaborate with members and can make it seamless for them to contribute to the success of the organization. Ultimately, it can lead to increased contributions, donations, and/or membership dues. The more efficient the communication strategy, the more success the organization is likely to have. As a result, the ROI for a social media initiative can be measured through the enhanced efficiency the organization achieves. This is the reason that optimizing an organization's communication strategy through social media is vital. It will lead to a more effective operational strategy for the organization both now and in the future and will ultimately save the organization time, money, and resources.

It is important to remember that social media is not just about marketing and getting "fans"; rather it is about enhancing the overall mission of the organization. Engaging a social media initiative can provide an organization with a connected network that can effectively, safely, and quickly reach members at any point of the day.

Applications

To better understand the ROI opportunity of social media, comprehension of the following is required:

1. The generation factor
2. The power of social marketing within niche networks
3. The power of a connected organization

The Generation Factor

We are currently in an age of a significant demographic shift in the professional market place (Jue et al., 2010). The baby boomer generation (born between 1946 and 1964) will soon be approaching the traditional retirement age. They have been by far the largest generation in the workforce until Generation Y (born between 1977 and 2000), more commonly known as the millennials, came along. The importance of understanding the millennial generation in organizations is vital. There are over 2 billion globally, over 40% of them in the United States are of non-Caucasian descent, and they are extremely accustomed to the use of technology (Bateman & Bateman, 2008). This generation has never known a world without electronic communication, instant messaging, and the Internet. They are referred to as "digital natives"; they expect everything within a matter of seconds, and they understand that news from an hour ago is ancient. They are always connected through their smart phones, laptops, and tablets (Artley & Mujtaba, 2006). They expect both their social and professional lives to be easily accessible and the communication with their friends and peers to be seamless. About 22% of individuals from this generation connect to social networks daily, and they make up the largest population of members on social networking websites (Jue et al., 2010). They view social networking as the major form of communication, and Fox Interactive has found that as social networking use increases among millennials, television, phone, and video game use decreases almost proportionately (Fox Interactive Media, 2007).

Millennials have been acknowledged as the generation that will make the largest contribution to the professional workforce. Unlike previous generations, they are expected to take action when it comes to pushing organizations to take more social responsibility. The approaching challenge for organizations will be to create an environment that will indulge these individuals while at the same time ensuring organizational success and value (Jue et al., 2010). This is a vicissitude that organizations must engage. Already, baby boomers are exiting the professional work force in record numbers and millennials are taking their place. Millennials will require interconnected networks that can be accessed quickly and effectively to accomplish objectives and missions. Organizations depending on traditional forms of member involvement and contributions will be left behind. Millennials will seek and quickly find those organizations that meet their requirements and needs for efficiency and communication.

The Power of Social Media Marketing Within Niche Networks

If you were offered the opportunity to promote your organization to a random group of individuals or to your direct-targeted audience, which one would you choose? It sounds like the choice would be obvious, but this point is made to clarify the power of social media marketing within niche networks. We all know social media is efficient in getting information out quickly, but we also know that without security and regulation, not only may the target audience never be reached but the information may get to individuals who should not have received it in the first place. This is why niche networks play a significant role.

The following is a case study conducted by the niche social networking provider Skipta. Skipta's verified network for pharmacists, called "Pharmacist Society," has more than 50,000 verified pharmacists and student pharmacists actively participating, and it provides this audience with a Web-based, mobile-connected solution to connect, engage, and collaborate with like-minded professionals. Within this network, pharmacy organizations, companies, schools, and manufacturers can establish a "Group" area in which they can also connect, engage, and collaborate with this target audience. Unlike traditional "open" social media sites, organizations have participated in very targeted member drives and advertising campaigns within this closed-loop verified network. The efficiency of sharing information, news, videos, and messages while maintaining control of who receives the content has been significantly enhanced. A study that Skipta conducted showed that within Skipta's Pharmacist Society, pharmacy organizations that participate have seen, on average, an increase of more than 150% in active reach to their intended audiences and have been able to actively and successfully integrate social media into their organizations by incorporating social media into their e-mail campaigns, membership drives, and member polling. With this increased reach, the organizations participating in Skipta's Pharmacist Society have also seen an increase, on average, of more than 30% in active involvement from their members within the site and now can both qualitatively and quantitatively evaluate feedback and initiatives using the analytics that are provided.

Social media marketing is powerful, but for organizations to get the most cost-effective, time-efficient, and safe use from this valuable marketing engine, niche networks are key. Engagement with a target audience in an environment where both the organization and the audience feel secure will produce results in both overall reach and impact factors that will speak for themselves. The ROI of social media is the opportunity to significantly improve communication, collaboration, and performance for the organization. This can be realized by streamlining efforts and going to the target audience directly by leveraging niche networks.

The Power of a Connected Organization

Collaboration with others to achieve common goals is key for organization leaders. In the digital age, efficient and effective outcomes are expected and organizations must stay ahead of the curve if they are to remain their industry's voices. Creating a private networking platform specifically for an organization will enhance its mission by streamlining member input to pressing issues and enhance results. Because social media can be tracked, analyzed, and evaluated through both qualitative and quantitative analytics, the discussions, feedback, and collaboration among members can provide vital information and direction for the organization. The right social media initiative can provide these data by allowing collaboration on networking tools such as virtual whiteboards, message boards, forums, and video conferences that can be securely accessed at all times. Tools such as these can provide connectivity to past, current, and future membership.

To ensure success for any social media initiative, companies must establish an internal strategy and work with a social media company that can integrate and streamline current organization tools and resources to make adoption seamless. One key objective is to use the internal social network as a "one-stop" shop for members, thus decreasing the time needed to find information, documents, and resources. Buy-in from organization leaders and board members is key. With buy-in, organization initiatives will become more streamlined and more positive outcomes will result. Leaders who are willing to lead by example will enhance the chances of success for their organizations.

In another example from Skipta, organizations that have formed private networking sites with that social technology provider have on average saved more than 90% of the cost associated with traditional communication to their members, saved more than $30,000 annually on technology solutions for virtual meetings and collaboration forums, and seen increases of more than 30% in membership involvement. These results exemplify how an integrated social media initiative can lead to a more effective operational strategy for an organization and ultimately save the organization time, money, and resources.

CONCLUSION

Social media has become a global phenomenon and is quickly becoming the major form of communication. Leaders everywhere should embrace the opportunity to make social media a vital and integrated part of their organizations. Organizations that work to connect their members and allow them to communicate, collaborate, and share information effectively are more likely to succeed; organizations that do not are likely to be replaced by others that do. In an organization's initiation of a social media program, it is important to streamline efforts, engage directly with the target audience, and incorporate a holistic approach involving both external and internal organization objectives. With this approach, a social media initiative is likely to be a success.

The professional members and workforce of the future will expect and demand instantaneous connectivity in their professional lives and will seek targeted networks for professional engagement. An organization's establishing a social media initiative will secure its position with its targeted membership and allow it to measure the ROI through the enhanced efficiency it achieves.

NOTE

1. IEG Sponsorship Report (www. sponsorship.com/IEGSR.aspx)

REFERENCES

Artley, J. B., & Mujtaba, B. (2006). *The art of mentoring diverse professionals* (p. 91). Hallandale Beach, FL: Aglob Publishing.

Bateman, W. K., & Bateman, K. A. (2008). Jessica and Jason meet Maslow: Gen Y and the hierarchy of needs. In R. C. Preziosi (Ed.). *The 2008 Pfieffer annual: Management development* (pp. 161–173). Hoboken, NJ: Wiley.

Cone Communications. (2007). *2007 Cause evolution and environmental study*. Retrieved from www. coneinc.com/research/archive.php

Fox Interactive Media. (2007). *Never ending friending*. Retrieved from http://creative.myspace.com/ groups/_ms/nef/images/40161_nef_onlinebook.pdf

Jue, A. L., Marr, J. A., & Kassotakis, M. E. (2010). *Social media at work* (pp. 2–35). San Francisco, CA: Jossey-Bass.

GOVERNMENT CONTRACTING AND HOW TO NAVIGATE FISCAL CRISIS[1]

Daniel Stid, Willa Seldon, and the Urban Institute[2]

An easily accessible and transparent database of contract information will bring sunshine into the confusing and sometimes shadowy practice of government contracting.
—Tom Coburn

Human service nonprofits shoulder a tremendous responsibility for the nation's well-being. Individual donors and foundations expect them to operate efficiently and produce meaningful results, clients depend on them to provide necessary services, and governments hold them to task for delivering programs efficiently and according to specifications. Even in good times, many nonprofits struggle to raise funds to meet these expectations.

Recessions can cripple the budgets of many nonprofits just as demand for their services rise. On top of revenue from donations and fees shrinking, many organizations struggle with reductions and ongoing payment problems from one of their biggest funders: government agencies. As a result, many are forced to cut services and staff or close program sites, hurting the communities they serve. Flaws in the government contracting system can exacerbate this financial stress, placing additional pressure on stretched staff and resources.

This chapter has two parts, the first of which is the findings of a national survey of human service organizations conducted by the Urban Institute in 2010. It documents the sheer scale and variety of the over 200,000 formal funding relationships that nonprofits have with governments. It provides an analysis of the organizations that contract with government agencies, the types of contracts they have, and the part of their revenue that is made up of government funding. The study discusses the numerous problems that nonprofits have with government funding, problems that were intensified as governments slashed funding during the recent recession. The steps that nonprofits took as a result of their decreased revenues, which damaged organizational capacities in ways that may take years to rebuild, are also discussed.

The second part of the chapter, from The Bridgespan Group, is a further discussion of the difficulties human service nonprofits have staying afloat and advancing their missions during times of government cutbacks. Governments issue "take-it-or-leave-it" contracts. Nonprofits have to compete for funding and accept poor contract prices and conditions in order to keep their missions afloat. This piece concludes with five approaches that some nonprofits are pursuing that enable them to seek and secure public funding while advancing their missions, sustaining their organizations, and retaining some room to maneuver in the process.

HUMAN SERVICE NONPROFITS AND GOVERNMENT COLLABORATION—FINDINGS FROM THE 2010 NATIONAL SURVEY OF NONPROFIT–GOVERNMENT CONTRACTING AND GRANTS[3]

Background

Governments rely heavily on nonprofits to deliver a range of critical services, from homeless shelters to child care to job training, but little has been known about the size and scale of these relationships—or how effective they are. This chapter offers a comprehensive look at the scope of government contracts and grants with human service nonprofits in the United States and documents the problems that arise. We also assess how these nonprofits were affected by the recession, how they responded to shrinking revenues, and how flaws in government contracting practices intensified their budget woes.

While donations and fees are crucial to human service nonprofits, many organizations rely heavily on revenue from government contracts and grants to expand their reach. Recent anecdotal press reports, regional studies, and small surveys describe a variety of problems related to government contracting: problems that are not new but that for many nonprofits were exacerbated by the recession, forcing them to make severe cutbacks in their staff and operations (Deffiey, 2010; DiNapoli, 2009, 2010).[4]

The findings reported here are based on a national study of human service nonprofits conducted by the Urban Institute, which surveyed a random sample of human service organizations with more than $100,000 in expenses in eight human service program areas (Table 12.1).[5] All estimates are weighted to represent the entire segment of the U.S. human service nonprofit sector that had government contracts and grants in 2009.[6] The Urban Institute explored the relationships between nonprofits and government contracting by program area, organization size, and level (federal, state, local) of government contract. Context is important; policies and practices differ in each of these categories. This study reveals how important government funding is to nonprofits, as well as how varied and often complex those relationships can be.

Government contracting with human service nonprofits is widespread and has grown steadily over the years. The collaboration between government and the nonprofit sector goes back to the colonial period (Salamon, 1987; Smith & Lipsky, 1993). Schools and hospitals, such as Harvard University and the Massachusetts General Hospital, received public funding in their formative years (Smith, 2006). However, it was not until the 1960s that government reliance on nonprofits started in earnest, with extensive federal spending on many new social and health programs including Medicare and Medicaid (Grønbjerg, 2001; Smith, 2006).

In 1960, public spending for services such as vocational rehabilitation, child nutrition and welfare, institutional care, and veterans' benefits accounted for less than $1 billion, about 4.4% of all public social welfare spending.[7] A portion of this outlay went to

TABLE 12.1 Examples of Nonprofit Human Service Organizations

Crime and Legal Related	Housing and Shelter	Human Service Multipurpose
Child abuse prevention	Affordable housing	Adolescent pregnancy prevention
Legal assistance	Senior citizens' housing	Adoption agencies
Dispute resolution	Subsidized housing	Child care centers
Domestic violence prevention	Low-income housing	Foster care
Juvenile delinquency prevention	Homeless shelters	Family counseling
Crime prevention	Home improvement and repair	Battered women's shelters
Rehabilitation for offenders	Transitional housing	Group homes
Ex-offender reentry	Housing services	Senior citizen centers
Community corrections		Centers for the developmentally disabled
		Immigrant centers

Employment	Public Safety and Disaster Relief	Hospice Care
Employment for disabled persons	Search and rescue	The Urban League
Job training	Disaster relief	YMCA/YWCA
Job placement assistance	Disaster preparedness	
Employment resource centers	Emergency response training	
Workforce investment		

Food, Agriculture, and Nutrition	Youth Development	Community Development
Food banks	Scouting	Urban planning
Food pantries	Boys and Girls Clubs	Rural development
Meal vouchers	Big Brothers Big Sisters	Community action agencies
Meals on Wheels	Junior Achievement	
Nutrition assistance and education	Leadership programs for youth	
	Youth service clubs	

nonprofits that rendered those types of services. Between 1960 and 1995, public spending for such services grew substantially, with government agencies increasingly using nonprofit organizations to provide desired services (Grønbjerg, 2001). As of 1997, an estimated 52% of federal, state, and local government funds for social services went to nonprofits (Salamon, 2003).

Direct grants, contracts, and fees for service are among the most important government tools supporting nonprofit activities in communities (Smith, 2006). However, Smith, in his 2006 article "Government Financing of Nonprofit Activity," points out that government financing of public services includes grants, contracts, and, increasingly, tax credits, tax-exempt bonds, tax deductions, vouchers, and fees for services. This diversification tends to mask the extent of public funding of nonprofits and, simultaneously, the increased centralization of government funding at the federal level in many areas such as health and social services.

Although the public often thinks that donations and volunteer work keep human service organizations afloat, as a group, the largest portion of their revenues come from fees for services, whether through private dollars or contracts and grants from local, state, and federal governments. According to the National Center for Charitable Statistics, fee-for-service income was the largest source of revenue for human service nonprofits in 2008; about 25% of total revenue for human service nonprofits came from fees for service from private sources and 24% from government sources. Private contributions made up roughly 13%. Another 7% of revenue came from government grants.[8]

State governments have long used nonprofits to deliver services. A considerable amount of money passes through state-administered programs that are financed entirely (e.g., food stamps) or largely by the federal government (e.g., Medicaid, Temporary Assistance for Needy Families). In some states, counties and other local government entities act as agents of state and federal government in managing contracts and grants (Bowman & Fremont-Smith, 2006). In June 2009, New York State had nearly 31,000 active contracts, worth $14.6 billion, with nonprofit organizations (DiNapoli, 2010). In Delaware, nearly half the annual budget of the Department of Services to Children, Youth, and Their Families was spent on contracting for services (Denhardt et al., 2008).

Some state agency representatives have said that if nonprofits were no longer willing or able to contract with governments to provide services, those services would stop or be severely disrupted. In particular, 45% of Delaware state government managers said they would not be able to provide services if their current nonprofit providers stopped contracting with the state (Denhardt et al., 2008).

The nonprofit sector has undeniably become an indispensable partner of governments in providing services to individuals and communities. Nonprofits nationally contribute just over 5% to the gross domestic product. They also contribute directly and indirectly to every state's economy. In Illinois, nonprofits employed more than 427,000 workers in 2007, almost as many as the three largest Fortune 500 companies in the state. These organizations pay their employees more than $16.5 billion annually, two and a half times Illinois's state government payroll. The sector creates 9% of Illinois's gross state product, about the same amount as the finance and insurance industries combined. In New York, the Office of the State Comptroller notes that in 2006, the state's 24,000-plus nonprofits reported $132.9 billion in revenue and provided nearly 1.2 million jobs, about 17% of the state's workforce.

Human Service Organizations

Among the 1.5 million nonprofit organizations in the United States, human service organizations stand out as the quintessential expression of the nation's benevolent spirit. They are a diverse group that includes local direct service providers, such as soup kitchens, child care, and youth mentoring organizations, as well as large national organizations such as the YMCA and YWCA, Boys & Girls Clubs of America, and the American Red Cross. This chapter focuses on eight categories of organizations as classified by the National Taxonomy of Exempt Entities classification system.[9] The categories break down by program area, as defined below and shown in Table 12.1. Figure 12.1 breaks down government contract spending by National Taxonomy of Exempt Entities category.

A Detailed Look at Government Contracts and Grants With Nonprofits

In 2009, local, state, and federal governments contracted with nearly 33,000 human service organizations. Their agreements extend from small grants (less than $500) to multimillion-dollar contracts. More than half of these nonprofits are multipurpose organizations that provide a range of programs and services for children, families, and the elderly. The second-largest category (18%) provides housing assistance and shelter. While governments

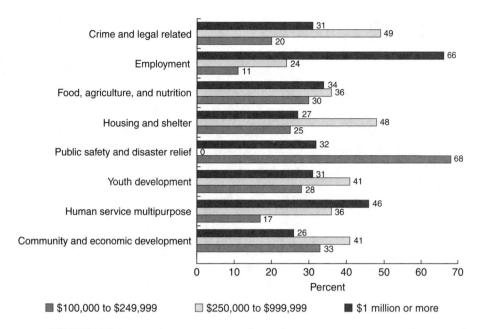

FIGURE 12.1 Human service nonprofits with government contracts, by type of organization and size.

contract with many small and medium-sized nonprofits, most contracts are awarded to larger organizations. Forty percent of nonprofits contracting with government have operating budgets of $1 million or more (large), and 39% between $999,999 and $250,000 (medium). Just 21% have budgets between $249,999 and $100,000 (small).

In 2009, the total number of contracts and grants awarded to human service nonprofits was nearly 200,000. On average, each organization had six contracts and grants but larger organizations averaged more than did small or midsized organizations: large organizations averaged nine contracts and grants; midsized groups, four; and small ones, three. The mean and median numbers of contracts do not vary much by level of government or type of organization (Table 12.2).

Nonprofits often work with multiple government agencies at the local, state, and national levels to deliver services. Over three-quarters have contracts and grants from two or more government agencies. Fifty percent of organizations have contracts at all three levels of government, while 19% only contract with agencies from one level of government (Table 12.3).

In 2009, governments contracted with human service nonprofits for over $100 billion worth of contracts and grants. For organizations with government contracts and grants, government funding accounts for 65% of total revenue. The amounts of government contracts and grants vary by nonprofit size and level of government. The median dollar value of local government contracts and grants ($80,000) is smaller than that for state ($200,000) or federal ($208,000) contracts and grants. The bigger the organization, the higher the median value of its contracts at all levels of government (Table 12.4).

While human service nonprofits have myriad revenue sources, such as fees, donations, and investment income, government revenue is the largest single source of funding for three out of five nonprofits (Table 12.5). That human service nonprofits with contracts and grants depend so heavily on government funding may have implications for their abilities to meet goals and expectations, especially in times of financial turmoil and low government revenues.

TABLE 12.2 Human Service Nonprofits With Government Contracts and Grants

Type of Organization	Number	Percent	Number of Contracts and Grants			
			Mean	Median	Total	Percent
Human service multipurpose	16,941	51.8	6	3	102,637	54.4
Housing and shelter	5,741	17.6	6	3	37,195	19.7
Crime and legal related	2,517	7.7	4	2	10,550	5.6
Community and economic development	2,401	7.3	6	3	14,637	7.8
Youth development	2,272	7.0	4	2	8,761	4.6
Employment	1,740	5.3	6	4	11,218	5.9
Food, agriculture, and nutrition	1,011	3.1	4	3	3,564	1.9
Public safety and disaster relief	70	0.2	2	2	158	0.1
Total	32,693	100.0	6	3	188,719	100.0

Note: Percentages may not sum to 100 because of rounding.
Source: The Urban Institute, *National Study of Nonprofit-Government Contracting and Grants* (2010b).

TABLE 12.3 Organizations With Contracts by Level of Government

Level of Government Contract	Number	Percent
Federal, state, and local contracts	16,278	50
State and local contracts only	4,457	14
Federal and state contracts only	4,045	12
State contracts only	2,354	7
Federal contracts only	2,100	6
Local contracts only	1,881	6
Federal and local contracts only	1,578	5
Total	32,693	100

Source: The Urban Institute, *National Study of Nonprofit-Government Contracting and Grants* (2010b).

TABLE 12.4 Median Value of Government Contracts and Grants by Size of Organization and Level of Government

Expenditure Size	Median Amount of Government Contracts and Grants ($)		
	Local Government	State Government	Federal Government
$100,000 to $249,999	30,000	60,000	79,500
$250,000 to $999,999	48,790	100,000	120,000
$1 million or more	200,000	650,000	600,000
Median	80,000	200,000	208,000

Note: Missing or not applicable answers are excluded.
Source: The Urban Institute, *National Study of Nonprofit-Government Contracting and Grants* (2010b).

TABLE 12.5 Single Largest Sources of Funding for Human Service Organizations

Funding Source	Number	Percent
Government (federal, state, or local contracts and grants)	19,657	60
Donations (individual, corporate, private foundations, federated giving)	6,124	19
Fees (public and private fees for service)	5,179	16
Other sources	1,663	5
Total	32,623	100

Note: Seventy organizations did not have a largest single source of funding and are excluded from the figure. The "other sources" category includes investment income, royalties, and other revenue sources. *Source:* The Urban Institute, *National Study of Nonprofit-Government Contracting and Grants* (2010b).

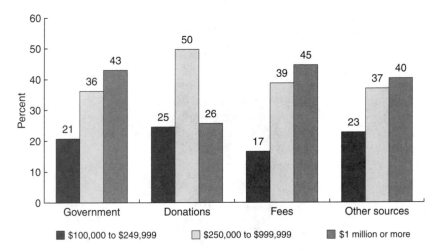

FIGURE 12.2 Single largest sources of funding by expense size.

Organizations that rely primarily on government contracts and grants for revenue are more likely to be large (with budgets of $1 million or more). Of nonprofits that count on government as their single largest source of funding, twice as many are large (43%) as small (21%). Human service nonprofits that rely mostly on donations tend to be mid-sized organizations that operate on a budget of $250,000 to just under $1 million annually (Figure 12.2).

In addition, nonprofits that receive most of their revenue from federal and state government contracts and grants are likely to be large, while those that receive their funds from local government are primarily midsized (Figure 12.3).

Funding from state government is the single largest source of government funding for two in five organizations. Just over a third of organizations receive the majority of their government funding from the federal government and about a quarter rely most heavily on local government (Figure 12.4). The origins of these resources, however, may be federal block grants or other federal or state programs that flow through to states, counties, and local governments.[10] This is a highly devolved structure of government contracting for basic human services.

The number of government grants and contracts varies substantially by state, ranging from an average of three per organization in South Carolina to an average of

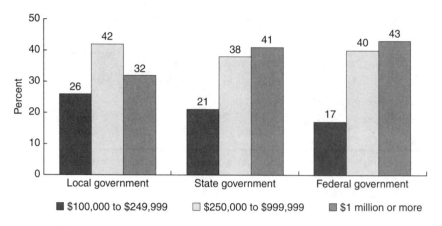

FIGURE 12.3 Single largest sources of funding by expense size.

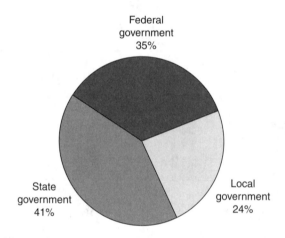

FIGURE 12.4 Single largest sources of government funding.

10 per organization in Arizona. These differences reflect states' diverse administrative, economic, and political environments. The resulting mix of government jurisdictions and agencies with different policies, procedures, and requirements can be difficult for non-profits to navigate.

Payment Methods
Federal, state, and local government agencies use a range of payment methods, matching requirements, reimbursement limitations, application processes, and reporting formats for their contracts and grants. The variety of practices by itself can divert significant resources from programs to administration, taking a toll on the ability of nonprofits to deliver services (Figure 12.5).

While payment methods vary somewhat by type of organization and by state, about half of human service nonprofits reported that cost reimbursement (paying all allowed expenses up to a set limit) and fixed cost payments (paying a negotiated amount, regardless of expenses) were their primary sources of government funds. Only 17% had any performance-based contracts (specifying outcomes, not methods).

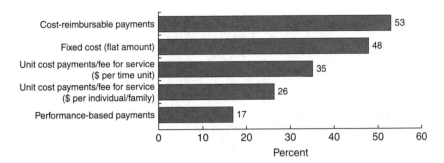

FIGURE 12.5 Types of payment methods.

Payment methods differed considerably across states. Seventy-seven percent of nonprofits in Delaware reported fixed-cost payments compared with 24% of organizations in Idaho. Sixty percent of organizations in Missouri said they had cost per time unit payments, while only 15% of nonprofits in Colorado did.

Matching Requirements

Government contracts and grants often require or suggest that nonprofits match their support with donations or other funding or otherwise explicitly share program costs. More than half of human service organizations reported that at least one of their government contracts and grants required them to match or share some costs. A third said that two or more contracts or grants had such requirements.

Among organizations that were required by their government contracts and grants to match or share some costs:

- Sixty percent had to match, on average, a quarter or more of their contracts and grants.
- Twenty-seven percent had to match, on average, 50% or more.
- Eighty-four percent of youth development nonprofits, 73% of housing and shelter organizations, and 71% of community and economic development groups had to match, on average, a quarter or more of their contracts and grants.
- Three out of four of the smallest groups (those with expenses between $100,000 and $249,999) had to match, on average, 25% or more of their contracts and grants.
- Thirty-three percent of organizations in Maine, Arkansas, and New Hampshire were most likely to have one contract that required matching, 40% of nonprofits in Missouri were most likely to have two to three contracts that required matching, and 31% of West Virginia nonprofits were most likely to have four or more contracts that required matching.
- Sixty-three percent of organizations in Arizona and 59% of those in Georgia, Oregon, Tennessee, Oklahoma, and the District of Columbia were least likely to be required to provide matching funds.

In this survey, it is not possible to identify whether there are distinctive characteristics of contracts and grants that require matching funds or if they are unique to nonprofit contractors, but matching requirements are a prevalent practice and should be studied further. The cost of raising matching funds would seem to limit such contracts to organizations with strong finances.

Program and Organizational Administrative Expense Limitations

A majority of nonprofits reported that government contracts and grants would not pay or would only pay a small portion of administrative or overhead costs. For about 60% of these organizations, the limit was 10% or less (Figure 12.6). Those costs include administrative costs directly related to programs and services (i.e., program administration) and overhead expenses for the whole organization (i.e., general administrative costs).

Management and general administrative expenses along with fund-raising expenses make up a nonprofit's overhead costs and cannot easily be allocated to individual programs. Such costs might include utilities and administrative staff (including finance, accounting, marketing, and contracting staff). Program administrative costs might include computer use, copying, rent, and telephone use. Governments and nonprofits, however, are inconsistent in their definitions of administrative, indirect, and overhead costs and their relationships to each other, which has made it difficult for them to classify costs consistently. Indirect costs are usually defined as costs incurred for common or joint objectives and are not easily assigned to cost objectives (e.g., to a particular program or award). Moreover, state and local governments differ in their reimbursement rates for indirect costs, if these costs are reimbursed at all. These differences largely depend on the policies and practices of the state and local governments that award federal funds to nonprofits.

Limits on administrative costs are a cause for concern because nonprofits must find ways to cover those costs. Trying to minimize overhead costs might lead nonprofits to offer low pay for administrative positions, making it difficult to recruit and retain skilled and experienced staff. Or they may forego investments in technology, reducing productivity and effectiveness. To cover indirect costs that are not reimbursed, nonprofits may serve fewer people, cut back on services offered, or forego or delay capacity-building and staffing needs.

> Covering operating costs of our organization (e.g., finance, executive director, grant manager) is the most difficult, and government contractors only want to pay "their fair share" of these costs. However, it is the government contracts that require the most time, data collection, and paperwork when compared to private funders and our individual donors. A fair share of our administrative, reporting, and data collection should be covered at a significant percentage by each government contract. (Survey Respondent)

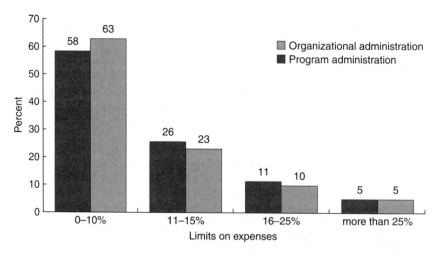

FIGURE 12.6 Limits on administrative expense recovery for government contracts and grants to human service organizations.

Among human service organizations in the study, most were allowed to expense program administrative costs of 10% or less.

- Seventy-five percent of public safety and disaster relief nonprofits, 69% of youth development organizations, and 65% of housing and shelter groups were more likely to be permitted between 0% and 10%.
- Medium-sized organizations (61%) were slightly more likely than were small (57%) and large (57%) nonprofits to be allowed less than 10%.
- A majority of organizations with state government contracts (59%), local government contracts (57%), and federal contracts (60%) were allowed less than 10%.

Most nonprofits were also allowed organizational administrative costs of 10% or less.

- Seventy percent of housing and shelter nonprofits and 69% of youth development organizations were more likely to be permitted between 0% and 10%.
- Medium-sized organizations (64%) were slightly more likely than were small (61%) and large (62%) nonprofits to be allowed less than 10%.
- A majority of organizations with state and local government contracts (62%) and federal contracts (63%) were allowed less than 10%.

Reporting to Government on Contracting

Most nonprofits are required to provide feedback to the government on the results or outcomes of their funded services. Reporting includes preparing narratives of program accomplishments, reporting on outcomes and administrative data, and audits. Nonprofits were most likely to provide feedback on contracting issues and procedures during meetings with funding agencies (76%) and less likely to do so through official government feedback mechanisms (42%). Over half relied on indirect advocacy through affiliated organizations or coalitions of organizations.

Large organizations furnish feedback at higher rates than do medium and small ones. Seventy-one percent of employment organizations and 63% of crime- and legal-related and multipurpose human services organizations provide feedback to the government.

Contracting Problems

Despite the importance of government contracting with nonprofits, we have little recent, comprehensive information on how well it works. Anecdotal press reports, regional studies, and small surveys, however, describe nonprofits' growing financial problems as a result of government grant and contract policies.

In 2009, New York State agencies reported that 82% of nonprofit contracts were approved late, forcing nonprofits to perform services without a contract in place, which resulted in late payments. Working without contracts and on-time payments has led to missed payrolls, reduction or elimination of services, and employee layoffs. In some cases, nonprofits have taken out loans or relied on credit to maintain operations. Louisiana nonprofits also reported financial troubles resulting from similar delays in state government contracts. They attributed contract delays to red tape, a lack of trained staff, and poor communication compensated for by deferring spending and cutting staff. These problems are not isolated to a few states. A recent report notes that government agencies in at least 19 states are delaying payments promised under existing grants and contracts to nonprofits.[11]

Contracting and grant problems are not new. In 2002, a survey of nonprofits showed that these organizations were burdened by the complexity of grants processes and the lack of uniformity in reporting requirements and definitions. This same concern was expressed more recently by Delaware nonprofits that reported being stressed by the volume of required paperwork to get state contracts and the lack of consistency among state agencies.

The U.S. Government Accountability Office also found inconsistencies in what qualifies as indirect costs and administrative costs, making it difficult for governments and nonprofits to classify costs and for nonprofits to be paid adequately. When nonprofits are reimbursed for less than the actual costs incurred, they are sometimes forced to make up the difference with actions that hurt their underlying mission, such as cutting back on the number of people they serve, narrowing the scopes of their services, or foregoing capacity development.

State government reimbursements to foster care nonprofit providers, for instance, do not cover the full costs of meeting the needs of children in their care. Although the Child Welfare Act requires states receiving federal foster care funding to cover necessary child care costs, states interpret this mandate in varied ways. Many states reimburse less than 80% of providers' approved costs.

The Urban Institute identified five problem areas in government contracting based on the literature and media reports: (a) payments that did not cover the full cost of contracted services, (b) complex and time-consuming reporting requirements, (c) complex and time-consuming application requirements, (d) changes made to contracts and grants, and (e) late payments.

The human service organizations were asked their perceptions of these five issues and were asked to rank them as "not a problem," a "small problem," a "big problem," or "not applicable" to their organization. They were also allowed to describe other issues they faced. Nonprofits reported some degree of difficulty in all five areas (Figure 12.7).

Failure to Cover Full Program Costs

Nonprofits often struggle with meeting their budget requirements, a challenge that is exacerbated when government contracts and grants do not cover the full costs of providing a service. More than two thirds of human service nonprofits reported problems with insufficient government payments (44% said it was a big problem and 24% said it was a small problem). This problem, however, is not uniform across all types of organizations. While almost three quarters of multipurpose human service nonprofits (73%) reported being underpaid for services, about half of youth development organizations (52%)

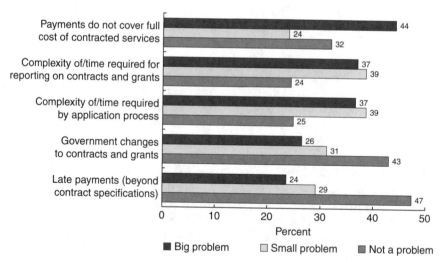

FIGURE 12.7 Key problems reported with government contracts and grants.

experienced the same thing. Seventy-seven percent of large nonprofits indicated that payments did not cover the full costs of contracted services. In contrast, 62% of medium-sized and 59% of small organizations reported this as an issue.

By state, Rhode Island had the highest percentage of nonprofits (84%) reporting insufficient payments for contracted services. Maine (82%) and Illinois (81%) came in second and third. New Hampshire, Iowa, Minnesota, Connecticut, Kentucky, Michigan, and Ohio round out the top 10 states where nonprofits had problems with inadequate payments.

Complex and Time-Consuming Reporting and Application Requirements

Nonprofit and government contracting has grown at all levels of government and so has the expectation of nonprofit accountability. Contracts and grants are more performance oriented, often with agency reimbursement tied to meeting specific performance measures. A majority of organizations (89%) had government contracts or grants that required them to report to funding agencies the results, outcomes, and impact of programs and services.

Eighty-one percent of nonprofits said that navigating different reporting formats was a problem, 76% said that inconsistent budget categories were a problem, and 75% struggled with different requirements for reporting on their outcomes.

> Reporting is a huge problem. For a small organization trying to serve special populations in rural areas, we often do not have the proper staff to report or even submit grants. However, we serve a population that needs the most help but we can't serve for the lack of administrative support. Many grants do not fund operations, only reimburse actual costs, and expect us to be self-sustaining. To be self-sustaining, we have to run our operation like a business and mark up our costs to pay the overhead. Many grants will not allow us to do that—just cost reimbursement. Many businesses across America would be out of business by that method. (Survey Respondent)

> Multiple audits by various programs for the same activities is an ongoing (annual) waste of resources, both ours and the funding programs'. (Survey Respondent)

While nonprofits welcome funding from government agencies, as from any other source, many find government contracting processes burdensome and costly. Over a third of nonprofits said the complexity of and time required for applications for government contracts and grants were big problems; the same percentage had problems with the reporting requirements. Three quarters of nonprofits said that the application process was complex and time consuming, with a similar percentage for reporting processes, which were a problem reported across all practice areas. Youth development organizations had the highest percentage of reporting this issue as a problem (76%).

Large organizations were slightly more likely to report that applications were complex and time consuming (79%) compared with small (71%) and medium-sized nonprofits (73%). The District of Columbia (92%) and Iowa (91%) had the most nonprofits reporting that this was a problem, while Arkansas (58%) had the fewest. The remainder of the top 10 states whose nonprofits found the contracting and grants process too complex and time consuming were Idaho, Vermont, Minnesota, Rhode Island, Alaska, Colorado, Maine, and Nevada.

Changes to Contracts and Grants

Another problem many nonprofits faced was government changes to contracts and grants after they had been approved. Nonprofits said some government agencies canceled or postponed their contracts or grants, cut payments, or made other costly changes. (It is not clear whether these changes are due to the recession or systematic changes.) About 58% of nonprofits regarded such changes as a problem; over a quarter characterized these changes as a big problem.

Sixty-six percent of employment organizations and 61% of human service multipurpose nonprofits reported that changes to contracts and grants were a problem. In contrast, changes were not a problem for 79% of public safety and disaster relief organizations. Large nonprofits were more likely to indicate that this was a problem (66%) compared with medium-sized (52%) and small (49%) organizations. The states with the most nonprofits reporting difficulties with these changes were Maine, Rhode Island, Illinois, Nevada, Louisiana, Kansas, Indiana, Connecticut, Hawaii, and Michigan.

Late Payments

Late government payments to service providers are frequently reported by nonprofits and government agencies alike. New York State's Office of the Comptroller found that the majority of the state's contracts with nonprofits did not meet prompt contracting time frames and that government agencies were late in paying nonprofits. In New York City, delayed payments to nonprofit organizations and other contracting problems prompted the Bloomberg Administration to propose an overhaul of the city's contracting system, which awards $4 billion in contracts every year. The Connecticut Association of Nonprofits reported that 42% of its members received late contract payments from the state, with 84% receiving Connecticut's Department of Social Services payments 60 days late.

> The problems our agency has experienced with government grants relate more to the application process itself (time-consuming, requires multiple letters of support and memoranda of understanding with collaborative partners, use of inefficient government websites to submit applications, etc.) and to time-consuming and repetitive reporting requirements for which instructions are difficult to understand and lead time to accomplish is very short. In short, they are not considerate of time and staff limitations, particularly for small nonprofit organizations—specifically the ones that need the help the most in tight economic times. (Survey Respondent)

In this study, 41% of nonprofits reported that government agencies made late payments (beyond contract specifications) in 2009, but 53% of nonprofits indicated that late payments from government were a problem for their organizations in general. There was substantial variation by level of government, organization size, program area, and the number of days payments were delayed. For those with late payments in 2009, almost half of large organizations experienced late payments—a higher rate than that of small and midsized organizations (Table 12.5).

Furthermore, 44% of employment and multipurpose human service nonprofits reported delayed payments, as did 46% of crime- and legal-related organizations (Table 12.6).

In general, more than half of human service nonprofits indicated that late payments were a problem, and almost one in four organizations considered it a big problem. Late payments affected different types of organizations to different degrees. More than half of human service multipurpose groups and employment organizations found late payments problematic.

Delayed reimbursement was more problematic for large organizations (59%) compared with small (46%) and medium-sized (49%) nonprofits. Illinois had the highest percentage of nonprofits reporting that late payments were an issue (83%). Maine and Connecticut followed, with, respectively, 80% and 73% of nonprofits indicating that delayed payments were a burden. More than 60% of organizations in the District of Columbia, Pennsylvania, Louisiana, Nevada, Indiana, New York, and Kentucky also reported late payments.

TABLE 12.6 Organizations With Late Payments by Size

Expense Size	Percent
$100,000 to $249,999	34
$250,000 to $999,999	38
$1 million or more	46

Note: Missing or not applicable answers were excluded.
Source: The Urban Institute, National Study of Nonprofit-Government Contracting and Grants (2010b).

TABLE 12.7 Organizations With Late Payments by Type

Type of Organization	Percent
Crime and legal related	46
Employment	41
Food, agriculture, and nutrition	28
Housing and shelter	34
Public safety and disaster relief	12
Youth development	37
Human service multipurpose	44
Community and economic development	34

Note: Missing or not applicable answers were excluded.
Source: The Urban Institute, National Study of Nonprofit-Government Contracting and Grants (2010b).

TABLE 12.8 Days Government Contract and Grant Payments Are Past Due by Level

Level of Government	Days (%)				
	30	60	90	Over 90	Total
Local	24	30	16	31	100
State	22	26	16	36	100
Federal	28	30	18	25	100

Note: Figures are based on organizations that reported past due payments.
Source: The Urban Institute, National Study of Nonprofit-Government Contracting and Grants (2010b).

Federal, state, and local governments were not equally late in their payments to nonprofits. State governments were most likely to be more than 90 days late, a delay that could reflect states' bleak financial situations during the recession. Federal government agencies were more likely than their state and local counterparts to make late payments within 30 days (Table 12.7).

In 2009, not only were state governments most likely to be 90 days late in paying nonprofit contracts and grants, but they also had the largest past due amounts per organization (Table 12.8).

Because some human service nonprofits cannot afford to cover late reimbursements, governments' delayed payments add a significant burden to their budgets and abilities to provide services to their communities.

The Recession's Effect on Nonprofit Revenue

The recent recession cut deeply into nonprofits' revenues just as demand rose for many basic human services. Payments from government agencies dropped, donations from individuals, corporations, and private foundations shrank, and investment returns and fee income fell.

At the state level, government spending declined in fiscal years 2009 and 2010. In fiscal year 2010, 40 states cut their general fund expenditures and 44 states estimated lower general fund expenditures than in the previous fiscal year. Fiscal year 2010 general fund expenditures are currently estimated to be $612.9 billion compared with $657.9 billion in fiscal year 2009, a 6.8% decline. Falling tax revenue squeezed state budgets, leading to cuts in all major service areas. Since 2008, at least 45 states and the District of Columbia have cut health care (30 states), services for the elderly and disabled (25 states and DC), K-12 education (30 states and DC), and other areas.

Nonprofits have been documenting the twin challenges of reduced funding and higher demand for services in Arizona, Kansas, New Jersey, New York, Wisconsin, and other states. In Louisiana, nonprofits report that funding and charitable giving have dropped off, while operational costs and demand for services have risen, yet they are still "demonstrating their tenacity, resilience, and innovation...just as they did after the hurricane in 2005 and then again in 2008." In Wisconsin, 41% of nonprofits said that despite financial challenges they would expand key services in the coming years.

Reduced Revenue

Our study documents the national scope and state variations in the recession's impact on nonprofits. We find that revenues from every source declined and that most human service nonprofits were affected (Table 12.9).

Government Funding

As tax revenues dropped during the recession, government contracts and grants to nonprofits shrank at every level. Fifty-six percent of organizations reported less revenue from state agencies, 49% lost local government funding, and 31% lost federal dollars. The larger the nonprofit, the more likely it was to report reduced government funding.

TABLE 12.9 Average Amounts Governments Still Owe Nonprofits by Level

Level of Government	Average Amount ($)
Local	38,937
State	117,679
Federal	97,635

Note: Figures are based on organizations that reported past-due payments and the dollar amount still owed.
Source: The Urban Institute, National Study of Nonprofit-Government Contracting and Grants (2010b).

Overall, federal government funding declined at the same rate for most types of nonprofit organizations. However, dollars for housing and shelter organizations fell the least, with just 19% of organizations reporting declines. The same was true for local government funding. Youth development and employment organizations reported the largest decreases in revenue from state government agencies, 63% and 61%, respectively.

Fee Income

Fee income was less likely to decline in 2009 than were other types of revenues. Among respondents that collected fees from government as a third-party payer (e.g., Medicaid), about a third received less revenue. Experiences differed greatly by program area. For example, 69% of youth development organizations reported that third-party fees had decreased while just 17% of community and economic development groups said fee income had declined.

Among nonprofits that collected fees from self-paying participants, 39% reported that collected fees had decreased, while 40% said that collected fees had remained about the same. Fifty-one percent of crime- and legal-related nonprofits said fees from self-paying participants had fallen, while 33% of employment groups reported no change.

Donations

Nonprofit budgets were further squeezed as donations fell. While contributions from corporations, individuals, private foundations, and federated fund-raising nonprofits (e.g., United Way) make up a smaller share of total nonprofit revenue, they still play a crucial role in supporting operating revenues, innovation, and other needs. Individual giving can provide a critical margin of unrestricted revenue. Shrinking contributions can seriously set back capacity building.

Donations are the largest source of funding for about one in five human service nonprofits. Midsized organizations are much more dependent on donations than are small or large nonprofits. In fact, half of all medium-sized organizations rely on donations as their single largest source of funding.

More than half of nonprofits reported declines in contributions from corporations (59%), individuals (50%), and private foundations (53%) and through federated giving (53%). With the exception of federated giving, smaller nonprofits experienced larger declines in donations than did larger organizations.

Investment Income

Reduced investment income was widely experienced during the recession—72% of organizations reported losses in 2009. Nonprofits of all sizes and program areas and in all regions saw their interest on bank accounts fall. Arizona nonprofits were hit the hardest, with 95% of nonprofits reporting a drop in such income. Investment income, however, accounts for only 4% of revenue for human service nonprofits. A third of nonprofits did not report any investment income revenue in 2009.

Coping With Reduced Revenue

To cope with lost revenue, human service organizations cut expenses and services, borrowed money, and, in some cases, closed offices or program sites. In 2009, 82% of human service providers scaled back their operations, with most organizations resorting to two or more cutbacks. Half of organizations froze or reduced salaries, 39% drew on financial reserves, and 38% laid off employees (Figure 12.8).

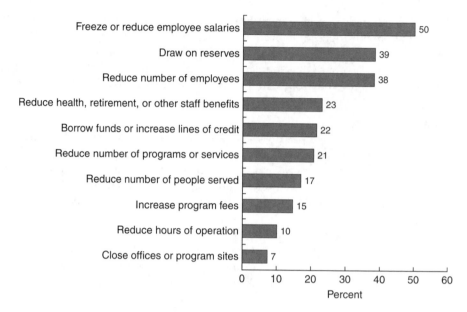

FIGURE 12.8 2009 Cutbacks by human service organizations.

Larger organizations were more likely to cut salaries, reduce benefits, and downsize staff than were smaller or midsized organizations. Three out of five crime- and legal-related nonprofits and the same ratio of youth development groups froze or reduced salaries. Three out of five human service organizations in Connecticut, Illinois, and Minnesota cut salaries, while only a quarter of nonprofits in North Dakota and Arkansas did. Organizations in Illinois were most likely to borrow funds or increase their lines of credit (42%), while groups in Montana were least likely to do so (3%).

Contracting Problems Intensified Reduced Revenue

During the recession, nonprofits that had had previous problems with government contracts were much more likely to make cutbacks than were organizations that did not report such problems. Late or inadequate payments, contracting changes, and the hassle of applying for and reporting on contracts and grants aggravated the financial stress of shrinking revenues and rising demand.

Looking at each of these problems individually, we found that nonprofits that were underpaid for contracted services were twice as likely to borrow funds or increase lines of credit (27%) as were organizations without payment problems (12%). These inadequately paid organizations were also more likely to freeze or reduce employee salaries, reduce benefits, lay off staff, and draw on reserves (Figure 12.9).

Human service organizations that reported problems with late government payments were more likely to freeze or reduce salaries, lay off staff, and draw on reserves compared with organizations that did not have late-payment problems (Figure 12.10).

Nonprofits that said government changes to contracts were a problem were more likely to freeze or reduce salaries, reduce employee benefits, lay off staff, cut back on programs or services, draw on reserves, and borrow funds or increase lines of credit than were nonprofits that did not say contract changes were a problem (Figure 12.11).

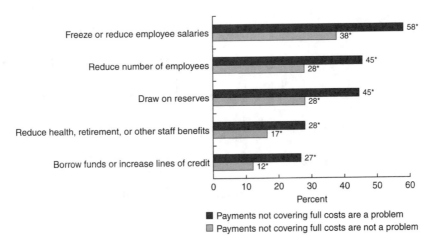

FIGURE 12.9 2009 Cutbacks by human service nonprofits by payments not covering full costs of contracted services.

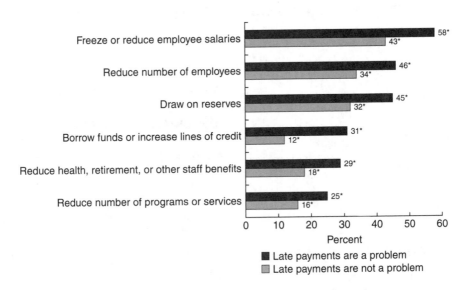

FIGURE 12.10 2009 Cutbacks by human service nonprofits by late payments.

Organizations that had a problem with the complexity of and/or the time required in applying for contracts and grants were significantly more likely to freeze or reduce salaries, lay off staff, and borrow funds or increase lines of credit compared with nonprofits that did not report these application problems (Figure 12.12).

Finally, nonprofits that found the reporting requirements complex and time consuming were more likely to freeze or reduce salaries and cut employee benefits compared with nonprofits that did not find the reporting requirements burdensome (Figure 12.13).

How Contracting Experiences Have Changed

In 2009, 64% of nonprofits reported having about the same experiences with government contracting as they had in prior years, while 31% reported that their experiences had gotten worse. Only 5% of organizations reported a better experience with government contracting in 2009 than they'd had in previous years (Figure 12.14).

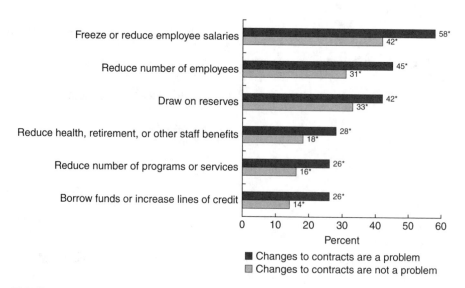

FIGURE 12.11 2009 Cutbacks by human service nonprofits by changes to contracts.

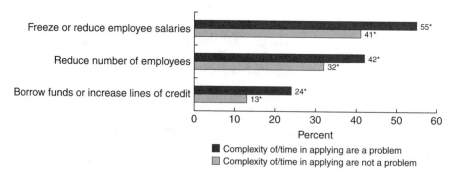

FIGURE 12.12 2009 Cutbacks by human service nonprofits by complexity of/time in applying for government contracts and grants.

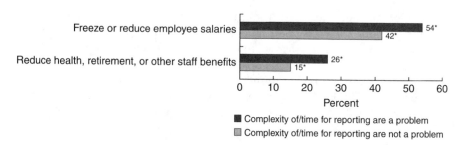

FIGURE 12.13 2009 Cutbacks by human service nonprofits by complexity of/time for reporting on government contracts and grants.

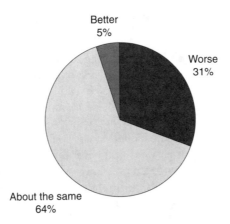

FIGURE 12.14 2009 Government contracting experience compared with prior year, national.

Large nonprofits were more likely to say that their experiences had been worse (36%) than were small (29%) and medium-sized (27%) organizations.

Contracting experiences varied greatly by state. Fifty-seven percent of organizations in Illinois and 56% in Hawaii said that their experiences with government contracting were worse in 2009 than in prior years, but only 11% of organizations in North Dakota and 6% in Arkansas said their experiences had gotten worse.

> 2009 was my 8th year as executive director here at our organization and I was the deputy director for the previous 4 years. This was without a doubt, THE most difficult year I've experienced, both internally and externally. Internally, we laid people off, used furloughs, cut benefits, all challenging ways to treat my staff who are working harder as the demands for our services remained the same and often increased over the year. Externally, the political climate while our state is in crisis has created additional tensions between nonprofits that are forced to compete at increasing levels when we should be working together. All my time is being spent putting out fires, making it harder to search for new money and new inspiration for an exhausted and overtaxed workforce. They say 2010 will be worse? I am concerned for my agency, as well as many others. (Survey Respondent)

This study marks a first step toward implementing workable solutions to the problems documented here: understanding the dimensions of government–nonprofit contracting and grants, the major problems, the impact of the recession, and the types of nonprofits most affected. The next steps will require concerted efforts to craft and test solutions and encourage governments and nonprofits to adopt those solutions. Following are five approaches that some nonprofits are pursuing that enable them to seek and secure public funding while advancing their missions, sustaining their organizations, and retaining some room to maneuver in the process.

FIVE WAYS TO NAVIGATE FISCAL CRISIS

The head of a large nonprofit that has been serving children and families since the 19th century and that gets most of its funding from state and local government recently told us,

> We have never had the chance to sit down across the table from government and discuss line by line what it takes to do the work. They call the terms, they put

the dollars on the table, they give the staffing patterns, and you can take it or leave it.

This is a problem, and it is only going to get worse. Indeed, for decades now, government has been outsourcing the delivery of human services to nonprofits. Helping homeless youth come in from the streets, bringing meals to the elderly, providing after-school programs for at-risk children—these are among the hundreds of essential services nonprofit organizations are providing every day. As reported above in the Urban Institute study, in 2009, nonprofits in the United States received more than $100 billion from government agencies via contracts and grants for the delivery of human services. For these nonprofits, government funding represented 65% of their total revenues. Roughly two thirds of this funding originates at the state and local levels. And increasingly, government agencies are outsourcing not only the delivery of these services but their financing as well by reimbursing nonprofits considerably less than what it costs to deliver them. These organizations are left to cobble together their own resources from other funding sources to make up the difference.

The long-term outlook for human services funding is bleak. The federal government is facing record budget deficits and interest payments to service its rapidly accumulating debt, the rising cost of health care, and the demographic challenge of paying for entitlement benefits for retiring baby boomers. Given that roughly a quarter of state government funding and a third of local government funding comes from Washington, DC, the federal budget squeeze will in turn impinge on human services budgets at these levels. Moreover, state and local governments have their own demographic time bombs to address, in the form of an estimated $1 trillion to $3 trillion in unfunded pension and retirement liabilities for current employees and retirees.

This brings us to the following questions: How can nonprofits that rely on government funding navigate this increasingly powerful undertow? How can they stay afloat? And can they even hope to make progress? The hard truth is that only a different turn in the political debate over what we owe the most vulnerable members of our society, along with a reversal of our nation's fiscal fortunes, can change this tide—and both appear unlikely in the foreseeable future. The sobering reality is that nonprofits will have to be even more entrepreneurial in their funding models, efficient in deploying their resources, and vigilant in serving their missions to make headway.

Here, at least, there are exemplars. The Bridgespan Group, a nonprofit advisor and resource for mission-driven leaders and organizations to accelerate social impact, works with social-sector leaders to help scale impact, build leadership, advance philanthropic effectiveness, and accelerate learning. Through consulting engagements and workshops with human service agencies across the country, The Bridgespan Group has observed—and confirmed through interviews with nonprofit leaders, sector observers, and government funders—that there are clearheaded, highly focused nonprofit agencies using a variety of strategies to sustain themselves financially while continuing to provide high-quality services as they carry out their missions. In an era of "take-it-or-leave-it" contracts, some agencies are finding room to maneuver.

Competing for Funding

Most people are familiar with the problem of monopoly, in which a dominant seller is able to effectively set prices for buyers. We tend to be less familiar with the equally imperfect market condition in which a dominant buyer is able to effectively set the price it will pay to the sellers that want to do business with it. For the record, this is called a monopsony, though many refer to it as the Walmart effect, given how that company systematically leverages its share of the retail market to put the squeeze on upstream producers of consumer goods. When it comes to the market for delivery of social services, government agencies wield something that looks like the Walmart effect on steroids.

The government agency typically sets the price and, in cash-strapped times like these, may keep it flat or reset it downward as it sees fit. Prices often fail to cover the full cost of those services. As stated in the above survey, 68% of respondents identified this failure to cover the full cost of delivery as a problem. According to the chief executive officer (CEO) of a large New York City nonprofit, "The contracting agency says they want us to have 'skin in the game.' Now, in reality, government has the statutory responsibility to provide the service. They are contracting out because they think they can get it cheaper."

Government also leverages its market power to further squeeze nonprofits by changing the terms and driving the execution of these contracts in its favor. The above Urban Institute survey reported that 57% of nonprofits responding saw government changes to contracts and grants as a problem. Agencies could suddenly be required to have an employee with a master's degree in social work delivering services that less credentialed employees had previously provided—with no increase in reimbursement to cover the higher labor costs. Along similar lines, 53% of nonprofits see delayed payments as a problem; for cash-strapped nonprofits, not getting paid on time means struggling to make payrolls (The Urban Institute, 2010a).

Faced with deteriorating conditions, why don't nonprofit service providers simply walk away? The harsh truth is they can't. Nonprofits are prepared to accept poor contract prices and endure readjustments in prices and terms and even badly delayed payments—simply to keep their missions going. The CEO of a successful multistate nonprofit bluntly observed of his government counterparties, "They know we are fighting for scraps, so everyone will just jump in to try to get that contract."

Can high-performing nonprofits escape this "commodity trap" dynamic by delivering better results and thereby standing out from the pack? After all, in private markets, companies often differentiate their products and services and compete on value instead of lower prices. Why can't high-performance human service providers do the same?

The idea of performance-based contracts came to the fore in the 1990s with the reinventing government movement. These contracts make some portion of the government's payment contingent on the nonprofit's realizing the desired outcomes (e.g., formerly homeless families remaining stably housed), in contrast with the usual focus on accountability for inputs (such as managing clients within specified caseload limits) or outputs (number of clients served; Martin, 2005; Osborne & Gaebler, 1993).

In theory, under performance-based contracts, nonprofits that are in a better position to hit the outcome targets and track the fact that they have done so would have a competitive advantage and, over time, could increase their shares of government funding. In several instances in which performance-based contracting has been systematically applied, such as with child welfare services in Illinois and Tennessee, or at the municipal level in New York City, there has been an improvement in outcomes for beneficiaries, sometimes with a reduction in the overall cost of services.

Yet for all the success of performance-based contracting in a few locations and policy domains, it has not been widely replicated. Among the obstacles are a lack of consensus on appropriate outcome measures, the difficulty and expense for nonprofits in tracking outcomes, and—not least—the complex challenges that government agencies themselves face in focusing on monitoring and paying for outcomes. As the CEO of a large Los Angeles–based nonprofit told us,

> Many of the government funding sources go through the motions of tying funding to outcomes, but it doesn't really work like that. There is a bit of smokescreen that

gives people the impression that it's going on, but in reality they are still counting heads and counting meals.

Lastly, nonprofits compete on influence and on relationships. This is not necessarily insidious—civil servants often grow to like and respect some of the nonprofit leaders they do business with and are naturally inclined to keep doing business with them. But politics clearly plays its part. As an entrepreneurial nonprofit CEO, who has been repeatedly frustrated in his efforts to expand his agency into new jurisdictions, told us,

> To get a contract now, you basically have to take it away from someone else. There is no new money on the table...If you are better friends with the government, then you will be keeping the contract.

It stands to reason that in a $100 billion market, there will be a lot of nonprofits that will vigorously defend their interests and their contracts, even when other providers have a better track record of demonstrating outcomes.

One retired state commissioner who had been frustrated in his efforts to bring in new high-performance providers to his state told us that the incumbent nonprofits were largely to blame:

> The old crowd is politically powerful. They were fighting tooth and nail for every penny they could get. Our approach was a direct threat to them, and they were able to work their contacts in the legislature like nobody's business to oppose what we were trying to do.

Approaches to Staying Afloat

In the highly constrained world of public funding, can a nonprofit delivering superior outcomes do anything more than take the price, accept the terms, provide the service, and hope that things do not get worse? Do nonprofits have any hope of agency, of having influence or exerting power?

Though there is nothing resembling a formula, some nonprofits are rising to the challenges as "tough times" becomes the new normal. These nonprofit leaders are pursuing strategies that enable them to seek and secure public funding while advancing their missions, sustaining their organizations, and retaining some room to maneuver in the process. Below are five approaches that seem to be working for the most ambitious human services nonprofits.

1. Get to Strategic Clarity

The first step in getting to strategic clarity is to set priorities for where, how, and with whom you seek to have impact. But establishing an organization's mission-critical priorities can be difficult. For larger nonprofits that have grown by taking on a range of contracts across different jurisdictions, government agencies, and policy areas, it is hard to make comparative judgments and set priorities across different kinds of programs and beneficiaries. The quest to win new contracts can take on a life of its own, and nonprofits can slip into what Peter Frumkin has termed "vendorism" (2002). Indeed, organizations that have solid infrastructures and reputations for doing the work specified within budget constraints are often recruited by government agencies to take on tasks that may not really be central to their missions.

Some organizations manage to avoid this pitfall by clarifying priorities, articulating the impacts they want to be held accountable for, and specifying how they will go about realizing those impacts. They define their missions at the next level down in more practical ways. The DePelchin Children's Center in Houston provides adoption, foster care, mental health, teen parenting, and other services from 60 sites across its service area. In addition to an overall mission statement, it developed a set of more specific statements aligned with each of its seven service categories. According to Peggy Pugh, its chief financial officer, these service-line-specific missions "enable us to apply that mission statement in making a decision about a given contract." For example, the more specific statements pointed toward gaps in autism programming and psychiatric services. After conducting a community needs assessment to verify that these gaps existed and that DePelchin was in a good position to help fill them, the agency went looking for government funding to support these services.

The second step in getting to strategic clarity is understanding the true cost of each program or set of services the agency provides. By "true," we mean *direct costs* (frontline staff, rent for service delivery sites) plus *indirect costs* (that program's share of management, information technology, and other agency-wide costs). It may sound simple, but in our experience even the most well-managed organizations have to work hard to understand the real costs of any particular program—especially how to allocate the indirect or so-called overhead costs that are harder to tie directly to a given program or service but that are essential for successful delivery of outcomes.[12]

"This is really about how general ledgers are set up," DePelchin's Pugh said:

Each division needs to maintain its own P&L (profit and loss statement) and timesheets. You also need to keep track of the units of service they provide. And this is not just the accounting people, but also the operational people. It is important to make program people accountable if they are not within their budget.

The third and final step in getting to strategic clarity is to make better decisions on whether or how to pursue a particular opportunity for government funding. The key here is for nonprofits to take into account both the potential mission and financial impacts of a given contract.

One simple but nonetheless powerful tool that helps human service nonprofits do this is what we term the program portfolio matrix. As depicted in Figure 12.15, the horizontal axis of the matrix shows programs' relative mission impacts. On the vertical axis, programs' net financial contributions are shown. The program portfolio matrix is a snapshot of the organization as a whole, created one decision at a time. In the ideal world, all programs would lie in the northeast quadrant—strongly aligned with the mission and with their full costs covered. But human services nonprofits do not operate in an ideal

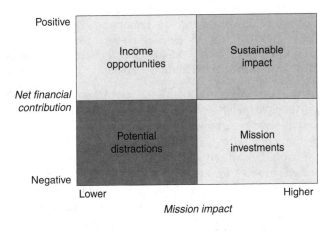

FIGURE 12.15 Program portfolio matrix.

world, and this quadrant is often sparsely populated. Thus, nonprofits need to look for opportunities to increase the financial contributions of their mission investments as well as develop and optimize revenues from income opportunities—provided this does not distract from realizing their missions. The trap to avoid, and in our experience a common pitfall, is maintaining a lot of potential distractions—programs that consume more cash than they bring in and do not have much mission impact. Nonprofits should pursue plans to either manage these programs into another quadrant in the portfolio or, if this is not feasible, opt out of them altogether.

Making decisions on how a particular contract will fit in the overall program portfolio, instead of deciding on it in isolation, helps an organization clarify and make trade-offs more effectively. Pugh told us, "At times we will take a contract that doesn't fully cover our costs if it is aligned with our mission and if it positions us for other opportunities, for example, in a different geographic area."

Another means for good decision making is establishing a formal process that brings to light and resolves questions about a given contracting opportunity. As agencies grow and diversify their programs, contracting decisions may become decentralized and big trade-offs are not reflected, let alone resolved. Pugh told us,

> People would submit a proposal for a contract without the management's approval. Now we have a grant funding meeting once a month...We discuss any new grants that come along, and drive the conversation from our operational mission statement.

In DePelchin's case, the program and finance sides of the house are both involved, each sharpening the other's perspective as well as that of the leadership team, which ultimately will be accountable for delivering services.

2. Diversify Government Funding Streams

For nonprofits that get the majority of their revenues from government sources, diversifying funding across different government agencies, programs, and contracts can help sustain organizations and their services against declining revenues. In fact, this is a common strategy. Most human service nonprofits hold multiple government contracts. But too often this diversification is driven by opportunism that strains organizations, not by a strategic design that plays to their strengths and sustains their missions.

Denise Cross, president of Cornerstones of Care in Missouri, described how her organization looks at diversification:

> Always be thinking about services you can provide that can be provided in a different way or provided in a different geographic area, so that you are better diversified...We developed an approach to support children with behavioral disorders in school settings. It's an evidence-based curriculum—we've done a lot of research around it—and we began thinking about who else could benefit from it. So we then took this same approach to children in foster care.

Note that this kind of diversification is *not* about opportunistically searching for new service populations to qualify for a different source of government funding. In the case of Cornerstones, it is about serving the same kids with the same well-developed intervention, only in a different setting.

Many nonprofits that rely on government funds for the majority of their revenues also receive some funding from nongovernment sources: corporations, foundations, and individuals. Supplementing government contract revenue with contributions from other sources may be essential in filling funding gaps. But being selective matters. As Cross told us, "We are more likely to take a contract that doesn't cover our full cost if we believe that there is broad community support for the service." For example, Cornerstones opened an emergency shelter for children removed from their homes because of abuse or neglect. It fund-raised from individual donors and foundations for start-up costs and secured a government contract to maintain the program. When more kids turned out to be using the shelter than had first been envisioned, Cornerstones went back to donors to fill in government funding gaps.

Cross also explained that her organization has been able to engage third-party payers for some services by "building relationships with insurance companies and structuring our programs so that they feel comfortable paying for them." For example, insurance may not pay for a 30-day stay, so services can be condensed into 3- to 5-day stays that are reimbursable.

3. Improve Productivity

The drive to improve productivity has long lagged in the nonprofit sector, in large part due to the prevalence of input-based funding and the ambiguity about what nonprofits are actually "producing." There are signs, however, that leading human services providers are sharpening their focus on productivity. In the current funding environment, this is a good thing for all parties, ranging from the taxpayers who ultimately pay for services and the more productive nonprofits who find it easier to live within their increasingly limited means to the beneficiaries who depend on the services provided.

Consider the observations and experience of Patrick Lawler, CEO of Youth Villages, a human services organization that works with more than 20,000 children and families in 20 states and Washington, DC:

> One of the challenges of our field is that we don't set the price. And most likely that price will not change in 10 years. So every day, you have to say, "How can we do this more efficiently and more effectively?" It's in our DNA.

Lawler's interest in productivity goes back two decades, to a business book entitled *Demystifying Baldridge* that he found while browsing in a bookstore. "It taught me about metrics and the use of data to improve quality. I wondered: Why can't a not-for-profit social services organization manage its quality and costs and processes in the same way?" Over the years, Lawler's question has led to a range of breakthroughs at Youth Villages. For example, team leaders realized that typing in case notes was taking up hours of clinician time, so the agency now uses electronic medical records and voice recognition software to allow clinicians to streamline their documentation, reducing time spent on that task by 40% to 50%. The productivity mind-set "is now a big part of what we do and it has transformed our organization," Lawler notes. "We are constantly looking at ways to manage time or cost more efficiently to produce the same or better outcomes for lower cost."

4. Measure Outcomes

Given the nascent state of performance-based government contracting, it may seem odd for this approach to show up on our list. Yet if the goal is to stay focused on mission, then measuring outcomes is essential. All too often, outcomes measurement is something nonprofits feel obliged to do for reporting to external parties about their retrospective performance. But the real power of measuring outcomes (and the appropriate starting point for nonprofits) is to drive internal reflection, learn about how the work is going, and plan how it can be improved. Viewed in this way, outcomes measurement can become a powerful way for leaders and staff to connect with and advance their organization's mission.

Consider the experience of the Hillside Family of Agencies in western and central New York, which provides a wide range of child and family services. As Hillside CEO Dennis Richardson explained, "We've purposely moved to being more data driven, a significant cultural shift for us. It wasn't that any public or private funder made us do those things. We wanted to know: Were we making a difference?"

A great example of Hillside's progress in outcomes measurement is its Work–Scholarship Connection, a nationally recognized youth development program shown to increase graduation rates and prepare students to enter college or the workplace. The agency began by tracking overall after-the-fact outcomes like graduations. It then moved on to measuring specific leading indicators, such as attendance and credit accumulation. As Hillside COO Clyde Comstock said,

> We can watch a whole cohort of kids as they are going through school, so we can tell if we have a cohort on target or in trouble. And we can do it with individual kids to tailor the services.

Hillside's measurement work continues to evolve. Comstock noted, "Now we are in a position to pose and answer questions like, 'Does extra tutoring help a kid who is more than 20% behind, or is it not a good use of resources?'" Outcomes measurement is thus a critical support for advancing productivity and tracking progress, or the lack thereof.

Looking ahead, Hillside plans to move its measurement work to the next level with a randomized control trial. CEO Richardson sees a clear link between Hillside's increasingly sharp focus on measurement and its future sustainability. "We started focusing more on measuring our outcomes as a result of our organizational curiosity: What are we doing that actually works?" he observed. "We also have come to believe—looking ahead to the future—that, if we couldn't answer that question, our funding would go to someone who could."

5. Move Beyond Vendorism

Among the nonprofit leaders we have talked to and worked with, the organizations most effective in engaging government are distinguished not so much by a particular set of activities as by a certain mind-set. They see the decision makers in government agencies as *customers*. They try to understand their concerns and unmet needs and to design compelling solutions to address them.

Achieving this mind-set isn't easy. After all, nonprofits tend to see the people and communities they serve, not the government that funds them, as the true customers. Also, government's power and its habit of wielding it arbitrarily are more likely to create anxiety, resentment, or a sense of helplessness than a customer-service ethic. Nevertheless, it is the nonprofits that are doing the selling and the government agencies that are doing the service buying.

By viewing government decision makers as customers and working to understand and address their needs, nonprofits can put themselves in a much better position to inform and shape government requests for proposals (RFPs). Youth Villages's Lawler observed,

> We try to form relationships with the highest level person in the government agency. We find out where the leadership's biggest needs and challenges are, and then look at what services we have that can help them solve the problem...We look over every word in new state budgets and the statements made by the governor or head of child welfare services and put together a plan for how to address the needs identified.

Richardson and his team at Hillside have developed a multistep cocreation process—intended to be completed before an RFP is issued—that involves bringing together the perspectives of families and funders, along with the team's, as the service provider to improve program design. Even after an RFP has been issued, it may not be too late to keep the conversation going. Richardson notes,

> We want to position ourselves as a source of solutions for funders. We will provide a proposal that violates the terms of the RFP but that accurately lays out what is really needed. More than once, that has led to the RFP being reopened and we have secured the rebid.

EXHIBIT 12.1 Managing in a Tough Government Funding Environment

THREE THINGS *NOT* TO DO

1. Crisis and Opportunity

Don't squander the chance to make important changes in your organization in terms of operations, leadership roles, or staffing. When significant cuts must be made, across-the-board reductions or leaving vacancies unfilled may seem like the fairest and least painful solution. But in doing so, you are postponing hard choices and losing the chance to resolve your budget challenges in ways that align with your mission and strategy.

2. Mind-Set

When the going gets tough, don't hunker down into a negative mind-set that causes you to hide or become isolated from potential sources of support. A crisis may turn out to be the best time to ask for help and to mobilize champions. Call on the community, your board—they may be more helpful than you think—and even other organizations, which may be able to take on programs you can no longer support to keep services alive in the community.

3. Stewardship

Don't let desperation guide your decision making and don't make decisions that are entirely about short-term financial solutions. Examples of bad decisions may include pursuing contracts because you need the money, not because the programs fit with your strategy; and underbidding in a way that starves your organization, burns out your staff, and hurts other providers, creating big problems down the road. (Your best people *will* go elsewhere if you don't treat them right during a crisis.)

Take It or Leave It?

"It is dangerous to be right," observed Voltaire, "when the government is wrong." In our conversations with leaders of human service nonprofits that are financially reliant on government sources, we have heard a lot about what government is doing wrong in its contracting processes. We have heard a great deal of anxiety that in an era of shrinking budgets, the current situation will only get worse, resulting in less funding at all levels of government and more limits on the already limited autonomy of nonprofits seeking to provide high-quality services.

But within this $100 billion sector—one on which so many vulnerable people depend—we believe there remains some room to maneuver. The approaches we have sketched out hardly guarantee success, and Exhibit 12.1 highlights some things you should specifically not do as you marshal your efforts. The most thoughtful strategy in

TABLE 12.10 Revenue Changes Reported by Human Service Nonprofits With Government Contracts and Grants in 2009

Source of Revenue	Percent		
	Decrease	Remain Same	Increase
Investment income	72	18	10
Corporate donations	59	28	13
State government agencies	56	30	14
Federated giving (e.g., United Way)	53	38	9
Private foundations	53	31	17
Individual donations	50	29	21
Local government agencies	49	40	11
Fees from self-paying participants	39	40	20
Fees from government as third-party payer (e.g., Medicaid)	34	47	19
Federal government agencies	31	39	30
Other	52	24	24

Note: Percentages for each source of revenue are based only on organizations that reported revenue from that source. The "other" category includes royalties, church/congregation donations, unspecified contracts and grants, and earned income from events.
Source: The Urban Institute, *National Study of Nonprofit-Government Contracting and Grants* (2010b).

the world can still come to grief when the government suddenly delays yet another payment or develops an RFP to solicit competitive bids for a service that your organization currently holds the contract to provide. Yet, within the system's numerous constraints, nonprofits have been employing these approaches to get beyond a take-it-or-leave-it relationship with their government funders, keeping their eyes on their missions and doing the best they know how for the people and communities they serve.

CONCLUSIONS

The chapter introduced nonprofits' contracts with government, the problems with those contracts, and the cutbacks nonprofits made in 2009, and Table 12.10 looks at the revenue changes of nonprofits that receive government funds have experienced, in part because of the changes and challenges in navigating government funding. While such a deep recession has accelerated and exacerbated longer-term structural conditions, the implications for people served by these organizations, the lost nonprofit jobs and institutional capacity, and the diminished flexibility of these organizations are costs that have been ignored or accepted without analysis or debate.

Government policies and practices play a substantial role in the ability of nonprofits to carry out their missions. This chapter documented the sheer scale and variety of the 200,000 formal funding relationships that nonprofits have with governments. Fully half of the almost 33,000 nonprofit human service providers have contracts with all three levels of government—local, state, and national; only 19% work with only one level of government. This devolved government contracting and grants system exacts a heavy toll on many nonprofit providers. Organizations must deal with government policies that differ from one agency to the next and often from contract to contract. The complexity of application processes and reporting requirements is not widely recognized, nor is the resulting need for professionally trained staff and administrative resources to support them.

Specifically, nonprofits have reported significant problems with government agencies' making late or insufficient payments, requiring complex and time-consuming applications and reports, and changing contracts and grants after they have been approved. The recession highlighted these problems as many nonprofits struggled to stay afloat. Yet while there are serious and widespread problems, good practices do exist. Nonprofits in some states reported relatively few contracting problems and could be studied as models for improving nonprofit–government funding relationships.

In addition, this chapter identified potential areas for reform. Governments need contracting practices that are more efficient and productive, including policies for improving proper and on-time payment to nonprofits, covering reasonable administrative costs for contracted programs, and using standard financial and reporting formats. Matching requirements could be dropped or reduced, particularly during times of economic stress. Nonprofits must be involved in efforts to structure more efficient and effective contracting practices. Collaborative approaches with formal feedback and consultation opportunities would help to facilitate positive changes. These improvements could, in the long run, save nonprofits and government agencies countless dollars.

Meanwhile there are steps that nonprofits can take to navigate fiscal crises, starting with gaining strategic clarity around their portfolios to determine what is in and what is out and including both diversifying funding streams and increasing productivity. In addition, nonprofits that measure outcomes may find that they can draw funding to what works and use their results to strengthen their performance and deepen relationships with funders.

NOTES

1. This chapter is based on an article by the authors that appeared in *Stanford Social Innovation Review*, "Five Ways to Navigate the Fiscal Crisis" (2012, Winter).
2. Collaborating authors include Elizabeth T. Boris, Erwin de Leon, Milena Nikolova, and Katie L. Roeger.
3. The Urban Institute (2010a).
4. A summary brief, *Contracts and Grants Between Human Service Nonprofits and Governments*, the methodology for the study, and a compendium of data by state are available on the Urban Institute website (www.urban.org/nonprofitcontracting.cfm).
5. Human service organizations comprise one of the major categories of nonprofit organizations under the National Taxonomy of Exempt Entities. The recreation and sports category was excluded from the study. See methodology section for sampling information.
6. The definitions of government contracts and grants often overlap and are not standard across jurisdictions. Both are payments for services that governments agree to underwrite.
7. Grønbjerg (2001) reclassifies components of the traditional categories of public social welfare spending (social insurance, including Medicare; public aid, including Medicaid; health and medical; veterans' programs, including medical and education; education; housing; other) into functional spending fields: insurance cash payments (social insurance without medical benefits), all education spending, all medical spending (health and medical, medical benefits), means-tested income assistance, welfare/social services, and other.
8. The Urban Institute, National Center for Charitable Statistics, www.nccs.urban.org
9. The National Taxonomy of Exempt Entities is the classification system for nonprofit organizations developed by the National Center for Charitable Statistics at the Urban

Institute and used by the Internal Revenue Service. It can be accessed at nccs.urban. org/classification/index.cfm

10. Examples of federal programs set up as large grants to state and local governments and then passed through to nonprofits include the Child and Adult Care Food Program (Department of Agriculture), the Emergency Shelter Grants Program (Housing and Urban Development), Medicaid (Department of Health and Human Services), Social Services Block Grants (Department of Health and Human Services), Temporary Assistance for Needy Families (Department of Health and Human Services), and the Workforce Investment Act Youth Programs (Department of Labor) (U.S. Government Accountability Office, 2009).

11. The 19 states in which nonprofits reported late payments are Arizona, California, Connecticut, Florida, Georgia, Hawaii, Illinois, Indiana, Louisiana, Michigan, Minnesota, Nevada, New York, North Carolina, Oregon, Pennsylvania, Rhode Island, Texas, and Wisconsin.

12. Nonprofits can find a free cost analysis toolkit at www.bridgespan.org

REFERENCES

Bowman, W., & Fremont-Smith, M. R. (2006). Nonprofits and state and local governments. In E. T. Boris & C. E. Steuerle (Eds.), *Nonprofits and government: Collaboration & conflict* (pp. 219–256). Washington, DC: Urban Institute Press.

Denhardt, K. G., Aristigueta, M. P., Foote, L., Auger, D., Miltenberger, L., Dodds, C., & Addison, C. (2008). *Forward together: Achieving better performance in nonprofit—State government contracting for human services.* Newark, DE: University of Delaware.

Frumkin, P. (2002). *On being nonprofit: A conceptual and policy primer* (pp. 167–169). Cambridge, MA: Harvard University Press.

Grønbjerg, K. (2001). The U.S. nonprofit human service sector: A creeping revolution. *Nonprofit and Voluntary Sector Quarterly, 30*(2), 276–297.

Martin, L. L. (2005). Performance-based contracting for human services: Does it work? *Administration in Social Work, 29*(1), 63–77.

Deffiey, R. D. (2010, December). *Nonprofit current conditions report: Analysis of a Minnesota Council of Nonprofits member survey.* St. Paul: Minnesota Council of Nonprofits.

DiNapoli, T. (2009). *Prompt contracting annual report: Calendar year 2009.* Albany, NY: New York State Office of the State Comptroller.

DiNapoli, T. (2010). *New York State's not-for-profit sector.* Albany, NY: New York State Office of the State Comptroller.

Osborne, D., & Gaebler, T. (1993). *Reinventing government.* New York, NY: Plume.

Salamon, L. M. (1987). Partners in public service: The scope and theory of government-nonprofit relations. In W. W. Powell (Ed.), *The nonprofit sector: A research handbook* (pp. 99–117). New Haven, CT: Yale University Press.

Salamon, L. M. (2003). *The resilient sector: The state of nonprofit America.* Washington, DC: Brookings Institution Press.

Smith, S. R. (2006). Government financing of nonprofit activity. In E. T. Boris & E. C. Steuerle (Eds.), *Nonprofit and government: Collaboration and conflict* (pp. 219–256). Washington, DC: Urban Institute Press.

Smith, S. R., & Lipsky, M. (1993). *Nonprofits for hire: The welfare state in the age of contracting.* Cambridge, MA: Harvard University Press.

The Urban Institute. (2010a). *Human service nonprofits and government collaboration: Findings from the 2010 National Survey of Nonprofit Government Contracting and Grants.* Washington, DC: E. T. Boris, E. de Leon, K. L, Roeger, & M. Nikolova. Retrieved from www.urban.org/uploadedpdf/412228-Nonprofit-Government-Contracting.pdf

The Urban Institute. (2010b). *National study of nonprofit-government contracting and grants.* Washington, DC: E. T. Boris, E. de Leon, K. L. Roeger, & M. Nikolova. Retrieved from www.urban.org/uploadedpdf/412227-National-Study-of-Nonprofit-Government.pdf

ADVOCACY STRATEGIES FOR POLICY CHANGE

Tine Hansen-Turton, Tess Mullen, Susan Sherman, and David Thornburgh

There is nothing more difficult to take in hand, more perilous to conduct, or more uncertain in its success, than to take the lead in the introduction of a new order of things.
—Niccolo Machiavelli

Very few social policy changes happen, either regionally or nationally, without some form of advocacy. When these efforts succeed, the results can be transformative. They happen because of creative investments in public persuasion, political activity, and legislative action. This chapter begins with a primer on how nonprofit leaders can become nonprofit advocates. It provides an overview of the legal guidelines that govern nonprofit lobbying. It details the process of developing a policy agenda, learning the legislative landscape, and executing the agenda, concluding with a review of the tactics of effective lobbying, such as working in coalitions, meeting with lawmakers, and cultivating relationships with legislative allies.

The chapter includes case studies that describe the advocacy process that went into the expansion of the role of nurse practitioners as primary care providers and the expansion of the retail-based convenient care clinic model. An additional case study discusses an assessment process on which advocacy for college access and success systems change can be built.

A GUIDE TO NONPROFIT ADVOCACY AND LOBBYING

In August of 2009, the Maryland chapters of the Alzheimer's Association received news that no nonprofit wants to hear. In an attempt to close a severe budget shortfall, Maryland was planning to cut $1 million in funding from its respite care program, an initiative that was vitally important to Alzheimer's patients and their families. As respite care providers themselves, the Maryland chapters of the Alzheimer's Association knew that many full-time, unpaid caregivers needed respite care subsidies to help them secure temporary care for their loved ones while they attended to their own personal needs. Even before its funding was halved, the respite care program's waiting list had already had hundreds of people on it.

With this knowledge, the Maryland chapters sprang into action. Drawing upon its extensive network of administrative and legislative contacts, the Alzheimer's Association launched a multi-pronged initiative aimed at preserving and increasing respite care funding. Over the next year, the association and the families it serves wrote letters to elected officials, testified at legislative hearings, cultivated the support of the Maryland Department of Human Services, and partnered with a number of social service and religious organizations to highlight the importance of respite care. Through its advocacy, the association shed light on the respite care program's human benefits and argued that increased respite care funding could ultimately save the state money by delaying the institutionalization of Alzheimer's patients. As a result of these efforts, the association and its allies accomplished a remarkable feat in an age of increasing fiscal austerity: They succeeded in restoring $250,000 in respite care funding for fiscal year 2011 and added $500,000 back into the program's budget for fiscal year 2012. Through successful lobbying, the Maryland chapters increased support for their clients in a very significant way (M. Douglas, personal communication, October 11, 2011).

Why Lobby?

In the past, many nonprofit leaders saw advocacy and lobbying as ancillary to their jobs but not core to their mission and success. In addition, the word "lobbying" often evokes negative connotations. More and more, however, effective nonprofit leaders have come to see that effective advocacy and lobbying are critical not only to their organizations' success but also to the larger issue(s) their organizations were founded to address.

Lobbying in and of itself is an activity deeply woven into the fabric of American democracy. The First Amendment to the Bill of Rights enshrines Americans' right to "petition their government for a redress of grievances." In its ideal form, lobbying is an activity through which citizens exercise that right and take an active role in shaping their country's future.

Nonprofits of all stripes—from environmental organizations to animal welfare groups—have unique insights into the challenges facing the country today. In the course of their daily work, many nonprofit leaders identify ways in which government programs could be administered better, laws could be improved, or public funding could be distributed more effectively. Given their unique insights into policies' real-world impacts, these leaders have an important role to play in informing legislative debates. By communicating with lawmakers and lobbying for proposals that they believe can make a difference, nonprofit leaders can magnify their impact and enhance their organizations' abilities to meet clients' needs.

This chapter focuses on how nonprofits can shape legislation by lobbying elected officials in ways that are in keeping with the Internal Revenue Service's (IRS's) definitions and requirements. It is important to note, however, that legislative bodies are certainly not the only arena in which nonprofit advocacy occurs. Working with administrators and executive agencies to improve government regulations and programs is another way in which nonprofit advocates can work to create positive change.

Nonprofit Lobbying: The Legal Landscape

When the topic of lobbying is broached, nonprofit leaders often express concern over whether it is actually legal for them to lobby. Let there be no mistake: It is legal for nonprofits to lobby. Before embarking on a lobbying campaign, however, nonprofit leaders need to make sure they understand the IRS regulations that govern lobbying. A 501(c)(3) organization that runs afoul of these regulations can face substantial penalties, including loss of its tax-exempt status and an excise tax.

A 501(c)(3) may lobby as long as lobbying does not constitute a substantial part of its activities. To evaluate whether an organization's lobbying activities are "substantial," the IRS takes into account a number of factors, including the amount of time and money a nonprofit reports devoting to lobbying on its tax returns (IRS, 2013b). Many nonprofits have found the IRS's "substantial part test" to be too vague and have elected to have the IRS evaluate their lobbying by another, more straightforward criterion.

By filing IRS Form 5768, 501(c)(3) organizations—with the exception of churches and private foundations—can elect to have the IRS evaluate their lobbying activities via an expenditure test. To pass the IRS's expenditure test, nonprofits must ensure that the money they spend on lobbying does not exceed a clearly defined percentage of their total expenditures. For instance, a nonprofit organization that spends less than $500,000 a year total can devote 20% of its exempt-purpose expenditures to lobbying. Once an organization elects to have its lobbying activities evaluated under the expenditure test, its election will remain in effect until it is explicitly revoked (IRS, 2013c).

When calculating how much a nonprofit spends on lobbying, it is important to remember that the IRS has a specific definition of lobbying. The IRS defines lobbying as an attempt to influence legislation by either directly contacting or encouraging others to contact legislators or their staffs to propose, support, or oppose a bill. Hosting educational meetings and producing educational materials on specific policy topics are not considered lobbying if they are not focused on a specific piece of legislation. The IRS does not consider contacting executive, judicial, or administrative officials to be lobbying (IRS, 2013a).

One final yet important rule of caution: Although nonprofits can lobby elected officials, they cannot campaign for them. Tax-exempt 501(c)(3) organizations are strictly prohibited from making campaign donations or issuing public statements to support or oppose a candidate for office. Voter registration activities, voter education efforts, and get-out-the-vote drives may be allowed as long as they are strictly neutral and nonpartisan (IRS, 2013d). It is important to note that although a nonprofit cannot engage in political activity, its staff can campaign for the candidates of their choice or contribute to political campaigns as long as they do so as private citizens and not as representatives of their organizations.

Getting Started: Deciding What to Do and How to Do It

As they prepare to enter the legislative arena, nonprofit leaders should think carefully about their policy priorities. When developing a nonprofit's policy agenda, it is helpful to review the laws, regulations, and programs that impact its work and clients. Often, a nonprofit's own casework will highlight a problem that needs to be addressed. Talking to staff and board members can also help future advocates identify new policies to be proposed or existing policies that should be changed. Throughout this process, it is important to be clear on each proposal's real-world impact.

To ultimately be successful, advocates must think critically about the resources at their disposal to support lobbying efforts. There are many different ways to lobby, each with varying degrees of expense. Some nonprofits only lobby occasionally and work primarily through large coalitions. Others hire outside lobbyists to represent their interests, while still others employ someone in-house. Each nonprofit must find the method or combination of methods that suits its unique needs. Nonprofits must also think about whether they can finance lobbying efforts with existing funds or whether new funds need to be raised for this purpose. Finally, in addition to reviewing the IRS's lobbying guidelines, nonprofits should review applicable city, state, and federal laws to see if they need to register as lobbyists.

Learning the Legislative Landscape

The old adage "knowledge is power" holds true when it comes to lobbying. Whether nonprofits are preparing to petition a city councilmember, a county commissioner, or a state or federal legislator, they need to have a basic understanding of how laws are made. Fortunately, in the age of the Internet, this information is often only a keystroke away. Many legislative bodies' websites have information that explains their inner workings. While advocates do not need to become legislative experts, having a basic understanding of the legislative process will help them strategize more effectively.

Advocates also need to familiarize themselves with the people and the politics that dominate the legislative bodies they plan to approach. Identifying and building a long-term relationship with an influential legislative champion are critical parts of the lobbying process. In most legislative bodies, the majority rules. Therefore, to get bills passed, groups need to secure the votes of at least half the legislature. Given that legislators often decide how to vote on a bill by looking at who supports it and who opposes it, it pays to court the support of legislative leaders who have the ability to influence their colleagues. Lobbying members who sit on the committee with jurisdiction over the issue in question is also critical. Similarly, since the majority party is in charge of setting a legislature's agenda, advocates should always try to secure the support of at least a few of that party's members.

To get a sense of the political landscape, advocates should monitor local newspapers and peruse well-known political blogs. They should take time to look at legislators' voting records, personal and professional biographies, and official websites. By tying their proposals to legislation that a lawmaker has supported in the past, they can enhance the effectiveness of their efforts (Center for Lobbying in the Public Interest, 2007c). Finally, studying the ways in which lawmakers present themselves, their records, and their positions on issues can provide helpful insights into which arguments will resonate with them. The better nonprofit advocates understand their audiences, the more effectively they will be able to persuade them.

Working With Coalitions: Finding Strength in Numbers

When it comes to lobbying, strength lies in numbers. By joining forces with other organizations and participating in one or more coalitions, a nonprofit can enhance its effectiveness in the public arena. There are many different types of coalitions: some are large national associations while others are loose collections of local organizations that share a position on a particular issue. Whether a nonprofit is joining a long-established coalition or engaging in a one-time joint issue campaign, working with others to secure support for a piece of legislation has numerous benefits. Local nonprofits can increase credibility by allying themselves with larger or better-known advocacy groups, while smaller nonprofits can benefit from a coalition's combined resources and the expertise of other coalition members (Center for Lobbying in the Public Interest, 2007d).

Even more importantly, forming a coalition with other organizations can enhance a nonprofit's ability to get its proposals enacted. Say, for example, that a fictional Philadelphia nonprofit named Caring for Kids wants the state to increase funding for programs serving at-risk teens. While this nonprofit may be able to secure meetings with legislators from the Philadelphia region, representatives serving other areas of the state may have little incentive to take its calls. By forming a coalition with other Pennsylvania nonprofits and having each nonprofit contact its own legislative allies, however, Caring for Kids could expand its outreach and increase the chance of securing widespread support for its proposal. By building a broad and diverse advocacy coalition, nonprofit leaders can bolster their abilities to build the legislative coalitions needed to enact their ideas (Pennsylvania Economy League, Eastern Division, 1997, p. 19).

Pitching Policy Proposals: The Value of Face-to-Face Meetings

There are a number of tactics that advocates use to convey messages to lawmakers. While phone calls, e mails, and letters are all valid forms of communication, face-to-face meetings are still the most effective vehicle through which to court legislative support.

Legislators receive hundreds, if not thousands, of meeting requests each year. To increase their chances of securing a meeting, advocates should try to submit meeting requests approximately 2 to 3 months in advance, providing a range of dates and times when they will be available. Given that legislators place a higher priority on meetings that include constituents, advocates should include constituents in their meetings when possible. In the event that a lawmaker is unavailable, advocates can, and should, ask to meet with a legislative aide. These aides are trusted advisors. By convincing them of a proposal's worth, advocates can increase the likelihood that that proposal will end up in a legislator's hands.

Before any meeting, advocates must prepare properly. Given that meetings are often only 20 minutes long, organization representatives do not have a moment to waste. Within the first few minutes, they should introduce themselves, their organization(s), and the proposal for which they are lobbying. To ensure that the meeting runs smoothly, it is best to designate one lead speaker and ensure that all attendees know their talking points (Center for Lobbying in the Public Interest, 2007c). When it comes to formulating talking points, advocates would do well to reflect upon the art of persuasion. In *The Art of Woo* (2007), authors G. Richard Shell and Mario Moussa explore this art, providing helpful advice along the way.

In their discussion, Shell and Moussa use the problem, cause, answer, and net benefits (PCAN) model as a guide. Using this model, the group leader should start the policy pitch by clearly defining the problem the nonprofit is trying to address. After briefly exploring the problem's root causes, he or she should explain how the proposal would rectify the situation. He or she should conclude by discussing the real-world impact of the proposal, highlighting why it is the best solution (Shell & Moussa, 2007).

Throughout the presentation, everyone who speaks should anticipate legislators' questions and opponents' counterarguments. Proactively addressing both will ultimately increase the effectiveness of the message. By listening to how a legislator reacts to the arguments, the whole team can identify ways to adjust their presentation to better address a particular concern and be prepared for future meetings.

The data, stories, and arguments that comprise the substance of advocates' policy pitches are critical to their success. To help make their pitches memorable, advocates should leave legislators with a compelling, personal story that gives a human face to the problem at hand. A group can add credibility to its arguments by sharing valid data that quantify the need for, and potential impact of, their proposals. Often, such data can be found in a nonprofit's records, on government websites, and in reports from well-respected think tanks and organizations. Before referring to any figures, however, advocates should make sure they are familiar with the data and how they were gathered. To maintain credibility, speakers must always be able to back up their facts if challenged (Center for Lobbying in the Public Interest, 2007a).

At the conclusion of a meeting, advocates should present the legislator with a one-page document summarizing the need for, substance of, and potential impact of their proposal(s). This one-pager will be a valuable resource for the legislators' staffs as the process moves forward. If the group has asked a legislator to introduce a new bill on their behalf, if possible they should provide him or her with a draft of the legislation. If drafting legislation is beyond their capabilities, advocates can facilitate the process by offering specific suggestions regarding the language and the provisions to be included. Finally, in keeping with good etiquette, advocates should always send a handwritten thank-you note to legislators after their meetings. With lobbying, as with so many other endeavors, manners matter.

Moving Forward: Building and Strengthening Relationships

Naturally, nonprofit advocates cannot expect to accomplish all of their goals in just one meeting. The legislative process is full of twists and turns, and therefore it is critically important to maintain contact with key allies. Finding effective ways to follow up with legislators and their staffs can help nonprofit leaders keep their policy proposals moving forward.

Building on the value of face-to-face interactions, nonprofits should consider inviting legislators to observe their work firsthand. Just as a picture is often worth a thousand words, site visits can often do much to help legislators understand the rationale behind a group's proposal. Similarly, if a nonprofit is announcing a new success or initiative to the media—such as obtaining a new federal grant or launching a new project—it should consider inviting a local lawmaker to make the announcement. Doing so will increase the likelihood that both the nonprofit and its legislative ally will secure favorable press coverage, which can ultimately help to strengthen ties between them.

It is also important to keep an eye on the legislative calendar. Staffers are much more likely to take someone's call if it provides helpful insights into the real-world consequences of legislation that is to be voted on imminently. If they have the capability, advocates may also want to offer to testify before a congressional or other legislative committee about the importance of a certain piece of legislation (Center for Lobbying in the Public Interest, 2007b). By consistently positioning themselves as helpful resources, groups can continually build beneficial relationships.

As they seek out opportunities to strengthen their connections with lawmakers, organizations should ensure that they do not only contact legislators when they want something from them. While legislators soon tire of groups that simply bombard them with new requests, they tend to appreciate those that remember to send brief updates on new programs and new successes. Most of all, legislators appreciate groups that consistently thank them for their efforts.

In the world of lobbying, the value of saying thank you cannot be overstated. If a legislator voted for a bill that is important to their agenda, advocates should look for venues in which they can thank that lawmaker. While a nonprofit cannot campaign for elected officials, it can publically acknowledge their efforts by writing letters to the editors of local newspapers, posting messages of thanks on lawmakers' social media sites, and highlighting legislators' actions in the advocacy updates it sends to supporters. All lawmakers like to have their work acknowledged. By publically expressing their appreciation, advocates can help turn one-time supporters into long-term allies.

What Is at Stake and Why It Matters

Today, in the context of record budget pressures, lawmakers at all levels are debating how to reinvent government operations and even the proper role of government and government spending in tackling the nation's challenges. Fierce debates over how to allocate limited funding, reform entitlement programs, and alter tax structures dominate the political landscape. There is no doubt that the decisions U.S. leaders make over the next few years will have a significant impact on the nation's future.

These decisions will also have a significant impact on American nonprofits and their clients. Organizations that have received government funding in the past likely face a leaner future. Those that serve vulnerable populations may also face new challenges if social safety nets are altered. Regardless of their missions or fields of operations, all nonprofits will be impacted by the new laws of the land. As such, it is in their best interests to take an active role in influencing the creation of those laws.

It is in society's interest as well, however. As entities that are devoted to serving the public good, nonprofits have a valuable perspective to add to legislative debates. Whether they are sharing their opinions about how current laws should be altered or casting a vision for new laws that should be created, nonprofit advocates can contribute to the greater good by sharing their expertise and ideas. Indeed, by taking the time to engage in lobbying and inform the legislative process, nonprofit leaders can render a public service the impact of which will be felt far beyond their local spheres of operations.

CASE STUDY: PRESCRIPTION FOR PENNSYLVANIA: RECOGNIZING ADVANCED PRACTICE NURSES (APNs)

In the culmination of years of carefully managed advocacy, APNs in Pennsylvania achieved legislative reforms through former Governor Edward Rendell's health care reform plan, the "Prescription for Pennsylvania." While APNs had argued for years that increased professional autonomy and recognition would lead to increased access to health care, that incentive alone was not enough to win legislative and regulatory battles.

Success: APNS and the Prescription for Pennsylvania

In January 2007, Governor Rendell announced the launch of his Prescription for Pennsylvania health care reform plan (commonly called "Rx for PA"; Pennsylvania Office of the Governor, 2007). It was one of first official acts of his second term as governor, occurring just 2 months after he had won reelection. This was not the first time the Rendell Administration had taken steps to establish health care as one of its high-priority policy issues. In January 2003, Rendell's first act as governor was to sign an executive order creating the Governor's Office of Health Care Reform (OHCR), which would develop and spearhead the Prescription for Pennsylvania (PA GOHCR, 2008b). Rendell appointed Rosemarie Greco, a former banking executive and consultant in strategic planning, to head the OHCR, as well as Ann Torregrossa, a former public interest law advocate. He also established the Governor's Health Care Reform Cabinet, comprising 10 senior officials including the Secretary of Public Welfare, the Secretary of Aging, and the Commissioner of Insurance to advise the OHCR (PA GOHCR, 2008a).

With the announcement of the Prescription for Pennsylvania in early 2007, health care once again became the central focus of the Rendell Administration. The plan centered on three categories of reform designed to improve the quality, affordability, and accessibility of health care in Pennsylvania. Each category contained a variety of reform strategies, some of which concerned access to health insurance. Most Prescription for Pennsylvania initiatives, however, addressed topics as varied as improving palliative care, reducing hospital-acquired infections, implementing the Chronic Care Model, creating new options for home-based long-term care, and ensuring smoke-free workplaces (PA GOHCR, 2007b).[1]

The accessibility category focused almost entirely on health care providers and included regulatory changes designed to increase the utilization of nurse practitioners, certified nurse midwives (CNMs), and clinical nurse specialists (CNSs). Indeed, APNs took center stage in the initial push for Prescription for Pennsylvania. While promoting the plan in Pittsburgh in January 2007, Rendell explained that access to health care would increase if state laws were changed to "free nurse practitioners to do anything they are capable of doing" (Mauriello, 2006). In the weeks following his initial announcement regarding the Prescription for Pennsylvania, Rendell declared that his health care reform plan would "unleash [the] tremendous potential" of APNs to care for more patients (Cholodofsky, 2007). A factsheet issued by the OHCR included the following description of the rationale behind the decision to include APNs and other nonphysician providers in Rendell's plan:

> Pennsylvania consistently lags behind other states in fully utilizing licensed health care providers that are not physicians. Prescription for Pennsylvania will eliminate the barriers in existing laws and regulations that limit the ability of health care providers to practice to the fullest extent allowed by their education and training. [PA GOHCR], 2007a)

Initially, the OHCR pushed to have its entire health care reform plan introduced as one comprehensive piece of legislation. The bill, HB 700, was introduced in the Pennsylvania House of Representatives in March 2007, two months after Governor Rendell announced the Prescription for Pennsylvania plan. The bill was referred to the House Committee on Insurance, and a public hearing was held the following month. It quickly became clear, however, that the bill contained too many controversial components and was unlikely to pass as drafted. Some of the most controversial components included a statewide smoking ban and provisions related to insurance reform (Fahy & Barnes, 2008; Worden, 2008).

As a result, a number of single-issue bills were removed from HB 700. Three of those bills were HB 1253, HB 1254, and HB 1255, were each designed to further define and/or enhance the scope of practice of certified registered nurse practitioners (CRNPs), CNSs, and CNMs, respectively. The three nursing bills that were part of Rendell's health care reform plan were among the first to be successfully enacted. In addition, four other pieces of legislation that were part of the initial Prescription for Pennsylvania push were signed on the same day, including bills designed to enhance the scopes of practice of physician assistants and dental hygienists and a bill to reduce hospital-acquired infections.

Laying the Groundwork: 1998–2006

The victories won by APNs in 2007 did not occur in a vacuum. They were the direct result of a grassroots advocacy campaign on the part of Pennsylvania's APNs and their patients that began in the mid-1990s. The focus of this campaign was not only to raise awareness of the role APNs can play in increasing access to health care but also to build relationships with members of both parties who would support the passage of future initiatives. By working collectively to address statutory as well as regulatory restrictions on scope of practice, APNs were able to win a series of incremental victories that paved the way for the larger reforms contained in the Prescription for Pennsylvania.

Act 68 of 1998

One of the first policy issues to unite Pennsylvania APNs was an effort to alter the legislative definition of "primary care provider" to include nurse practitioners. In 1998, Pennsylvania moved to amend the statute governing the operations of the state's managed care organizations (MCOs). At the time, few state policy makers fully understood the role of nurse practitioners, and the statutes governing MCOs permitted only physicians to act as primary care providers. Pennsylvania's decision to review its managed care law presented APNs with an opportunity to address this issue.

Nursing groups in Pennsylvania, including the Pennsylvania State Nurses Association, the Pennsylvania Coalition of Nurse Practitioners, the Pennsylvania Chapter of the National Association of Pediatric Nurse Practitioners, the National Nursing Centers Consortium (at that time, the Regional Nursing Centers Consortium), and others came together and quickly implemented a two-pronged strategy to educate policy makers and demonstrate the impact that nurse practitioners were already having on the Commonwealth's health care safety net. APN representatives presented eight different sets of testimony at hearings on the proposed amendments to the insurance law that would come to be known as Act 68.

Nursing groups submitted both written and oral testimony that highlighted the ability of APNs to expand access to health care services for the underserved. Being defined as primary care providers in Act 68 was especially important for APNs because Pennsylvania was in the early stages of moving from a Medicaid fee-for-service model to a managed care model.[2] At the time (as is the case now), nurse practitioners played a large role in serving Medicaid patients through nurse-managed health centers and other community-based primary care settings. This fact was highlighted in APNs' testimony to legislators. To further demonstrate their impact on the safety net, APNs and their patients sent thousands of postcards to legislators calling on them to ensure that Act 68 would allow APNs to serve as primary care providers.

Ultimately, the strategy proved successful. The final version of Act 68 was signed into law by Governor Tom Ridge on June 17, 1998. It included language explicitly authorizing nurse practitioners to act as primary care providers for managed care enrollees. APNs had learned the value of speaking with a unified voice. They had also identified key bipartisan supporters in the General Assembly, including Republican Representative (now Senator) Pat Vance and Democratic Representative Kathy Manderino, on whom they could rely for support in upcoming initiatives.

Nurse Practitioner Prescriptive Authority

In 1998, Pennsylvania was one of only three states in the nation that had not yet granted prescriptive authority to nurse practitioners (Jenkins, 2002). This was due in large part to repeated disputes (and ensuing gridlock) between the Board of Nursing and the Board of Medicine, which at the time had dual authority to regulate nurse practitioners. For more than 20 years, the Board of Medicine had resisted attempts to reform regulations governing nurse practitioner prescriptive authority. During and immediately following the Act 68 campaign, however, APN groups implemented new strategies that caught the attention of former Governor Ridge, in addition to several key legislators. These strategies helped push the issue of nurse practitioner prescriptive authority to the forefront of policy issues in the Pennsylvania General Assembly.

One of the first things members of the APN community did was solidify the unity of their message by forming a group called the Alliance of Advanced Practice Nurses (the Alliance). The founding members of the group included representatives from the Pennsylvania State Nurses Association, the Pennsylvania Coalition of Nurse Practitioners, the Pennsylvania Association of Nurse Anesthetists, the Regional Nursing Centers Consortium (now the National Nursing Centers Consortium), and the Pennsylvania chapters of the American College of Nurse Midwives, the Pennsylvania Association of School Nurses and Practitioners, and the Psychiatric Advanced Practice Nurses of Pennsylvania. Under the banner of "One Alliance, One Voice," the group quickly initiated a legislative visit and letter-writing campaign designed to highlight the need for nurse practitioner prescriptive authority along with other APN reforms.

In March 1998, the APN groups again turned to Representatives Vance and Manderino to introduce HB 50. The bill proposed comprehensive amendments to the state's nurse practice act that not only would have extended prescriptive authority to nurse practitioners and CNSs but also would have modified the law governing the practice of certified registered nurse anesthetists. After more than 500 APNs rallied at the state capitol in Harrisburg, the bill was introduced with 124 cosponsors. Other groups expressed their support for the bill as well, including the Hospital and Health System Association of Pennsylvania, the Chamber of Commerce, and other key business allies. However, the bill quickly lost momentum as the Pennsylvania Medical Society mobilized in opposition; cosponsors began to withdraw and the bill became stranded in committee hearings (Pennsylvania Coalition of Nurse Practitioners, 1999).

Although the bill was eventually abandoned, the introduction of HB 50 served an important purpose: It brought the issue of nurse practitioner prescriptive authority to the forefront of the political landscape and helped bring about a series of historic meetings between the Alliance and the Pennsylvania Medical Society. It was the first time the Medical Society had met with a group representing such a diverse collection of professional nurses. With further encouragement and pressure from the governor's office, the Board of Medicine and Board of Nursing would enter a series of negotiations that would ultimately lead to limited prescriptive authority for nurse practitioners (Jenkins, 2002).

In April 2000, almost two years after the process began, a compromise agreement was reached between the Board of Nursing and the Board of Medicine regarding nurse practitioner prescriptive authority. The approval of both boards meant that nurse practitioners had gained prescriptive authority, but the Alliance was unsatisfied. The regulations contained controversial provisions, including a requirement that a physician could not collaborate with more than two nurse practitioners prescribing medication. Specifically, the Alliance felt that this provision would hinder the practice of nurse-managed health centers operating in medically underserved communities.

In the following months, the Alliance voiced its concerns. Ultimately, the Pennsylvania Independent Regulatory Review Commission[3] disapproved the regulations because they were "against the public's interest," sending them back to the boards of medicine and nursing for revisions (Pennsylvania Coalition of Nurse Practitioners, 2000). In December 2000, after yet another series of negotiations, the boards reached agreement on a revised version of the regulations (Jenkins, 2002). The struggle was over, and nurse practitioners in Pennsylvania had won prescriptive authority.

The policy debate over prescriptive authority highlights the importance of having the support of the governor's office when proposing statutory or regulatory change. The Ridge Administration worked closely with the boards of medicine and nursing in drafting new regulations, and the governor's involvement helped the process move along more rapidly than it might have otherwise. Another important factor was the face-to-face meeting that took place between the Alliance and the Pennsylvania Medical Society. In the future, APNs would again rely on support from the governor's office and face-to-face communication with physician groups to earn scope-of-practice reforms under the Prescription for Pennsylvania.

The End of Dual Regulation

The third major victory of the Alliance prior to the Prescription for Pennsylvania was to ensure that the Board of Nursing had sole authority to regulate advanced nursing practice. For 27 years (from 1975 to 2002), nurse practitioners in Pennsylvania were the only group of regulated professionals in Pennsylvania required to answer to two different regulatory boards (Jenkins, 2002). As highlighted in the struggle for prescriptive authority, working collaboratively with the Board of Medicine was sometimes difficult. Regulations often had to go through many revisions before the boards of medicine and nursing could agree upon a final version.

In 2001, the Alliance approached Republican Senator Jane Earll in an effort to address the issues created by the system of dual regulation. In November of that year, Senator Earll introduced SB 1208. The main purpose of the bill was to end the authority of the Board of Medicine to regulate nurse practitioners and place the profession under the sole jurisdiction of the Board of Nursing. After its introduction in the Senate, the bill was referred to the Consumer Protection and Professional Licensure Committee, where it stalled.

The Alliance again engaged in a grassroots campaign of letter writing, legislative visits, and mass rallies. Thanks to continuing advocacy by Senator Earll, the bill was voted out of committee in June 2002 and received a vote for final passage from the full Senate in October. After its passage in the Senate, the bill was sent to the House, where it underwent many revisions based on input from several physician groups, the governor's office, and Representative Vance, among others (Pennsylvania Coalition of Nurse Practitioners, 2002). After the addition of these amendments, the legislation was unanimously approved by the full House.

On the last day before the legislative session ended, the amended version of SB 1208 was sent back to the Senate. At 6:40 p.m. that night, just prior to the close of the session, the Senate voted unanimously to approve the amendments offered by the House (Pennsylvania Coalition of Nurse Practitioners, 2002). Governor Mark Schweiker signed the bill in December 2002, effectively ending the era of dual regulation and giving the Board of Nursing sole authority to regulate nurse practitioner practice in Pennsylvania.

In this effort, the Alliance again saw the value of nurturing bipartisan support and building strong relationships with key legislators. Senator Earll's support of the bill was a key factor in its success. In 2002, she was slated to become the Republican nominee for lieutenant governor in the general election that took place later that year. Although the Republicans did not win the election, her position on the ticket helped to win support for the bill among Republican legislators.

In addition to ending dual regulation, SB 1208 clarified nurse practitioner scope of practice. The changes offered by the legislation indicated that nurse practitioners could fill the role of primary care provider and emphasized their ability to function independently. It would be this ability of nurse practitioners to expand access to primary care that would later capture the attention of Governor Rendell, who took office in 2003.

Governor Rendell's First Term

Although the practice environment for APNs in Pennsylvania had improved significantly, in 2003 there was still much work to be done. During Governor Rendell's first term, the Alliance began building a relationship with the new administration as its members pressured the legislature to continue making reforms. Prior to the Prescription for Pennsylvania, the major issue facing APNs was that the state's laws and regulations had not been updated to accommodate their expanding role. For example, until 2004, the law stated that only physicians could sign the form certifying that a person was entitled to a disability parking placard, even though both nurse practitioners and physicians were qualified to perform the placard examination. Thus, if a nurse practitioner performed the disability assessment examination, she would have to ask her collaborating physicians to sign the form. Although this gap in the law was relatively small, when added with other inconsistencies it made it difficult for nurse practitioners to act fully as primary care providers. Many legislators agreed that these inconsistencies should be corrected but also feared that making all of the necessary changes would lead the legislature down a slippery slope of never-ending revisions.

The disability placard issue was resolved in 2004 through the passage of HB 1912, introduced by Representative Vance, which amended the motor vehicles statute to allow nurse practitioners to sign the certification form (Commonwealth of Pennsylvania, 2004). However, there were other statutes and regulations to be updated, and the strategy of addressing each issue one at a time through legislation was frustrating and time consuming. APNs recognized the need for a comprehensive piece of legislation that could make all necessary revisions at once.

In February 2005, the Alliance published a white paper that laid out all the areas of the law that needed to be revised in order for nurse practitioners, CNSs, nurse midwives, and nurse anesthetists to practice to the full extent of their training (Alliance of Advanced Practice Nurses, 2005). The document also clearly provided the rationale for the Alliance's position that the increased utilization of APNs would lead to increased access and a general reduction in overall health care costs, noting:

> Advanced Practice Nurses are positioned to significantly expand the capacity of the Pennsylvania health care delivery system...Pennsylvania has already acted to create a

statutory foundation for Nurse Practitioners and Nurse-Midwives to perform their full scope of practice…Barriers to performing their scope-of-practice continue, despite statutory authority. Outdated state statutes and regulations, third party payor provider contract rules, and confusing federal funding rules restrain nurse practitioners from providing their full scope of care to needy individuals. It is in the Commonwealth's best interest to alleviate these restraints, freeing Advanced Practice Nurses to provide care to people in a satisfying as well as cost effective way and in a wide variety of underserved health care settings (Alliance of Advanced Practice Nurses, 2005).

The white paper was brought to the attention of staff at OHCR, and its suggested changes quickly became the blueprint for the Prescription for Pennsylvania's APN reforms (Plant, 2007).

Also in 2005, a new ally entered the picture as Take Care Health Systems (Take Care) and began to establish itself in Pennsylvania as an operator of retail-based health clinics. Because Take Care's clinics were primarily staffed by nurse practitioners, the company was aware of the regulatory barriers to effective nurse practitioner practice in Pennsylvania and was willing to devote company resources in the effort to reform laws. In addition to providing public relations in support of the plan (at a time when this emerging model of care was already receiving media attention as the next big thing in health care), Take Care clinics in the Pittsburgh suburbs also served as press-friendly sites for Rendell's stump speeches in support of increased utilization of APNs and his health care reform plan (Chodolofsky, 2007; Ereudenheim, 2006).

Allies from outside of the health care industry were also a welcome addition to the efforts. Private academic institutions with nursing schools and several health systems helped APNs in Pennsylvania make the case for policy change. For example, the University of Pennsylvania put effort and resources into developing relationships with key policy makers in Harrisburg. Funders such as the Independence Foundation also supported nonprofit nurse-managed health centers throughout the process and helped convene meetings with key members of the governor's staff. By developing relationships with community allies with an interest in improving the regulatory environment for nurse practitioners, the nursing community was able to build a stronger case for legislative change.

Lessons for Advocates

The work of the Alliance in the first term of the Rendell Administration paved the way for success during his second term. Prescription for Pennsylvania would give nurses the comprehensive legislative vehicle they needed to address almost all of the barriers to APN practice in Pennsylvania. However, the success of the nursing component of Prescription for Pennsylvania was not inevitable by any means. In fact, the mere *inclusion* of provider issues in a state health care reform plan was unprecedented at the time (Aiken, 2007). In many ways, the most important and crucial work came months and years before the Prescription for Pennsylvania plan was officially introduced, as nursing groups and supporters throughout Pennsylvania developed relationships with policy makers and educated legislators about the untapped potential of APNs to provide care. So, what lessons can be learned from the Pennsylvania experience?

Lesson No. 1: Building Strong Alliances Within the Nursing Community

Having a unified nursing community was crucial to the development and eventual success of Prescription for Pennsylvania's nursing provisions. As noted, the Alliance of Advanced Practice Nurses worked to raise awareness of the contributions of APNs from different specialty areas and develop talking points about barriers to practice. The collaborative process of creating advocacy documents (such as the Alliance white paper) and mutually identifying important issues ensured that nursing leaders throughout the state were able to speak to policy makers with a unified, coherent voice about the issues that mattered most to them.

Lesson No. 2: Building Relationships With Policy Makers

Over the course of many years, nursing groups built relationships with both Republican and Democratic policymakers throughout the state. In addition to identifying and nurturing relationships with General Assembly members on both sides of the aisle, earning the support of sitting governors was crucial to policy advocacy efforts. By providing high-quality, succinct, trustworthy, and lucid information about APNs to policy makers, the nursing community was able to build the case for legislative change. By developing relationships with legislators and executive branch members with significant political capital, the Alliance was also able to ensure that when legislative momentum began to lag and bills stalled, it did not signal the end of reform efforts.

Lesson No. 3: Finding New Allies

Strong support from the private sector was important to the success of Prescription for Pennsylvania's nursing reforms. Having learned the value of private-sector support when the Chamber of Commerce supported prescriptive authority for nurse practitioners in 2000, nurses in Pennsylvania again sought to identify new allies to support Prescription for Pennsylvania.

CONCLUSION

As evidenced by the Pennsylvania experience, strong advocacy and alliance-building efforts (both within the nursing community and outside of it) can have a great impact on the success of legislative reform efforts. In addition, the success of Prescription for Pennsylvania also rests with the Governor's Office of Health Care Reform and its focused team of professionals who were willing to recognize and address established health care traditions that were behind the times. By speaking with a unified voice and building solid, long-standing relationships with a broad range of bipartisan policy makers, funders, civic leaders, business leaders, and legislative advocates, the nurses of Pennsylvania were able to gain broad support for pro-nursing reforms as part of a bold and comprehensive health care reform agenda.

NOTES

1. This sampling of issues addressed by the Prescription for Pennsylvania is meant to provide the reader with an understanding of the breadth of topics covered by the reform plan. It is not intended to be an all-inclusive list. A discussion of the full range of topics addressed by the reform plan is beyond the scope of this article, which focuses only on the nursing-related components of the Prescription for Pennsylvania.
2. Pennsylvania first initiated mandatory managed care for Medicaid beneficiaries in selected regions in February 1997.
3. The Pennsylvania Independent Regulatory Review Commission is an independent state agency that reviews all regulations promulgated by state agencies on the basis of statutory authority, legislative intent, public interest, economic, or fiscal impact and clarity.

REFERENCES

Aiken, L. (2007, September 5). *Workforce policy solutions to health care reform.* [Web blog post]. Retrieved from http://healthaffairs.org/blog/2007/09/05/pennsylvania-workforce-policy-solutions-to-healthcare-reform/print

Alliance of Advanced Practice Nurses & Pennsylvania State Nurses Association. (2005). *Solving one piece of the health care delivery puzzle: An action agenda for the Commonwealth of Pennsylvania* (white paper). Washington, DC: Alliance of Advanced Practice Nurses. Press Release available at: www.prweb.com/releases/2005/02/prweb204736.htm

Center for Lobbying in the Public Interest. (2007a). *Finding & using data*. Retrieved from http://clpi.org/images/pdf/07_data.pdf

Center for Lobbying in the Public Interest. (2007b). *Making a difference for your cause in three hours a week*. Retrieved from www.clpi.org/images/pdf/difference_3hours_perweek.pdf

Center for Lobbying in the Public Interest. (2007c). *Personal visits with a legislator*. Retrieved from http://clpi.org/images/pdf/07_personalvisits.pdf

Center for Lobbying in the Public Interest. (2007d). *Working in coalitions*. Retrieved from www.clpi.org/images/pdf/07_coalitions.pdf

Cholodofsky, R. (2007, January 25). Governor lauds clinics operating in drug stores. *Pittsburgh Tribune-Review*. Retrieved from www.highbeam.com/doc/1P2–11276574.html

Commonwealth of Pennsylvania. (2004). *Governor Rendell signs 18 bills*. Retrieved 3 July 2008, from www.state.pa.us/papower/cwp/view.asp?A=11&Q=437426

Commonwealth of Pennsylvania, Governor's Office of Health Care Reform (PA GOHCR). (2007a). *Rx for access*. Retrieved from www.gohcr.state.pa.us/prescription-for-pennsylvania/Rx-for-Access.pdf

Commonwealth of Pennsylvania, Governor's Office of Health Care Reform (PA GOHCR). (2007b). *Rx for quality*. Retrieved from www.gohcr.state.pa.us/prescription-for-pennsylvania/Rx-for-Quality.pdf

Commonwealth of Pennsylvania, Governor's Office of Health Care Reform (PA GOHCR). (2008a). *The governor's health care reform cabinet*. Retrieved from www.ohcr.state.pa.us/health-care-reform-cabinet/index.html

Commonwealth of Pennsylvania, Governor's Office of Health Care Reform (PA GOHCR). (2008b). *Meet our staff*. Retrieved from www.gohcr.state.pa.us/about-the-office/OurStaff.html

Ereudenheim, M. (2006, May 14). *Attention shoppers: Low prices on shots in clinic*. The New York Times. Retrieved from www.nytimes.com/2006/05/14/business/14clinic.html?_r=2&oref=slogin&

Fahy, J., & Barnes, T. (2008, January 13). *Rendell vows to press ahead on health care*. Pittsburgh Post-Gazette. Retrieved from www.philaup.org/health/2008_0113PPG.html

Internal Revenue Service (IRS). (2013a, April 18). *Lobbying*. Retrieved from www.irs.gov/Charities-&-Non-Profits/Lobbying

Internal Revenue Service (IRS). (2013b, April 18). *Measuring lobbying: Substantial part test*. Retrieved from www.irs.gov/Charities-&-Non-Profits/Measuring-Lobbying:-Substantial-Part-Test

Internal Revenue Service (IRS). (2013c, April 28). *Measuring lobbying: Expenditure test*. Retrieved from www.irs.gov/Charities-&-Non-Profits/Measuring-Lobbying-Activity:-Expenditure-Test

Internal Revenue Service (IRS). (2013d, September 3). *The restriction of political campaign intervention by Section 501(c)(3) tax-exempt organizations*. Retrieved from www.irs.gov/Charities-&-Non-Profits/Charitable-Organizations/The-Restriction-of-Political-Campaign-Intervention-by-Section-501(c)(3)-Tax-Exempt-Organizations

Jenkins, M. (2002). Abbotsford Community Health Center and Pennsylvania politics. In D. J. Mason, J. K. Levitt, & M. W. Chaffee (Eds.), *Policy and politics in nursing and health care* (pp. 87–91). Philadelphia, PA: Saunders.

Mauriello, T. (2006, December 12). Rendell wants more health care by nurse practitioners. *Pittsburgh Post-Gazette*. Retrieved from www.post-gazette.com/pg/06346/745432–85.stm

Pennsylvania Coalition of Nurse Practitioners. (1999, September). *HB 50 Cosponsor withdrawals*. Pennsylvania NP Issues.

Pennsylvania Coalition of Nurse Practitioners. (2000, August). *We're almost there! IRRC disapproves proposed CRNP regulations*. Pennsylvania NP Issues.

Pennsylvania Coalition of Nurse Practitioners. (2002, December). *After 27 years…It's finally over*. Pennsylvania NP Issues.

Pennsylvania Economy League, Eastern Division. (1997). *Roadmap to Harrisburg: A practical guide to working with Pennsylvania state government*. Philadelphia, PA: The League.

Pennsylvania Office of the Governor. (2007). *First pieces of Governor Rendell's "Prescription for Pennsylvania" signed into law* [press release]. Retrieved from www.prnewswire.com/news-releases/first-pieces-of-governor-rendells-prescription-for-pennsylvania-signed-into-law-52755127.html

Plant, M. (2007). We make the road by walking. *Pennsylvania NP Issues*. Retrieved from www.pacnp.org/newsletters/Sept%202007%20Newsletter.pdf

Shell, R. G., & Moussa, M. (2007). *The art of woo.* New York, NY: Penguin Books.

Worden, A. (2008, February 25). Pa. Smoking ban: Not if, but how. *Philadelphia Inquirer*. Retrieved from http://articles.philly.com/2008–02-25/news/24989291_1_public-places-smoking-ban-restrictive-ban

APPENDIX A

Methodology for the Independent Sector NGen Fellows Project

1. REVIEW RELEVANT LITERATURE

To ground themselves in current thinking on leadership development and succession planning, NGen Fellows conducted a review of relevant literature. The following references were found to be most valuable:

- 2009 NGen Fellows Project report. (2010, July) *Independent Sector*. Retrieved from https://www.independentsector.org/uploads/NGen/ngen_fellows_09_report.pdf
- Campbell, M., & Smith, R. (2010) *Developing high potential talent*. Greensboro, NC: Center for Creative Leadership.
- Cornelius, M., Corvington, P., & Ruesga, A. (2008). *Ready to lead? Next generation leaders speak out*. Baltimore, MD: Annie E. Casey Foundation.
- Deal, J., Peterson, K., & Gailpor-Loflin, H. (2001). *Annotated bibliography of emerging leadership*. Greensboro, NC: Center for Creative Leadership.
- Kunreuther, F. N. (2005). *Up next: Generation change and the leadership of nonprofit organizations*. Baltimore, MD: Annie E. Casey Foundation.
- Kunreuther, F., & Corvington, P. A (2007). *Next shift: Beyond the nonprofit leadership crisis*. Baltimore, MD: Annie E. Casey Foundation.
- Kunreuther, F., Kim, H., & Rodriguez, R. (2008). *Working Across Generations*. San Francisco, CA: Jossey-Bass.
- Tchume, T., & McAndrews, C. (2008). *Working Across Generations: The Next Generation of Nonprofit Leadership*. From Changing Our World, The Centre on Philanthropy 2011 Conference.

2. INTERVIEW THOUGHT LEADERS

To build on the existing body of research, during the first 2 weeks of January 2011, three informational interviews with experts in the nonprofit sector were held to help shape the overall project and identify questions to be used in the focus groups. The following experts were consulted:

- Caroline McAndrews, Director of Leadership, Building Movement Project
- Shera Clark, Manager, Nonprofit Sector, Center for Creative Leadership
- Jennifer Deal, PhD, Senior Research Scientist, Center for Creative Leadership

3. CONDUCTED INTERGENERATIONAL FOCUS GROUPS

Four focus groups were held in February and March of 2011 to help Fellows better understand succession planning in the nonprofit sector. Three were held in person (Washington, DC; Philadelphia, PA; and Minneapolis, MN) and one was virtual. Groups consisted of 5 to 23 people who met for approximately 2 hours. Fellows reached out to participants through referrals, personal connections, and the assistance of local nonprofit intermediaries. To ensure a diverse cohort of participants, Fellows targeted individuals with varied backgrounds and characteristics (i.e., race, gender, and age) as well as diversity in professional background (i.e., size of their nonprofit, issue focus or organization, experience across sectors). Before each focus group, all participants received an article on succession planning (Cornelius, Corvington, & Ruesga, 2008), an overview of the project, and the list of standard questions.

During each focus group, Fellows focused on three primary areas: (a) personal experience; (b) organizational issues; and (c) sector-related issues. A standard set of discussion questions was used but each conversation flowed naturally. All participants were encouraged to speak during the discussion.

Focus Group Demographics

Across the four focus groups, there were 49 participants (41% male and 59% female; 23% boomers, 31% millennials, and 46% Generation X; 62% White, 16% Hispanic/Latino, 10% African American, and 12% other).

Focus Group Questions

Focus group discussions were based on the following questions, categorized as personal experience, organizational, or sector-related.

- Personal Experience
  - How did your career evolve? How was it different in your 20s, 30s, 40s, 50s, and 60s (as relevant)?
  - Who mentored you effectively? How did it benefit your organization and impact your career path?
  - What can people in their 20s and 30s learn from those in their 40s, 50s, and 60s? Vice versa? Without this cross-generational conversation, what will be missed?
- Organizational
  - What organizations are doing succession planning and leadership development well?
  - What is required to do it well?
  - Within organizations that do it well, what are the broader benefits observed?

- Does this work for all types of organizations? Are there organizational structures that work better than others?
- What are the biggest challenges?
- Have you experienced "founders' syndrome"? What impacts has it had?
- Sector-Related
  - Compared with the for-profit sector, is there something unique to the nonprofit sector that prevents organizations from performing succession planning and leadership development well? For example, are there financial constraints that hinder such planning?
  - What can other organizations learn from their example? What is transplantable to other organizations? What is critical to an effective organization's culture?

APPENDIX B

Design and Function of the CCAT

The Core Capacity Assessment Tool (CCAT) is a 146-question online survey that measures a nonprofit's effectiveness in relation to four core capacities in addition to organizational culture. The CCAT allows organizational leaders, including senior executives and board members, to independently and anonymously rate their organizations on very specific behaviors. Based on survey results, the CCAT generates scores for each of the core capacities as well as a set of subcapacities. It also gathers historical data (over a 3-year period, inclusive of the year the CCAT is taken) on a comprehensive set of business metrics such as operating budget, staffing, volunteers, funding sources, number of active board members, and so forth, which offer an organization insights into how its capacity and business metrics are intertwined.

The CCAT measures four core capacities, shown in Figure B-1:

- **Adaptive Capacity**: The ability of a nonprofit to monitor, assess, respond to, and create internal and external change.
- **Leadership Capacity**: The ability of organizational leaders to create and sustain the organization's vision, inspire, model, prioritize, make decisions, provide direction, and innovate.
- **Management Capacity**: The ability of a nonprofit to ensure effective and efficient use of its resources.
- **Technical Capacity**: The ability of a nonprofit to implement all of its key organizational, programmatic, and operational functions.

There are 36 subcapacities that are measured within these four main capacities. The four capacities work separately and together to maximize a nonprofit's effectiveness and efficiency.

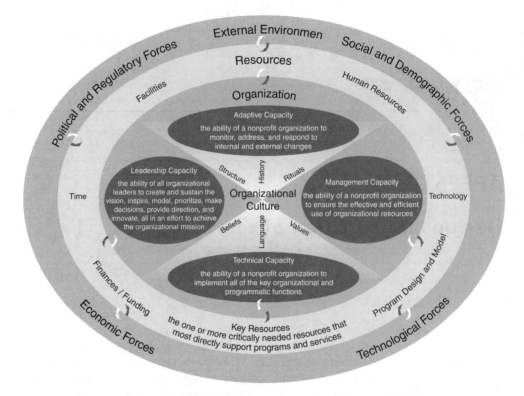

FIGURE B-1 The CCAT capacities.

While all are necessary, the leadership and adaptive capacities are the most critical. If these are weak, it will be difficult for a nonprofit to flourish, even if it is managerially and operationally strong.

The CCAT also helps organizations identify their life cycle stage, which affects how capacity should be developed and assessed. Organizations taking the CCAT are placed along a life cycle continuum and given capacity-building recommendations statistically proven to help organizations in that position advance to the next stage of development. The CCAT describes three nonprofit life cycle stages, shown in Figure B-2:

- **Core Program Development**: A set of programs central to mission success has been developed and has begun achieving a consistent level of desired results for those served.
- **Infrastructure Development**: An organizational infrastructure has been developed, as have operations necessary for supporting core program replication and progressively increasing the number of clients or service recipients.
- **Impact Expansion**: Impact expansion has been achieved that brings together an organization's programs and leadership with other community resources. This often involves engaging in activities such as collaboration, strategic alliances, partnerships, and joint policy and advocacy efforts to create greater change.

The CCAT generates a customized capacity-building plan that highlights an organization's top priorities for improving effectiveness. The report presents these recommendations in order of importance in relation to items that TCC's data analysis have revealed are most critical to advancing along the development continuum.

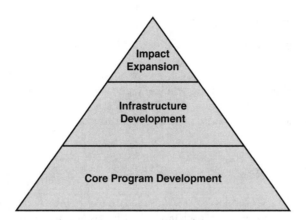

FIGURE B-2 The CCAT life cycle stages.

HOW THE CCAT IS USED

The CCAT is used by nonprofits, funders, and capacity builders. Nonprofits use it to assess their own organizations' capacities, frame strategic planning efforts, devise capacity-building plans, and track progress over time. Funders as well as nonprofit associations and networks typically use it to measure the organizational effectiveness of sets of nonprofits, often to inform the development, implementation, management, and evaluation of capacity-building initiatives. Capacity builders and capacity-building organizations use it to assess capacity-building readiness, diagnose organizational problems or challenges, and strategically target capacity-building interventions as well as evaluate progress over time.

The CCAT also offers nonprofit leaders access to real-time benchmarking that allows organizations to create reports comparing each of their capacity findings with a self-selected and dynamically selected comparable group of nonprofits within the national database. More than 2,500 nonprofit organizations across the country have taken the CCAT, representing a full spectrum of nonprofit subsectors, ranging from small, grassroots organizations to large institutions with multimillion dollar budgets.

The following examples demonstrate how the CCAT has been employed at the organizational, cohort, regional, and fieldwide levels.

Individual Nonprofit Organizations

The New Jersey Audubon Society (NJAS), the oldest conservation organization in the state, used the CCAT to develop a 3-year strategic plan. Operating 10 nature centers and 34 wildlife sanctuaries around the state, the Society serves over 500,000 people annually. It is also a leader in supporting environmental legislation and encouraging sound environmental policy.

As one of the first steps in its strategic planning process, NJAS senior staff and board members completed the CCAT. At the outset, the CCAT results helped the organization focus its data-gathering efforts on information related to those areas that senior staff and the board deemed most in need of improvement. The findings enabled NJAS to set priorities about where to invest resources and build specific capacities.

According to society president Thomas Gilmore,

> The comprehensive nature of this strategic planning process led to close examination of both New Jersey Audubon's mission and the internal structures that enable us to achieve it. Every aspect of our organization was reviewed for opportunities to enhance capacity, hone efficiency and ensure long-term sustainability. The plan provides clear direction and attainable steps that will enable the society to carry out its mission and expand its legacy of quality conservation through the next decade.

Cohorts of Nonprofits

The Oregon Arts Commission (OAC) used the CCAT to help determine the need and desire for capacity-building assistance among its grantee organizations. Based on the CCAT results of 70 organizations, in 2009 OAC designed a tailored capacity-building initiative that provided workshops, webinars, annual meetings, and peer exchanges statewide. When the program ended in June 2011, OAC again administered the CCAT to measure any changes in organizational capacity among its grantees.

The longitudinal analysis for organizations that took the CCAT in 2008 and 2011 found that they had made statistically significant advances in capacity. In particular, they had experienced gains in each of the four core capacities as well as all but two of the 36 subcapacities. The greatest increases were seen in the leadership and adaptive capacities, the two areas the initiative focused on reinforcing. One of the capacities that declined was the ability to support staff resource needs, likely because of the 2008 financial crisis and its aftermath.

The Jordan Schnitzer Museum at the University of Oregon in Eugene benefited from the initiative. F. Gregory Fitz-Gerald, president of the museum's Leadership Council, recounts that when the museum first took the CCAT in 2008, it confirmed that the organization had many weaknesses to confront. The museum's leadership spent the next three years systematically and steadfastly addressing these concerns. Fitz-Gerald says,

> The CCAT is an excellent self-assessment tool that provides a systematic and structured analysis of an organization's strengths and weaknesses. We used it three years ago and again this year to measure our progress in fixing our weaknesses. Happily, we have made great progress.

Ecosystem of Nonprofits in a Region

TCC Group recently worked with the Weingart Foundation to conduct a comprehensive study of the capacity-building needs of, and resources available to, nonprofits in Los Angeles County, which has more nonprofit organizations than any other county in the nation and more than most states. Through this effort, more than 250 nonprofits completed the CCAT, which provided confidential, individual organizational diagnoses as well as robust aggregate data for regionwide research. The participating nonprofits also completed a supplemental survey that assessed their experience with access to capacity-building service providers. Figure B-3 displays the community nonprofit ecosystem of a variety of different cohorts, including the region of Los Angeles County.

The study found that Los Angeles County nonprofit organizations have important strengths like inspiring staff leaders and a clear understanding of the needs of the communities they serve. But they are less effective in equally critical areas like strategic learning, board development, financial management, and fund raising. The research also revealed that nonprofits are not well-informed consumers of capacity-building services and perceive

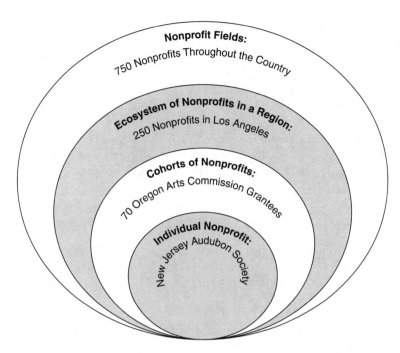

FIGURE B-3 The ecosystem of nonprofits in a community.

available consulting, peer exchange, training, and other services to be fragmented and of mixed quality. The study also determined that the capabilities of capacity-building providers in the region need improvement. Moreover, most Los Angeles funders are seen as providing inadequate and uncoordinated support for nonprofit capacity building.

The final report was shared with nonprofit, capacity-building, and philanthropic leaders in the county to initiate a candid discussion about ways to address identified issues. A series of forums were held to reflect on the findings and cocreate a strategy to build nonprofit capacity in the region. The study also stimulated discussion about how funders can modify their behavior to support nonprofit governance and how capacity builders can strengthen their own organizations. Weingart Foundation President Fred Ali observed,

> Los Angeles County depends on nonprofit organizations to provide vital services, fuel social and cultural innovation, and advocate for change. Yet these nonprofit organizations are struggling as demand for many services increases and revenues decline. While some of them have proven to be resourceful and resilient in providing quality services during these tough times, many are facing serious challenges in their leadership, governance, management, and operations. If the capacity of these organizations is weak, then their programs and services are bound to suffer. [The Foundation wants the study] to stimulate change that enables more Los Angeles County nonprofit organizations to be well led, reflective, sustainable, adaptive, and ultimately achieve greater impact.

THE NONPROFIT FIELD

A few years ago, TCC Group mined the CCAT database for information on the keys to nonprofit financial sustainability. TCC conducted a statistical analysis of the factors correlated with sustainability for approximately 750 nonprofits that had used the CCAT.

Through this research, TCC found three central factors that determined a nonprofit's sustainability: organizational leadership, adaptability, and program capacity. During a period of economic stress, this study helped funders and nonprofit leaders alike to determine ways to enhance the financial sustainability of nonprofits in their communities.

The study found that nonprofits that score well on internal leadership and leader vision are significantly more sustainable than are those that do not. Leaders should be responsible for developing and communicating the organization's mission and vision as well as for motivating employees to achieve organizational goals. A nonprofit can strengthen leadership by combining capacity-building strategies, such as executive coaching and peer exchange programs, with assessment, program evaluation, and strategic planning.

Adaptable program management and staffing were also important predictors of sustainability. These elements encompass an organization's ability to make the necessary staffing changes to increase and improve service delivery and ensure that staff members have the knowledge and skills to deliver those services. Finally, fund raising and financial management correlate with sustainability. To build fund-raising capacity, the CCAT analysis recommends that nonprofits put strong financial plans in place and, using board members, engage the community to invest time and money with the organization.

These findings point to a formula for organizational sustainability that consists of leadership, adaptability, and program capacity. They also indicate that strategic planning and evaluation are critically important.

So, what does a financially sustainable nonprofit organization look like? New York Cares, which addresses pressing community needs by mobilizing New Yorkers to service, is one of the small number of organizations that met all of the threshold criteria for the capacities that predict sustainability on the CCAT survey. The organization has strong leadership, is highly adaptive, and excels in both external and internal relationships. Diversification, engagement, and transparency are the mantras of New York Cares's fund-raising efforts and have helped the organization increase revenue at an average rate of 10% to 15% per year over the past decade. According to executive director Gary Bagley, "We regularly engage the philanthropic community in our work, giving donors the opportunity to experience, firsthand, the quality and impact of our projects." New York Cares also strives to satisfy internal stakeholders and keep staff morale high. Bagley observes that activities like annual staff outings and all-staff volunteer projects, "although low on budget, are high on enthusiasm and fun." When a position opens up, New York Cares rarely has to look beyond its strong "bench" to find a highly qualified replacement. In fact, 28% of current employees have held more than one staff position.

Another example of how the CCAT has been leveraged to strengthen the nonprofit field is its use by The Reimagining Service Council, a national group of government, philanthropic, and nonprofit leaders in the field of volunteer engagement. TCC conducted an analysis of national CCAT data to examine if and how the engagement and effective management of volunteers strengthened organizational capacity and found that organizations that engage at least 50 volunteers and manage them well are significantly more effective than are nonprofits that do not.

APPENDIX C

How to Research Funding Sources

In addition to asking board members, staff, local experts, funders, and peers for recent information specific to the organization's domain, other general approaches for researching funding sources are given below.

FOUNDATION FUNDING

It is unlikely that any one foundation will be a perfect fit for a given organization. Instead of looking for that silver bullet, identify those foundations that seem most aligned with the organization's strengths and start building relationships from there. The most useful information may come from the peer research discussed in Step 2. Look at the websites of similar organizations. Though there may be lists of funders on the websites of peer organizations, organizations are unlikely to find actual amounts there. These can be found (sometimes) on the funders' websites, and (always) on their 990 forms, available through the Foundation Center (www.foundationcenter.org) or Guidestar (www.guidestar.org).

The Foundation Center's *Foundation Directory Online* database is a great resource for researching potential foundation funders. This database requires a subscription, but several options are available with reasonable rates. (See the sidebar, "How to Use Foundation Center's *Foundation Directory Online* Database.") The database can provide two very important pieces of information. First, it can give a sense of the overall foundation funding available in your organization's area, which can help you to develop realistic goals for how much you could raise. Second, it can help pinpoint the foundations that may be your most likely funders.

Once likely foundation funders have been identified, it is necessary to assess your organization's fit with their missions. Here, diving into foundation websites directly to determine any common characteristics of their grantees may make sense. For example, some foundations may say that grantees from a fairly wide geographical range are eligible, but an examination of the list of agencies actually funded will provide a clearer sense of the geographic areas in which they are most interested. *Getting specific about the criteria they use to evaluate grantees is crucial since foundations that on the surface look similar may in fact have very different priorities.*

Take the experience of BELL, a youth development organization. While working to identify potential new foundation supporters, the organization developed a list of foundations that had historically supported youth development efforts. Further research revealed, however, that less than a quarter of those foundations focused on efforts like BELL's. The foundations that focused on early childhood advocacy, for example, were out. Those that focused on direct service provision of out-of-school-time experiences, however, were squarely in.

Digging deeper into the out-of-school-time foundations, BELL found that some placed a premium on evidence of impact and depth of experience while others preferred to fund newer, less-proven innovations. With its proven programming, BELL was a better fit with foundations in the former camp. Those were the foundations BELL ended up targeting.

In addition to looking at the criteria foundations use to assess grantees, you should also consider the requirements they place on their grantees. Make sure that the costs to meet those requirements will not trump the value of the grant.

With foundation research, as with hunting for jobs or spouses, actually talking to people trumps Internet research. Find opportunities to meet key staff from targeted foundations. Advocacy forums, "meet-the-funders" events, ribbon-cuttings, and a variety of other local and regional events offer opportunities for funders and nonprofit leaders to meet. Alternatively, ask someone to make an introduction, or simply send a note.

GOVERNMENT FUNDING

Federal, state, and local government funding sources will all require different research approaches. In all cases, though, interviews with government officials will be essential

---

HOW TO USE THE FOUNDATION CENTER'S *FOUNDATION DIRECTORY ONLINE* DATABASE

1. From the *Foundation Directory Online* home page, click "Search Grants." There, you will be able to determine total annual giving to the issues and locations it addresses.
2. Once in "Search Grants," restrict your search for grants by the categories most relevant to your organization. These include location (from broad countries to narrow zip codes), recipient type, subject (i.e., issue area), types of support (e.g., building/renovation, program evaluation), and keywords. It is advisable to do a few searches with different combinations of categories and keywords since some areas are more narrowly defined than others. For example, a search for "crime, public policy" yields about half as many grants as a search for "crime, reform."
3. Also in "Search Grants," you can filter results by grant year and grant amount.
4. Once a list of grants has been compiled, export the data to Excel for easier manipulation.
5. Also in the Foundation Center database, you can research specific funders. If one funder seems particularly promising, navigate to "Search Grantmakers" to learn more about them. There, you can view historical giving patterns, purpose and activities, primary fields of interests, and application information.

to truly understanding the relevant eligibility rules and process requirements. The political climate is also an ever-present consideration. Are government priorities shifting in a way that would affect the funding stream being researched? Has that stream lost its key champion? Will economic considerations lead to an increase or decrease in dollars? These are all questions you should bear in mind when considering a government funding source.

The good news about researching government sources is that for the most part, all information must be public. The bad news? Much of this information can be difficult to access or understand. Setting up phone calls with the appropriate officials early and often will be key to an organization's ability to answer its most important questions. To identify those officials, do an Internet search of the specific funding source. If this approach fails, reach out to the government agency overseeing the funds (e.g., the Department of Education for Title I money) for help in identifying the right person. Also consider how to tap board members, colleagues at peer organizations, and other contacts to facilitate introductions to and conversations with government decision makers. Though it may require some persistence to schedule a meeting, the benefits of those direct conversations can be huge.

BELL found that one-on-one conversations with government officials were essential. BELL needed to understand if a particular government funding source would require the organization to provide transportation to its students (something BELL did not do). An in-depth online search yielded no clear answer, so BELL reached out to the appropriate federal administrator. When that person did not respond right away, BELL leveraged its relationships with donors, intermediaries, and board members. Through that process, BELL was able to get the clear answer it needed: Transportation would be required in most cases, so the source might not be a good fit for the organization.

As with foundations, getting a sense of past funding patterns is critical for understanding which government agencies are providing funding, and who and what they are funding. For federal grants, some agencies make it easy to find this information. For example, the Substance Abuse and Mental Health Services Administration, which oversees much of the government's substance abuse and mental health funding and some of its homelessness and HIV funding, lists grantees by year and program category; within its state-by-state reports, it provides brief summaries of each funded project. The Centers for Disease Control and Prevention, on the other hand, which is by far the largest source of disease prevention funding, often makes it hard (or impossible) to figure out who and what it has funded. One place to look for grantee listings is in an agency's news releases, which often include announcements of funding awards and can usually be easily located on agency websites.

Grants.gov (www.grants.gov) is a great source for real-time information on currently available funding and for funding that has previously been available. It provides links to current and past funding announcements, which contain extensive detail on program requirements including eligibility. As with foundations, a gap may exist between the kinds of organizations that are theoretically eligible for funding and those that actually get funded. The National Institutes of Health, for example, almost always lists a broad range of eligible entities in its funding announcement but in practice directs the great bulk of its awards to academic institutions.

Subsidy Scope (www.subsidyscope.org), an initiative of the Pew Charitable Trusts, is another helpful website. It allows organizations to identify specific organizations that are receiving different types of government grants.

For state-level sources, consider starting with the home page of the state department with responsibility for a particular issue area (e.g., the Department of Education for an education nonprofit, the Department of Justice for a juvenile crime organization).

Many of these state department home pages will provide links to specific state funding sources. This may take a bit of digging.

Finally, for local grants, the best approach is generally to go straight to the source, whether it be the mayor's office, the school district, the county services office, or some other local body. Online information may be scarce for local streams, so conversations with key government staff will be particularly important.

OTHER PRIVATE GIVING

Though finding information on other forms of giving (such as corporate and individual) is often harder, there are some sources that may enable an organization to come up with rough estimates of annual donations in its issue area. The Center on Philanthropy at Indiana University produces Giving USA, an annual report on philanthropy (including individual giving) that breaks out donations by domain (e.g., human services, education). The center also has a searchable database of individual donors who have made gifts over $1 million (called their Million Dollar List), which can be a useful tool for determining whether peer organizations have been successful in securing major individual and/or corporate investments. Other academic bodies and think tanks—such as the Center for High Impact Philanthropy at the University of Pennsylvania and the Urban Institute's Center on Nonprofits and Philanthropy—allow users to search their rich compendia of research. When looking for state-specific information, it may be worth a quick Internet search to see if there are sources that compile high-level data for a particular state. For example, Associated Grant Makers in Boston produced a 2005 report on average levels of individual giving in Massachusetts.

Note that researching individual and corporate giving may require more time and result in a less complete answer than would be the case with foundation or government sources. As with much of this process, success will hinge on a willingness to move on when the research is "complete enough."

While outside data can provide essential evidence that significant individual and/or corporate giving exists in an issue area, it says little about an organization's ability to actually secure those funds. Whether the organization is competitive depends on a variety of factors, including the strength of the narrative, the skill of its development team, and the organization's ability to speak to individual passions and interests. Historical success in securing individual and corporate gifts is also an important factor to consider. Research has shown that growing individual giving, in particular, is often a slow process. At some point, it may make sense to bring in external specialists—such as fund-raising consultants—to advise on how to increase the likelihood of success.

APPENDIX D

Recommended Readings

CHAPTER 1

The Jossey-Bass Handbook of Nonprofit Leadership and Management. (2005). Robert D. Herman and Associates. San Francisco, CA: Jossey-Bass.

Nonprofit Management 101. (2011). Darian Rodriguez Heyman. San Francisco, CA: Jossey-Bass.

Forces for Good. (2008). Leslie R. Crutchfield and Heather McLeod Grant. San Francisco, CA: Jossey-Bass.

The Toyota Way. (2004). Jeffrey K. Liker. New York, NY: McGraw-Hill.

CHAPTER 6

The Innovator's Dilemma. (2003). Clayton Christensen. New York, NY: HarperBusiness.

CHAPTER 7

Joining a Nonprofit Board: What You Need to Know. (2011). Marc J. Epstein and F. Warren McFarlan. San Francisco, CA: Jossey-Bass.

CHAPTER 8

Leading Across Boundaries, Creating Collaborative Agencies in a Networked World. (2010). Russell M. Linden. San Francisco, CA: Jossey-Bass.

CHAPTER 9

Driving Results Through Social Networks. (2009). Rob Cross and Robert J. Thomas. San Francisco, CA: Jossey-Bass.

The Jossey-Bass Reader on Nonprofit and Public Leadership. (2010). James L. Perry. San Francisco, CA: Jossey-Bass.

Good to Great. (2005). Jim Collins. New York, NY: HarperBusiness.

The India Way. (2010). Peter Cappelli, Harbir Singh, Jitendra Singh, and Michael Useem. Watertown, MA: Harvard Business Review Press.

Six Degrees of Connection. (2010). Liz Dow. Philadelphia, PA: LEADERSHIP Philadelphia.

CHAPTER 10

The End of Fund Raising: Raise More Money by Selling Your Impact. (2011). Jason Saul. San Francisco, CA: Jossey-Bass.

INDEX